Public Relations
WRITING

STRATEGIES & STRUCTURES

From the Wadsworth Series in Mass Communication and Journalism

General Mass Communication

Biagi, *Media/Impact: An Introduction to Mass Media*, Twelves Edition

Fellow, *American Media History*, Third Edition

Hilmes, *Only Connect: A Cultural History of Broadcasting in the United States*, Fourth Edition

Lester, *Visual Communication: Images with Messages*, Sixth Edition

Overbeck, *Major Principles of Media Law*, 2015 Edition

Straubhaar/LaRose/Davenport, *Media Now: Understanding Media, Culture, and Technology*, Ninth Edition

Zelezny, *Cases in Communications Law*, Sixth Edition

Zelezny, *Communications Law: Liberties, Restraints, and the Modern Media*, Sixth Edition

Journalism

Bowles/Borden, *Creative Editing*, Sixth Edition

Davis/Davis, *Think Like an Editor: 50 Strategies for the Print and Digital World*, Second Edition

Hilliard, *Writing for Television, Radio, and New Media*, Eleventh Edition

Kessler/McDonald, *When Words Collide: A Media Writer's Guide to Grammar and Style*, Eighth Edition

Kessler/McDonald, *Cengage Advantage Books: When Words Collide: A Media Writer's Guide to Grammar and Style + Exercise Book*, Eighth Edition

Rich, *Writing and Reporting News: A Coaching Method*, Eighth Edition

Public Relations and Advertising

Diggs-Brown, *Strategic Public Relations: Audience Focused Approach*

Diggs-Brown, *The PR Styleguide: Formats for Public Relations Practice*, Third Edition

Drewniany/Jewler, *Creative Strategy in Advertising*, Eleventh Edition

Hendrix, *Public Relations Cases*, Ninth Edition

Newsom/Turk/Kruckeberg, *Cengage Advantage Books: This is PR: The Realities of Public Relations*, Eleventh Edition

Sivulka, *Soap, Sex, and Cigarettes: A Cultural History of American Advertising*, Second Edition

Research and Theory

Baran/Davis, *Mass Communication Theory: Foundations, Ferment, and Future*, Seventh Edition

Sparks, *Media Effects Research: A Basic Overview*, Fifth Edition

Wimmer/Dominick, *Mass Media Research: An Introduction*, Tenth Edition

ELEVENTH EDITION

Public Relations WRITING

STRATEGIES & STRUCTURES

Doug Newsom
Professor Emeritus, Texas Christian University

Jim Haynes
Southern Methodist University

CENGAGE

Australia • Brazil • Mexico • Singapore • United Kingdom • United States

Public Relations Writing: Strategies & Structures, **Eleventh Edition**
Doug Newsom, Jim Haynes

Product Director: Monica Eckman

Product Manager: Kelli Strieby

Content Developer: Jeffrey L. Hahn, JLHCG

Associate Content Developer: Rachel Schowalter

Product Assistant: Alexis Mackintosh-Zebrowski

Marketing Manager: Sarah Seymour

IP Analyst: Ann Hoffman

IP Project Manager: Farah Fard

Manufacturing Planner: Doug Bertke

Art and Design Direction, Production Management, and Composition: Lumina Datamatics, Inc.

> For product information and technology assistance, contact us at
> **Cengage Customer & Sales Support, 1-800-354-9706 or support.cengage.com.**
>
> For permission to use material from this text or product, submit all requests online at **www.cengage.com/permissions.**

Library of Congress Control Number: 2015947424

ISBN-13: 978-1-305-50000-6

Cengage
20 Channel Street
Boston, MA 02210
USA

Cengage is a leading provider of customized learning solutions with employees residing in nearly 40 different countries and sales in more than 125 countries around the world. Find your local representative at: **www.cengage.com.**

Cengage products are represented in Canada by Nelson Education, Ltd.

To learn more about Cengage platforms and services, register or access your online learning solution, or purchase materials for your course, visit **www.cengage.com.**

Printed at CLDPC, USA, 10-19

*D*edicated to all public relations practitioners, educators and students who care about communicating clearly and effectively.

Brief Contents

Contents

PART   2   Writing Principles   33

CHAPTER THREE
Writing to Clarify and Simplify the Complex: Style and Content   34

CHAPTER FOUR
Grammar, Spelling and Punctuation   58

CHAPTER   FIVE
Social Media Writing   75

P A R T   3   Preparing to Write   93

C H A P T E R   S I X
Research for the Public Relations Writer   94

CHAPTER NINE
Writing for Public Media   179

C H A P T E R   T E N
Email, Memos, Letters, Proposals and Reports 221

CHAPTER ELEVEN
Newsletters   245

Preface

Welcome to this 11th edition of Public Relations Writing. The authors are the same, Doug Newsom and Jim Haynes, PRSA Fellows with years of practice, university teaching and many workshops at home and abroad. What is different is a slight change in the book's subtitle to Strategies and Structures.

Inside you'll find many changes in the chapters, since the field is constantly in flux. We welcomed a new colleague to handle the social media chapter for us: Steve Lee, whose business has been digital communication since its inception in 1998 and thus the focus of his teaching experience as an adjunct and workshop presenter. The Internet and social media have affected the way all of us communicate, professionally and personally. To quote Lee, "Social media has become such a vital tool for public relations practitioners that the majority of public relations and communications managers believe that understanding how to use and manage social media channels is essential to success."

Use the text as a home base to alert you to "learning/teaching" examples you encounter daily. Practitioners and professors always are sensitive to incidents in all media that create learning opportunities. Public relations practitioners—especially those in firms and agencies—discover, discuss and critique incidents daily to help guide their practices. For professors, such incidents are the next presentation for their classes, and the examples are always at your fingertips to show, talk and tell.

We, as authors, cannot update any textbook fast enough to keep up, but we welcome your inquiries, ideas and initiatives. You can find us at doug.n@att.net and jhaynes1102@sbcglobal.net.

Doug Newsom and Jim Haynes

Acknowledgments

We would like to express our gratitude to colleagues, practitioners and students who offered informal comments on the book and to more formal directions from reviewers who recommended changes and offered guidance and suggestions for this edition.

We also are very grateful for the many who signed permissions for us to use materials that appear in the illustrations.

We'd also like to thank the dedicated team at Cengage Learning for their support, mainly Kelli Strieby, Product Manager, and Jeffrey Hahn, Content Developer. Thanks also to Jyotsna Ojha, Project Manager at Lumina Datamatics.

PART 1

PR Writing: Role and Responsibility

Finding facts, communicating effectively in all media, knowing the law and being ethical—all are essential for the PR writer.

CHAPTER ONE

Public Relations and the Writer

What an exciting time to be a writer. Your message can be crafted for any medium you can imagine, from an electronic app to moving billboard to a tweet, a blog, a newspaper or magazine piece, a video feature, a television story or a serious white paper for research and policy recommendations.

The key words are *story* and *purpose*. The audience is a given.

In a world of instant communication, all messages are simultaneously local and global.

You will be telling an organization's story whatever you write.

The story must be told concisely with clarity, accuracy and memorability.

Writing coach Paula LaRocque in a twist of the idea that all one learns about living is absorbed in kindergarten says to think of nursery rhymes.

"[W]hen approaching a story, we'll do well to remember that old Mother Hubbard went to the cupboard to fetch her poor dog a bone. And that the cow jumped over the moon, And that the owl and the pussycat went to sea in a beautiful pea-green boat.

"Actor, action, acted upon: the clearest and most logical syntax English can devise. No wonder the bright beginnings of nursery rhymes have pleased readers for centuries."[1]

Good advice for engaging attention is being clear and memorable.

Your pattern for development of every piece of writing, regardless of medium, will be:

Purpose—telling an organization's story in terms of what it is, what it does and why it matters.
Building relationships—tying the organization to those exposed to the communication, however, wherever and whoever these might be.
Writing strategically—delivering a message effectively to get the desired response.

Communication is wasted if it fails in any of these three.

You should be able to state the purpose in a single declarative sentence, keeping in mind the expected reaction or response so your message will bring the intended results. You also want to know if there are unintended reactions or responses, so you need to keep in mind how to monitor messages to produce prompt, thoughtful reactions.

How Strategic Public Relations Writing Is Different

You may be thinking that you have been writing this way all along. You have sent text messages, posted and responded to Facebook comments, sent Instagrams, shared videos and such. The difference is that these were your creations for your own purposes or reasons. When you write for an organization either as an internal public relations writer or for a client in an agency or a firm, your message is to achieve a business goal for that organization, whether it is nonprofit or for profit.

Public relations is the strategic management function that helps an organization achieve its goals and objectives through building and maintaining goodwill with its various stakeholders/publics. Effective public relations writers are critical to that success. Your writing is purposeful, persuasive and principled. Principled? Absolutely. You didn't see "spinning" in that sentence, did you? Clients and employers may not understand this, but it is imperative that you do, as a writer. What PR writers do, the legal and ethical responsibilities involved and what they accomplish for their employers, institutions or clients, is the topic of this first section.

As more public relations units identify their titles as "strategic communication," that often indicates an integrated communications practice involving both advertising and public relations. Technological changes have already blurred the lines anyway in presentation, format and the interactivity of users with a medium. Additionally, many different tools go into other PR writer responsibilities such as preparing materials for promotions, special events, campaigns, crises and specialized areas, such as investor relations.

Because PR writers are responsible for tailoring all types of messages for any medium and a variety of individuals, writing for public relations takes many forms, as you will realize as you go through these chapters. The more you know about different media and diverse publics, the more facile you are with all writing assignments, the better off you will be in the kaleidoscopic job market.

Always and remaining critical talents for public relations people are the ability to recognize potential stories and anticipating how these might be received by global audiences. Choosing words and illustrations requires a keen understanding of the complex, and often conflicting, values held among diverse publics. The demands on today's writers are for more versatility, greater understanding of the repercussions of convergence among traditional media and the impact and connectivity of social media and the requirements of different media as well as increased competence in using visuals and sounds to help convey a message.

What is traditionally called "social media" have joined the list of media for any organizational message. You may be tweeting or posting on an organization's Facebook page or posting videos as part of a media mix you are using. However, you also will be responding to comments that come in to the organization from its electronic sites.

Social media content for clients and organizations provides needed feedback. Interactive websites and blogs are well within the PR writer's job description, and although some organizations hire social media specialists for Facebook and YouTube channels, PR writers may be the ones hired just for this aspect. Appropriate responses in online communication are critical to an organization's credibility. Remember, most social media postings are user-generated, unedited content with instant and global distribution.

As the demand for versatility in PR writing grows, there is more emphasis on accountability—evidence that the messages work. Employers want measured proof of results from communication efforts. There is no open budget line for communication. Yet there is no need to despair. The writer who is genuinely good at the task of researching information, learning its meaning and communicating that effectively is and always will be needed. You must understand what makes public relations writing different, although, from literary writing, news writing or selling, although you may be drawing techniques from all three. The major focus for public relations writing is persuasion.

Public relations writers prepare messages for any medium that can convey information. Furthermore, most of the time, these messages—words, images and sound—are conveyed electronically. Potentially these messages can be received anywhere in the world.

The difference for strategic writing lies in the power and responsibility of the public relations person who is in the position of brokering goodwill between an institution and its publics. There are two aspects to this responsibility. Strategically, public relations practice involves the ways an organization's operations and policies affect people—the face-to-face interaction of employees with customers or clients and the organization's participation in the affairs of the community. Tactically speaking, though, good policies and good performance are worth little if people don't understand the policies and don't know about the performance. The heart of public relations practice remains in communication, particularly writing.

Good public relations requires communication skills, expertise in dealing with all media, the dynamics of public opinion and the principles of persuasion. Further, the communicator must know when and what to communicate. This involves analysis, judgment, counseling and planning—in addition to and prior to communicating. In this chapter, we'll try to clarify the nature of this complex task and the writer's role in it.

Job Descriptions Vary

Because practitioners have different backgrounds and experiences in different parts of the world and that experience is affected by the social, political and economic environment, the demands on writers vary. Some ingredients to look for are "ethical," "socially responsible," "trusting relationships," "reliable communication," "anticipation of consequences," "counsel to client/organization" and "evaluator of outcomes."

Analyzing, Predicting and Counseling

The main roles of the professional are "analyzing trends, predicting their consequences, counseling organization leaders." These roles fall into the management context, in which personnel help to frame, implement, adjust and communicate the policies that govern how an institution interacts with its publics. It is through public relations that an organization acts with responsibility and responsiveness—in policy and information—to the best interests of the institution and its publics.[2]

The management of communication is now seen by many public information writers as the key to the corner office. According to *The Wall Street Journal,* "Today most CIOs (chief information officers) have a more expansive role—and a set of aspirations to match. Now that the CIO manages the ever more complex information flow that drives a company's internal decisions as well as its links to customers globally, the job has the look of a corporate stepping stone to higher ground." Topics such as artificial intelligence and cybersecurity, as well as management and economics, were part of the second annual meeting of a network of CIOs from around the world in San Diego, California, in February 2014, hosted by *The Wall Street Journal.* Most of the attendees report directly to the corporate executive officer (CEO), and most were women. A wide and diverse collection of industries was represented. The information officers said they wanted to be seen "as an essential and versatile player, able to represent the company and participate in the big decisions. And to lead."[3]

What is important to remember is that these CIOs are senior employees. It is the staff writers on whom the weight of writing falls on. That is what you can expect and must be prepared for to climb that ladder. Doing this job well requires a broad educational background, expertise in many areas and, most of all, good judgment. Unlike the corporate attorney or accountant, the public relations practitioner cannot refer to a body of laws or procedures that prescribe behavior under given circumstances. Instead, the public relations person must know human behavior and combine that knowledge with specific information about people within the institution and people outside whom the institution deals with. For example, the PR director for a bank must consider the views of bank officers and bank employees as well as those of customers, the community, legislators and government regulatory agencies. The public relations person for the local school district must be aware of the feelings of students, parents, voters and the regional accrediting agency. Any institution has many publics, and the public relations director must be able to advise management about the possible impact on those publics of various plans, policies and actions.

In addition to analyzing publics and counseling management on the effects of policy, the PR person must be alert for signs of change. The right policy today will not necessarily be the right policy tomorrow. People's attitudes and opinions evolve, and the composition of the public changes. The capable PR person notes trends in public opinion and predicts the consequences of such trends for the institution.

Usually, the public relations director also serves as a spokesperson for the organization and overseer of the entire public relations program. The PR person at the top of the department spends little time on basic public relations techniques such as writing.

Frank Wylie, a former president of the Public Relations Society of America, described the division of public relations labor in this way: Senior-level public relations people are likely to spend 10 percent of their time with techniques, 40 percent with administration and 50 percent with analysis and judgment; at entry level, it's 50 percent techniques, 4 percent judgment and 45 percent "running like hell."[4]

Competence in Convergence

Message delivery is in its second decade of mixing Internet and related personal electronic devices with printed materials and traditional media such as television, radio and news magazines and papers. The decline of staff in traditional media opened opportunities for writers of all kinds, from citizen journalists and freelancers to organizational writers. Traditional media put much of their content online and developed their own Twitter and Facebook pages as well as using websites, email and actual online subscriptions to keep audiences.

In addition to becoming familiar with all avenues of communication, a writer has to develop competence in using them to craft messages for the most effective delivery. One key in talking about media choices is understanding different references to media access. Think of the acronym POSE that represents your control over the writing: paid, owned, sponsored or earned.

Paid seems clear. It includes advertising in all media from pop-ups on your computer when you get email to paid programing on various television channels, and most familiar are those in print media including special sections.

You buy the time or space and have a contract that allows you to control the content, including the design and time of presentation. The only exception to control content would be restrictions cited in the contract you sign. Paid can also include something where your organization has made a contribution so its logo can be used. Think of tee-shirts for special events that have all sorts of logos on the back representing organizations that made donations and allow for their logos to be used.

Owned obviously means that your organization owns the medium, which might be a newsletter or magazine—print or electronic. These are often referred to as "house ads" because they promote something the publication is doing or offering. When you see something on television or hear it on radio that is called a promo. It calls your attention to an offer or event on that station or something that station is sponsoring such as a collection of toys for children.

Sponsored means that a publication or program has been paid for by an organization, often a trade or professional group, whose members have articles about their organization displayed in the publicity. The organization itself controls the representation, words, pictures and such, but doesn't have to pay for the exposure. Videos and films are often paid for by a trade group or association or even a company to tell its story in the public interest, and these sponsored programs are offered free of charge not only to public media but also for educational use in schools.

Earned indicates that the information is considered valuable enough to a medium's publics, that the medium uses the material, but not always as sent. The medium controls the presentation.

Reactions and Responses

What management expects from exposure, regardless of the medium, is a report of what happened as a result. An investment has been made, and the organization making it expects a report.

How did various publics respond? How was that demonstrated? Did reactions indicate any preferences? How might that affect methods of reaching various publics in the future? Did some reactions indicate unfamiliarity with the organization, misunderstandings about its activities, suggest policy modifications or more?

Communication is not a one-way street. Going one way, the PR person analyzes public opinion and the needs of the community, and opens channels of communication that allow such information to flow into the institution. Using this information, the PR person advises management on the policies that are likely to be of mutual benefit to the institution and the public—or at least acceptable, if not beneficial, to the public.

Then—going the other way on the street—the PR person opens channels of communication that reach out from the institution to the public. The viability of channels may be shown in using various types of media to interpret the institution's policies and actions to its various audiences. Social media specialist, Lida Citroen (www.lida360.com), has a formula: Values + Action = Credibility. With values clearly posted on websites, anyone can compare what is said with what is done. If facts or perceptions don't show a valid equation, then credibility is lost and reputation jeopardized. Communication in this direction is largely the responsibility of the PR writer. Exactly what is it then, that PR writers do?

The variety of publics is so vast that PR people often find it useful to divide the publics they deal with into two broad classes: internal and external. *Internal publics* are groups within the organization (such as employees or the board of directors). *External publics* are groups outside the organization (such as the media, your company's customers or the state legislature). The distinction between the two is not always clear-cut; stockholders, for example, though essentially an external public, can have close ties to the institution. One definition of internal publics is "all those who share the institution's identity."

Stakeholders/Publics, Channels and the Role of the Writer

It is a simple thing to say that the task of public relations writers is to communicate with the public. But in practice, there is nothing simple about it. With most communication electronic, "publics" include some "stakeholders," people who identify with an issue, action or event, though they may have no investment in the organization, its products or services. Something is posted on the Internet that they like or don't like or that conflicts with their values, threatens them or maybe is something that they want to support. Furthermore, there is no homogeneity to any group, even if they have a name. It's not as though there were one single "public" to write for. Rarely is a public relations message important to everybody in the "public."

For example, news that a theme park is creating a new thrill ride is important information to youngsters who enjoy such entertainment, but what they want to know about it is quite different from what businesses and residents near the theme park want to know. Concerns of businesses and residents are about increased traffic to the area and more noise. What that group is concerned with is different from what the city's safety engineers and the theme park's insurance people want to know. These groups' needs are all different from what the local and state tourism departments want to know. The tourism departments' needs for information are different from those of investors in the theme park, and even those are not the same. If the theme park belongs to a publicly held company, its stock is traded on the open market, so securities analysts are another public. Publicly held companies are also responsible to the Securities and Exchange Commission. If the theme park is your client or your employer, you have to prepare information to reach all of these publics, and the information for each has a different focus. This focus is not a "spin." It is a responsible communication to satisfy the information needs and interests of particular publics.

A *public* is any group of people tied together by some common factor. And as public relations writers soon discover, there are many, many such groups. The *public* in public relations should really be *publics*. Even then, how do you analyze them? The easiest way is statistically, by gender, education, income, etc. That can be an indicator, but won't tell you as much as if you have the *psychographics*. Psychographics classify people by what they think, how they behave and what they think about—their special interests, such as gardening, cooking and hiking. Psychographic information is not merely helpful to the PR writer; it is often necessary. Consider the public relations director responsible for a university's alumni association magazine, who admitted with some dismay that she didn't know how to appeal both to an 80-year-old graduate of the engineering school and a 22-year-old sociologist. She did a research study that revealed a psychographic pattern binding all the alumni to the institution. This information suggested the sorts of articles that would interest alumni. The public relations director was then able to make informed decisions—and she now felt a great deal more confident in her choices.

Setting Priorities and Selecting Channels

What a writer must do is engage an organization's publics. That is necessary to attract them to the story you want to tell. The story has to be honest and contribute to the organization's transparency. This becomes easier to do when you analyze the possible publics and set priorities.

Select the publics that are most important for the communication effort. They may include the group that a new policy will affect the most or the groups whose opinions are especially important. (See Table 1.1 for a formula to prioritize publics.)

The next step is to select channels for the message that have the most significance to the priority public and to which they have easy access. Channels may be individuals

| TABLE 1.1 | *Discovering and Prioritizing Publics*   Prioritizing publics may be done in a number of ways. One informal method is called the PVI: *P*, the Potential to influence a public, plus *V*, the Vulnerability of the organization to that public (which may change over time and in different situations), equals *I*, the Impact of that public on the organization. Here is a tabular form for "computing" a PVI index. |

	P	+	*V*	=	*I*
Audience or Public	Potential for Organization to Influence (Scale 1–10)		Vulnerability of Organization to Be Affected (Scale 1–10)		Importance of Audience to Organization
_____	_____		_____		_____
_____	_____		_____		_____
_____	_____		_____		_____

Source: Jim Haynes, *Instructor's Guide for This Is PR*, 3rd ed. Doug Newsom and Alan Scott (Belmont, Calif.: Wadsworth, 1985), p. 63.

or media and may be mass media or specialized media and print or electronic or both. Each medium has characteristics that make it suitable for sending a particular message to a particular audience at a particular time.

Specialized Media These media offer an opportunity to control the message and its delivery. Since they are designed for a particular audience they are called specialized to distinguish them from media accessible by any audience. Specialized media include the internal publications or intranets that institutions produce to communicate with employees, staff, management and others close to the institution, such as directors and stockholders. Also included in specialized media are an organization's computerized message boards and audiovisuals intended for internal use only. Among these specialized media are electronic information networks of personal computer users.

Accessible Media Such media include any channel that is relatively unrestricted by ownership or government. In most democracies, government sends public information through its organizational channels, such as the Food and Drug Administration. When an organization posts messages in accessible media, these are likely to be seen by unintended audiences. Because neither the circulation nor the audience of such media is controlled by the organization that sends the information, such media are mostly for communication with external publics. Public relations writers using such media to reach large audiences must remember that these media are seen by internal publics as well. For example, a leading metropolitan daily newspaper's female employees objected to a promotional campaign that displayed women as sex objects. French police did not like billboards portraying them as "helpful" rather than as crime fighters facing danger.

The Role of the Writer

Public relations writers must be knowledgeable not only about publics and channels but about all aspects of their own institution as well. The PR writer for a social services agency must understand welfare eligibility rules and federal funding guidelines. A writer for the highway department must know about everything from road-building materials to traffic laws. PR writers must know enough about the financial aspects of a business to prepare the right message for securities analysts and to develop an annual report that stockholders can comprehend and auditors will approve.

In addition to possessing a broad knowledge of their company's business, public relations writers must be able to research specific subjects to determine what is and what isn't important. They must be able to borrow ideas from other fields—psychology, social psychology, sociology and political science, for example—to help put their research in perspective. PR writers must be alert to changing patterns of thought and behavior in society and must fully comprehend to the issues of the day.

Finally, and most important, the public relations writer must be an expert in communication. If you want to be a public relations writer, you must know how to write effectively in many different styles and for all media. You must understand the principles of good writing and be familiar with the vast body of scientific research on communication, persuasion and public opinion. Your goal is to be an efficient, effective communicator. You must accept that your writing is management-oriented strategic communication and therefore most likely to be persuasive in nature. Because of the scope of your communication, you must command a knowledge of publics and their cultures—their corporate or work environment culture, their personal or lifestyle culture and their indigenous or ethnic culture. Beyond that, you must know the international communication networks and media systems and how they operate. To be responsible in your communication, you must know and understand thoroughly the organization itself—what it does, where it is, who it serves, regulations affecting it and criticisms of the institution's policies, actions or consequences of how it conducts itself.

No matter what message you communicate, what audiences you communicate with and which media you use to reach those audiences, you have to know which words will work and why. Preparing you for these varied writing tasks is what this book is all about.

You are critical to maintaining the reputation of the organization you are representing. The advice from Daniel Tisch, APR, FCPRS, Global Alliance, is as follows: (1) define what you do in terms that your employer or clients will value; (2) know your professional responsibility; (3) plan your professional development; (4) start a conversation: "Are we a communicative organization?"; (5) what are your organization's character and values?; (6) build a listening strategy by collaborating with other disciplines; (7) is your organization sustainable?; (8) measure the quality of your organization's communication.[5]

Exercises

1. Collect materials from your college's website and admissions office about your school. Analyze them for message statements. Are different appeals addressed to first-year students, transfers, graduate students, older-than-average students? What are these appeals? What about your school's website, easy to navigate?

2. Examine the different types of messages and media used by your school's public relations office. List all of the publics these suggest.

3. Examine ads and broadcast spots for your school. Compare these public message statements with the admission materials. What message statements are consistent? Are any of them inconsistent? For example, does admission material suggest it is easy to get into the school while publicity talks about the high standards for admission? How are sponsorships for community events on campus presented? What about public access and parking for events on campus. Are they open to the public?

CHAPTER TWO

Ethical and Legal Responsibilities of the PR Writer

As you will see in this chapter, ethical and legal responsibilities are anything but straightforward. They are, let's face it, complicated. In this arena nothing is written saying, "do this and don't do that." One complication is the continuing conflict between the right to privacy and the right to know. Transparency is one part of that issue.

A lack of transparency is being blamed for many of the world's problems. From economic disasters and government disorders to cyber crises, all sorts of systemic failures seem to have a root cause—obfuscation, if not deliberate dishonesty, thus the demand for transparency.

Public relations practitioners have included transparency in their "best practices" list for a long time for many reasons, but focus on just four. First, public relations practitioners have a highly developed sense of personal and professional ethics that drives them to meet the spirit of the law as well as its explicit provisions. Second, they believe that their highest professional obligation is to advocate policies and techniques that are socially responsible. Third, they uphold the idea that looking after the best interests of priority publics is in the best interests of their organizations. Fourth, they want the organizations for which they work to be managed by people who are proactive in outlook and behavior. Thus, they counsel transparency at the management level, not only to command public trust but also to set standards for employees at all levels. Public relations professionals and their organizations that don't meet those standards often cause problems for themselves as well as others, and earn the title of "spin doctors" from their critics.

All organizational communicators are not professional public relations practitioners, bound by codes of ethics, though. In an attempt to alleviate that situation, the Global Alliance for Public Relations and Communication Management introduced the Stockholm

Accords in 2010, which included a code of ethics designed for universal application. The Global Alliance is a coalition of professional communication organizations representing 70 countries.[1] Although the code is a good guide as an effort to consolidate international consensus, it is not enforceable. Furthermore, of all the messages you receive in a day, how many are from professional communicators anywhere in the world?

There is an expectation that messages, from whatever source, should be genuinely sensitive to the feelings and needs of others and treat others as the messenger would want to be treated. That doesn't always occur. Ethics are founded on moral principles that are themselves grounded in effects. Moral principles consist of a set of beliefs and values that reflect a group's sense of what is *right* or *wrong*—regardless of how these terms are defined in formal rules, regulations or laws.

This is the case whether you agree with the idea that a moral judgment must fulfill *formal conditions* or you think a moral judgment must also meet some *material conditions*. The difference is that formal conditions call for moral guidelines or rules that are regarded as universal and prescriptive. But material conditions represent considerations that deal with the welfare of society as a whole and emphasize basic human good or purpose. For example, agreements in the Geneva Convention are prescriptive, but they do not address restrictions on the freedoms of individuals within a society, such as apartheid or immigration quotas.

If you ask for a public's view of your organization's ethics, don't be surprised if your organization is seen as unethical. The public's view of an organization's ethics is likely to be based less on a definition of morality than on the consequences of what the organization says and does, which will be seen as either moral or not moral by each and all of its publics. This sense of rightness, even if it later proves to be in error, is the stuff on which *public opinion* is formed.

Clearly, public opinion is important. Much of what you will do as a professional will be directed toward influencing, if possible, the opinion of publics. Since we live in a global society, you need to remember that, as a public relations practitioner, not everyone in the world is free to express a personal opinion.

In many parts of the world, some expressions of opinion, or even fact, are not legal. This will affect the way you, as a public relations person, do your research and communicate your messages, including illustrations.

In the USA, the country's First Amendment is treasured, in a real sense the product of public opinion. That's a sobering thought because it implies that the First Amendment can be abridged or voided if public opinion no longer supports it. So if you write, say or do something that violates society's sense of "rightness," you may be undercutting your constitutional right to free speech. That's a heavy responsibility. As a PR writer, how can you meet it?

Core Values and Personal/Professional Behavior

Our core values are based on our personalized belief system—what we believe to be right or wrong. We are influenced in these by our family, friends, education and a faith we endorse, if we do. We take this core of values into the world where it is often tried and tested, but probably no more so than in the workplace.

The reason is that organizations, like individuals, develop around a core set of values that often are set forward in a mission statement or even a formal statement of values. These values are operationalized in the corporate culture that is often set by the organizational leadership. In looking for a place to work, you need to find an organization that fits within your own value system. In all probability, the organization that hires you will be looking also for a "good fit" between the corporate culture and a potential employee.

Even when there is a "good fit," initially, situations change and so may your level of comfort in working there. One way to understand ethical responsibility is to look carefully at the interplay of different levels of influence on your personal and professional behavior.

Dynamics

Pressures in the workplace come from the economic, political and social system in which the organization exists. As we live and work in a more global society, these pressures have increased significantly. It's an understatement to say there is little consistency in cultures. You are more likely to hear the term "cultural conflicts."

Governments are a big part of that. Governments change and with them the philosophy of governance as well as the laws themselves and the rules of regulators. Public relations is a recognized discipline, but it is practiced in many different ways around the world because it too must be responsive to the environment in which it functions in representing businesses and nonprofit organizations. Additionally, the organization itself for which you as a public relations person work is responsive to standards and practices set by its own industry. If you work for a PR firm or agency, you may have clients from a number of different industries. The relationship between you and an organization changes with time. Provisions of communication law are always in flux because a new court decision may put a different interpretation on a law, rule or regulation. And society's expectations and judgments about what is right or wrong are notoriously capricious. An example of changed expectations is the effect of what's happening in cyberspace to the old protocol of a clear division between advertising and editorial content. Website editorial independence is seldom carefully defined, and search engines finding information on a topic cannot sort out the independent news from the sponsored information.[2] Compounding the problem are the many organizations that have placed their websites in the hands of management information systems specialists instead of public relations people. Because building and maintaining relationships are not necessarily high on their list of priorities, the result can be damaging to the corporate image.[3]

Trying to follow your own moral compass in the swirl of this cultural, social, legal and economic storm is not easy. You can easily get "off course," confused in your ability to know with certainty your ethical and legal responsibilities as a writer. Adding to the confusion is the increasing diversity of the population, especially in the USA. With this mix comes a complexity of value structures. Although these may be difficult to tease out in research about your publics, it is crucial that you do so.

Changes simply occur. What is wrong today may be right tomorrow, or vice versa. It is your responsibility to be sensitive to these changes; otherwise, you and your organization may get into lots of trouble stemming from the volatility of today's values.

Values

The concept of *values* is another way of talking about ethics. The study of ethics falls into two broad categories: *comparative ethics* and *normative ethics*. Normative ethics are studied by theologians and philosophers. Comparative ethics—sometimes called *descriptive ethics*—are studied by social scientists, who look at the ways different cultures practice ethical behavior. Values form the foundation of our institutions and organizations, as well as of our own informal and formal rules of behavior, which may change during our lifetime.

We're taught from an early age that some values are eternal verities. But if we see them violated repeatedly without sanctions, we begin to wonder whether they really are verities or eternal. A deceptive public relations practice, for example, may go unpunished or even unnoticed, and its users may gain significant advantages to the detriment of others. Which are the values we are expected to exhibit as responsible public relations writers?

Remember that ethics, being value based, are different in different cultures, something to be sensitive to when communications go to other countries and something to be aware of in other countries, such as the USA, that also have diverse cultures. When the *limits* of what your primary public will tolerate turn out to be narrower than those of your organization or yourself, your ethical behavior will be open to public debate, which may result in censure or withdrawal of support. In such cases, your first concern should be with examining your own personal and professional standards.

Influence of Personal Standards

Your personal and professional ethical standards come from your core values. If you find that your own standards are in conflict with those of your colleagues (especially your supervisor) in an organization, it can be personally and professionally upsetting.

Suppose that your task is to write, say or do something that, although legal, can't readily be reconciled with your own standards. What is your responsibility? To resolve this problem, you must explore your options realistically. Four basic strategies are apparent: (1) try to educate those in your organization to your standards; (2) refuse the task; (3) ask that you be given another task or (4) take the assignment.

Educating

You can try to convert those around you to your point of view. The character of an organization tends to reflect its top leadership. The leadership hires managers, who then hire people whom they perceive as fitting into and contributing to the goals of the organization. To say that you must be a clone of the top leadership is absurd, but it is equally absurd to believe that you would be in the job if those doing the hiring had not assumed that you "fit the mold" to some extent.

That assumption will be in your favor as you attempt to educate others in the organization to your point of view, because you are presumed to be much like them. If you use this identification tactic, you'll probably find that some colleagues are open-minded but others aren't. If your organization encourages dialogue, however, your chances of getting a fair hearing are greater. But even with a fair hearing, you may not convert them to your view of the world; besides, you may be wrong. A lot depends on how carefully and thoughtfully you have drawn the personal and professional circles of influence around yourself.

How pliable is your position? What is the absolute limit beyond which you will not compromise? What justification can you offer to support your position? Is the basis of your justification appropriate to the situation? You must ask yourself and carefully answer these questions and many like them before you attempt to implement a strategy of conversion.

Suppose you ask and answer such questions to your own satisfaction and mount a campaign to change the organization's course of action. Can you win? Yes. Even if you aren't successful at converting your colleagues, you still may win in two important ways.

First, your colleagues will respect a well-articulated, well-reasoned argument, even if they disagree with it. That's because the subject of contention is a matter of judgment. Neither you nor they can be absolutely certain of the truth of the matter, but each of you may recognize and appreciate sincere efforts to divine it.

Second, you also win because, when you articulate a different or unpopular standard, you accept the highest responsibility of being a professional public relations person. You are expected to counsel your organization against doing something you believe is wrong. Any lesser standard of behavior is not worthy of being called professional.

If you don't convert the others to your point of view, you can then adopt a strategy of refusal.

Refusing

A position of refusal is often greeted with arguments that "It's OK because everybody does it." If those arguments don't succeed, they are often replaced by anger—even retribution— that may get you fired. Your willingness to risk being fired is the severest test of your conviction. If your belief is strong enough, getting fired may be a personal and professional favor to you. That's because it tells you clearly that the organization does not respect you or your professional judgment and abilities. You need to know this so you can find another organization that does. Also, you will not be subject to criticism when the action of the organization draws fire.

No one and no organization can make you do something you believe is wrong, even if it is not illegal. If you cave in because you need the money, you like your position, you're really counting on an attractive retirement program or the like, your convictions are mostly for show. That's your fault. Don't blame the organization, society or some generalized "other" for the bottom-line decisions you make.

If you don't have the courage of your convictions, you may tend to assume that others don't either. This may be true of some, but not of all. And such an assumption is likely to make you less sensitive to the feelings, needs and values of others. As a result, you may write, say or do things that are harmful to pertinent audiences, without even recognizing it. Thus you may feed on and perpetuate stereotypes, confuse form with substance and promote behaviors detrimental to the best interests of your publics/stakeholders. If left uncorrected, this behavior can end in alienation and loss of support for your organization, thereby setting the stage for program or organization failure.

To paraphrase the Golden Rule, the way you are treated as a writer is a reflection of how you, as a writer, treat your target publics/stakeholders.

Requesting Reassignment

If you like what you are doing and your prospects for the future look good, you may seek an alternative to refusing the task. One approach is to ask that you be assigned to something else of equal or greater importance. The problem is that there may be no one else to take the assignment. Assuming that someone else is available, this strategy will produce three important results. First, by stating your case clearly, calmly and logically, you will find out just how persuasive you really are. Second, whatever the response to your request, you also discover how you are valued by your supervisor and organization. Third, you'll get a clearer picture of the people you work with and for—what their values are and how they relate to the organization and industry with which they are identified.

Taking the Assignment

Taking the assignment, even if you are sincerely opposed to it, labels you as a team player who puts the values and needs of the organization above personal values. You are seen as fitting into the culture of the organization. You won't rock the boat. You will safeguard the values of the organization because you are loyal and trustworthy. You may even get a raise, a promotion or both.

The problem with all this is that you may be expected to write, say or do things that, although not strictly illegal, may violate a primary public's sense of right and wrong. If you push beyond what your target public will tolerate, you are likely to find yourself on trial in the court of public opinion. The judgments can be harsh. Even if you later clean up your act, you may never win an appeal or get a pardon. That will depend to some extent on the values and standards of practice exhibited by your organization and industry.

Influence of Organization and Industry Standards

Will having high personal and professional standards mean that you'll always be swimming upstream in your organization? That depends on the organization you work for and the industry sector it is part of. Some organizations and industry sectors are seen as monoliths whose only purpose is to make more money or gain additional power and influence. Such perspectives often are based not on facts but on perceptions that masquerade as facts. Some organizations and industry sectors seem more gifted than others at keeping facts and "facts" in close harmony.

Perceptions

Responses to a crisis, especially initial ones, are critical to perceptions of an organization's ethical standards and sensitivity to all stakeholders. The response should fit neatly into an organization's mission and values statement. If the response contradicts either or both of those statements, the credibility of the organization is damaged for a very long time, perhaps even permanently. Occasionally, an organization even changes its name in an attempt to escape a bad reputation triggered by a thoughtless or ill-considered response.

Organizational Culture and Values

When you start a new job, you'll go through a period of training in the culture and values of the organization. This may include attending a formal training program whose announced purpose is to acquaint you with the principal processes, techniques and policies that are to guide your behavior as an employee. These also reflect, but often not as obviously, the values and culture of the organization. But much of your training comes from simply watching and interacting with your new associates. That's how you learn the rules governing how you should behave in an organization. These rules of conduct may become so much a part of you that you hardly notice them. You may even respond automatically to new cues.

Automatic Responses

When you do things automatically, you're less likely to question your behavior or that of the organization. And if you don't question how, what and why you do things, you aren't much more than an automaton. The only real difference is that you draw a salary. Automatons are machines whose greatest expense comes in the form of an initial capital investment, supplemented by routine maintenance to keep them productive. When they wear out or become outdated, they are simply replaced.

A responsible public relations writer should be a thinking, constructively critical and contributing member of the organization. In fact, the highest contribution you can make is not your technical skill but your sensitivity to the needs of your organization's relevant publics. If you become so immersed in the culture and standards of the organization that you lose touch with the values of those publics, you can do little more than a machine can do.

Problems may arise when the messages you shape undergo significant changes in the process of obtaining necessary approvals. The challenge for you is to see that these changes don't affect the sense of what must be communicated. This problem is aggravated by "editors" who excise segments or change things just to prove they can. You are supposed to be good enough with words and language that you can retain the sense of the message without compromising its integrity and without challenging the ego of those who have authority to approve what you write.

Because you are part of your organization, you are expected to know as much about what you write as anyone in the organization. You can't rely on your wordsmithing skills alone. You must know your organization and its industry thoroughly. You won't get much support or respect if you repeatedly make simple mistakes, such as using jargon incorrectly. You are supposed to know, and you shouldn't have to be told over and over. That's part of an organization's culture and values. But the practice of professional public relations also has its own culture and values, thus representing another area of influence on your behavior.

The complexity of this overlay of influences makes ethical decisions anything but clear-cut.

What Happens When You Aren't Told?

Unfortunately, there's yet another scenario to consider. One has to imagine that many investor relations (IR) people experienced this during the recent global financial meltdown. You are not told about decisions that have moral, and sometimes legal, consequences.

The reason that "best practices" in public relations has the top PR person reporting directly to the top manager of the organization is that to communicate responsibly, you have to know the facts. Some top managers don't agree and hide facts from their public relations people, assuming that "what they don't know won't hurt them," and certainly won't "get outside." They are just wrong.

When a crisis is brewing, or even seems likely, the public relations person has to know as much as can be known, and as soon as it is known. It is the responsibility of top management to tell its board of directors, even if it is a nonprofit organization, and to arrive at an action plan that should be shared with the top public relations person immediately. Be sure that such procedure is in place before you take a job or you are accepting unnecessary personal and professional risk. If you are not told, what do you do when you find out? You have to meet with top management to determine why you were not told and then determine why you were not told and then evaluate your situation. If you can't persuade management to take an ethical and responsible communication of the situation, you are better off leaving. Leave gracefully, without accusations or threats. If legal possibilities are involved, you also need to get a lawyer. Yes, you'll have to bear the cost, but whatever that is, it is not as costly as the loss of your reputation, which could make you unemployable in the industry. Or, the result could be a substantial fine or imprisonment, if the event involves legal matters.

Influence of Public Relations Standards of Practice

The reason you could find yourself unemployable is due to a tainted professional performance. Every professional field has its own code of ethics and standards of practice. One of the most widely acknowledged codes in public relations is the one adopted in 2000 to replace the 1988 code. (The Public Relations Society of America [PRSA] adopted its first

Source: "Shoe" © MacNelly. King Features Syndicate.

code in 1950.) The code has much to say about the standards of practice, but a few key points are especially pertinent to your role as a writer.

Accuracy

Credibility with priority stakeholder/publics is probably the most important asset a writer or an organization can have. Without credibility, it is very difficult to succeed at what you want to do. Factual inaccuracies usually are pretty easy for primary publics to detect. The more difficult such inaccuracies are to discover, the more damaging they may appear in the eyes of your audience. Publics may conclude that you have deliberately distorted or misrepresented the facts for some ulterior motive.

They may label you and your organization as dishonest—and you are, if you misrepresent the facts. But you and your organization can also make "honest" mistakes. These may seep into your writing as a result of rushed, sloppy editing, failure to verify details and the like. But if you simply rationalize them as "honest" mistakes, you're really not being very responsible. You are paid to do things correctly, and this includes preventing "honest" mistakes from getting by.

To illustrate, the annual report of a major oil company contained an out-of-place decimal that dramatically reduced estimates of its oil reserves from those it had claimed in previous reports. The financial community immediately became alarmed because it feared the company had been puffing up earlier estimates of its reserves. Frantic phone calls and a dramatic drop in share prices ensued. The company quickly issued a corrected estimate, so the damage, though costly, was temporary—all because the writers, editors and proofreaders made an "honest" mistake. You can also bet that market analysts and brokers looked at the next year's annual report with an extra dose of skepticism. "Honest" mistakes are sometimes no less damaging than dishonest ones. For example, in the global environment of instant communication if a response to an inquiry in social media doesn't match a statement about the same issue on your website, the world will know about it in seconds.

Honesty, Truth and Fairness

The concept of honesty goes beyond the idea of accuracy and raises questions of truth and fairness. You can deal with documentable facts as a writer and still be dishonest, untruthful and unfair. So factual accuracy is not enough. The selection of facts and the way you weave them into the fabric of a message are what establish you as honest, truthful, fair and credible.

Must you use all the facts, even the bad? No. But to ignore the negatives is not fair. Even if recipients of your primary message are not highly sophisticated, they are not dumb. If you fail to acknowledge damaging information, you simply invite disbelief. Not only will you not be believed, you may also be perceived as unfair. Honesty and forthrightness served American Airlines well when one of its jets ran into a mountain in Colombia. The airline's chief pilot said, "Human error on the part of our people may have contributed to the accident."[4] Years ago, the legal department might have been in an uproar because of concern over protecting the company from liability. Now most organizations see that a greater loss may come from a failure to speak out. A loss of credibility translates to a loss of customers.

Illustrations matter too, and often that is a question of fidelity to truth rather than an attempt to mislead or deceive. A digitally altered photo released from the USA's Army regarding promotion of Ann Dunwoody to four-star general involved keying in the USA flag as background instead of her desk in front of a bookcase. The USA's Department of Defense claimed not to have violated Army policy in altering the photo, but the Associated Press (AP) suspended use of photos from the USA's Department of Defense as a result of its policy of not altering any content from an image.

That situation probably is a more ethically defendable one than another issue involving the USA's Department of Defense. The Pentagon Public Affairs office had sent around retired military officers as spokespeople supporting the government's military decisions. Many of the retired military analysts were said to have undisclosed ties with military contractors. Many retired military officers have gone to work as advisors to companies that are defense contractors. The uproar that disclosure of this practice created was over the law against "domestic propaganda."

False or Misleading Information

Misleading information can lead audiences to make bad decisions. When they discover they have been misled, they withdraw their support. Although you and your organization may enjoy some advantage because of a deception, the advantage is usually temporary. And the consequences of misleading people can be enormous as well as long term. In fact, disaffected audiences may seek retribution through legal actions, boycotts or other means.

The excesses of false and misleading information that came from Enron and WorldCom provoked the Sarbanes-Oxley Act of 2002 designed to make publicly held companies more accountable. As a result, the Securities and Exchange Commission (SEC) and the New York Stock Exchange issued new orders. Although the public relations implications fall largely on the IR specialists, other corporate communications people must also be watchful. One has to wonder about some deliberate and confessed decisions during the financial meltdown that are in direct contradiction to Sarbanes-Oxley and even SEC regulations.

The Sarbanes-Oxley regulations requiring more explicit information about earnings emphasizes the SEC fair disclosure regulations made in 2000. That SEC regulation requires that investing decisions be made more accessible to the public and that anytime material information is intentionally disclosed, it must be made available simultaneously to all publics. That did not happen when Bank of America acquired Merrill Lynch. The bank officer blamed the regulators for telling him not to make the disclosure. So that action was intentional. When unintentional, the undisclosed information must be made public as soon as possible. Disclosure also has to be made through a combination of means to reach as broad an audience as possible. Many IR officers now post news releases immediately on the corporate website as well as sending them on all of the wire services. Public relations practitioners also were affected by the Campaign Reform Act of 2002 that created new disclosure requirements and requires prompt compliance with earlier regulations so that there's more public information available about politically active groups and individuals.[5] Truth has a way of emerging in spite of extraordinary efforts to keep it hidden. In the vast majority of cases, false information is destined to fail. PR writers who knowingly write and distribute false information, for whatever reason, violate one of the trusts explicit in the PRSA code and risk losing the respect and acceptance of their primary publics. False information corrupts not only a writer but also the channels of communication used to distribute it. Hence, false information supplied to a newspaper and relayed to readers damages the reputation of the newspaper, as well as the primary source, in the eyes of the readers. The result is that the newspaper may be reluctant to accept subsequent information from you. Moreover, not only will you find it more difficult to get information into that newspaper, but also will all other public relations people. The assumption will simply be that all public relations professionals or other official spokespersons are alike, and you can't trust any of them.

In 2012, what provoked an attack on the USA's consulate in Benghazi killing the US Ambassador to Libya was reported to USA news media by then ambassador to the United Nations Susan Rice as reaction to a film "The Innocence of Muslims." When conflicting evidence surfaced, Rice said in formal testimony that what she reported was given to her as the official version of what was known at that time. Within hours after her announcement, though, the Libyan Congress disputed her report and said no protests against the film had occurred. The attack was the work of Islamic militants fighting in Syria, Libyan officials said. When US survivors were debriefed later back in their country, they confirmed the Libyan government's version. The result has been accusations of a cover-up by the USA that is likely to resonate for years.

Influence of Laws and Regulations

Everything you communicate has the potential to spark litigation. You must know your freedom under the First Amendment (if you are in the USA) and the laws governing commercial speech as well to bulletproof your writing as much as possible. If your material is going into other countries, check on your rights and restraints there too. You can't fully immunize it from legal action, but you can minimize the potential for losses. And you don't have to be an attorney to do this. Just follow some simple guidelines.

Negative Laws

The first guideline is to realize that laws are generally negative. They define what is not legal. They generally don't define what is legal. You may suppose that something is legal because it has not been defined as illegal. But although that may be true at the time, you may be in for a surprise later.

A further guideline is to remember that case law is built on a series of court decisions, each citing previous decisions. Even when a substantial line of cases evolve from a seminal decision—often one that turns on some question of constitutionality—each new case has the potential to produce a different interpretation of what is illegal, thereby setting a precedent. One thing you should guard against is doing something that will turn you or your organization into a legal precedent.

A case in point was a USA Supreme Court decision in 1989 declaring that the copyright of creative work is the property of the freelancer or vendor unless its ownership passes to someone else in a legal contract at the time the work is authorized. Organizations and PR agencies have sometimes acted as if they owned such creative work, even when no contract existed. The only way they can own it now is to contract for it ahead of time or to obtain permission to use it, which may involve paying fees for each additional usage. That now includes making the print version available on a website.

Simply because you or an organization have always done things in a certain way does not mean that those procedures will be acceptable tomorrow. It is your responsibility to keep up with court decisions and new laws affecting communication in general, and your organization and industry specifically. Copyright laws continue to change regarding materials available through cyberspace.

That brings us to another guideline. Read and study each weekly issue of *Media Law Reporter*, published by Bloomberg BNA. This publication specializes in timely reports and summaries of laws and court decisions affecting every aspect of mass communication, including public relations. If you have any doubts about a new law or court decision, consult an attorney who specializes in communication law. Don't depend on other attorneys, because they may know no more about communication law than you do.

Contracts

You'll find that your organization probably uses lots of outside vendors—writers, producers, photographers, printers and the like. Because they are working for you, you are responsible for their actions in the process of preparing and presenting their material. You must know the nature of agreements with each of these suppliers. Otherwise you are liable to make a grievous error that may cost your organization lots of money and perhaps you your job. One of the most important contract areas is work done "for hire." Unless a vendor signs away ownership of his or her creative work to your organization in a legal contract, you may not use it for any additional or subsequent purpose unless you get legal permission and, sometimes, pay additional fees. This applies to all kinds of creative work.

Additionally, any time a photographer—whether staff or freelancer—supplies you with pictures, each one that includes people (especially professional models) must be accompanied by a photo release form duly signed, thus "releasing" his or her likeness for use in the specified situation. If you're using a freelance photographer, determine who owns the rights to the images before shooting begins. Ownership of the images may fall under the "for hire" provision, too. But unless a contract says otherwise, the photographer retains the original images and controls subsequent uses of them.

One contractual arrangement now simplified is for the organizational use of music—either for meetings or to entertain phone callers put "on hold." The American Society of Composers, Authors and Publishers (ASCAP) has an umbrella contract covering the playing of copyrighted music in public. Some organizations play their own promotional jingles, which for copyright reasons they usually have written especially for that purpose unless they use music "in the public domain," music on which the copyright has expired. There are some risks here because special arrangements of such music and performances of it may still carry a copyright, especially now with changes in the USA and the European Union (EU).

In addition to explicit contracts governing outside vendor relationships, there is an implied contract between you and your employer that you will maintain confidentiality. Some firms actually write this into a separate employee contract, although most of the time it's understood that you will keep to yourself what you learn about a client or an organization. That you will protect confidential information is an implied contract. You won't share information with anyone outside the organization and will use a "need to know" basis inside. Such discretion is especially important when you're dealing with financial matters that may constitute "insider information" and thus be of concern to the SEC. The fact is that if you tip someone who uses that information for personal gain in the stock market, you are as guilty of "tipping" as they are of "insider trading."

Commercial Free Speech

In the USA, no First Amendment rights for organizations are constitutionally guaranteed. However, over the years, a commercial free speech doctrine has evolved. Advertising is clearly covered. The doctrine is less clear about public relations communication, as Nike discovered in defending itself from a lawsuit filed by activist Marc Kasky. Nike had been accused of using sweatshop labor in contracting factories abroad to make its shoes and not monitoring working conditions there. Nike wrote letters to educators and opinion leaders defending its operations and also wrote op-ed commentaries for newspapers as well as sent news releases to the papers.

The US Supreme Court has always supported First Amendment privileges for *political* free speech, even when it is inaccurate. But, Kasky sued Nike for false *advertising*. So, the question really is the definition of Nike's action: commercial speech, as Kasky claimed, or noncommercial, as Nike claimed. Commercial speech is held to high standards of truth so consumers will not be deceived. Earlier cases, like the 1983 Texas Gulf Sulphur case where a news release was held to be "false and misleading," suggest that news releases are also under the umbrella of truth.

Convergence and integration of message distribution, though, brings up some potential challenges. Integration of media for messages, especially, may make what would be clearly recognizable as advertising less distinguishable from what could be otherwise seen as noncommercial communication.

The problem is that commercial free speech is determined by case law, to which the Nike case contributes. In the past, decisions have moved back and forth across the spectrum of just how free are organizational and institutional voices.

Beyond case laws, organizations and institutions also have to deal with possible contempt of court in trying to defend themselves in lawsuits. Litigation journalism (or litigation PR as some prefer to call it) has relaxed some earlier threats. But all it takes is for the opposing side to make the case to the judge handling the case that anything being said about the case is likely to prejudice the jury. When that occurs, you can't write a position paper about the case that you make public, or write commentaries or interpretations of the case for public consumption without inviting a contempt of court charge. Furthermore, you can't go on talk shows, issue news releases, buy advertising space or time or take other actions to convey the position of your organization on the case. This can be very frustrating because it effectively gags an organization until the case has been decided.[6]

Libel Laws and Privacy Issues

When you defame someone in writing, it's libel and to do so in speech that is not written is slander. Defamation is an attack on someone's character, good name or reputation.

If people believe they have been libeled by what you have written, they can bring legal actions for actual and punitive damages. Your best defense against libel is to be accurate and truthful to a fault—so much so that you can document anything you say. Public figures (elected officials and people in the public eye) who bring libel actions must prove you libeled them "with malice." You should realize, however, that current case law makes it difficult to determine exactly who is a public figure.

You need to be very careful when dealing with both public and private figures. Stick with provable facts. You can't play fast and loose with words and avoid libel actions. Any time you use words that could impinge someone's character, such as "gangster," "villain," "cheat," "drug addict" and so on, you are inviting a court appearance. Check current libel laws for other words and usage that can be interpreted as an unfavorable attribute, such as "unprofessional," "paramour," "hypocrite" and so on.

Privacy laws are most often of concern when you want to use a person's likeness and name in publicity, advertising or other promotional materials. People in pictures of crowds at public gatherings represent fair use, but you can't single out people in the crowd and use them for promotional purposes without their consent. If they happen to be celebrities, you'll also need a legal contract to back up the usage. Otherwise, you may be guilty of invasion of privacy.

Libel is another issue, and one that is changing, in many ways due to the Internet. First of all, the person or institution suing for libel must prove damage. In the defense of libel claims, the documentable *truth* must be admissible in court, and that's up to the judge.

One closely watched Massachusetts state court case was *Noonan v. Staples*, in which an executive of the office supply company, Staples, had sent an email to employees explaining that former employee Alan Noonan had been terminated because he violated company travel and expense policies. Noonan's suit for defamation rested on his proving that the truthful email was sent with "actual malevolent intent or ill will." "Actual malice," from the *New York Times v. Sullivan* case, has consistently been interpreted to mean "reckless disregard for the truth," leaving provable truth a defense. The first decision was based on a 1902 state law that predates the *New York Times v. Sullivan* decision and says truth is a defense to libel unless actual malice is proved.

The case wound up in the hand of a jury and was tried in Boston. A one-page verdict form filed by the jury found in favor of Staples. The debate was over "actual malice." Remember this was a digital case involving an email.[7]

Another email case was a much more private email. Lawyers for the producers of the Broadway musical, "Rebecca," sued the show's former publicist Marc Thibodeau for sending an email to a potential investor in the show warning the investor that the show was in trouble. Thibodeau used the name "Sarah Finkelstein" in sending the email. His lawyer did say that his client had used the fictitious name in his warning. Lawyers for the producers of the musical sued for defamation and breach of contract and fiduciary duty because the investment was hoped to save the show financially. Long-time Broadway publicist Thibodeau was labeled by his lawyer as "an innocent whistle-blower." The publicist also had sent emails under the name of "Bethany Walsh" to the investor's lawyers. In addition to this lost investor, Rebecca show producers discovered that four other investors it was counting on were "ghost" investors from a middleman. The production is being delayed.[8]

A question that these two cases did not address is who owns digital accounts, particularly social media accounts? There seems to be clarity on email accounts in that if you are using your employer's email account then the employer owns the account.

Oops. What if your social media accounts are also on your employer's electronic account and not on a separate, private account? Or, even you have them on a private account, and think you own your Twitter, LinkedIn, Facebook and so on, your employer may consider these should be valued as trade secrets.

Your content on social media is not the value; it's the connections. Employees in marketing, advertising and public relations consider contacts built through relationships to be essential professional connections that will help them wherever they are employed. Even the federal courts may decide that in some cases social media accounts are an organization's trade secrets and thus their property.

Some guidelines you might want to consider come from Cayce Myers, Ph.D., J.D., LL.M., Virginia Tech, Department of Communication.
For PR Practitioners:

- Establish up-front who owns what social media account. When a practitioner is working in-house this may be established by social media policy. However, when working freelance or for an agency with multiple accounts, this ownership question may not be answered by a policy. Establishing boundaries and expectations up-front in a written contract reduces the risk of litigation over ownership.
- Create and maintain personal social media accounts, specifically LinkedIn, and use them only for personal reasons. This may require practitioners to set up personal and professional accounts. While this may not be optimal for unity of professional branding, it provides a demarcation between professional and private accounts.
- Do not do promotions for clients or organizations on social media accounts. Using personal social media accounts for promotional or sale purposes, specifically creating promotional events or groups creates an argument that the account is the property of the organization. While it is tempting to use personal accounts that already have built in followers, it blurs the lines between professional and personal, creating the potential for ownership disputes.
- When selling a PR practice or leaving a job you should establish what social media accounts you are taking with you. Merely changing the name or affiliation of an account does not eliminate an organization's ownership interest. Remember what's at stake is the connections, followers and friendships on the account. (For advice to organizations, refer to this source in the footnote.)[9]

Privilege, another libel defense, is a fair and true report of a public, official or judicial hearing, but who determines whether the report is "fair"? The *fair comment* defense—which used to protect people, such as reviewers and columnists, who often exaggerate statements about public figures for humor—has suffered some severe blows in the courts. Some claim that now such protection doesn't exist. At the federal level, public figures still must prove malice in their libel suits, although, in some instances, their defense has been privacy. The privacy issue is often ignored within organizations when they assume that because people work there it's all right to use their names and pictures without permission. This is not true, and problems multiply if the representation is in something designed to make money for the organization, such as an ad or a brochure. There are also problems if the employee no longer works for the organization. The protection is a release form giving you *permission.*

Copyrights and Other Rights

The premise of a copyright is that creators of creative works should own what they create. Consequently, it provides a means of protecting a person's or organization's creative property against unlawful appropriation and use by others. By copyrighting what you write, you serve notice that the work is yours. Always use the copyright symbol (©) with the word *Copyright* adjacent to it. Copyrighting does not automatically invoke legal action in instances of suspected infringement. It only makes it possible for you to seek legal redress. The initiative lies with you, not with the law. Copyright protects the specific expression of an idea, but ideas, as such, are not protected. You must file for copyright protection with the Library of Congress (http://www.loc.gov/copyright/) for that protection.

Digital technology is affecting copyright law, so that you need to look for changes in that as well as the extension of copyrights on existing materials, even after the creator is dead. You should also be aware that many publications routinely copyright their contents. However, unless the individual messages in these publications were written by staff personnel, their creators retain ownership of what they have created.

Violations of copyright often take the form of plagiarism. Public relations writers have to be acutely aware of not usurping others' creations while doing research. If you quote a source, put your notes in quotation marks, and register all of the information you will need for attribution. Furthermore, if you want to use more than 100 words from one source, fewer words if it is a song, poem or relatively small work, you must get written permission from the copyright owner of the source.

Much to the dismay of fans of historian Doris Kearns Goodwin, in 2002 she admitted to copying passages from other sources and using them in her own. She was asked to take a leave of absence from PBS's *NewsHour* and resigned from the Pulitzer Prize Committee. She is not the only high-profile public figure to admit to incorporating others' work into her own. In the election campaign for the 44th president of the USA, artist Shepard Fairey created a poster based on a photograph taken by an AP photographer of the then candidate Barack Obama. Neither the photographer nor the AP was given credit. Fairey's position was that artistic license changed the image so substantially that no permission or credit was needed. The AP then countersued Fairey and his companies claiming they knew the image was copyrighted by AP and still used it as a basis for posters and other merchandise sold and distributed through various channels without permission or compensation.

If you, as a public relations person, plagiarize someone's work, not only will you be fired when it is discovered, you will also have to find your own attorney and pay all of the expenses. Furthermore, it is highly unlikely that you will be able to find PR employment again.

When you use somebody's trademark, service mark, trade character or the like, make sure that you show the ownership. For example, the ™ symbol must appear immediately after the mark, usually accompanied by a line of small type that says something like "[product name] is a registered trademark of [company name]."

You do need to realize that many individuals and countries see copyrights and trademarks as unfair protectionism and argue for more freedom of appropriation of creative work.

Government Regulators

Most of the things you write will fall under the purview of four major government agencies. One is the USA Postal Service. That agency is concerned with classes of mail, fraud, lotteries and the like. The range of regulations is staggering. And you'll find the interpretation of some of them varies significantly, depending on whom you ask. So, if you're not sure about something, ask the postmaster at the site where you expect to do a mailing. That's the only way you can really be sure.

The SEC is especially concerned with information dealing with or relating to the stock market and the financial community in general. Particular concerns that may affect you as a writer involve executives and their compensation, annual reports and news releases dealing with the financial condition or direction of your organization and potential opportunities for insider trading. The Internal Revenue Service also watches financial reports.

The Federal Trade Commission (FTC) has a wide range of interests. In relation to writers, however, the FTC is most concerned with maintaining fair competition. Hence, seemingly deceptive advertising or other promotional materials draw FTC's attention and action.

The Food and Drug Administration (FDA) watches over information from food and health industries and is very protective of the consumer. In fact, it considers information drug companies circulate about their products to be promotional, and it closely monitors educational or scientific activities.

Other regulatory groups can affect what you write too. In fact, the Bureau of Alcohol, Tobacco and Firearms threatened to close Leeward Winery in California because the winery quoted in a newsletter to customers information from a CBS *60 Minutes* show that suggested red wine may help reduce the risk of heart disease. Another winery got into trouble for using similar information in an ad. A liquor store was also stopped from using an in-store wine sales campaign that had heart signs reading "Wines to your health" and "Be heart smart."

Your responsibility is to know the applicable rules and regulations affecting your organization and industry. If you don't know the answer, ask someone who does. But you'd be wise to go to the original source, rather than risk acting on someone's well-intentioned but possibly wrong advice. For protection, some advertising/public relations agencies and other profit-making companies have internal legal counsel and a policy of reviewing all information, especially public announcements of any kind.

If you get into legal trouble, though, one point to remember is that when you work for an organization you do have some legal protection. Furthermore, if your organizational legal counsel asks you for help in crafting responses to any litigation or a litigious situation, you are more likely to be considered as legal counsel as they themselves are and protected from being subpoenaed by the opposing side. You may be under the legal umbrella of attorney-client privilege. Federal courts are more likely to see those who craft strategies, especially in time of crisis, as part of the organizational team.

Quite the contrary if you are self-employed. You are likely to have to turn over any and the all material related to the case, even what you would consider confidential because it could compromise the person or organization you have worked with that is getting sued. For that reason, you may want to contact an attorney who knows something about media law in advance of any possible litigation and make arrangements. When a case occurs, you probably will want to put the attorney on a retainer because cases tend to drag on with occasional spikes demanding an instant response.

If you work for an agency, although you may have responsibility for one or more clients, the agency itself usually has a lawyer or law firm on retainer. The client probably has legal staff too. Your protection in such a situation is less clear, and it may depend on where the suit is filed. Although the lawyers have attorney-client privilege, you probably will not. The courts have been ambiguous in their rulings regarding public relations writers.

Influence of Priority Publics

Although the four major areas of influence already mentioned are vital to your success as a writer, none is more important than the influence of primary publics. Every organization, public or private, profit making or nonprofit, must be keenly aware of the influence of its primary publics. Indeed, the organization can exist only with their permission.

Permission does not always mean approval of all that the organization is doing. However, the critical limits of an organization's ethical and legal behavior are determined by its primary or closest stakeholders/publics—those who share organizational identity, such as employees and (often) former employees, and those with whom it has an ongoing relationship, such as suppliers, distributors and customers.

Shared Values

The stronger a public's identity with the organization, the stronger its reaction will be to what the organization is saying and doing. Primary publics perceive themselves as having shared values with the organization. Any violation of these values is often reacted to very strongly and personally.

Relationships can be considered at three different levels: developmental level, sometimes called the cultivation stage, the maintenance level and the quality level or strength of the connection of an individual to the organization.

To have a strong connection to the organization, people need to feel they have easy access, are being listened to in a positive way and are responded to honestly and fairly. The underlying consideration is trust in the organization and the credibility of its communications, both created by transparency.

Transparency is an expectation of openness and disclosure of information that significantly affects all publics. The Internet provides multiple opportunities for any organization to develop unique and personal connections. These are easy to establish, but require high maintenance.

Nevertheless, the quality of an organization's relationships with its publics is a measure of good management. Even those who may not agree with the organization should respect it.

Source: Dilbert, © by Scott Adams, United Feature Syndicate, Inc. 2-1-09

Adversarial Groups

Maintaining connections with and respect from adversarial groups is critical and, there-fore, their reactions are anticipated in the planning process and closely monitored there-after. Adversarial groups may include regulators, competitors, special-interest groups and activists concerned about certain aspects of society (the environment, endangered species, animal rights and so on). These groups typically perceive themselves as having a different, not shared, set of values. That's not always the reality, but it is almost always the perception. For this reason, adversarial groups exhibit little tolerance for "mistakes" or "poor policy decisions."

Although the closest publics may respond quickly and personally to something they don't like or something they see as a violation of shared values, they are much more forgiving than adversarial publics. These two groups set the boundaries within which an organization must operate to be successful. Understanding their ethical standards and values is, therefore, crucial to planning and setting policies.

Exercises

Situation: You are the vice president for corporate communication at Enodyne, a conglomerate. You are in a corporate board meeting, having just finished presenting the budget for next year, when an emergency phone call from Ben McConkle—the public relations director of a subsidiary, Fielding Works, which manufactures industrial solvents and other chemicals—advises you that a Fielding transport on its way to a toxic waste dump had an accident near North Platte, Nebraska, about three hours ago. The truck turned over three times and several containers of toxic chemicals ruptured, posing high danger to people on the scene and to people within a 5-mile radius, depending on the speed and direction of the wind. No one was seriously injured, but the driver and his companion suffered minor abrasions and bruises. The driver is Burl B. Benton, 33, an employee of 10 years with a spotless record. The companion is Helene A. Haven, 30, a female nonemployee. McConkle wants quick guidance on how to handle inquiries, especially those related to these facts: (1) tests showed that Benton and Haven had been drinking; (2) neither was legally drunk; (3) tests showed that Haven had traces of cocaine in her system and (4) McConkle has not yet notified Mrs. Benton and her two children of the accident. McConkle needs your advice now, not later, because the news media will pick up these facts very soon.

1. What guidance will you offer McConkle? Is your guidance fully responsible to Enodyne, to the driver and his family, to the driver's companion and her family, to the people in the area of the accident and to others? How so? Why so?
2. Write a one-page summary of the ethical problems involved in this situation, and explain how they might affect you as a PR writer.
3. Write a one-page summary of the potential legal problems in this situation, and explain how they might affect you as a writer.

PART 2

Writing Principles

Remember that all readers, listeners and viewers of PR writing are volunteers! Make their experience rewarding.

Writing to Clarify and Simplify the Complex: Style and Content

Public relations writers seldom prepare materials that are required reading, listening or viewing. Occasionally, as a PR writer, you may prepare a handbook or manual or training video that eventually is required consumption for some audience. Even if it is "required" reading, you still have to make it accessible. The point of these materials is usually instruction, so the audience must be able to understand the message first, and second it must be compelling enough to remember.

Most audiences for whom you research and write, though, are volunteers. You have a great deal of competition too, at all levels. You have to compete for attention with all kinds of insistent messages. A primary source for information about your company, its products and its services is on a website. That website won't have many visitors if it isn't viewer-friendly and offers information that is easy to understand. When you are trying to get messages into a medium over which you and your organization have no control, just to get the material accepted you have to compete with materials prepared by skillful staff writers and freelance sources worldwide. That means you have to be a very good writer, offering excellent information in an extraordinarily interesting way.

Most important, you need to remember that good writing is writing that succeeds in communicating. Bad writing is writing that fails to communicate.

Writer and teacher of writing at Yale William Zinsser says that every successful piece of nonfiction should leave the reader with one provocative thought not previously held. Not two thoughts or five, just one.[1] But all the advice in all the books about writing is worthless if you don't learn the most important point first: *Write so people will understand what you mean.* That is the one provocative thought you should take from this chapter. To do that, you must consider both style and content.

You won't be very successful in communicating if you simply enter words into a computer without giving them much thought beforehand or if you are more concerned with displaying your vocabulary than with communicating with your readers. You have to think about who your readers or listeners are. What do they know? What do they think they know? You can't get by with just telling them what you want to and in words that you choose. Furthermore, much of what you write is expected to have a specific effect. PR writing is results-oriented, and it is a craft that must be learned and practiced.

How do you produce prose that succeeds in communicating? There is no magic formula, but you start with the basics—message, recipients (intended and unintended), medium. Then be sure the message, however complex, is simplified.

Message, Recipients, Medium

An important part of good writing is being properly prepared before you start. You must do the necessary research on the subject matter so you will understand the material, know what is important and have in mind just what you want to communicate and what results you want. You must also know who will receive your communication and how best to reach them. In short, you must know your message, your recipients and your medium.

Message

Most writing, whether for public relations purposes or otherwise, has one goal: to convey a message. The goal of any writer is to transfer thoughts to other people's minds, whatever the medium. Step one, then, is deciding just what you want to say. If you don't understand what you're trying to say, neither will others.

This means you must know exactly what you are trying to say. Don't express your message in hazy, abstract terms. Make sure you understand the message before you begin to write. If you can't write a short, simple sentence that summarizes the point you want to make, you probably need to do a little more thinking. Remember: What do you want to happen as a result of your communication effort? Results, the effects of your writing, are what those who employ you will be measuring. In short, your job depends on effective, measurable results.

Recipients: Publics/Stakeholders and Others

It is not enough, however, for you to understand your message. You must phrase it so others also will understand. Knowing who your intended readers or listeners are (see the discussion of priority publics in Chapter 1) means awareness of their characteristics, values and beliefs so you can reach them (see the discussion of demographics and psychographics in Chapters 6 and 7).

Otherwise, you won't be able to communicate effectively. In short, you must tailor your message carefully and deliberately for intended recipients. However, you have to remember that your message also will reach unintended recipients accessing your organization through apps; social media; and countless other text, audio and video media. The challenge is being culturally aware while tailoring your message to reach your priority publics/stakeholders. Instant global access to communication also means cultivating a sensitivity to how unintended recipients are likely to react. Building good relationships, not creating bad ones, is the responsibility of the public relations writer. You want all of the informal (social) network buzz you might create to be positive. Tailoring your message also means realizing that even publics able to read and comprehend complex information have too much to read and too little time in which to read or pay attention to a specific message that is being offered, but not necessarily sought. For publics who only hear your message, complexity is too much of a challenge. The medium is your other consideration.

Medium

An important part of tailoring your message consists of choosing the right medium to reach that public. In addition, different media are appropriate for different types of messages. Choosing the right medium is an important aspect of successful communication.

The choice of medium in turn affects the way you should frame the message. Articles written for magazines are done in an entirely different style than public service announcements for radio. You must use the style appropriate for the medium, being aware of the medium's technological advantages and limitations.

These three rules—(1) know your message, (2) know your recipients (your publics/stakeholders) and (3) know your medium—will take you a long way toward successful writing. Both the substance and the style of what you write depend on these three elements. Your job is recrafting your message for each medium you will be using.

Success in delivering the message applies only to the planning stages of writing. Even if you know your message, your audience and your medium, your writing may fail. The execution is just as important as the preparation. So add three other rules for successful execution: Write clearly, make what you write engaging and simplify the complex to make information easily accessible.

Style

Clarity, of course, is the number one aim of writing style. If your audience doesn't understand what you've written, your efforts will have been wasted. But even if your writing is clear, if it isn't engaging you will lose your reader or listener before you can deliver a message. You need to initiate a relationship that attracts because it offers a reward to the recipient.

Readability/Listenability

Given a strong enough motivation, a person will "plow through any complexity of words, signs or hieroglyphs," says readability expert Robert Gunning.[2] That's true. Someone intensely interested in a subject will read through the worst writing trying to glean the slightest bit of new information. Usually, though, interest is not that high. People bombarded from all sides with innumerable public relations messages from different communicators are likely to ignore any messages that demand too much time or effort.

The problem today may be that although the desire to understand may be strong, the ability is inadequate. It is for 43 percent of the population. A 2003 study measuring skills on three levels—prose, document and quantitative—revealed 29 percent have difficulties with basic reading exercises and another 14 percent can't even manage that much. Some of the reading challenges may be medical, such as dyslexia, a lack of educational opportunities or due to having English as a second language. Only 13 percent read at the highest level and just 44 percent are average.

The figures had changed little in 2013, causing this comment, "Stagnation is unacceptable. Today's 12 graders are performing no differently in mathematics and reading than they did in 2009, said David P. Driscoll, chair of the National Assessment Governing Board, which sets the policy for NAEP (National Assessment of Educational Progress)."[3]

What this means was made clearer in a *USA TODAY* piece by Greg Toppo. "A long-awaited federal study (2009) finds that an estimated 32 million adults in the USA—about one in seven—are saddled with such low literacy skills that it would be tough for them to read anything more challenging than a children's picture book or to understand a medication's side effects listed on a pill bottle."[4]

What qualities make writing "easy to read"? This question has been the subject of a vast amount of research, finally focusing on two key qualities: sentence length and word length.

Sentence Length   The first principle of readable writing is to keep most sentences short. For the meaning to be clear, the reader must be able to grasp at once the relationship among the words in a sentence. Long, tangled sentences tend to obscure those relationships.

Of course, not every sentence should be short. An endless stream of short sentences makes for dull reading. And it is possible for long sentences to be clear—if they are properly constructed.

The key to readability, then, is average sentence length. An occasional long sentence is no problem. But a never-ending series of long sentences leaves readers dizzy. According to Gunning, modern prose read by the public has an average sentence length of about 16 words.[5] If your sentences are much longer than that on the average, your prose probably isn't as readable as it should be.

There are two major reasons why sentences are too long. One is that writers tend to connect independent clauses with coordinating conjunctions or add details that could be left for later sentences. The other is that too many unnecessary words are present. The cures are easy: Use more periods and fewer words.

Some long sentences, for example, can simply be cut in two with a period at the right spot. Avoid connectives like "however." Use a period and start a new sentence. Look at this example:

> Students inclined to fall into the habit of binge drinking are very likely to become alcoholics; however, students who are willing to learn how to drink responsibly and moderately may require external pressure and special incentives to change a habit perhaps learned in high school or earlier.

A revision might be: Binge drinkers are inviting alcoholism. A habit of alcohol abuse learned at an early age may require incentives or external help to change.

A sentence of 47 words becomes two, one 5 words and another 18. See if you can trim the second sentence to a desired maximum of 16 words.

Excessive words in much writing result from temptations to overwrite—overusing modifiers, especially words that intensify and may be redundant. Some modifiers are so trite they are meaningless, such as "spectacular" or "amazing." Some are redundant, like "dog puppies" or "young children." The fewer words, the stronger the statement. Look at this example:

> The Provost said he never in his 10 years at the university ever had witnessed such a debacle, and he was surprised and shocked by the students' outrageous and destructive behavior at the game, although he realized it was not all students, just a disruptive few.

It is better to say, "The Provost said the students' outrageous and destructive behavior at the game shocked him."

The original sentence would have been worse if the attribution had not been clear. Much writing is made murky by needless attribution. Introductions and personal commentary also inflate, and commentary is not welcomed in news releases. These writing flaws are quite common in what is euphemistically called "business writing."

An example is: "Structural integrity has been found to be difficult to measure." All you need is: "Structural integrity is difficult to measure." If the statement is something that needs documenting, cite a source. Don't write around it.

Weak information also causes protracted introductions. Another cause may simply be a lack of focus. People are in a hurry and if you want to be on their agenda, you have to earn the right with a clean, clear appeal.

Look at this example:

> Students, faculty and staff are asked to provide their cell phone numbers by email to the university's safety alert email address (safety@xxx.edu) so they can be called in the event of severe weather. A notice of when the university will be officially closed due to severe weather will be on the university website, Facebook page, Twitter and on the university's main phone as well as given to the local news media to announce.

Try this: "University closings on bad weather days will come as a direct call to registered cell phone numbers. To be notified, send your cell phone number to safety@xxx.edu. Weather closings will also be announced on the main university website, Facebook, Twitter and phone and by local radio and television stations." The 73-word message was cut to 49 words and made more specific. Can you make it even better?

The personal commentary problem is so common in letters that one of the authors forbids students from using "I" to begin any sentence in a cover letter, memo or media advisory. The reason? People are likely to intuitively respond with "Who cares?" Of course few are rude enough to express it, but the reaction is there. An "I" disengages the reader, whereas a "you" involves the reader.

Keeping sentences short is just the starting place in writing clearly, though. Short sentences won't make reading easy if the words within those sentences don't make sense. You can't write clear sentences if you don't use clear words.

Word Length   A student with an exceptional vocabulary once turned in what he thought was an especially well-written paper. The professor's comment scribbled across the top of the paper was simply: "Avoid sesquipedalianism." Because the student's vocabulary wasn't *that* large, he scurried to a dictionary to look up *sesquipedalianism*. He found it to mean the excessive use of long words.

The professor could easily have written, "Don't use so many long words," and the student would have understood immediately. The point for public relations writers is twofold. First, if you use long words, some readers won't understand them. Second, even if the long words you use have well-known meanings, they slow the reader down.

There is no need to say *precipitation* when you mean *rain*. There is nothing wrong with saying *use* instead of *employ* or *utilize. Fair* is just as good a word as *equitable*.

Some writers can't resist filling their prose with important-sounding phrases like "integrated conceptual analysis" or similar verbose nonsense. At least twice in every sentence they use words ending in -*ment*, -*any*, -*ial*, -*ization*, -*action* and -*ability*. Avoid such words when you can. They make reading more difficult and diminish the forcefulness of your statement. As public relations writer Alden S. Wood asks, who would have responded to these words?

> Retain your earth! Abstain from engagement in interpersonal ballistic relationships unless the power incumbents initiate these relationships. If, however, it becomes apparent that overt hostile interaction is to commence, let this commencement have its genesis in this geopolitical region.

The average sentence length in this paragraph is less than 14 words. But the words are so foggy that the meaning is completely lost. Fortunately, Captain John Parker didn't talk like that. Instead he uttered the famous command, "Stand your ground. Don't fire unless fired upon. But if they mean to have a war, let it begin here."

Why do long words make reading more difficult? One reason is that long words tend to be abstract. Readers comprehend more quickly if words are concrete—that is, if they evoke visual images and avoid ambiguity. If an oil company says it's spending money on "petroleum exploration facilities," for example, the average reader won't have a very clear notion of what the company is buying. They will, however, if the company says "drilling rigs."

Long words are often unfamiliar to readers. Common words, which readers recognize immediately, are usually short. Why say "remuneration" when "pay" will do?

Readability Formulas   Short sentences and short words are the prime ingredients of clear writing. These ideas have been incorporated into various formulas to gauge the readability of a piece of writing. Such formulas—notably those devised by Gunning (Fog Index) and Flesch (reading ease) and Flesch-Kinkaid (grade-level)—can be very useful to writers who want to check the clarity of their prose. Readability is much easier to check now that most word-processing software comes with readability formulas. To test your writing, use readability Microsoft Word's statistics. Everything from industry's technical writing to the often-obscure prose of accounting is now being measured for clarity by using readability formulas. This shift toward plain language almost demands that writers measure their writing for level of comprehension. Keep in mind, though, that a high readability score doesn't guarantee good writing. Readability formulas are actually nothing more than measures of structural simplicity, and as Gunning points out, "nonsense written simply is still nonsense."[6] (See more on testing readability in Chapter 6.)

Besides, clarity may be the first goal of writing, but it's not the only one. Clear writing can be stilted and unnatural. Writing can be so simple that it's just plain boring. Clarity is worthless if the writing isn't also interesting, because writing that isn't interesting usually isn't read.

What makes writing interesting? Primarily, the subject matter. Some subjects are interesting to some people but not to others, which is why you should know your publics/stakeholders and be aware of their situations and experiences.

Here, though, we're concerned with style. The basic goals of style are, in addition to clarity, the logical development of ideas and a smooth transition from one idea to the next. Of course, style must also help maintain the reader's interest. Writing must be lively, with generous use of active verbs and vivid phrases. Interesting writing sounds natural, is not monotonous and, in general, is "pleasing to the ear." Interesting writing uses personal words such as you and people to enhance human interest. Thus besides the fundamental goal of clarity, good writers strive for naturalness, variety, euphony and human interest.

Naturalness

Reading is easiest if the style is conversational. Readability experts agree that one of the basic rules of readable writing is "write like you talk." Of course, you can't write exactly like you talk. There is a difference between written and spoken language. Spoken sentences are not carefully structured, and they often contain much repetition. In speaking, meaning can be shaded by intonation, inflection, facial expressions and gestures. You can't duplicate such features of the spoken language in your writing. But you can write prose that sounds natural, as though someone could have spoken it.

The following sentence, for example, is clear, but it sounds like a written, not a spoken, sentence:

> Smith was not disturbed that Johnson had submitted his resignation. He said that the position held by Johnson was not of high significance.

The same thing could have been written in a more natural, conversational manner:

> Johnson's resignation didn't bother Smith. He said Johnson's job wasn't that important, anyway.

A good test of naturalness is to read aloud what you've written. If you stumble over phrases and your tongue gets twisted, the sentence is not easy enough to read. Try again. If you still have trouble writing sentences that sound natural, try this approach. Write what you want to say as you would say it in conversation. Then go back and rewrite the sentence with proper syntax, making sure the pronouns are in the right place and the meaning is clear.

Just be sure you have the correct word, especially if you are using a commonly known quote. Wordsmith and author Paula LaRocque had this example in one of her writing columns:

> Feature writer: "After the city's bustle, she's only too glad to reside, as Thomas Gray wrote, far from the maddening crowd."
>
> Gray wrote "far from the *madding* crowd." "Madding" means tumultuous or restless, which may or may not be "maddening."[7]

Part of making writing conversational is using active, not passive, verbs.

Notice the improvement that results when we substitute the active voice for the passive in the following sentences:

> *Passive:* Everything possible was done by company engineers to restore service.
> *Active:* Company engineers did everything they could to restore service.
> *Passive:* It was requested by the company president that the exhibit be kept open by the museum officials.
> *Active:* The company president asked museum officials to keep the exhibit open.

Paula LaRocque, as well as Strunk and White (*The Elements of Style*), remind us that the passive voice is often the most effective, especially in technical or scientific writing, as she notes, because of "the focus on finding, process or method—on action rather than on actor." She uses this example in a column:

> *Active:* The researcher (technician? lab worker? scientist?) then heats the compound and adds the catalyst.
> *Passive:* The compound is then heated and the catalyst added.[8]

Grammatically, though, you need to be sure you know what to do with tenses.
One example she uses, "They got out of the car and lifted out the walker. It sunk in the snow." Her comment: "It sinks. It sank. It has sunk. It will have sunk."[9]

Grammatical use of conversational style involves another device that helps writing sound natural: the contraction. Use contractions freely. Everybody uses contractions in speech, and no matter what your grammar school teacher told you, there is absolutely nothing wrong with using them in writing. You suffer no loss of meaning when you use *don't, won't* or *can't* instead of *do not, will not* or *cannot*. Avoiding contractions does nothing but slow the reader down, and readers don't like to be slowed down. Just be sure you are using a contraction. One of the most common grammatical errors occurs with *it's,* a contraction of *it is* and not the pronoun *its.*

Variety

Monotony can poison an otherwise good style. You haven't gained anything by stringing clear and natural sounding sentences together if their structure and vocabulary are so similar that readers get bored. You enrich meaning and help comprehension when you search for different words. Refreshingly new words help the pace too. The style must push readers along and keep them going. Readers shouldn't feel they have to force themselves through sentence after sentence.

Variety means following the rules wisely. For example, we already mentioned that not all sentences need to be short. True, a series of long sentences makes it hard for a reader to follow the flow. And it's easy to get lost in a maze of adverbial and prepositional phrases. But an occasional long sentence, if constructed properly, can improve the flow of the narrative. A compound sentence can take the reader from one idea to the next. An occasional inversion of subject and verb reduces monotony and can emphasize the action in the sentence. You need to be cautious with this technique, however, to avoid altering meaning.

Many writers, although aware of the need for judicious variety in sentence structure, still go too far in trying to achieve variety in word choice. This leads to the use of three or four words to describe the same thing. For example,

> When my books arrived, I took the hardbound texts from the package and placed the treasured volumes on my bookcase next to my other bound publications.

Usage experts call this pitfall "elegant variation." "There are few literary faults so widely prevalent," says one expert.[10] No doubt the problem stems from the widespread belief that you should never use the same word twice in one sentence. But no such prohibition exists in any rulebook, and a single repetition is seldom as terrible as some writers think. Of course, repeating the same word several times can get boring. But you don't have to thumb through a thesaurus to find a synonym. And often a pronoun works well enough: "I took the books out of the box and put them on the shelf with my others."

In other cases, there's no need to repeat the word at all: "Jones, Smith and Brown all won races; it was Jones' first win, Smith's third victory, and Brown's fourth triumph." But the vocabulary lesson is unnecessary. It's just as clear to say, "It was Jones' first win, Smith's third and Brown's fourth."

If there's no way to get around repetition, go ahead and use the same word again. It won't hurt you. And the reader won't have to figure out whether you used different words because of some real difference or because you were trying to avoid repetition at all costs or, worse, trying to show off your vocabulary.

As for the thesaurus, don't throw it away. But use it only when you are looking for a specific word, the exactly right word, which you know but just can't think of at the moment. It is rarely wise to pick a word you've never heard of or used before. Always check a dictionary to make sure the word you choose is appropriate.

Euphony

The main reason so many writers worry about sentence uniformity and word repetition is that they want to achieve euphony in their writing. Indeed, writing that is rhythmic and makes proper use of figures of speech is usually more enjoyable to read than straightforward stilted prose.

The only way to achieve euphony is to read good writing and develop an ear for it. If you discover a good style that is used successfully by someone else, don't worry about copying it. Just don't get carried away. As one observer puts it, a "concatenation of mellifluous phrases may indicate more polish than insight."[11] First make sure your thoughts are clear and your message is pleasing to the mind. Then worry about pleasing the ear.

Human Interest

If you are writing about people, your writing will naturally contain elements of human interest. But if your subject is something mechanical, impersonal or abstract, your task will be more difficult. How can you achieve human interest when writing about inanimate objects? The trick is to remember that you're writing *to* people even when you're not writing *about* them. When appropriate, address the reader as *you*. Use the pronoun *we* to refer to people in general when discussing common knowledge, as in, "We know today that the world is round." Rhetorical questions and direct quotations help give writing a personal sound. If you don't find any and you never use *we* or *you,* your prose isn't likely to be very interesting.

Trite Expressions

"The performance *highlights* …," "The series *features* …" and similar noun-into-verb conversions are trite. News releases burdened with such creaking turns of phrase as "colorful scenery," "dramatic new move" and "spearheading the effort" deserve their usual fate—a quick trip to the trash. Clichés make your copy seem old because the words are so familiar. Public relations writing demands freshness and vitality. But don't try to freshen a cliché. And don't try to be coy by putting it in quotes—as though you really know better but are speaking colloquially—as that just calls attention to its triteness. Simply avoid using expressions you constantly hear or read.

Occasionally, a mistake can be ludicrous as in this one by a political writer: "we're beating our heads against a dead horse."[12]

Eliminating Bias

A writer's word choice can be unintentionally disparaging. A careless construction can offend people with disabilities, members of ethnic groups, people in certain age groups—especially the very young and the very old—or women. Using gender-neutral language should become routine for you. Avoid expressions like business*men*, which excludes businesswomen. Use "businesspeople" or be specific: "merchants," "retailers" and so on. Avoid using the masculine pronoun in a generic sense. Either use a noun or use the nongeneric plural pronoun (they, them, their). Gender-neutral language is much more common now as state constitutions have adopted changes as have most businesses.

You need to watch titles too. Don't make assumptions about gender in addressing a letter. Be sure your professor has an earned doctorate before using Dr., but if he or she has a Ph.D., use it. Some women on campus find students using Dr. for all male instructors and using Mrs. for females, when that is inappropriate. More than one student has been castigated for using a social title in a business setting by a female professor. Having students use Dr. in addressing them has embarrassed some male instructors without the doctorate.

When you are writing about a couple in a story, be sure you give equal identification to each partner. For example, in a story that appeared in the business section of a newspaper, a couple who are partners in a real estate development company that bought a downtown property were not equally identified. He was identified as an accountant, but she, also a CPA, was only identified as his wife. It would have been just as easy to eliminate the bias by writing: Accountants Jane and Jim Smith, partners in the Heritage Building Co., are listed on the deed as new owners of a parking lot across the street from their downtown building at 500 Main Street. Although this example of bias is probably the fault of the reporter, you will be writing news releases, so don't make a similar mistake.

Don't mention ethnicity or disabilities unless they are important to content. Be careful not to use stereotypes in language or art. Active seniors are offended by rocking-chair representations of their age group, and children resent being portrayed as miniature, but imbecile, adults.

Quotes

As a public relations writer, you will be using many quotations in your releases. If that is what the person said, then you must use it. No. Paraphrase the quote to weave it into the story in which you may incorporate partial quotes.

Just stringing quotes together makes for formidable reading.

Edit your copy mercilessly. You can do this better if you put it away for a day and go back to it. Get others to read it and offer critiques. The checklist in Table 3.1 provides a guide for assessing drafts of writing.

Internet Language Use

Although Chapter 5 provides a discussion of social media, something needs to be said here about the stylistic mix of participatory media. Citizen news reporters often bring the most current events to our attention. Blogs too, come from individuals, not institutions,

TABLE 3.1	*Writing Checklist*

1. Is the message clear? Have you said exactly what you want to say?

2. Have you identified important publics? Does your writing speak to those publics?

3. Is the style of writing appropriate for the intended medium?

4. Are your sentences instantly clear? Are they free from confusing constructions?

5. Are sentences, on average, fairly short? Have you avoided stringing long sentences together?

6. Is your writing concise and free from needless words?

7. Have you used common, concrete words that evoke visual images?

8. Is your language natural? Can your writing be easily read aloud?

9. Is the sentence structure varied?

10. Are most sentences in the active voice?

11. Have you made sufficient use of personal words and sentences?

12. Have you substituted creative language for trite expressions?

13. Is your writing free from bias?

14. Is this your best effort?

© Cengage Learning

although the authors of some blogs may be officers in organizations that are reaching out to their publics in a less traditional way. Blogs usually invite feedback, so the result is often conversational, rather than expository.

Institutions are positioning themselves in the social media. Some broadcast media specifically say that their audiences can reach them on their website as well as in one or more of the social media sites, such as Twitter or Facebook. Brevity especially is a requirement for Twitter with its 140-character limit. Messages there need to be simple and clear as well as brief. Economy and specificity demand appropriate punctuation for clarity, but lean on language with powerful verbs.

Content: Simplifying the Complex

The need for clear and simple writing has never been greater. With email messages flashing through cyberspace and faxes going around the world, your prose will be translated and interpreted in the idiom of another culture, another experience.

If you always remember to use simple language, you'll be able to write clearly about even the most complex ideas. That is important because the world has become exceedingly complex.

See Figure 3. 1 Less Than Zero from the *Smithsonian* magazine, April 2013, p. 23.

As a general interest publication for a widely diverse, well-educated audience, Smithsonian's *magazine challenges readers with simplified, but not "dumb-down" articles. Note the imagery used in this piece to make it understandable.*

BORDERS TEMPERATURE

Less Than Zero

If you can't break the laws of physics, work around them.

When a cold snap hits and the temperature drops, there's nothing to stop it from falling below zero, whether Celsius or Fahrenheit. Either zero is just a mark on a thermometer. But drive a temperature lower and lower, beyond the coldest realms in the Arctic and past those in the most distant reaches of outer space, and eventually you hit an ultimate limit: absolute zero.

It's a barrier enforced by the laws of physics below which temperatures supposedly cannot possibly go. At minus 459.67 degrees Fahrenheit (or minus 273.15 Celsius), all the heat is gone. Atomic and molecular motion ceases. Trying to create a temperature below absolute zero would be like looking for a location south of the South Pole.

Of course, scientists perceive such barriers as challenges. And now some lab trickery has enabled researchers to manipulate atoms into an arrangement that appears to cross the forbidden border. With magnets and lasers, a team at Ludwig-Maximilians University Munich in Germany has coaxed a cloud of 100,000 potassium atoms into a state with a negative temperature on the absolute scale.

"It forces us to reconsider what we believe to know about temperature," says Ulrich Schneider, one of the leaders of the research team.

As a bonus, the weird configuration of matter might provide clues to some deep mysteries about the universe.

Schneider and his colleagues relied on laser beams to trap the atoms in a grid, kind of like the dimples in an egg carton. By tuning the lasers and applying magnetic fields, the team could control the energy of the atoms, key to manipulating temperature.

Ordinarily, not all the atoms in a sample possess the same amount of energy; some are slow-moving, low-energy sluggards, while others zip about like speed demons. A higher proportion of zippy atoms corresponds to a higher temperature. But most of the atoms are always slower than the very fastest—when the temperature is positive.

With their magnet-and-laser legerdemain, the German scientists pushed the majority of the potassium atoms to higher energies, the opposite of the usual situation. Though that may not seem like a big deal, the switch messed with the mathematics that determines the gas's temperature, leading to a negative

value. Technically, physicists define temperature as a relationship between changes in entropy (a measure of disorder) and energy. Usually more energy increases a system's entropy. But in the inverted case, entropy decreases as energy increases, flipping the sign of the relationship from positive to negative. The atoms had a temperature of minus a few billionths of a kelvin, the standard unit on the absolute scale.

The catch is that scientists reached temperatures "below" absolute zero in a mathematical sense only. While the negative temperatures were numerically lower than absolute zero, they weren't colder. In fact, the gas was superhot, hotter than anything with a positive temperature could ever be.

Besides achieving a weird temperature state, the new work replicates a peculiar feature of the universe. Negative temperature systems also possess negative pressure, which on cosmic scales is causing the universe to expand faster and faster. Physicists call the universe's negative pressure field "dark energy," but they haven't been able to figure out exactly what it is. Perhaps negative pressure in a lab could offer insights. —TOM SIEGFRIED

Absolute zero, the temperature at which all atomic and molecular motion stops, is much colder than anything ever experienced by people here on earth.

ILLUSTRATION BY **Traci Daberko**

"A mature person is one who does not think only in absolutes."
—ELEANOR ROOSEVELT

Smithsonian Magazine.

In his first paper on the theory of relativity, written in 1905, Albert Einstein penned one of the simplest sentences you'll ever find in a scientific paper. In explaining a point about time and simultaneity, Einstein wrote (in English translation):

> If, for instance, I say, "That train arrives here at 7 o'clock," I mean something like this: "The pointing of the small hand of my watch to 7 and the arrival of the train are simultaneous events."[13]

You can't get much simpler than that.

Einstein treasured simplicity in writing, and though his scientific papers did get technical in places, his public writings were always clear and readable. Einstein could write simply on subjects like relativity because he understood them so completely himself. He could write clearly, without too many technical terms, because he knew his subject well enough to express the ideas in plain language and retain absolute accuracy.

Public relations writers are not likely to be as knowledgeable about any subject as Einstein was about physics. Yet they are still called on to translate complex subjects into understandable language. There is nothing simple about nuclear power, pollution chemistry or petroleum economics. Medicine, urban affairs and social services can be as complex as advanced calculus. Yet such issues are becoming more and more important to the average citizen. Public relations people must be able to explain the implications of government and corporate actions in these areas, as well as to interpret the latest research findings. It's advisable to have authorities check the final drafts to be sure your translations are accurate. It takes special writing skills to simplify the complex without explaining it inaccurately.

Some authorities think it's impossible to explain complex things like scientific research to the general public. Even Rudolf Flesch, the ultimate advocate of simplifying the complex, advises writers not to try to give complete scientific explanations. You can describe the meaning of a discovery, he says, and indicate its importance. But a complete scientific explanation? Flesch wouldn't even try that with his own readability formula:

> Here I would have to get into statistical regression formulas and multiple correlation and whatnot, and nobody who hasn't had a course in statistics would know what I am talking about.... There is only one bit of advice I can offer in this business of giving laymen an exact scientific explanation: don't try.[14]

Not everybody agrees with this attitude. William Zinsser says, "a complex subject can be made as accessible to the layman as a simple subject. It's just a question of putting one sentence after another."[15]

In practice, explaining subtle scientific principles to nonscientists isn't often of much use—not because lay readers can't understand, but because most aren't really interested. If a reader is interested in a subject, however, a good writer can explain it. You can even explain statistics to people who haven't had statistics courses, if they are interested enough to follow what might be a fairly lengthy explanation.

Today, in many cases, people aren't merely interested in scientific explanations. They demand them. If your company is building a chemical plant near a town, you'd better be able to explain to the people who live there what that plant will do and how its safety systems will work. You won't get by with saying, "Don't worry—it's safe."

Conflicting scientific advice also gets into the public agenda, leaving people confused about what to believe or to do. With people increasingly concerned about health issues, in 1998, the Harvard School of Public Health and the International Food Information Council Foundation convened an advisory group of experts. Later this was broadened to include nutrition researchers, food scientists, journal editors, university media relations officers, broadcast and print reporters, consumer groups and food industry executives. The result was a set of guidelines to provide a context in which people can evaluate information.[16] With search engines, most health issues and ways to treat them are easy to find, but not so easy to evaluate.

A solution for PR writers of health, disease and treatment issues is to use the same system of getting a diversified panel of experts both internally and externally to develop a document called a position paper. (See Chapter 6.) Documents should be developed internally for any issue relating to the organization with input from legal, marketing, customer service, operations, public relations and public affairs and consideration of opposing points of view from activist groups and competitors. Position papers then provide a launching pad for all public statements on an issue about a product, service or project.

And if the public doesn't ask technical questions directly, news reporters and electronic journalists will. Today, all media deal with more technical subjects in greater detail than ever before. When reporters, freelancers or bloggers working on such stories don't understand something themselves, they often go to PR people for explanations. PR writers, frequently trained only in journalism or English and not in the technical fields they must try to interpret, often find themselves at a loss. When an activist group accuses your company of cheating on taxes, how do you explain the complexities of accelerated depreciation and the investment tax credit? How does the public relations person for a factory suspected of polluting the air explain the difference between primary ambient air standards and secondary emission limits? How does the spokesperson for a nuclear plant explain the meaning of "10 picocuries of radioactivity"?

It isn't easy, but these things can be explained. You can simplify the complex, and you can simplify it accurately—but only if, like Einstein, you know your subject.

Know Your Subject

There is an old saying among newspaper editors that a good reporter can cover any story. If the reporter doesn't know much about the subject, he or she can simply call an expert, ask a few questions and then explain it all to readers in words they'll understand. Or so the theory goes.

This adage may have been true once, but it isn't anymore. And it's no truer for PR writers than for reporters. Nevertheless, pamphlets on complex subjects are often written this way. An engineer produces a technical description of some process or machine in words specific to the profession. The copy is given to the PR person, who edits and rewrites to simplify the language but keeps the facts as the engineer wrote them. In theory, the PR person needs to know nothing about the subject; the engineer provides the facts. The PR writer just needs to know how to write clearly.

The problem is that you can't simplify complex writing unless you know what it means. You must understand it thoroughly yourself before you can explain it to somebody else. You must know more about the subject than you'll ever put into print. If you don't, you won't be able to tell when a simplified statement can stand alone or should be qualified. And you won't know the difference between a correct statement and a false one.

Consider this example from a writer trying to describe the dangers of cigarettes in simple terms:

> Opening another front in its war on smoking, the federal government plans to publicize a new peril—carbon monoxide—to prod the cigarette industry to reduce its use of that substance in cigarettes just as it has reduced tar and nicotine.

This sentence is simple enough, but also sheer nonsense. Carbon monoxide is not a substance that exists inside tobacco, waiting to be unleashed. It is a gas created when carbon (in the tobacco) combines with oxygen (from the air) as tobacco burns. The writer simply didn't know much about the subject. The sentence is also nonsense because carbon monoxide is not a "new peril." It's neither new in the sense of being a new phenomenon associated with burning cigarettes nor is it new in the sense of being recently identified as a health hazard by scientific evidence. "Hyping" a story, often with carelessly chosen adjectives, damages credibility.

The same is true of the reporter who attempted to describe nuclear fast breeder reactors:

> The fast breeder gets its name … because the chain reaction is so much faster than in conventional … reactors.

Again, this is a readable simplification of a complex idea. It's also an incorrect simplification. The fast in "fast breeder" doesn't refer to the rate of the chain reaction (which would be measured by the number of atoms splitting per second), but to the speed of neutrons—small subatomic particles that fly around inside reactors and split atoms. In ordinary nuclear power plants, atoms are split mostly by slow neutrons; in fast breeders, speedy neutrons do most of the splitting.

How can you avoid making such mistakes? You simply must research your subject thoroughly before you begin writing. Get help from experts on points you don't understand. Recheck any passage containing statements you're not absolutely sure of.

Finally, don't try to tell readers everything you know. That always takes you to fringe areas, where your knowledge gets a little shaky and errors begin to creep in. Statements perfectly consistent with what you know might be inconsistent with what you *don't* know. Besides, if you tell the readers everything *you* know, you're probably telling them a lot more than *they* want or need to know. Give readers just what they need to get the message.

For example, if you wished to continue the story of carbon monoxide in cigarette smoke, you might be tempted to write something like this:

> Carbon monoxide, a molecule that consists of a carbon atom bonded to an oxygen atom, is dangerous because of its chemical affinity with hemoglobin. Hemoglobin, a complex chemical substance containing iron, serves as a transport mechanism for oxygen in the bloodstream. Because the affinity of carbon monoxide with hemoglobin is greater than the affinity of oxygen with hemoglobin, carbon monoxide impairs the ability of hemoglobin to carry oxygen.

This explanation, while essentially accurate, is too long. Unless you're writing for medical students or biochemists, just say that carbon monoxide impairs the ability of the blood to carry oxygen throughout the body. *You* should know all about hemoglobin and oxygen transport. But you don't need to tell everybody about it. The more you know about a subject, the easier it will be to simplify, and the less likely you will be to make mistakes.

There is one danger, though, in knowing a lot about a subject. When you have written on the subject for a while, you may find yourself using the jargon of the discipline. This is the fatal flaw in most writing on technical subject matter. If you want the audience to understand what you write, avoid using technical terms. Instead, follow the golden rule of simplifying the complex: Use plain English.

Use Plain English

Most people know plain English when they hear it. It is everyday language, free from the long words and technical terms that plague the prose of scientists, engineers, economists, doctors, lawyers and writers in other specialized disciplines. All professions and trades have special vocabularies that members use when they communicate among themselves. Unfortunately, some members use the same words—the jargon of the field—when they try to communicate with people *outside* the discipline. It doesn't work. To write plain English, you must avoid using words with "insider meanings." It is especially wrong to use such language in a calculated effort to mislead your readers. That is unethical.

Misleading language confused and outraged USA taxpayers when the public wound up "owning" the insurance giant American International Group (AIG) that distributed much of the taxpayers' money as bonuses to executives, which were part of the failing institution's problem. Although staffer Serena Ng did a credible job of simplifying the financial tangle in a front and page two story on Wednesday, March 18, 2009, in *The Wall Street Journal,* it took reading the story more than once to get a grasp of the situation. Here is one reader's much more succinct, yet clear, account:

> Before the taxpayer-engaging bonus payout to executives of American International Group (AIG) the insurance company's new "financial products division" attempted to profit from investing in the unfamiliar and speculating out of bounds.
>
> While few of the very savvy on Wall Street were betting that the real estate boom would bust, as it historically had, the insurance giant—now in the mortgage market—risked it all and lost it all.
>
> As the low-rate mortgages offered to over-extended homebuyers were bundled, bought and sold between loan companies, investment banks and financial funds, AIG left itself exposed as the last rung of a weak ladder.
>
> AIG set the corporation up to regain only a fraction of a penny on every dollar of protection they provided in case these mortgage bundles lost too much value. So, when homeowners did default and the economy plummeted, AIG was holding a heavy, but empty, bag.
>
> American taxpayers' anger at AIG was directed toward the insurance company's bets against the economy that proved true, especially since their gambling was completely unregulated by the government.
>
> **Summary courtesy of W. M. Newsom, used with permission.**

Much of the problem with the AIG situation was the use by AIG of misleading terminology and language. Semanticists refer to misleading language as *doublespeak.* There are at least four kinds, according to William Lutz: euphemism, jargon, gobbledygook (or bureaucratese) and inflated language.[17] In some cases, doublespeak fails to communicate simply because it is confusing or vague. In other cases, it is deliberately misleading, and therefore unethical and irresponsible. Misunderstanding may occur, but without serious consequences, with jargon and inflated language. Intentional deception is often the motive underlying gobbledygook and euphemism.

Avoid Doublespeak   Euphemisms may mislead deliberately, like the USA State Department's decision in 1984 to use "unlawful or arbitrary deprivation of life" instead of "killing" in its annual reports on the status of human rights around the world. Some euphemisms are just foolish, such as calling garbage collectors "sanitary engineers." Some euphemisms may be considered useful, to protect sensitivities or to respect cultural taboos.

Within any profession, jargon has its uses. A jargon term may stand for a complicated concept that would take paragraphs to describe in full. Once members of a profession agree on such a term, they can use it freely, because everyone within the discipline knows what it means. But to people not trained in the field, it sounds like gobbledygook. (See Figures 3.2 and 3.3.)

Writers must also recognize another type of jargon that may cause problems— common words that have special meanings to the members of a given group. Printers, for example, use words like *flat* and *signature* in an entirely different way than most people.

FIGURE 3.2

This warning about the use of abbreviations illustrates how readers not "in the know" can be left uninformed and confused.

Mind your FDDFSs and ACCs

HONGKONG — If the opening of Hongkong's new airport at Chek Lap Kok was a headache, then reading the official inquiry report is daunting.

The 702-page tome released yesterday was awash in acronyms.

The report used short forms of better-known companies, but also spewed out impossible gobbledygook like HO.KIA-ASP, AMFSRC and FDDFS.

Try this.

Referring to a passenger who had a heart attack and was not taken fast enough to hospital, the commission said steps were being taken to improve efficiency.

"AA and FSD are arranging a direct line to be installed between FSCC and ACC so that, in future, requests for ACC escort vehicle do not have to go through AMFSRC," it said.

— REUTERS

Source: From *The Straits Times*, Singapore, January 23, 1999, p. 28. Reprinted with permission from Reuters.

FIGURE 3.3

Doublespeak Quiz   *Test your skill at deciphering by taking this quiz.*

DOUBLESPEAK QUIZ

1. ___ safety-related occurrence
2. ___ incomplete success
3. ___ fiscal underachievers
4. ___ service technician
5. ___ non-goal oriented member of society
6. ___ single-purpose agricultural structures
7. ___ downsizing personnel
8. ___ advanced downward adjustments
9. ___ collateral damage
10. ___ experienced automobile
11. ___ media courier
12. ___ unauthorized withdrawal
13. ___ digital fever computer
14. ___ organoleptic analysis
15. ___ nail technician
16. ___ philosophically disillusioned
17. ___ kinetic kill vehicle
18. ___ ultimate high-intensity warfare
19. ___ social-expression products
20. ___ career associate scanning professional

A. to smell something
B. used car
C. pig pens and chicken coops
D. thermometer
E. repairman
F. newspaper delivery person
G. accident
H. failure
I. the poor
J. bum, street person
K. firing employees
L. budget cuts
M. bank robbery
N. civilian casualties during war
O. grocery-store checkout clerk
P. anti-satellite weapon
Q. scared
R. greeting cards
S. manicurist
T. nuclear war

ANSWERS: 1-G, 2-H, 3-I, 4-E, 5-J, 6-C, 7-K, 8-L, 9-N, 10-B, 11-F, 12-M, 13-D, 14-A, 15-S, 16-Q, 17-P, 18-T, 19-R, 20-O.

Source: From Richard Lederer, "Gobbledygook: The Quiz," *AARP Bulletin*, March 2005, p. 46.

Writers must make sure that readers understand when a common word is being used with a special meaning.

The lack of understanding special terms can be extremely dangerous too. Low literacy in understanding medical terminology or health care instructions can be fatal. Public relations practitioners working in the various health care fields have some serious challenges. Most health materials are written at the 10th grade level or above. Furthermore, few are translated into other languages. People often are too embarrassed to admit they don't know what they are reading or understand the directions or consequences.[18] Pretest all messages with the intended audiences.

Inflated language consists of fancy words used for common concepts, as when members of a given group use long or obscure words instead of short familiar ones that mean the same thing. Specialists, for example, often use technical terms to sound impressive. Consider the following sentence, written by an engineer explaining some of the drawbacks of solar-electric power plants:

> All solar-thermal systems must accept diurnal transients and rapid transients from cloud passage during daily operation.

He was trying to say that it gets dark at night and that clouds sometimes block the sun. The idea isn't any more complicated than that, and there's no reason to make it sound complicated.

Bureaucratese is also called *gobbledygook*. A good bit of it originates with our largest institution—the federal government. In 1981, Malcolm Baldridge, then Secretary of Commerce, decided to purge at least his area. He issued a memo banning certain expressions and discouraging the creation of new ones. He warned commerce staff to steer clear of "bastardized words, nouns and adjectives used as verbs, and passive verbs." Included were these miscues: finalized ("finished" is OK); impact a situation (you're on safe ground if you "control" it or "affect" it); parameters to work within ("specific limits" are acceptable); I share your concern (Who cares? You still have to say "yes" or "no").[19]

Sometimes it is deliberate deception. With people trying to eat healthier foods, the idea of some marketers is that if you say it is on the package, then it is. What they are counting on is hasty purchasers not reading the fine print. If and when they do, or when it is pointed out to them in news stories, then there is a loss of credibility, and a likely loss in sales.

As examples, labels on some foods are deliberately misleading according to a study by Temple Northup titled, "Truth, Lies and Packaging," which appeared in the journal *Food Studies.* A report of Northup's findings made its way to the front page of the June 21, 2014 issue of the *Fort Worth Star-Telegram,* which carried this quote from Northup, "When you see words like antioxidant or gluten-free, you automatically associated that with health. But the products aren't necessarily healthy." The fine print required by the Food and Drug Administration is missed by hurried shoppers who tend to read the big print on the labels. Be sure you don't capture some of the label language when you are writing promotional material for a campaign. The FDA may not ignore that misstep.

A similar, but separate story from *Consumer Reports* magazine was also referenced in the newspaper story about labels. The *Consumer Reports* study showed that 59 percent of consumers look to see if a product is labeled as "natural," although there is no verification system for that term. Consumers tend to assume there is and it means ingredients grown without pesticides, or genetically modified organisms or artificial ingredients. Not so.[20]

In some cases, though, unfamiliar terms may just have to be explained because common words won't do the job as well. If a word that has no plain English equivalent is essential to your subject, you have no choice but to use it. But make sure you explain to your readers what this new term means.

It may be that all you need to do is supply a simple definition when you introduce the word. But usually there's more to simplifying the complex than defining technical terms; in fact, dictionary definitions are frequently as confusing as the terms themselves. And your purpose is not to build the readers' vocabularies but to convey an idea. Often you can get the idea across more clearly by *describing* the new term than by defining it.

Describe, Don't Define   Assume you're writing about the use of the chemical element lithium as an agent for treating psychological depression. It seems like a good idea to begin by defining lithium. So you turn to the dictionary and find: "lithium: a soft, silver-white element of the alkali metal group. Atomic number 3, atomic weight 6.941." This is not a very useful definition. If this is all you tell your readers, they won't really know much more than they did before.

Instead, you could write, "Lithium is a silvery-white metal that is very light; in fact, it's the lightest metal known. It's also very soft and can be cut with a knife. Its name comes from the Greek word *lithos*, meaning 'stone.'" Now your readers will have a picture of lithium in their heads. You've removed some of the mystery behind the name and can go on to discuss the uses of lithium.

For the same reason, it does little good to define *kilowatt-hour* as "the amount of energy consumed when an electrical demand of one kilowatt is maintained for one hour." You're much better off if you describe a kilowatt-hour as the amount of electricity it takes to run a handheld hair dryer for an hour, or as the energy needed to toast three loaves of bread. These are not good scientific definitions of a kilowatt-hour, but they are good descriptions—and they're much more likely to be understood.

Whether you use definitions or descriptions, though, you shouldn't introduce too many new terms. Using technical terms is a luxury to be indulged in sparingly. Don't expect a reader to assimilate several new terms at once. Of course, some writers operate on the "define and proceed" principle. This is a favorite method of textbook writers. They introduce a new term—or five new terms or however many they need—define them and go on with the story, using the new terms freely. The unfortunate students find they must refer to the original definitions every 10 seconds or so to keep track of what they're reading.

Textbook writers don't have much choice, however, because their purpose is often to teach students the vocabulary of a new field. And this goal requires definitions. But public relations writers have a different aim: to communicate a single message. You can't do that if you introduce new terms just to educate the audience. You have to convey the main part of your message in words the audience already understands. In other words, use plain English as much as possible.

If you're writing a medical brochure about *interferon,* a protein substance in the body that helps to fight disease, you must use the term interferon. But you don't need to give your readers a complete lesson in biochemistry. Avoid the temptation to use words like *fibroblasts* or *lipopolysaccharides.* Even if you define these terms, using them will obscure what you're trying to say about interferon.

What if such terms are essential to the discussion? The point is, they're probably not. At least the terms themselves aren't. Fibroblasts might be important, but you can just as easily say "connective tissue cells." Describing such things without naming them will be easier for you and your readers.

Of course, you can't describe technical terms without knowing what they mean. So whenever you're writing on a specific technical subject, keep a specialized dictionary on hand. If you're writing about geology, for example, you should have a dictionary of earth science or some comparable reference work at your fingertips.

What if you replace jargons with common words where possible and do a good job of describing any necessary technical terms, and the message is still too complex for the average reader? In that case, you simply must give readers enough background so they will understand. But you have to be careful not to give too much background at once. Take one step at a time.

Take One Step at a Time

You can confuse readers by telling them too much at once. A reader can accept one new fact if you use understandable words, but don't expect to transfer several new thoughts at the same time. The reader's mind will flash "overload" and stop taking in anything. It's like blowing a fuse when you plug too many appliances into the same outlet. The brain, like an electrical circuit, can stand only so much flow.

You have to introduce one new idea at a time. And you must do so in logical order. The first idea should help explain the second, the second the third and so on.

If you start with the simplest idea and proceed one step at a time, you can eventually take the reader to a high degree of sophistication. This is Isaac Asimov's description of how he wrote a book on mathematics:

> It was about elementary arithmetic, to begin with, and it was not until the second chapter that I as much as got into Arabic numerals, and not until the fourth chapter that I got to fractions. However, by the end of the book I was talking about imaginary numbers, hyperimaginary numbers, and transfinite numbers—and that was the real purpose of the book. In going from counting to transfinites, I followed such a careful and gradual plan that it never stopped seeming easy.[21]

Using the one-step-at-a-time approach, you can eventually explain almost anything. The key is to make sure the first step is in the right place. After you've identified the main points and put them in order, look at the first point. Will your audience know what you're talking about? Naturally, that depends on the audience and their level of knowledge about the topic. Knowing where to start, though, depends on a clear definition of all steps. You must determine at the outset what the central points are. Many writers do this well enough, but somewhere between the start and the finish the central ideas get lost. Communicating the complex is bound to fail if only the writer knows what the central ideas are. Make the central points clear to the reader.

Make the Central Points Clear

Whether you're writing on a complex subject or a simple one, the objective is still the same: to convey a message. Messages must be supported with facts, figures, descriptions and explanations. You can't leave out important details. Too often, though, writers let details and descriptions obscure the message. The central point is buried in a paragraph of statistics or turns up at the end of a series of equivocal qualifying phrases. Don't lose track of your purpose. Make sure the main idea stands out.

Usually you do this by stating your main point clearly and forcefully at the outset, leaving the details for later. It is much easier for readers to follow a chain of explanations if they know the point of the story ahead of time.

If you don't make the main point clear, your audience not only won't get the message, but they also won't attach much importance to what you have to say.

When you get sick, you may see a physician because you think the doctor will be familiar enough with your ailment to diagnose and treat it quickly. But if you aren't able to explain the symptoms clearly, your doctor may be stumped, at least at first.

Explain the Unfamiliar with the Familiar

Readers don't easily understand complicated explanations of things they know nothing about. But if you can tie your subject to something within the reader's experience, you can skip several steps of definition and description and get right to the explanation.

Simple analogies can work wonders in getting people to understand why things are the way they are. The energy business is difficult to explain, and especially natural gas because it's usually not visible. When gas utility customers read about a British Thermal Unit (Btu) as a measurement for gas, it's not easy for them to visualize. The explanation in Figure 3.4 helps.

FIGURE 3.4

Explaining the Unfamiliar   *"Counting Energy," reprinted with permission from Straight Talk, ONEOK Quarterly, publication of ONEOK, Inc., Fall 2001.*

Counting Energy

We buy gasoline in gallons, coal in pounds, wood in cords and natural gas in cubic feet. Each of these resources has a measurable amount of heat energy stored in it. To compare the energy potential of these different resources, we convert each to a common measure.

A common measure of heat energy is the British thermal unit (Btu). Each Btu is the heat needed to raise the temperature of one pound of water one degree Fahrenheit.

A gallon of gasoline has about 125,000 Btu; a pound of coal, about 11,125 Btu; a cord of wood, about 28 million Btu; and a cubic foot of natural gas, about 1,000 Btu.

Numbers of that size are difficult to understand, especially since we don't think of water by the pound. An easier way to understand the energy value of a Btu is to remember that burning a kitchen match releases about 1 Btu. It takes about 60 Btu to heat the water for a cup of coffee.

Scientific subjects especially call for explanations in familiar words. A natural science writer helped readers understand a known but seldom-experienced natural phenomenon, the northern lights, in this way:

Scientists today believe that the Aurora Borealis is caused by the "solar wind" particles interacting with the earth's geomagnetic field beyond the upper atmosphere in the area called the magneto sphere. According to Syun-Ichi Akasofu of the University of Alaska's Geophysical Institute, the solar wind generates huge quantities of electricity in the magneto sphere. This energy accelerates particles into the upper atmosphere where they strike atoms of various gases, producing the characteristic colors and staining the sky with dancing light.[22]

Analogies help audiences visualize the unfamiliar. *Quill* columnist and *The Dallas Morning News'* former writing coach Paula LaRocque cites some succinct examples. David Stipp of *The Wall Street Journal*:

These are, to be exact, spotted salamanders. Black, six inches long and spotted with bright yellow polka dots, they resemble baby alligators in overtight clown suits.

And William Grimes, *The New York Times Magazine*:

It's a quiet site. You can hear the gentle sizzling of high-tension wires from the electrical substation serving the construction works. Hundreds of precast concrete tunnel segments lie baking in the sun—Snack Chips of the Gods.[23]

Helping people see something can also be aided by using concrete words instead of abstractions. Abstractions are vague and open to interpretation. The farther you move away from words that are specific and concrete, the more you leave to the audience's imagination.

Use the checklist in Table 3.2 when reviewing a draft of your work on a complex subject.

Make the Message Accessible

Presentation of the message also makes a difference in simplifying material. Some typefaces are easier to read, for example. Most serif type is easier to read than a sans serif because we recognize whole words, not characters, and we tend to scan lines, stopping at intervals. Our eyes catch the tops of the serif type, and we identify the word without even seeing all of the characters. (See Chapter 7.)

In discussing ways to make materials more accessible, Kathleen Tinkel, writing for *Adobe Magazine,* distinguishes between legibility and readability. She says *legibility* refers to the ease of distinguishing one character from another. *Readability* refers to the type as it is set and can include size, spacing, column measure, leading, page layout and other such variables.[24]

Recommendations Tinkel makes include (1) using natural letterfit and close word spacing; (2) indenting the first line of a paragraph; (3) avoiding low contrast and small sizes if you think the audience may have impaired vision; and (4) not using designs with fine hairlines, colored inks or colored papers if the lighting is likely to be poor.

TABLE 3.2	Checklist for Simplifying the Complex

1. Have you researched your subject thoroughly? Do you understand its complexities and the precise meanings of the terms you use?

2. Does your writing stay within the range of your knowledge?

3. Have you told readers only as much as they need to know to understand the point?

4. Have you used plain English as much as possible and avoided unnecessary jargon? Have you substituted common words for technical terms whenever no loss of meaning results?

5. Have you fully described all technical terms you can't avoid?

6. Have you made sure all technical terms used are really necessary to communicate the message?

7. Have you taken the readers one step at a time? Have you started with a point your readers will understand?

8. Have you identified the central points you want to make? Are they made clearly and not obscured by explanation and detail?

9. Have you used familiar ideas to explain unfamiliar concepts?

10. Have you used concrete words rather than abstractions?

11. Have you made the material as accessible as possible?

© Cengage Learning

Tell Stories

You are trying to attract and engage an audience with a memorable message. To do that, use all of the techniques of this chapter to simply deliver your message as a story, one that gives the readers/listeners a reason to be interested, an easy way to follow you to the desired conclusions. This will keep them in the story with all of the tactics of good fiction and leave them with something to use and share.

Exercise

Storytelling: Think of some situation you can get information about and determine the purpose of a story that would encourage readers/listeners to provide support for a cause, accept a major change or to embrace an idea. You want to write a memorable message through the story. Use the techniques discussed in this chapter to capture attention and retain it by developing the story with simplicity and clarity. Employ all of the tactics of good fiction to leave readers/listeners with a story to use and to share.

Grammar, Spelling and Punctuation

"Language is a living thing,"[1] you've heard, and certainly always changing because people are using it. Social media, though, seem to have put English on steroids. Dictionaries are adding new words with increasing frequency, revising the usage of existing entries[2] and changing their designation as parts of speech too.

How about this question:

Google is:
    a. a noun
    b. a verb
    c. both.

Answer: C. Google is a name, so it is a noun, but if you are looking for something, you are told to "Google it." Remaining question: If you are talking about the search engine, Google, it has a capital letter, but is that also true, if you use it as a verb?

Taking grammar, spelling and punctuation for granted can get us into a lot of trouble. One edition of this text actually got into print with the headings in the upper corner of each page in this chapter reading "Grammer." Authors don't handle headings, but the error wasn't caught in the page proofs either. Talk about the loss of credibility—that is a good example. Spelling caused a credibility problem for the IRS too when its publication for tax practitioners appeared with "Practioner" on its cover. The "grammer" mistake didn't get any publicity, thank goodness, but the IRS's mistake did. A New York City tax expert called this to the attention of *The Wall Street Journal,* which put the information in its front page "Tax Report" column, along with this question from the tax expert: "How can we rely on what is inside the manual if the outside is incorrect?"[3] The loss of credibility is more serious than the embarrassment.

Computers make it easy for us to check spelling and grammar, but careful reading is necessary too. Editors of a church bulletin were embarrassed when the following message was printed: "The Senior Choir invites any member of the congregation who enjoys sinning to join the Choir." Spell-check won't catch that error because *sinning* is a word and was spelled correctly.

As a public relations writer, you enter the world of professional writing. You join the ranks of skilled wordsmiths. Not only will you be expected to write expertly yourself, but you'll also be editing the writing efforts of others. You'll be relied on to know the rules and when to break them in order to communicate.

"Language is for communicating," writes direct-mail expert Luther Brock. "Words are simply a means of expressing one's self and, in our business, of convincing people to do business with us."[4] Writing grammatically correct prose, he points out, isn't always the best way to communicate.

"Unfortunately," writes Brock, "traditionally correct language is dishwater-dull. Why? Because it is not a reflection of the way most people talk. And talk-language just about always outsells grammar-book language."[5] As Brock indicates, the purpose of writing is to get a message across to a reader. In many respects the rules of grammar help achieve that end. But sometimes they get in the way. When they do, the experienced writer may ignore them. That doesn't mean you shouldn't bother to learn the rules or you shouldn't obey them most of the time. But you should keep the rules in perspective. "Rules," says Robert Gunning, "are substitutes for thought."[6] That's true, but they still can be useful. In many cases, it's easier to follow a rule than to waste a lot of time thinking. However, when it comes to making decisions about writing readable prose, rules are no substitute for thought.

Writing expert and syndicated columnist Stephen Wilbers makes the point that writing often calls for deliberate breaking of the rules.[7] He cites at least three cases when, although your computer may advise you to use the active voice, the passive voice is better. One of these is when you intend to emphasize the receiver of the action. The example he uses is: "Millions of people have read *The Hunt for Red October*" (active voice), compared with "*The Hunt for Red October* has been read by millions" (passive voice).[8]

Another example of when the passive is the better voice, Wilbers says, is when you are trying to create coherence between sentences. The illustration he uses is: "We must decide whether to increase our prices. The possibility that we will lose some of our customers should influence our decision." Using the passive voice connects the sentences better: "We must decide whether to increase our prices. Our decision should be influenced by the possibility that we will lose some of our customers."[9]

Sometimes the passive voice is just more diplomatic, Wilbers says. A letter that says "You disregarded the terms of our contract" is likely to create more hostility and less compliance than one that says "The terms of our contract were disregarded."[10]

Just as "always use the active voice" can be ignored at times, so can other "rules." Take the "like" versus "as" case. One of the main principles of good writing, says Gunning, is to "write like you talk." A lot of English teachers part company with Gunning here, some simply because the rules of grammar dictate that "write as you talk" is the proper way to state the principle. But Gunning responds with three good reasons for using *like* instead of *as*.[11] First, many good writers have used *like* as a conjunction (Norman Mailer for a modern example, and John Keats if you prefer the old-timers). Second, "write as you talk" breaks the rule as it states it. When speaking, people say "write like you talk"—and everybody knows what they mean. That brings us to the third point, which is that "write as you talk" has two possible meanings. It can mean "write the same way you talk" or "write while you are talking." But this is ambiguous, and unintended ambiguity is one of the worst of all possible writing sins.

Ambiguity and Grammar

The main reason grammar exists is to avoid ambiguity. Many grammar rules help us keep our meaning clear. Dangling participles, for example, are condemned by grammarians, and they should be; they can obscure the meaning of the sentence. (Sometimes a dangling participle sounds so silly that the true meaning is obvious, but even in those cases, the sentence is awkward and should be rewritten.)

That Versus *Which*

The common misuse of *that* and *which* is an example of how bad grammar can tangle meaning. Using *that* and *which* correctly is important, for it involves questions of both ambiguity and naturalness. In speaking, *that* comes more naturally. "I picked up the books *that* were on the table; where are the keys *that* I left on the shelf?" In writing, for some mysterious reason, people feel compelled to use *which*. "Attached are the copies *which* I promised to send you."

Rudolf Flesch, in *The Art of Readable Writing,* explains at great length why *that* is better in such cases.[12] His discussion is worth looking up and reading. Not only is *that* the more natural word, it prevents confusion about the meaning of the sentence. In the above examples, the clauses beginning with *that* are restrictive; *which* should not be used to introduce a restrictive clause. When you say, "Bring me the books *that* are on the table," you want *only* the books on the table—not any of the other books nearby. The clause is restrictive. When you say, "Bring the books, *which* are on the table," you're not restricting the books; you're simply telling where they are. The comma is the clue. If the sentence reads correctly without the comma, you should use *that* instead of *which*. (In fact, try to avoid *which* clauses altogether. Clauses with commas slow readers down.)

The desire to tighten copy sometimes tempts writers to eliminate the word *that*. Often this can be done without injury to sense, but you need to watch for three problems that can occur if you strike a *that*. First, when a verb is delayed, readers might have to review the sentence to get the proper meaning. For example: "The registrar revealed the grades of the athletes being disciplined met academic standards." You need a *that* before "the grades" to make the meaning clear. Second, the time element may be rendered ambiguous. For example: "Stockbrokers said last month the decreasing bond and stock prices were a mystery." Either stockbrokers made the statement last month, or they made it recently about last month's mystery. The placement of the missing *that* will clarify which is the case. Third, smoothness may be interrupted because a clause is being used in apposition.

For example: "The president's decision is one only the students will understand." A *that* between "one" and "only" makes the sentence much more readable.

Subject–Verb Agreement

Another rule that aids clarity is that the subject and verb in a sentence must agree. Subject-verb agreement helps us avoid confusion over who's doing what. There is a difference, for example, between "Growing vegetables is interesting" and "Growing vegetables are interesting."

Furthermore, merely misidentifying the subject is no excuse to break the rule. A headline in a major newspaper once said, "Workings of the SEC no longer is so mysterious." The subject is workings, not SEC; the verb should be *are* and not *is*. There is no excuse for making the mistake in less obvious cases either, as in "The general, along with his men, are marching tomorrow." The subject here is singular; the additional phrase does not make it plural. The corrected sentence reads "The general, along with his men, is marching tomorrow." If that sounds awkward, simply say "The general and his men are marching tomorrow."

Like any other rule, this one is no substitute for thought. When you write, "The *data* you need are on page 17," you are going out of your way to show that you know there is such a thing as a "datum." Most people would say "The *data* is on page 17," and there's no good reason not to. Your meaning will still be clear.

The plain fact is that in modern American usage *data* can be construed either as a singular collective noun or as a plural. The *AP Stylebook* points out that in a sentence like "The data is sound," *data* clearly refers to a collective unit, and not to the individual bits of information that collectively make up the data. If you want to emphasize the individual entities in a collection of data, of course it is correct (grammatically) to write "the data are."

The word *datum* is not a plural of data. It means a single piece of information and is rarely found in any type of writing today—even in surveying or civil engineering, where *datum* has a special meaning and the plural used is *datums*.[13]

Another awkward case of subject–verb agreement is the pairing *none is,* which grates on the ear and calls attention to itself. "None of the boats is going out to sea today" sounds silly. Always using a singular verb after none—no matter what the rest of the sentence says—is nonsense. Furthermore, any legitimate dictionary or usage manual says so. More often than not, the sense of *none* is plural. Theodore Bernstein, in *The Careful Writer,* says that the rule to follow is "Consider *none* to be plural unless there is a definite reason to regard it as a singular."[14] For example, when *none* is followed by a prepositional phrase with a singular object, the singular verb sounds better. "None of the cake have been eaten," by contrast, sounds awkward.

Myths of Grammar

Why do most people think *none* is singular and should always be followed by *is* or some other equally out-of-place singular verb? Even the *Oxford English Dictionary* says *none* is usually plural. Well, at some time in the ancient past, a grammar teacher decided that *none* meant "not one" and that it should be singular. That teacher passed it on to a student who became a teacher and passed it on to another student and so on. And all of these teachers were steadfastly devoted to the cause of rules as substitutes for thought. These are the teachers who, as Rudolf Flesch puts it, "tell students from grade school through college that they'd better learn not to write 'it's me' and never split an infinitive; or they'll get shunned by society in later life and never get a decent job."[15]

Some of these grammar "pitfalls" are important; others are merely grammar myths. The old *it's me* or *it's I* question, for example, isn't worth the time it takes to quibble. Almost everybody uses *it's me* these days, and most experts accept it, even though a predicate nominative is supposed to use the subject form of the pronoun. Another contraction you hear is, "aren't I." Literally it is "are not I." This is still not generally accepted.

Also, few good writers would say "between you and I." This is not only grammatically wrong but, worse, it is stilted and unnatural. In this case, the correct form is also the most natural one: "between you and me." The same is true for the common misuses of *myself* when *me* is the right word. "He sent a message to John and myself" is a self-conscious and awkward way of avoiding the use of *me*. *Myself* should be reserved for intensive or reflexive use, as in "I hurt myself" or "I myself will do it."

Split Infinitives

As for split infinitives, every good writer knows that infinitives should sometimes be split. Let the situation be your guide. If avoiding a split infinitive makes a sentence awkward, go ahead and chop the infinitive in two and get on with writing the story. Consider E. B. White's observation in *The Elements of Style*:

> The split infinitive is another trick of rhetoric in which the ear must be quicker than the handbook. Some infinitives seem to improve on being split, just as a stick of round stovewood does. "I cannot bring myself to really like the fellow." The sentence is relaxed, the meaning is clear, the violation is harmless and scarcely perceptible. Put the other way, the sentence becomes stiff, needlessly formal. A matter of ear.[16]

Keep in mind, though, that split infinitives sometimes cause confusion, especially if the insertion of several words turns the split into a gorge. "He wanted to quickly, skillfully and perhaps even artistically complete the project" is widening the split a bit too far. Remember, clarity is the goal.

Sentence-Ending Prepositions

The split infinitive taboo originated with the fact that Latin infinitives are single words and thus can't be split. The same archaic logic led to the myth that you should never end a sentence with a preposition. Some people who remember nothing else at all from their grammar-school days remember this "rule." But in fact, this is just another example of somebody learning grammar from Latin in the Middle Ages and passing it down through the centuries until everybody says it's so but nobody knows why. In Latin, it's very difficult to end a sentence with a preposition. Why allow English to do something denied in Latin?

Fortunately, some noteworthy language experts have ridiculed this rule to the point where few people still follow it. To writers, Winston Churchill's most famous line was not about blood and tears and sweat but the one in which he called the rule against sentence-ending prepositions an impertinence "up with which I will not put." Nowadays, almost all usage manuals repudiate the "rule." As a personal guide, know the "rule," before you decide to ignore it.

Usage Manuals

Once writers realize they are free from the chains imposed by grammar rules, some go off the deep end. If rules are made to be broken, why follow any of them? Well, not all rules should be broken. *Rules should be broken only when, by doing so, you can make the writing clearer, more natural, and easier to understand.* Feel free to dismiss the pedantry of critics who rank split infinitives on the same plane with arson or man-slaughter. But do strive to use the language carefully and accurately.

It is no pedantry, for example, to insist that words be used in keeping with their proper meanings. *Allusion* is not the same as *illusion,* for example, and *imply* and *infer* are not interchangeable. *Parameters* are not *perimeters,* either. Countless words are misused simply because they sound like others. (See Table 4.1.)

Many writers scoff at such criticism, saying, "The reader will know what I mean. Lots of people use the word that way." If you adopt this philosophy, you put yourself in the position of confusing the members of your audience who *do* know the correct meanings of words. The intelligent reader is left to wonder if the writer is using this word correctly, in which case it means something else. Using words imprecisely can lead to such ambiguity. Choose words carefully.

Even some grammar "rules" deserve a little thought before they are rejected or accepted. Any given rule can be good for some situations—possibly even most situations—though bad for others. How can you decide when to follow a rule and when not to? You must decide, of course, but it never hurts to get some advice. Check a few basic reference books. Besides a dictionary and a standard grammar handbook, you should have at least two language-usage manuals that discuss points of grammar and usage in depth. One manual you should always have and use is the latest *Associated Press (AP) Stylebook.* In 2014, some of the changes surprised long-time users. For example, the *AP Stylebook* now permits "over" for all larger numerical numbers when previously the stylebook required "more than" for clarification, to prevent ambiguity. Another change that caught users' attention was the use of Wal-Mart for all references to the organization, stores or corporate. AP's explanation from David Minthorn, the *AP Stylebook* editor, was "The language evolves, the usage evolves, and we're trying to be sensitive to it."[17]

You need to get new stylebook manuals each year when there is a new edition: Regular English usage manuals as well as the *AP Stylebook* and *The Economist Style Guide* for British English. A subscription to Vocabula Review online (bounce@vocabula.com) will give you daily examples of the wrong use of words, ways to make your writing more concise and some words that are rarely used with their meaning and use. The same organization also has books at www.vocabula.com/VocabulaBooks.asp. You can go to blogs like *After Deadline* handled by Philip Corbett who manages *The New York Times* style manual. Such manuals analyze many of the tricky usage questions that writers stumble across.

TABLE 4.1	*Commonly Confused Words* Here is a list of pairs of commonly confused words. If you don't understand the differences between the members of each pair, consult a usage manual, *The Associated Press Stylebook* or *Words Into Type*.		
absorb, adsorb	assure, ensure	doubtful, dubious	parameter, perimeter
accrue, acquire	baited, bated	dual, duel	pedal, peddle
adapt, adopt	canvas, canvass	farther, further	poison, toxin
adhesion, cohesion	cement, concrete	flaunt, flout	pore, pour
affect, effect	complement, compliment	fortuitous, fortunate	practicable, practical
all ready, already	compose, comprise	grisly, grizzly	principal, principle
allusion, illusion	continual, continuous	imply, infer	rebut, refute
alternately, alternatively	credible, credulous	infect, infest	reign, rein
apparently, obviously	deduction, induction	mantle, mantel	stationary, stationery
appraise, apprise	discreet, discrete	minister, pastor	suspect, suspicious
arbitrate, mediate	disinterested, uninterested	naval, navel	whereas, while

© Cengage Learning

When you read some of these manuals, you'll find that usage rules aren't as restrictive as you've been taught. You'll be surprised to learn what some language "purists" like Fowler and Follett have to say about split infinitives, for example. You'll also, no doubt, run across subtle but important usage matters that have escaped your attention until now. Cappon's book has a chapter called "Bestiary: A Compendium for the Careful and the Crotchety."

Perhaps the most important lesson you'll learn from reading usage manuals is that there is considerable disagreement among the "experts" over what should or should not be allowed. So don't let anybody tell you there is always a right and a wrong where grammar and usage are concerned. Gather some opinions, think about each problem and then make up your own mind. Just be sure that, when you break a rule, you break it for a reason and not because you didn't know. You also need to remember your audience. Materials for international use by English-speaking people need to follow more strictly traditional usage.

Verbs

Where's the action? The action of PR writing is in the verbs: they should keep things moving, capture attention and hold it.

Use active-voice verbs, and avoid using the passive voice. Recast the sentence if you have to. One simple way to put movement into your language is to limit your use of forms of the verb "to be." Consider these examples:

An honor code is being considered by student government representatives, who want to talk with university faculty about the idea. [Passive]

Student government representatives considering an honor code for the university want to talk with faculty about the idea. [Active]

When writing broadcast copy, you should stay out of the past tense. The idea underlying this practice is that all broadcast news should sound as immediate as possible. A new rule on college athletes' eligibility passed yesterday by the NCAA would be written: "College athletes must make higher grades now to stay on the team." The present perfect tense is used most often by broadcasters. It implies immediacy, although the action is over. You just write "has been" instead of "was" and "have been" instead of "were." For instance, "I've been in India" sounds as though you've just returned.

Be sure you choose the correct tense to capture the meaning: "High winds on the lake sunk the boat." No. "The boat sank during the storm." Or, "When they went to the dock, they found their boat had sunk." Or, "High winds flooded many boats causing some to sink." *Lie, lay* and *laid* are other sources of problems. "You may lie a book on the table where it lays." Or, perhaps, "That table is where I laid the book."

Emotive and Cognitive Meaning

Cognitive meanings are information based. Emotive meanings may be positive or negative or mixed. You must be sensitive to these two different types of meaning. Emotion-charged words are often used in public relations writing, but it is imperative that you know, in advance, the emotion a word is likely to elicit from the audiences it will reach. Negatively charged words are those that evoke bad images, such as prejudicial terms used for ethnic groups. Positively charged words are those that encourage "good feelings," such as "peace," "love" and "freedom." Some words may have mixed emotive meanings, and these can be the most dangerous to use. Words like *globalization* have different meanings to people with different value systems.[18]

Spelling

You might expect that spelling would be rather clear-cut, but it isn't. For example, you can spell *benefited* with one *t* or *benefitted* with two. You must decide which one you will use for your organization; you thereby establish the style for that organization's publications. On the other hand, if you are writing for *other* publications, you have to spell words the way *their* style dictates.

With more international communications in English, you have to ask, "Whose English?" Will you use the *s* in spelling *organisations* or the *z* as in usage in the USA? Perhaps some global standardization for English is in sight, since the European Union has chosen English as the preferred language, and it is the major language of the Internet.

Who cares about spelling? Well, the people who hire PR writers for one, so if you want a job, you'll take spelling seriously. There's no excuse for *not* spelling correctly. Just keep a dictionary within arm's length whenever you're writing. If you're not *absolutely certain* that a word is spelled correctly, look it up.

Face it. If your prose is riddled with spelling errors, your readers just might conclude that your facts are also suspect. (They might also conclude that you're not too bright.) Therefore, why should they believe what you've written or even read it at all? It's little consolation to say that most readers won't catch the spelling errors. Then only the educated people will think you're wrong.

Spelling errors do crop up now and again, even in prestigious publications. Even though you make every effort to eradicate mistakes, a spelling error will someday appear in one of your finished products anyway. That's not a reason to be less diligent in your efforts. If you operate with the attitude that "just one error" isn't so bad, you'll end up with many. The old saying that "to err is human" should be applied only as consolation after the fact, not as a license ahead of time to make mistakes.

Sometimes mistakes result not from lack of diligence, but from overconfidence. Some people spell so well that they're sure they can spot any spelling mistakes. Thus they don't look up the words they should. To avoid such overconfidence, good writers and editors should occasionally test themselves on lists of commonly misspelled words. Even good spellers will find some surprises. Test yourself by counting the number of words spelled *correctly* in the list contained in Table 4.2. Word processing systems can check spelling, but if (for example) you have used *there* instead of *their,* the system will not find the error. The system will only find words that are misspelled as nonwords, such as *thier* for *their*. It will miss homophones (words that sound alike but are spelled differently) and misspellings that produce other true words (such as *study* for *sturdy* or *sandbag* for *handbag*). (See Table 4.3.)

Ten common misspellings that slip by spell-check may be created by your errors too. Contractions are the most common. The contraction of it is, *it's,* versus the possessive *its* and the contraction *you're* versus possessive *your*. When you meant *sales,* you could find

T A B L E 4 . 2	*Unassisted Spell-Check*		
How many of these words are correctly spelled?			
badmitton	barbiturates	procede	innoculate
sacreligious	Limosine	comittee	pantomine
chaufeur	corollary	comission	inocuous
diarhea	wierd	priviledge	perogative
embarass	cemetary	knowledgable	excell
Farenheit	mispelling	sieze	
flourescent	preceed	satelite	
If you counted two correct, you're right. Only *barbiturates* and *corollary* are spelled correctly.			

© Cengage Learning

T A B L E 4 . 3	*Spell-Checker*

Eye halve a spelling chequer

It came with my pea sea

It plainly marques four my revue

Miss steaks eye kin knot sea

Eye strike a key and type a word

And weight four it two say

Weather eye am wrong oar write

It shows me strait a weigh

As soon as a mist ache is maid

It nose bee fore two long

And eye can put the error rite

Its rare lea ever wrong

Eye have run this poem threw it

I am shore your pleased two no

Its letter perfect awl the weigh

My chequer tolled me sew

Source: Dana Summers, reprinted by permission of Tribune Media Services.

"sails" as a computer-generated substitute or "affect" the verb for "effect" a noun. Perhaps you wrote "would of" for "would not." That will slip by. Another common slip is if you misuse "supposed." "Supposed to" refers to a responsibility or duty, whereas "suppose" means to think. Other wrong words include such as "threw" for "through," or "then" versus "than" or "wonder" versus "wander" and "farther" versus "further."[19]

Problems are likely to occur with plurals and possessives in spell-check. Some grammar software may recognize such distinctions as "the bee's sting" (one bee) or "the bees' sting" (more than one bee). The key to possessives is the apostrophe. With the simple plural, bees, there is no apostrophe, but there is one when you are using a plural possessive. Another area of confusion occurs with the apostrophe when it's used in contractions—*it's*, as just used, for "it is." *Its*, a singular possessive, has no apostrophe. Sometimes *its*, the possessive, as in "The dog buried its bone," is misused for the contraction, as in "Its going to be difficult to find the bone the dog buried." Think of the apostrophe in contractions as standing for the missing letter.

If you answered Table 4.2 correctly without any help, you're a pretty good speller and should have no trouble with the following test. Read the passage and circle the words that are spelled *incorrectly*. Assume that the piece is part of a feature story that is to appear in a newspaper, and follow *AP Stylebook* spelling rules.

> The scientists could not reach a concensus. One physicist argued that his experiments superceded earlier findings.
>
> Beseiged by numerous complaints, the director of the labratory devised a stratagy to accomodate the researchers. He alotted each one 15 minutes to speak. One said everyone had benefitted from the experiments on liquefcation of nitrogen, but he saw no correllation between those results and the experiments on parafin.
>
> "It would take a whole battallion of scientists to solve this dilemna," another scientist said. "We do high calibre work, but when you liquefy a miniscule amount of gas, there's no way to avoid all possible arguements about the results." Another suggested that a questionaire should be drawn up and sent out. "If we could get them all filled out, that would be quite an achievment," he said.
>
> "That's an inovative idea," said the physicist. "I'd like to save my copy of the form as a memento of this occassion."

You should have circled 20 words. If you didn't find them all, a trip to the dictionary (or perhaps the *AP Stylebook*) is in order. By the way, although dictionaries accept *benefitted,* the AP allows *benefited* only. Some dictionaries also accept *liquify.*

Source: "Shoe" © MacNelly. King Features Syndicate.

Word Choice and Meaning

Sometimes misspelling a word interferes with your intended meaning. A report from an organization warned that the scholarship fund was jeopardized because some of the *principle* had been used, instead of just the interest. No. What the writer intended to say was some of the principal, the initially invested amount, had been used. Confusing the two words is fairly common, as is use of the word *attain* when *obtain* is intended. Another common error is the use of "reign in," meaning to contain or control when the correct word is "rein in." Writing coach Paula LaRocque found these examples of misused words:

> Here's a headline on a story about celebrities that refers to "Marquis" names instead of "marquee" names. Another about an athletic field that refers to "sewn" grass. Another that declares, "Frost Belt Unthawing." Unthawing? When something frozen thaws, it unfreezes. So, if it is unthawing is it refreezing?[20]

Writers caught in these mistakes often say, "Oh, well, you know what I mean." No. Not really.

Another error that creates confusion is the use of single quotation marks to emphasize words. A conference paper on the "Going Green" ecology effort referred to 'green' products and 'green' consumers, using the single quotation marks for emphasis. Unfortunately, this error often appears in newspaper headlines. The newspaper headline writers might use the excuse of saving space, but what about using italics? In American English, single quotation marks go inside double quotation marks. The reverse is true in British usage where commas also go outside quotation marks. (See the Global English? section.)

Punctuation

Whereas grammar is mostly a matter of making meanings clear and spelling is basically a matter of convention, punctuation is a little of both. True, proper punctuation is usually just a matter of following the rules. But the underlying purpose of punctuation is to help make the meaning clear, and subtle changes in punctuation can change the meaning of a sentence. For example, the sentence "Woman without her man is an animal" can be punctuated "Woman—without her, man is an animal." The late Liz Carpenter, former press secretary to Lady Bird Johnson, liked to have people punctuate this sentence as a test for sexism.

Apostrophes are a common source of confusion about meaning. Probably the most common error occurs with the word "it's," the contraction of "it is," with the possessive word "its," with no apostrophe. In this case, "its" indicates possession like the pronouns "his" or "hers" or "theirs." However, possessives such as "Jane's book" or "Joe's pencil" use the apostrophe. Acronyms cause much of the confusion about punctuation. For example, use apostrophes in the case of single letters such as P's and Q's or A's and B's, but only an "s" after multiple letters such as "four VIPs." You create a possessive with "The four VIPs' choice of a restaurant was The Original BBQ."

Most reputable publications follow a fairly rigorous set of punctuation rules and apply them consistently. The virtue of consistency is simply that readers can pay attention to the message without being bothered by changes in the manner of punctuation. Sentences, for example, usually end with periods. Readers know this, and they don't have to think about it. They know that, if a writer ends a sentence with some other mark, it is an intentional act to tell the reader something—as when a question mark is used to indicate a question.

Inconsistent punctuation calls attention to itself. Anything that calls attention to itself takes attention away from the message, and that hinders communication. When you're trying to communicate, there's no excuse for introducing anything that distracts the reader, however slightly.

Sometimes punctuation conventions defy logic, but these conventions are so entrenched that violators expose themselves immediately as amateurs. The prime example involves the use of periods and commas with quotation marks. Whenever a period or comma follows a quotation, it is placed *inside* the closing quotation marks. Always. Without exception (at least in the United States). It doesn't matter whether the quote is a complete sentence or a title or a single word. For example:

John's article, called "The Hands of Time," is well written.
I didn't know he wrote an article called "The Hands of Time."

The rule still applies if single quotes are used inside double quotes:

He said he "wrote an article called 'The Hands of Time.' "

Other punctuation marks, such as question marks and exclamation points, are placed according to the sense of the sentence:

Did he write an article called "The Hands of Time"?
He asked John, "What is the title of your article?"

This may seem trivial, but many public relations writers are their own editors. If you want your material punctuated correctly, you need to know the rules. And in the case of this particular rule, there is nothing to be gained by breaking it. It is followed uniformly (in the United States), and departures from the convention call attention to themselves.

For many other punctuation rules, convention is not as binding. Often, standard "rules" should be broken to make the reading easier or to make the meaning clear. People are taught in school, for example, to place commas before direct quotations, as in

John said, "What's going on here?"

Sometimes the comma is an intrusion, however, and can be dropped with no confusion:

"What did he say?"
He said "Let's go!"

Not all rules should be so casually violated. Some are important for keeping the meaning clear; most rules of this type involve the comma.

There are dozens of rules regarding commas, and it doesn't hurt to know them. Most help keep sentences clear and prevent readers from stumbling over tricky passages or linking clauses to wrong elements. In general, comma rules are helpful.

Some writers overdo their use of commas, though, and stick one in wherever they can. Too many commas clog up the works and make for slow reading. The best practice is to use commas only when they are necessary to avoid confusion.

The careful use of commas with nonrestrictive clauses, for example, helps avoid confusion. Restrictive clauses, which are necessary to make the meaning of a sentence clear, are not set off by commas. Consider these examples:

> Restrictive clauses, which are needed for clarity, are not set off by commas.
> Clauses that are needed for clarity are restrictive.

All restrictive clauses are needed for clarity. Therefore, the "which are needed" clause in the example is merely explanatory and is not essential to the meaning of the sentence. It is a *nonrestrictive* clause and is set off by commas.

Not all clauses are needed for clarity. But the "that are needed" clause is essential to the meaning of the sentence: it *restricts* the types of clauses under consideration. It is therefore a *restrictive* clause and is not set off by commas.

Restrictive and nonrestrictive clauses are also called *essential* and *nonessential* clauses. They don't always use *that* and *which*. *Who* can be restrictive or nonrestrictive, and this fact makes proper punctuation all the more important. Consider these examples from the *AP Stylebook*:

> Reporters, who do not read the stylebook, should not criticize their editors.
> Reporters who do not read the stylebook should not criticize their editors.

The first sentence says that reporters—all reporters—do not read the stylebook. Therefore, they shouldn't criticize their editors. The second sentence says that some reporters—those who don't read the stylebook—shouldn't criticize their editors. There's a big difference.

Another comma error that can make sentences unclear involves appositives. An appositive is a phrase that stands for a noun and bears the same relationship to the rest of the sentence that the noun does. Here is an example:

> Joe Smith, the captain of the football team, signed a contract today.

The appositive following "Joe Smith" is set off by commas. The comma after team is essential. "Joe Smith, the captain of the football team signed a contract today" reads as though someone were telling Joe Smith (whoever he is) that the captain of the football team signed a contract.

Don't set off short titles with commas, however. "Team captain Joe Smith signed a contract" is perfectly correct. "Team captain, Joe Smith, signed a contract" is not. A similar problem sometimes comes up with restrictive appositives, when a descriptive phrase is needed for full meaning. "The American League baseball players, Daniel Nava, Jackie Bradley, Jr., and Grady Sizemore, are outfielders" is not properly punctuated. This sentence makes them the only players in the American League. Omit the commas after *players* and *Sizemore*, and the sentence is correct. Avoid related mistakes, too, such as the one made by a textbook author who wrote "In his novel, *The Deer Park,* Norman Mailer describes…." There should be no comma after *novel;* Mailer has written more than one.

You have to watch carefully for brief use of language on posters, billboards and signage. Proper punctuation is critical there. A retail store avoided all punctuation and posted the following:

ATTENTION
Toilet
   ONLY
for
DISABLED
ELDERLY
PREGNANT
CHILDREN

Thank you for shopping with us.

Many punctuation rules other than those mentioned here are equally important. It's impossible to cover all of them in a single chapter. Conscientious writers take punctuation seriously, however, and consult such books as the *AP Stylebook* for help on the fine points.

Of course, experts sometimes disagree about proper punctuation. Don't think that every rule should be followed in every instance. But make sure you know the rules. And when you break one, know why.

Global English?

All English is not the same. Not in spelling, not in word meanings, not in punctuation and not, in some instances, even grammar. The question is, which version of English do you use, the British or the American? The answer is, it depends on the medium and/or the public. You use what is accepted and familiar, not necessarily to you. Remember: public, message, medium. Choosing *exactly* the right word does matter.

Think of Mark Twain's comment: "The difference between the almost right word and the right word is really a large matter—it's the difference between the lightning bug and the lightning." The "hood" of a car in American English is a "bonnet" in British English, and your weight in "pounds" will be different in British "stones," which are 14 pounds. Measures of all kinds may be quite different, from temperatures to clothes sizes to cooking.

Even if the word is the same, the spelling may be different. Many publications using the British spellings will have "organisations," not "organizations," for example. In British-language publications, you'll often find "whilst," which is considered "quaint" in the USA. British-language publications are likely to use "venue," whereas American-language publications use "place." Names of things are not the same, as you may know from traveling. An "elevator" is a "lift" in places using British English. British English uses different forms of punctuation too. Where American English uses double quotation marks with other punctuation inside ("."), British English uses single quotation marks with other punctuation outside ('.).

Fortunately, you can use a computer language system to help. Most computers use American-English spelling, grammar and punctuation, but you can get a British-English system to use when needed. The question may be which system will eventually prevail. Some think it is the American-English system because of technology. Most people who buy computers get the American-English system automatically and have to get the British-English system separately. Time will tell.

To be good public relations writers, you need to be aware of and sensitive to the differences. Fortunately, there's help available, online. At www.tardis.ed.ac.uk, you'll find *The English to American Dictionary Index*. Another source for help is the Association of British Language Schools (ABLS) stylebook and usage guide.

If you are attempting to communicate in another language, be cautious about using the Internet for free online translations. You may not be sending the message you intended. For example, http://www. translate.google.com offers English, French, German and Spanish. However, if you use a site like this, be sure to translate the supplied translation back into English. English input: *When I go to town to shop, I enjoy taking a long walk in the park before I return home in the afternoon.* Spanish translation: *Cuando voy a la ciudad a hacer compras, disfruto tomando un paseo largo en el parque antes de que yo vuelva a(en) casa por la tarde.* English translation of the Spanish: *When I am going to the city to do buys, I enjoy taking a long walk in the park before I return to (in) house in the evening.* Some words have to be translated in the proper context. A good example is the Polish word *baba*. When a baby says it, the meaning is "grandma," but it can be translated as a derogatory word for "woman."[21]

If you are preparing materials in another language, hire someone fluent in both languages and someone who has recently traveled in the other country where the materials will be used. Language usage changes over time in a country. Also, as you know from experiences with American English and British English, there are significant differences in word choices, spellings and meanings between the two versions of English. This is also true of other languages.

Always Check

At every level of your writing, check to be sure you are saying what you intend to say. With your initial product, reread, read aloud, revise or rewrite completely. When you have what you think is a final copy, then edit it severely. When you have something to send for publication and get back a proof, edit it again carefully (see Table 4.4) for suggestions at each level.

Words of Advice to Post on Your Desktop

This list of bad practices to watch for in your writing comes from author Paula LaRoque:

- A dreary march of long words, sentences and paragraphs.
- Sentences that "back in" with words and dependent phrases.
- Opening sentences burdened with heavy proper nouns.
- Untranslated or unnecessary jargon.
- Abstract rather than concrete terms.
- Visual clutter—acronyms, symbols, parenthetical intrusions.[22]

T A B L E 4 . 4	*The Quality Controlling System*	
Quality Controlling for Some Tasks		
Revising	**Ideas**	
	• paragraphs	• change
	• headings	• add
	• bullets	• reorganize/reformat
	• graphics	• eliminate
Editing	**Language**	
	• sentences	• voice
	• words	• tone
	• symbols	• conciseness
		• parallelism
		• modification
		• diction
		• punctuation
		• mechanics
Proofreading	**Hard-copy appearance**	• headings, footers, margins, spacing
		• font consistency
		• common mistakes
		• typos

Source: Reprinted from *ETC: A Review of General Semantics,* Vol. 58(1), Spring 2001, by permission of the author, Philip Vassallo, and the International Society for General Semantics.

zimmytws/Shutterstock.com

Exercise

Verbal Energy by Ruth Walker, "Test your grammar 'smarts' " reprinted with permission from *The Christian Science Monitor Weekly,* November 19, 2012.

The exercise for Chapter 4 is online and was developed by The Christian Science Monitor and Ruth Walker. To test your grammar "smarts," please go to: www.CSMonitor.com/grammar-quiz/

Social Media Writing

Mastering Social Media Writing

It's not difficult to see what an incredible impact the Internet and social media have had on all communications—public relations, advertising, marketing. The move to digital communications has been swift and all-encompassing, forever changing how we communicate personally and from organization to stakeholder or stakeholder to organization.

Social media has become such a vital tool for public relations practitioners that the majority of public relations and communications managers believe that understanding how to use and manage social media channels is essential to success.

What Is Social Media?

Ask anyone the question, "What is social media?" and you're likely to hear a reply with "Facebook" mentioned. While Facebook is the best-known and largest of the social channels in terms of users, it is barely the tip of the social media iceberg.

A simple online search for social media will reveal 20–50 systems, categories or groupings of activity that someone will fit into the social media space. The more well known include these:

Blogs: owned (corporate) or free, like Wordpress or Blogger
Microblogs: Twitter
Social Networks: Facebook, LinkedIn, Google+, Tumblr
Social News: Digg, Reddit, Delicious

Virtual Communities: DelphiForums, Mumsnet, AARP
Podcasts: audio or video
Video Sharing: YouTube, Vimeo, Instagram, Vine
Photo Sharing: Instagram, Flickr, SmugMug
Messaging: Instant messaging, texting
Wikis: Wikipedia
We will focus on content developed for blogs, social media networks and Twitter.

The Digital Diamond

While social media is unique and important, it does not operate in a vacuum. The digital communication world conveniently divides into four parts—the Web, email, blogs and social media, Figure 5.1. Even though each element stands alone, they are far more effective when used together in harmony.

Website   Your website is the cornerstone of your digital communications. It's where audiences come to hear it "from the horse's mouth," so to speak. This is where your reputation begins and purchase decisions take shape. Your website must be up to date at all times, easy to navigate and quick to search with fast page-load speeds, delivering clear, concise information. The reputation of your organization is affected by your website, and consumers use website information in the decision-making process. Bottomline, your website is critically important for your organization's reputation, and sales.

Email   Permission-based email provides pure marketing power, preferred by audiences that value who you are and what you offer. The user, in this case, holds all the power, deciding what brands and individuals can communicate to them via email. When they

FIGURE 5.1

Digital Diamond, Copyright © 2013, QSI Group; used with permission.

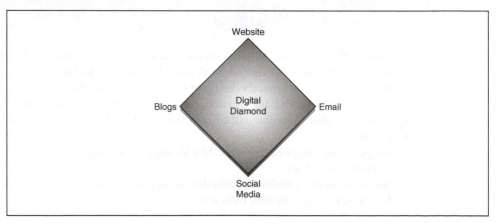

give you permission to communicate with them you enter into an agreement to send only certain information or offers. Break that agreement and they will flee. Honor that agreement and they will stay and listen and act.

Email is the first two-way dialogue system in your digital communication array. Always accept and listen to email replies. This feedback is a valuable resource to detect problems and opportunities.

Blog   While the website is where you put all your important corporate and product information for reference, your blog is where you share the latest news and information with your stakeholders. Your blog is a conversation, where you tell your stories and invite your readers to respond. It's the ideal venue for two-way communications, so encourage comments and be ready to listen as much as you speak. A regularly updated blog connected to a website can significantly increase overall website traffic.

Your blog is an ideal place for announcements, sharing accomplishments, helping solve your customer's problems and sharing key information. For some organizations blogging has replaced other external communications functions like media relations. It is a direct channel where your story is told in your own words without the filters imposed by news media, analysts or others.

Blogs are great places to inform, entertain, intrigue and inspire. They are the "Wild, Wild West" of writing—not patterned, no formulas, almost anything goes.

Social Media   Social media networks are where we can speak directly to our fans, followers, customers and connections in their preferred location. Some people love Twitter, while others are Facebook fanatics, and still others are most comfortable in LinkedIn or Tumblr. We communicate differently depending on the audience and the channel, but we never forget that we're talking to them on their home turf. Social media is social, meaning that brands and organizations must tread somewhat carefully or risk being exiled for inappropriate actions. Serve instead of sell. Inform instead of intrude. Being relevant is a great goal.

Social media can be serious, thought-provoking, entertaining, insightful and even silly at times. Unless your audience is overly serious, like some government stakeholders, have some fun. A channel like Twitter is full of clever thinking and fun photography. Match your style to the audience and the social media channel for the best success.

Channel Indulgence

No matter what social media channel you personally use, as communicators we must be channel indulgent and place our messages in **every** channel used by our key audiences. Avoid the temptation to simply copy and paste your beautiful prose into each social channel. Instead, customize your messages to fit the personalities of the specific social channel and audience.

Social communication is the closest thing we have to actual interpersonal communication. We don't say the *exact same thing* when we speak to others on the telephone, send them an email, write them a letter or talk face-to-face. Just like these different methods of communication, social channels each have personalities, strengths and weaknesses. To be most effective, you must tailor your communication slightly in each channel to accommodate these differences.

The Voices of Social Media

Each social media channel is unique, with differing personalities, strengths and weaknesses. Understanding these differences and knowing as much as you can about your audiences is the key to digital success.

Blogs   Blogs are wonderful companions to their website parents. While websites are the cornerstone of digital communication, blogs are the ongoing conversations. Topical, diverse and current, blogs allow you to speak to the latest news and information, the latest trends and rumors. But remember that with this conversational nature, blogs have a shorter shelf life than content on your website.

Facebook   Facebook is the origin of the "friending" system, and as such it remains personal and private. Facebook is a means of personal communication for many, allowing them to keep up with their friends and family members without the burden of real-time human connection. Likewise, for organizations Facebook allows interested fans (those who "like" you) to keep up with the latest information about your organization and its products and services, and a way to share directly with your other Facebook fans.

Twitter   Without some taming, Twitter truly is a chaotic mess. Imagine three close friends standing in a circle talking fast and with incomplete sentences. Short, choppy, staccato. That's Twitter—fast and fun. Perfect for the quick thought, breaking news or clever twist on the trends of the day. It's where the world has its say during major events. For organizations, Twitter is good for announcements or to drive traffic to a new blog post, discount or product offer. But don't be selfish. Share what's fun and interesting as well as your deals and spiels.

LinkedIn   LinkedIn is certainly the place for promoting your job openings and finding jobs. But it's so much more. It's a great place for business news, group discussions, industry-specific Q&A and business networking.

Beyond personal, LinkedIn offers a way for audiences to connect directly with your organization, keeping up to date via your posts. Then there are LinkedIn Groups where individuals from the organization can participate by asking and answering questions. This is a great way to demonstrate your expertise in important industry subjects.

LinkedIn is not fun and games but "all business, all the time."

Google+   Google+ is social media on steroids. In most social media channels you have one group of friends, whereas in Google+ you segment those individuals into numerous circles, each specific in one or another way. The result is that your updates can be tailored to specific audiences.

With the future of Google+ in doubt, it's important to note the other extras Google packs around Google+. Hangouts are like quick webinars for small groups, Hangouts Live are a great way to learn, while Communities offers closed and private group sharing.

Finally, Google offers some hidden SEO benefits when you blog using the same username as your Google account.

Pinterest   Say "Pinterest" in most circles and the reply you're likely to hear is "clothes," "shoes" or "girls." While those limited perceptions may be accurate, Pinterest is a powerhouse, offering you the chance to show and tell like no other social channel.

Pinterest is where you can be completely selfish, pinning your best products in hopes of inspiring and interesting your audiences.

Keep it short and simple. Great photographs are a must because they are displayed in a small format. Short descriptions must tell what the photo is about. The goal is to interest readers so they will click on your pin and visit an associated Web page or blog post.

Photo/Video Sharing   There are a myriad of photo- and video-sharing channels. Some are hot, others not, but all offer opportunities if the photo or video is high quality and well thought out.

For photo sharing, Instagram has emerged as the leader, but don't completely discount Flickr, SmugMug and others. Never forget that even the most boring and mundane products can be photographed in ways that make them fascinating. It takes a bit of thinking and hard work but it's worth the effort.

Video sharing has grown from the dominate YouTube to include similar services like Vimeo. Both have their strengths, and both should be used, even simultaneously.

In recent years, short video sharing has exploded. Vine started the craze with its six-second videos, and Instagram soon followed to accommodate both video and photo sharing.

The magic of photo and video sharing is "capturing a moment in time." Any written content must also tell the story of that moment.

The Content Challenge

Content is everything in digital communication, be it copy, graphics, photos or videos. Everything we use to communicate should be viewed as valuable content. Having an abundance of content is not necessarily a good thing. Avoid the temptation of trying to say everything at once and all the time. Limit messages to achieve clearer communication and be always mindful of what your audience needs and wants to hear.

At the simplest level you can begin to determine the best content with a message audit stemming from the answers to three questions: (1) What is the content your audience *needs and wants?* (2) What is the content your organization *wants* to communicate? and (3) What content do you have available? List the answers to those questions and look for similarities. Where the answers intersect is where your optimal content lies. Lean too far to your audience's needs and you do not do justice to your organization. Lean too far to the wants of the organization and you run the risk of being a selfish communicator. (See Figure 5.2.)

The most difficult challenges digital communicators face is how to be invisible and unselfish.

FIGURE 5.2

Three Circles Graphic

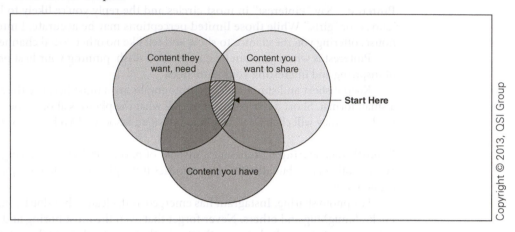

Being Invisible

When we blog or post on social channels as ourselves, it's personal. We use "I" and "me" frequently and casually. But when we are creating content for our organization, our personal opinions get in the way of good communication. What we think is really not relevant or appropriate for our organization and often clouds the message we're trying to convey.

The first step is to eliminate all "I" and "me" references. Then understand that "we," "us" and "our" refers to what the organization says about a topic, not what *you* say.

Write from a neutral point-of-view, without editorial or personal slant. It takes practice, so write as often as you can.

Being Unselfish

We've all seen selfish content. The individual or organization spews all their canned spiels and deals without regard for what the audience needs or wants. Selfish communication is quickly disregarded and sometimes ridiculed.

There is a sweet spot between (1) What your audience needs and wants to hear and (2) The content your organization has and wants to communicate. Focus on that sweet spot, and you can create a win-win scenario where your serve both the key audience and your organization.

This approach requires that you know much more about your key audiences. You need to get beyond age, sex, marital status and income and learn their traits and habits. The more you know, the better you can hone your content to be what they need. Satisfy your audience and they will stay or come back.

Insidering

Have you ever learned a bit of information that the rest of the world does not yet know and proudly shared it with your friends and close associates? That's "insidering" —the concept of bringing your audience into your organization and showing them something the rest of the world might not know.

Blogs and social media are the perfect places to share insider information. It makes your audience feel like they are "in the know" and closer to your organization. Whenever possible, share special information as rapidly as possible with the audiences that read your blogs or follow you on social media.

Writing for SEO

Let's assume that your content is spot on target—tight, concise and perfect GSP (grammar, spelling and punctuation). But no matter how great your writing is and how worthy your message is, it doesn't matter if your audience can't find you. That's where search engine optimization (SEO) comes in.

Writing for SEO is a bit of art combined with a bit of science. We supply the art, and Google, the dominant search engine in the USA, controls the science. We must accommodate these SEO requirements to achieve a high-page rank. The goal is for your story to appear in the first few pages of a Google search. If users don't find what they want in the first few pages, they tend to go back and amend their original search. So listing on the first three pages is important.

What We Know and Don't Know

Google uses more than 200 proprietary algorithms, or criteria, to determine how high on the results list your Web page or blog page is. Some of these algorithms are public, but Google keeps the rest secret. Each time you enter a search in Google, they apply their algorithms to the massive store of data they've amassed on every Web page and blog page, resulting in a numerical score. The higher the score, the higher your page appears in search results.

Determining Keyword Phrases

Optimal keyword phrases are three to five words. Your challenge is to define exactly what your reader will type into Google to find your content. Generally, if you use only one or two keywords, your content gets lost in a sea of generality.

An entire industry has been built around determining the best keywords to use for your content. Many online tools exist to help you research the best keywords, but the real question is simpler: "What will your readers search for in Google to find your content?" That is the start and end point for determining keywords.

The Science of SEO

Now that you have your three- to five-word keyword list, you must place it in *seven key locations* on your page or post so Google's bots will read it for optimal SEO.

Let's assume, for example, that your keyword phrase is "Writing for SEO."

The on-page elements are as follows:

URL—This usually occurs automatically with well-built blogs

Title (H1 or Heading 1)

Subhead (H2 or Heading 2)

Body Copy—Use your keywords in the first sentence and three to five times in each page or post

Page Description—The snippet you write that Google uses to describe your page or post

Graphics—One or more graphics with alternative tags in place

Outbound Links—One or two links to more information on other pages or posts

For some writers, the requirement of using an identical phrase in all these key places will seem a terrible intrusion. But with slight changes in your writing process and a little practice, keyword placement will become more natural.

Blog Writing

It's tempting to assume that all of your audiences are perfectly comfortable with digital communications. However, since most adults 40 years or older grew up with print before digital became common, the idea of social media might feel somewhat foreign to them.

Those who prefer to read print will scan multiple columns on each page and while reading get the feeling of speed as they run down the columns with their short lines of copy. Readers can hop through the story, repeatedly jumping back and forth to read and reread sections.

Digital reading is more linear, forcing your readers to focus on one wide column as they scroll vertically.

For clarification, blog content is commonly referred to as a blog post, article or story.

One-Mississippi, Two-Mississippi …

Blog readers are quick, giving you about four to eight seconds to interest and intrigue them into continuing with your article. The rule for blog writing is "be quick, be sharp, be concise." Your headline and first paragraph are critical to enticing them into reading the entire article. This puts a great deal of pressure on the quality of your title and lead paragraph.

Break the Rules

You can throw away most of what you've learned about news and public relations writing when it comes to writing for blogs. No inverted pyramid, no formula or patterns, no AP style, but yes, perfect GSP. Remember that blog writing is the "Wild, Wild West" where almost anything goes.

If blogs are conversations, then they come in all shapes and sizes. Some are serious and heavy with information, while others are fun and entertaining, full of puns and innuendos. Every possible writing style is available to blog writers. Just make sure the style matches the reader audience.

Avoid long posts in favor of short, concise pieces. For SEO purposes, your target is 350–500 words for a blog post. It's far too easy for readers to simply "click-off" if you ramble or veer off course. Digital readers appreciate brevity, so make your point quickly and conclude.

This generally means you must limit each post to one clear message. Keep it brief and on point, and your readers will stay with you to the end. Avoid tangents, tributaries and those wonderful sidetracks where you go on and on about a minor point and keep piling on word after word until the original thought is lost forever in an obscure fog of something that seems to have less and less to do with the one point you're really trying to make in your bloated blog post. Whew! Got it?

Staying short and sweet and single-purposed makes blog writing much easier for the writer than other forms of writing.

Change the Writing Process

You have an idea, do a bit of research and start writing. That's the normal process. But we're going to blow up that process because of SEO requirements, audience-centric focus and single message limitation. You have some work to do before your actual writing can begin. Let's examine the process step by step:

1. Picture Your Audience   Close your eyes and picture in your mind the face of one member of your audience. Be clear about who they are, what they're like and what they need from you. Now hold on to that picture as you write. Talk *with* them not *to* them. Remember, you are being unselfish and communicating what *they* need to hear, not just what *you* want to say.

2. Determine Objectives   Objectives are clearly defined outcomes you wish to see come from your communication efforts. Without clear objectives, your communication can too easily drift into aimless talking. Without clear purpose, you will rarely know if you succeeded.

Determine the objective for each piece of content you create with the needs of your audience and organization in mind. Now let this objective guide your messaging decisions.

3. Message   One point, one thought. What is it? Write it down and refer back to it often. As you develop your blog post it's okay to come back and modify your message as necessary. Blog writing is an ebb and flow to get the right balance.

Good blog articles are engaging and two-way. Rather than demanding your audience "sit down, shut up and listen" to you, engagement is your aim. Ask them what they think and feel instead of just feeding them your information. If you want comments on your post, *ask* for comments. If you want them to pass your story to their friends and associates, *suggest* that. If you want them to take action, *call for that action* in your post.

4. Keywords   Now that you have your audience, objective and message in mind, you should know what your blog is all about. Create a three- to five-word keyword phrase that your audience will use to find your article when they search Google. Not too general or your post will be lost in a sea of other stories. Not too specific or you risk missing a large portion of an interested audience. What would *you* type into a Google search to find your blog article?

Test your keyword phrase by searching for it in Google and checking the results. If those results are off target, then rework your keywords until you see more appropriate results. You're not completely alone with your content. There are more chances of posts similar to your article. Continue working on your keywords until you're satisfied you have found the right search phrase.

5. Style   What type of article do you intend to write? Announcements are short bursts. Reference pieces are long and winding and full of information—usually good for later reference. Serious pieces can be full of emotion, even first-person commentaries. Is your intention to entertain your readers with something fun or humorous? Remember, there are few rules to good blog writing.

You have a blank canvas to fill, so you can be creative in how you communicate. Maybe your post will be an actual conversation between two persons with opposing views. Or a series of tweet-like bursts. Or a limited amount of words and a large number of graphics. In any event your post is a reflection of how your audience accepts communication and the message you want to deliver.

There is a caveat that comes with creativity. Be careful that your chosen style does not confuse or bewilder your readers. Do not let your creative style get in the way of good communication. Boring as it may sound, when in doubt keep it simple and to the point.

6. Write   Finally you can begin writing. Write your title and lead paragraph first. Don't obsess over making them perfect. They are merely placeholders at this point, and you should expect to come back and edit them time and again. Don't forget that your keywords must be placed in your title and the first paragraph.

It's a good idea to briefly outline your article so you don't forget your key points as you write. Some writing applications like iA Writer Pro, which was used to write this chapter, accommodate notes and outlining in their workflow.

Now tell your story—quickly, clearly, completely. Don't forget to include your keyword phrase three to five times in your post. Quote other sources or other people, and be quotable yourself.

Assume this first draft will be heavily edited or completely rewritten if necessary. Repeatedly refer back to that picture of your audience in your mind and talk directly to them. Stay focused on your message, and engage your audience where possible. Ask them to comment on or share your post with others. Include a call-to-action if possible.

7. Edit   When the first draft is finished, step away from the keyboard. Take a short break, answer emails, read and enjoy yourself for a moment. Then dive back in and begin editing your piece.

Constantly ask yourself: "Is this what the *audience* needs or wants?" and "Is this what the *organization* needs or wants?"

Check that your keywords are perfectly placed in the title, first sentence, a subhead and three to five times in the body. Determine what graphic or graphics you will use and what alt tags they will carry (alt tags [alternative tags] are snippets of copy embedded with Web and blog graphics which are read [spoken] by readers for the sight impaired.)

Be hard on your writing. Tighten it and remove all unnecessary verbiage. Are those adjectives absolutely necessary or just dead weight? If you find a tangent that strays from the message, remove it.

8. Edit Again   Take another short break. Stretch, freshen your drink, check Twitter, then return with clear eyes and read your story again.

9. Copy and Format   Copy and paste your content into your blog and format the heads, subheads, graphics and outbound links. Always create an excerpt so your post appears correctly in a blog list. Excerpt is a blog feature that presents only the title and lead paragraph of your article in a list of the most recently published blogs. You can include a visual in your excerpt for interest.

Preview your post to see exactly how it will appear, then go back and amend everything necessary to improve presentation.

10. Publish and Listen and Learn   Your job doesn't end when your article is published. It's now time to listen.

Monitor traffic to your post and determine how many came to the post and presumably read your article. High traffic usually is driven by a good title and lead paragraph, solid SEO and using social and other tools to push traffic to your post. Watch how long they stay on your post. Read and respond to comments. Learn and remember what content resonates with your audience.

Perform a Google search to see how high your post appeared in Google's page ranking, and look for other articles or posts that may have been spurred by your article.

To hone your skill as a blog writer you must listen, learn and repeat.

Social Media Writing

Writing for social media "pushes" is really simple compared to blog writing. But you must follow many of the same social communication rules, no matter which social media channel you use.

For clarification, in social media when you publish, or "push" something, it is commonly called different things for differing channels. In Facebook a push is called an *update*, in Twitter a *tweet*, in LinkedIn, Google+ and other channels a *share*.

Relevant, Useful and/or Entertaining

Social content must be relevant, useful and/or entertaining for your audience. Communicate what they need, not just what your organization wants to say.

Invisible

You, the writer, must be completely invisible. Use of "I" or "me" will be misunderstood as coming from the organization, not an individual. The exception to this is if your organization has an iconic brand mascot like the Jack in the Box, Jack Ball (head) or the Geico gecko. In those cases you can let the mascot do the speaking and use "I" and "me" as needed.

Use Hashtags

Hashtags are typically one or two words preceded by a "#" symbol in Twitter, Facebook and Instagram posts. Hashtags may be embedded in the copy, as seen in the Jack in the Box tweet in Figure 5.3, or added to the end of the copy before any short link. Hashtags are used to group social pushes into specific subject areas. Readers can search hashtags—instead of individual words or phrases—to see all social pushes on the same topic.

FIGURE 5.3

Tweets with Hashtags Are Easier to Search

Twitter, Inc.

For example, if you're talking about your organization's latest spring styles in women's clothing, your hashtag might be #springstyles. You can include multiple hashtags including your brand name and other descriptors.

Include a Link (URL)

In most cases you will be communicating about a subject that requires more information, so you should include a link to that additional information. In these cases your push is simply a clever or compelling means to interest your reader into seeking more information.

But, there will be times when you just want to say something quickly. Those pushes don't require a link, but don't leave your reader hanging. If there is any chance they will need additional information, provide an appropriate link to that information.

In social pushes you will rarely include a full link because it is far too long and cumbersome. Instead you reduce your full link to a short link. Several groups provide this service. For example, if you want to shorten your full link you might visit the shortening service Ow.ly at http://ow.ly/url/shorten-url. Paste your full link into Ow.ly, for example, https://en.forums.wordpress.com/topic/what-is-a-shortlink?replies=7, and it would be shortened to http://ow.ly/Lbq03.

Be Quick, Be Clever

You have only a few seconds to entice your reader to read more. Your writing should be laser sharp and concise. The shorter the better, as long as you get your point across.

Write for the Channel

The style, tone and length of your social media push must match the requirements and personality of the specific channel you're using. Following are brief tips for writing in particular social media channels.

Facebook   Remember, for its users, Facebook is generally personal and private. Your Facebook updates should be sensitive to the fact that Facebook users operate in a closed sea of friends, family and close associates. If your pushes are selfish and irrelevant, your update will be viewed as an inappropriate intrusion. Imagine you're invited into someone's home, their Facebook home, and be respectful. Write Facebook updates in conversational tones as seen in the Figure 5.4 Facebook update telling how a student captured a stunning photo. Use hashtags whenever possible.

Depending on your relationship with and the needs of your audience, Facebook can be a very powerful tool. Keep your updates more on the personal side, using "we," "us," "our," "you" and "your" as appropriate.

Your Facebook updates can be far longer than pushes in other channels. Be careful. Don't go on and on just because you can. Keep it to one thought, be concise and keep it as short as possible.

FIGURE 5.4

Facebook Updates Should Be Personal When Possible

Twitter   Twitter is a writing challenge. Your content, hashtags and short link must fit within a 140-character limit. If you run over this limit your tweet will still be available intact, but your readers will not be able to see all of the tweet easily without opening the Twitter app. Avoid that nuisance.

Ben & Jerry's in Figure 5.5 conveyed their message in a fun way using a perfect visual, included a hashtag and got in a link for more information, all within the Twitter character limit.

Twitter is exceptional when you have alerts, announcements or anything that resembles breaking news. Tweets are more first-person than other channels. Still, don't use "I" or "me" unless the tweet is coming from you, the person, rather than the organization. Use hashtags as much as you can.

FIGURE 5.5

With Twitter the Challenge Is to Say a Lot in Few Characters

LinkedIn   What did we say about LinkedIn? "All business, all the time." This is not a place for fun and games. Convey only meaningful and important information, but don't forget to be human when possible. AT&T in Figure 5.6 shows its appreciation for its employees in a very business and human manner.

You have two choices in LinkedIn—be a subject matter expert (SME) or share information about the organization and its people, products and services. This is not a venue for sales messages, but a perfect place to show off your personal or organizational expertise in a particular area. Remember that recruiters for all kinds and sizes of organizations use LinkedIn to search for prospective employees. Keep your LinkedIn posts business-like and relevant for a business reader. Time is money.

Google+   Google+ has become much more freewheeling over the years—more tolerant of long posts, but never tolerant of bad writing. Be quick and concise, and have some fun. Be clever, turn a quick phrase or say something with tongue-in-cheek. But remember, if you're clever and your audience doesn't understand what you're trying to say or takes it the wrong way, they may be quick to publicly criticize you.

Pinterest   Visuals rule on Pinterest. Photography should be excellent, even in the small format in which it is presented. Keep your description under 10 words wherever possible and match perfectly the photograph you're pinning. Many marketers include a brand name

FIGURE 5.6

LinkedIn Is a Great Place to Talk about Your Organization and People

AT&T At AT&T, we appreciate all of our Administrative Professionals and the important work they do. Join us and help energize the future of innovation, ideas and technology: http://soc.att.jobs/2dto

Linkedin

in the descriptions. A link should always be embedded in your pin. This link should go to a Web page or blog page specific to the photo and description in your pin. Avoid linking to your website's main page.

As an example, Figure 5.7 uses an excellent visual with descriptive copy and mentions the brand.

Instagram   Like Pinterest, Instagram is all about the visuals. But, like Facebook, you can write and write and write describing the photo or video you're posting. Don't abuse the privilege and ramble.

Posting interesting photographs and videos will get followers, so think different, colorful and unique perspective. Many brands show their people and products in cool, fun and different ways.

Use lots of hashtags, and don't hesitate to embed usernames or hashtags in your description.

The Science of Short Writing

Digital writing has spawned an emerging art of saying as much as you can in a compelling manner with very few characters. There is research into the use of action verbs and words that trigger visual images to make short writing more compelling. Articles, object phrases and punctuation are usually omitted such that "The Steps You Would Use for Good Blog Writing" would shorten to "Steps to Good Blog Writing."

Email subject lines, blog titles and social media pushes all pose a test of your short-writing ability. Good social media short writing comes with practice and observation. Watch what others write and learn.

FIGURE 5.7

Pinterest Is All about the Visual and Description

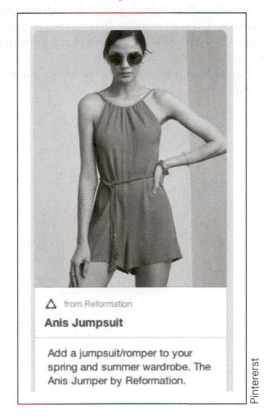

from Reformation

Anis Jumpsuit

Add a jumpsuit/romper to your spring and summer wardrobe. The Anis Jumper by Reformation.

Pintererst

In the End

Be it Web pages, emails, blogs or social pushes, good content is first about the audience and second about the organization. *Be as unselfish as you can, and focus on the needs and wants of your audience.* In digital it is incredibly easy for the reader to ignore or abandon your content if it gets too "salesy" or self-centered.

There is no art to digital writing. Success comes from experience and listening. Writing and publishing are only half the job. Watch and listen to see what resonates with your audience and what falls flat. Learn from this and repeat the topics, styles and approaches that work best.

Just like in other forms of writing, the more you produce the easier it becomes. Practice, practice, practice. Write just for fun. Treat your personal blog and social media the same way as you do your work writing. Watch what engages and learn how to reproduce that technique.

Remember to follow the best blogs and social pushes you see. What engages you will likely engage others as well. Learn from what others do to succeed. Research and follow the best blogs and social media. There is likely a reason they have achieved great followings.

Social media is lightning quick, so audience exposure is often more spontaneous than purposeful. Users often visit a favorite site out of habit—just checking in, or impulsively—wondering what's new on a photo-sharing site. It's your job to interest them and cause them to stop for your content.

Happy blogging, updating, tweeting, pinning, posting, insidering, showing and sharing!

PART 3

Preparing to Write

Going on a long journey requires planning and preparation. You need to know where you're going, what you need to take and where you'll stay. Similarly preparations—that is, answering questions—are necessary before writing is begun.

CHAPTER SIX

Research for the Public Relations Writer

*A*nswering *questions* is the purpose of public relations research. Because research of various types can be used at every step of the public relations process, it's obvious that the number of questions that we might like to have answered is huge. The continuing rapid growth in the use of social media has added tremendously to the number.

Planning for Research

You may not be directly involved in public relations planning, especially early in your career, but you still need to know a good bit about research because you'll use a lot of information unearthed through research. This information generally falls into six broad categories:

1. Policy and purpose
2. Background material
3. Public, audience, constituency
4. Message
5. Media
6. Program evaluation

All six are important in every PR situation, but rarely are they all equally important. Your sensitivity to the problem at hand will help you determine which category or combination of categories is especially important in a particular case.

When you analyze the steps you take when you consider making a major decision to stop smoking, go on a diet to lose weight or purchase a car, you find that you go through four steps in a specific sequence, which often is referred to as "A-I-D-A":

- *Awareness*—The first step is to become aware that the product, service or practice exists.
- *Interest*—Next, you probably would check out the advantages and disadvantages you might have in adopting the product, service or practice.
- *Desire*—If you continue developing interest, and if the product, service or practice seems to be right for you, you might develop a preference, or desire, for the product or service.
- *Action*—Finally you make a decision. You toss out the tobacco products; figure out what diet seems practical; or evaluate your finances, find that you can scrape by, take a test drive in that new-smelling auto and make a down payment.

Even in a world of interactivity, online communications and social networking, consumers still need to be *aware* of a product, express *interest* in it based on some degree of knowledge about the products' attributes and benefits, *desire* the product because it is relevant to their needs, wants or interests before they will make a purchase decision or take another *action*.[1] As you will see in Chapter 7, public relations writing is all about *persuasion*. Our role is—or should be—to always help members of our publics move through the AIDA process toward specific *actions*.

To do that, we need information. In this chapter, we examine what might be one part of such a plan—that is, how we help people move toward the actions we want them to take. For this we need information about the products, services or practices that we want to encourage. We need to know what benefits they offer, where they are available, what they cost and so on. We need information about the kinds of people most likely to take such actions.

It is much easier and quicker today, but a lot riskier, to find information. You simply tell a search engine what you're looking for, and it will scour the Internet for the information. The problem is that the search engine can't recognize the difference between biased and unbiased information. Only you can make that distinction.

Getting information from the Web is problematic, because there are no traffic cops on the information superhighway. Wikipedia.com, which bills itself as "the largest reference website on the Internet,"[2] is "the communal encyclopedia that anyone can edit." Using Wikipedia is convenient, but it provides no way to track the source of information it contains, making accuracy questionable at best. You may find that you still must visit a traditional library now and then, or do some original research on questions that can't be answered by existing information.

You must develop basic strategies that help you select and use information. One approach is to rely on information from reputable sources, including the websites of organizations such as the U.S. Census Bureau and other government agencies, *The New York Times* and *The Wall Street Journal*. Even then, the information may be less than dependable. The Institute for Public Relations Research provides reports of research on 23 topics at its website, http://www.instituteforpr.org/.

An extensive database on public opinion is available from Pew Research Center, one of the world's leading archives of social science data, specializing in data from surveys of public opinion. Pew is a nonpartisan "fact tank" that provides information on the issues, attitudes and trends shaping America and the world. It does not take positions on policy issues.

Reliable information on the status of public relations was made available online on June 16, 2014, at http://www.annenberg.usc.edu/gapstudy. This is the eighth biennial Communication and Public Relations Generally Accepted Practices (GAP VIII) Study by the USC (University of Southern California) Annenberg Strategic Communication and Public Relations Center (SCPRC). According to the GAP VIII report, "The purpose of the GAP Study is to provide senior communicators with timely guidance as they manage their organizations, develop strategy, and prepare for the future. Participants included the most senior communications professionals in corporations, government agencies and non-profit organizations."

Good references for events and issues of the day are *Facts on File* and encyclopedia yearbooks. The database for most communication materials is ERIC—the Education Resources Information Center.

The point is that when searching for facts, be prepared for ambiguity that sometimes may be hard to reconcile. It's important to keep careful records of where the information you use came from, quote the sources and use footnotes when appropriate for the type of writing that you're doing.

Information from newsgroups and independent electronic newsletters may or may not be biased. That doesn't mean you can't use it. It does mean, however, that before you use it you must seek other sources to confirm it.

Keep in mind that action data, according to the newsletter *pr reporter,* is what is needed by public relations writers, including data that:

1. *Answers questions essential to planning projects, programs and campaigns.* The most desirable research methods focus on the latent readiness of audiences to behave in certain ways and on how audiences get information and how they use it to arrive at decisions.
2. *Tests, if possible, and deflates assumptions.* Conventional wisdom—often what leads senior management to decisions—may be wrong.

T A B L E 6 . 1	*Prewriting Checklist*

1. Gather the facts of the matter and get them right.

2. Gather authoritative opinions and interpretations of the matter.

3. Evaluate facts and opinions for their pertinence. Discard those not directly related to the matter.

4. Synthesize the remaining facts and opinions into a cohesive body of information.

5. Organize the information for writing.

6. Develop a writing outline that moves logically from one point to the next.

7. Write. Edit. Rewrite.

3. *Produces baseline data that permits accurate evaluation.* Good baselines help us know how far we've moved, if at all, whether a process is working and whether behavioral change goals are met.[3]

Research, then, is a key element in professional success—research at the beginning and at the ending of any endeavor. Research is as important to a beginner as it is to a senior counselor, although the focus of research may change as you move up the career ladder. Because most entry-level jobs in public relations are directly related to the writing process, it is important for you to learn as much as you can about research and how to use it as a writer.

For this reason, you should review and remember the prewriting checklist in Table 6.1.

Research in Public Relations

Careful planning is central to the process and practice of professional public relations. Plans are generally successful in direct proportion to the quality of the information on which they are built. That's why research is so important to the overall success of a public relations plan. Planning usually begins with what is known as a *situational analysis*. This is where answers are sought for all sorts of questions.

Mission Statement   What is your organization's *mission statement*? The mission statement should establish the scope, domain and fundamental purpose of the organization and provide a guiding philosophy. The mission statement should be a clear, simple statement of the overall purpose of the organization, provide a focal point for objectives, goals and activities and define success for the organization. Southwest Airlines' mission statement meets those criteria: "The mission of Southwest Airlines is dedication to the highest quality of Customer Service delivered with a sense of warmth, friendliness, individual pride, and Company Spirit."[4] (See Chapter 14 for more information on mission statements.)

Objectives   What are senior management's most important *objectives*? In some organizations, the term *goal* is used to denote long-range outcomes desired, while *objective* is used for short-term outcomes. Other organizations reverse the meaning, with objective meaning long range and goal referring to short term. Neither is incorrect, but it is important to clearly identify the meaning of each:

- Based upon the organization's mission statement
- A long-term desired outcome
- An open-ended statement of purpose (see Table 6.2.)

Goals   Whereas objectives are long-term and open-ended, goals are:

- Short range
- Specific as to time
- Fully measurable
- Extensions of objectives

A goal should answer the question, "What one result do we want to accomplish?" Well-written goals are close-ended statements of purpose oriented toward an *end result* or *outcome*. (What happens *after* the special event occurs or the annual report is delivered?)

T A B L E 6 . 2	*Criteria for Objectives*
	The Objectives Need to Be:
Relevant	**Do the objectives support the overall company/brand goals?**
	Objectives must be directly aimed at what the business wants to accomplish. Anything not pertinent to that should be eliminated.
Realistic	**Can I/we fulfill the objectives and what will it take to do so?**
	There needs to be a belief that it is possible to achieve them, but at the same time that it is not too easy. Objectives should not be set too low.
Specific	**Who do I want to affect with what?**
	Objectives should be clearly articulated. They cannot be vague. It is not only the desired effect within a set time, but also considers the target audience.
Measurable	**What measurements should I consider to establish success?**
	The objectives need to be specific enough to be measurable and monitored to determine progress. Different objectives need different types of metrics.
Timely	**Over what period of time am I/are we looking to achieve these objectives?**
	Without a time frame, it is possible to determine success but impossible to determine lack of success.

Source: Katharine Delahaye Paine, Pauline Draper and Angela C. Jeffrey, "Using Public Relations Research to Drive Business Results," Copyright © 2008, Institute for Public Relations, used with permission.

Each well-written goal contains the following four components:

1. What is being measured (awareness? attendance? contributions?)
2. A starting point or base against which to measure
3. Quantities or percentages to be achieved
4. A deadline or amount of time for accomplishment

Evaluation of success is only as good as the quality of the goals. By including these components, you're setting the stage for measuring your success. If the goal is related to awareness or another factor that can't be counted (like attendance at an event can be), research may be necessary to determine the starting point—"where you are," so to speak.

Here are two examples of how weak goals can be made stronger by including the four components listed previously:

Example 1

Weak: "Enhance our public image."
Stronger: "Improve recall of important facts about our organization—from three to five—among key media representatives by June 1 of next year."

In this example, what's being measured is *recall of important facts*. The base—where you are now—is *recall of three facts by key media representatives*. The quantity to be achieved is *five*—two more than the starting point of three. The deadline is *June 1 of next year*.

Example 2

Weak: "Increase fundraising."
Stronger: "Increase by 10 percent—from $60,000 to $66,000—the monies raised from our annual fundraising event by the end of the year."

As you see in both examples, the intangibles—"public image" and "fundraising"—have been converted to terms that are measurable. It's important to keep "targets," or results to be achieved, reasonable. A 10 percent increase in funds raised may sound small but would be a major accomplishment and might be a "stretch" to reach.

Define and Segment Publics

Segmenting each public into homogeneous segments who will respond in similar ways can help you make communications more targeted and effective. This kind of segmentation is accomplished using one or a combination of two criteria—demographics and psychographics or lifestyles.

Demographics

Demographics are the statistical characteristics of human populations and include such factors as:

- Age
- Gender
- Race
- Geographic location
- Occupation
- Marital status
- Education
- Household size
- Income or household income

Knowing any of these factors about the members of a target public can be of great help in public relations planning. For example, if you work for a grocery retailer, marketing research might indicate that the company's target audience is a married female between the ages of 26 and 34. The research might also indicate that a typical shopper is employed as a professional, has one or two children and prefers to shop at the end of her workday, stopping at a store on the right side of her homeward drive. With this information, you could develop a public relations plan for new store openings focused on events to include children and emphasizing products that offer both nutrition and ease of preparation. One large grocery chain which determined that its target audience fit this demographic profile decided to build new stores on the right-hand side of evening drive-time traffic arteries to make stopping on the route home from the office more convenient for the women shoppers.

However, if you work for an organization making pet food, you are interested in reaching people whose lifestyles involve pets, regardless of the people's age, sex, race or other demographics.

Psychographics and Lifestyles

Psychographics involve identification of personality characteristics, interests (like children, music, art, pets, travel or hobbies) and attitudes that affect a person's lifestyle and purchasing behaviors. Psychographic data points include opinions, attitudes and beliefs about various aspects relating to lifestyle and purchasing behavior.

Other Questions   What are the significant trends? What is the overall economic situation? What are the political considerations for the action we are contemplating? How is our organization perceived by target publics? How are our competitors viewed by target publics? How much support can we expect from affected publics? These and other questions unique to the situation must be raised and answered.

Two Basic Types of Research

The two basic types of research are *quantitative* and *qualitative*. The research that results in numbers, such as a survey, is quantitative, because we can attach quantities in response to questions: "On a scale of 1–7, with 1 being 'Poor,' and 7 being 'Excellent,' how would you rate the performance of the new mayor?" And so on. It's a good idea to allow respondents to opt-out by using a zero indicating "Don't know; don't care to answer."

Qualitative research includes interviews, focus group interviews, case studies and pilot studies. Although the results of qualitative research often are used as a part of the decision-making process, it is most common in exploratory research, where a problem or its scope is being defined. For example, focus group interviews often are used to explore what questions should be asked in an upcoming survey and how well each question is understood. In-depth interviews and focus groups are used for input in deciding characteristics, and even names, for products/services being developed.

Although analysis of survey data requires training and experience, the results are statistical, more objective and thus less likely to be influenced by prejudices of the researchers. A thorough research study, such as a communication audit, often incorporates both qualitative and quantitative research methods in evaluating an organization's public relations or internal communications program.

Categories of Research for the PR Writer

Policy and Purpose   The "company line" is a euphemism that hardly does justice to the full concept behind the term *policy*. Policy is a considered statement of purpose, position or direction that is expected to guide the behavior of those it covers.

Every organization in both the public and private sectors has a set of policies. Anyone working for or with the company or organization is expected to know the provisions of applicable policies.

Policy is of two general types: internal and external.

Internal policy is that of your employer. It is a set of guidelines that directs and controls the collective behavior of the organization and the job behavior of each employee. Such policies may range from a policy governing employee benefits to a policy of public candor in the face of a community crisis.

External policy comes from a source outside the organization's immediate control but bears on the organization's behavior toward its constituencies. For example, if you are writing the annual report for a publicly held company, you must know and observe certain Securities and Exchange Commission policies and requirements. It is critical that you know applicable policies in order to avoid problems. This not only may save your job, it may even get you promoted.

Some policies you may need to know are available to you only in oral form. Oral policy can be especially frustrating, for three main reasons. First, oral policy is easily distorted. What you believe today to be a clear understanding of the policy may be completely obsolete a year from now. Second, management may be unsure of itself and thus reluctant to put a decision in writing. Third, management may have a hidden agenda. To understand this point, suppose you are about to write a series of releases for the local media about your country club's gala next month, some proceeds of which will go to the United Negro College Fund. Club policy does not bar African-Americans from membership, but there are no African-Americans in the club. And you are told, when you ask the club manager, that no African-Americans are invited to or expected to attend the gala. Written policy may say one thing, but unwritten policy may say something else.

If you find yourself relying more on oral than written policy, urge management to put the oral policy in writing. If management resists this suggestion unreasonably, start looking for another job.

Background Material   Successful public relations writing is based on a solid, fully developed body of facts. The kinds of facts needed will vary, depending on the situation.

For example, suppose you are retained to write a brochure in support of a bond election to double the community's hospital bed space. What facts do you need to know before you begin to write?

For starters, here are a few: What has been the community's rate of growth over the last 20 years? How much is the community expected to grow in the next 20 years? What accounts for this rate of growth? What is the ratio of community patients to patients from outside the community? Why? Has this ratio changed in the last few years? Is the ratio expected to change in the future? Why? Is the interest rate on the bonds favorable? How do local financial leaders view the bonding program? Why?

The questions you might ask about this project may number into the hundreds. The number is not the issue. The point is that public relations planning, decision making and writing depend on the careful accumulation of facts and ideas.

As you begin the task of assembling background materials, you should assume the traditional role of the news reporter by asking who, what, where, when, how and why— especially why. As you get answers to these questions, you'll begin to build an elaborate, sophisticated, project-specific system of information that will help you handle assignments ranging in diversity from staging a small symposium to handling a crisis at a chemical plant.

If your search for the proper background material leads you into legal or government documents and you find that an office or agency is uncooperative, you may want to request the needed information, if it qualifies, under the Freedom of Information Act (FOIA). For guidance and materials on how to make an FOIA request, contact the Freedom of Information Clearinghouse. Go online to http://www.citizenarchive.org/litigation/free_ info/ or write to 1600 20th St. NW, Washington, DC 20009.

One of the key points to remember about background materials is that, even if the public relations situation is new to you, it is not new. Others have faced the same situation or a similar one. Learn from their experiences if you can.

Public   As noted earlier, public relations professionals are fond of talking about publics, audiences, stakeholders or constituencies. These terms are used synonymously. It is rare in public relations that you will deal with a single public. Even when it appears that way, closer examination usually turns up two or more subsegments, each with its unique characteristics, concerns and needs.

Thus the question is: How can you identify the public or subsegments? This requires research, perhaps at different levels of sophistication. To illustrate this point, consider the following situation.

You are director of public relations for a new bank with a national charter in a metropolitan area. The bank's management is aware that deregulation allows savings and loans and investment companies, such as Fidelity, to provide many financial services previously available only at banks.

Your management decides to market the bank to certain types of potential customers—specifically, those whose annual incomes are $100,000 or more. This rules out many potential depositors from your target audience. And it focuses attention on specific segments of the community, such as physicians, dentists, attorneys, retailers, owners of manufacturing or service companies, architects, designers and engineers.

In this situation, you will first try to divide the priority public into segments by using demographic information—income, sex, education, occupation, race, ethnicity, marital status, home ownership and the like.

In March 2014 the U.S. Census Bureau provided evidence that accuracy in gathering demographic data is not so easy. "The Census Bureau has embarked on a years-long research project intended to improve the accuracy and reliability of its race and ethnicity data. A problem is that a growing percentage of Americans don't select a race category provided on the form: As many as 6.2% of census respondents selected only "some other race" in the 2010 census, the vast majority of whom were Hispanic."

The Census Bureau undertakes a complete USA census (nearly 309 million people in 2010) every 10 years, in years ending in "0." "Many communities, including Hispanics, Arabs and people of mixed race, have said they're unsure of how to identify themselves on census forms. This pattern of response led to the bureau's 'most comprehensive effort in history to study race and ethnic categories', according to Census officials Nicholas Jones and Roberto Ramirez. 'Increasingly, Americans are saying they cannot find themselves' on census forms, Jones said.' "[5]

Once a demographic profile is complete, the picture of this public comes into sharper focus. But does it tell you all you need to know? Perhaps. Perhaps not.

What you may need now is psychographic information—information about lifestyle, attitudes and behavior. Information of this type may give you important clues indicating that your public relations program should communicate differently with, say, physicians and dentists than with retailers and manufacturers. For example, physicians and dentists may be more concerned with long-range financial planning, whereas retailers and manufacturers may be more concerned with managing cash flow. If so, messages going to these two groups must be different.

Research helps you understand to the fullest extent the needs of your public and its components so that you can shape messages that speak to their distinct needs.

Message   What you say and how you say it may have a great deal to do with your success. Recall our discussion about publics. If you are lucky enough to have a single public with which to communicate, your job will be easier. But when you have several publics, it can be complex.

Whether it is one public or several, you are generally well advised to begin by reducing your message to a single simple idea. Remember, though, that a single simple idea is not necessarily an insignificant or simpleminded idea. Reducing what you want to say to this level is necessary to help keep you on the right track as you shape your message.

Because different methods can be used to construct a message for maximum impact, you should select an approach based primarily on your purpose for the message. Is the purpose to change or to reinforce behavior? If it is to change, you must remember to make a reward obvious to the receiver of your message. If it is to reinforce, your message must avoid information that contradicts current behavior.

Should you use a conclusion-drawing technique? In this method, you select and present information that will lead your audience to draw the conclusion you want it to draw. Communication-research literature suggests that this is a good method of communicating with sophisticated audiences. However, this technique can be fatal if used with unsophisticated audiences.

There are many techniques of message presentation in addition to the ones discussed. You should review the communication-research literature and develop a personal understanding of these methods. What are they? How do they work? Under what conditions do they appear to work best? A good way to begin is to review Chapter 7.

Media   As you work your way through a public relations problem, you will have to make choices about which channels of communication to use and how to use them. Before you can make these decisions, however, you need to know the characteristics of the various media available to you. What are their technical qualities and requirements? What can they or can't they do? What are their emotional qualities? How do people react to them? How and why do people use them as they do? Should you use general or "traditional" media, specialized media, social media or a combination of the three types? These are serious questions, the answers to which are not easy and may involve large amounts of time and money. But you need to know, not guess. Review the Competence in Convergence section in Chapter 9 that discusses media choices using the POSE (paid, owned, sponsored, earned) formula.

Once you have chosen the media, you'll need to assess whether they are effective and efficient in implementing this particular public relations program. This suggests that you'll need to monitor progress and evaluate success. Four questions are important here. Did you reach your priority public? Was your message really heard and accepted? Was your message acted upon? Was the use of the media cost-effective?

Storing and Retrieving Research Data

Public relations professionals would have more serious communication problems if intensive spadework in policy, background material, public, message and media were fresh with each new program. However, professionals routinely accumulate pertinent research information, initiate research for later use and plan for future research needs.

A large proportion of public relations research is borrowed from the social sciences, especially from behavioral areas. Useful research studies are accumulated and indexed for future use. Research about publics and media is continually reviewed and stored. Much of the information about publics comes from comprehensive studies done by the commercial media about their audiences. Other studies come from product and service institutions concerned about their own publics. Research on internal policies is mined from organizational sources, whereas external policies are gleaned from various municipal, state and federal organizations, professional or associational groups and the like. (Review the section of Chapter 3 that discusses messages that go to both intended and unintended audiences and how watching cultural sensitivities can cause problems from those unintended audiences.)

A particular public relations situation may require some original fact-finding. In conducting original research or in hiring a research company to do it, the public relations practitioner must know clearly what is needed. Otherwise, the resulting information may be imposing but inadequate.

Organizing   Because public relations information comes from such a wide variety of sources, organizing it can be a problem. One common organizational pattern is to categorize information according to policy (pertinent internal and external guides), background material (substantive facts bearing on the situation), public (facts about the people you want to reach), message (facts about successes of message types in similar situations) and media (the most effective ways of delivering your message).

Presenting   The organization of the research should reflect the ways in which it will later be presented and used. In presenting this information, it is important to explain the implications of the findings when these are not obvious and to suggest what bearing the research has on the situation. The information should also indicate what other research is needed to make the picture clearer.

Updating   Organization of the research should allow for easy updating, especially when ongoing research, such as periodic opinion measurement (as in an election campaign), is critical. Today, most organizational information is stored in computers, including cloud computing storage by third parties. The PR professional must know enough about the method of storage to use the system effectively. What works best for information technology (IT) people may not always be what works best for the public relations person trying to use the information.

Reusing   Adding to or reusing research information is difficult if the information is not readily accessible. The retrieval process is critical. PR professionals must work with IT people to tell them how the information will be used—what will be needed, under what conditions, when and in what form. Don't be timid about asking for help. For PR research needs, the system must be designed so that data is well organized, is presented in a meaningful way and can easily be updated.

Sources for PR Writers and Researchers

Writers and researchers of all types—not just public relations professionals—depend on research from two basic sources: paper and people. Of course, "paper" doesn't always mean books. It can mean Internet sites, digital recordings, video and audio recordings, films, DVDs, or some other forms of storage. The important point to remember is that sources are either secondary (paper or other form of stored information) or primary (people).

Secondary Sources for Research

Every public relations writer should have at least a working library in the office that contains a dictionary, a thesaurus, appropriate reference volumes and bibliographies, and pertinent professional and technical journals and documents. Completing this working library is a file system where information can be placed for easy and immediate access. This office library will be your first line of attack when you need secondary information. For some writers, all of this will be in one place—their computer. Computer software and the Internet can include many language references and fact-storage packages.

If you need help, call a reference librarian. You will save time if you can succinctly describe the information you want. Some reference librarians will answer simple questions on the phone.

Library   Most universities and metropolitan areas have public libraries containing resources for basic research. They also usually have cooperative agreements with other libraries to get information on loan. College and university libraries contain scholarly material you may need. Some university libraries are repositories for government documents. These documents represent a large body of research in many different areas. Some churches have substantial holdings of religious works and genealogical data, and many cities have law libraries. Some libraries have special collections that are open to qualified researchers.

Reference Works   The primary tools of both the reference librarian and the researcher in the library are collections of information and reference works. These are "maps" that enable you to find the treasures of information you seek. Standard reference works include encyclopedias, biographical dictionaries, dictionaries of quotations, concordances of the Bible and other famous works, atlases and gazetteers, chronologies or other books of dates, handbooks and sourcebooks such as dictionaries of all languages and areas of specialization.

Bibliographies   One reference source that is especially important is the bibliography. In compiling and categorizing bibliographies, authors provide you with paths through mazes of footnotes. Bibliographies usually identify reliable sources of information that you will want to tap. Many libraries offer electronic access to stored bibliographies so that you can view on a screen all the most likely sources. Hard (printed) copies also are available from materials listed in these databases.

Periodicals/Databases   One resource accessible in electronic systems is *The New York Times Index* of more than 13 million articles. Using this database, online at http://www .nytimes.com/ref/membercenter/nytarchive.html, you can track, call up and read any story that appeared in *The New York Times* as early as 1851. Because *The New York Times* makes an effort to be a newspaper of record, it is possible to do a great deal of research through this index alone.

LexisNexis, CompuServe, Dow Jones News Service and others are electronic databases that can be tapped through the Internet by public relations writers for research purposes. Many newspapers in addition to *The New York Times,* such as *The Washington Post, The Oklahoman* and The *Fort Worth Star-Telegram,* provide database services that may be helpful. The Associated Press and larger media chains such as Gannett can be rich sources for information. For commercial publications, the most useful index is the *Readers' Guide to Periodical Literature.* You can also find indexes and databases that focus on highly specialized fields, such as law (LexisNexis®) or medicine (MEDLINE®).

Public Records   Government records at all levels—local, state and federal—are available to you unless they contain classified information. Some government agencies offer significant research assistance. For example, the Library of Congress (LOC) is helpful in locating information and will often offer advice to put you on the right trail.

Government Records   Most government offices are storehouses of information, and many government offices distribute their own materials. The federal government has published its materials by the USA Government Printing Office (GPO). A central store in Washington, D.C., contains information on every imaginable subject, as do GPO regional offices in cities with federal centers. Ask to be put on the GPO's mailing list.

One essential source of information for PR people is the U.S. Census Bureau. A huge amount of data is available on the www.census.gov website. For information about countries around the world, *The World Factbook,* maintained by the Central Intelligence Agency (CIA), is an excellent online resource.

Public Access to Information   FOIA has opened many files of both public and private institutions to examination. This means that normally you now have access to all documents—titles to property, budgets of state institutions, court proceedings and the like—that have been filed in a public place. A wealth of information exists in these documents.

Primary Sources for Research

When you must research primary sources, generally you have two ways of gathering information from people. One is the interview, and the other is the questionnaire. Whether you're asking questions face-to-face or through a questionnaire, you must prepare yourself ahead of time so the answers you receive will give you the information you want. Let's look at each of these methods.

Interviewing   After you have done some fundamental research, you are ready to begin asking questions of people who might be knowledgeable in your subject. In any interview you may want to begin by asking yes/no questions, but always use these as the basis for asking open-ended questions in the body of the interview. Find authorities through your research, then develop questions for them and follow up any leads they may give you.

Although some people seem to have a natural talent for getting information from others, every public relations person should develop and practice interviewing skills. Like people who play musical instruments by ear, natural interviewers—and all others—become even better with practice.

Go to an interview prepared with questions on paper, and be sure to explain how and where the information will be used. As the interview proceeds, keep information in mind that you have gained from your research. Then, if the opportunity arises, you can follow a different line of questioning. Take notes and use a recorder, and try not to rely solely on one or the other. It is unquestionably ethical to advise your interviewee that you want to record the conversation and to seek consent. No federal law requires prior consent in a face-to-face interview, but if the interview is recorded from an interstate telephone, prior consent is required. A few states require prior consent to record intrastate telephone conversations. Be sure to check out legal provisions in the state where you work.

One service that can enhance interviews is Skype, an Internet-based service that allows users to communicate by voice using a microphone and an interactive video using a webcam. The advantage is that the interviewer can view the body language of the person or persons being interviewed, and that can be valuable in phrasing questions. Some network administrators have banned Skype on corporate, government, home and education networks, citing reasons such as inappropriate usage of resources, excessive bandwidth usage, and security concerns.

Listen to what the person is telling you, and try to remember the information by putting it into the context suggested by your prior research. Encourage full responses by asking relevant questions and by participating in the conversation. Avoid being judgmental. You are asking, not telling. Table 6.3 provides an interviewing checklist.

T A B L E 6 . 3	*Checklist for Interviewing*

1. Research your subject before the interview.

2. Know something about the person you are interviewing.

3. Prepare a list of questions in advance.

4. Inform the interviewee in advance of the kinds of questions you will be asking.

5. Whenever possible use a tape recorder *and* take notes. Never put complete trust in a machine or in your memory.

6. Ask for explanations if you don't understand something.

7. Ask specific questions. Vague questions elicit vague answers.

8. Ask one question at a time. Don't throw several questions into the same sentence and expect the interviewee to answer—or even to remember—them all.

© Cengage Learning

Some of the important information you get from the interview will come from keen observation of the behavior of the person you are interviewing. Watch for nonverbal communication cues, and note both physical characteristics and environmental factors that could be telling. In particular, note gestures that indicate personality characteristics, and remember emotional emphases. The latter are particularly evident in the way something is said: the inflection of the voice, the expression on the face. Be cautious, however, about reading more into these details than is there. Be aware of your own bias and involvement with the subject, so you don't misinterpret what you experience. To safeguard against misinterpretation, some researchers prefer to videotape interviews so that they can capture this information and isolate it later.

Keep in mind that there are several characteristics of a good interview. First, you need to present yourself as a warm, responsive person to the interviewee. If you cultivate that impression consistently, people you interview will respond warmly to you. That goes a long way toward convincing respondents that their interaction with you will be both pleasant and personally satisfying. Second, you need to create a permissive atmosphere in which the person being interviewed does not feel inhibited by your questions but that invites candid responses. If respondents see your interview as important, they'll tend to be more cooperative. Third, you must be sure not to apply pressure of any kind, real or implied, on the person you are interviewing. If you maintain a detached but permissive posture in the interview, respondents are more likely to "open up" with more candor than you may have expected.

To achieve these purposes, you should follow these steps:

1. Introduce yourself by name and explain your affiliation (show documentation if it is needed or asked for).
2. Explain clearly what it is that you are doing.
3. Explain to the interviewee how he or she was chosen to be interviewed.
4. Adapt your behavior to the personality of the person being interviewed.
5. Build rapport.

Focus Group Interview   A focus group interview is with a group, not an individual. Its original intent was as a preresearch tool to help researchers identify and use terms in their questions to respondents that had common meanings to people in a target public.

The procedure for such an interview is to select 8–12 people from a target public, bring them to a central location and talk with them for 1–2 hours on some topic. While the atmosphere should appear to be casual, the moderator always works from a prepared script—a list of questions designed to get participants to begin talking and interacting with each other. Their conversations often are recorded, sometimes with video. A transcript of the dialogue can be analyzed to identify words or phrases that people use consistently to mean certain things. These words and phrases may then be used to form questions to be asked in a survey.

Suppose your client is a materials testing laboratory that does nondestructive and destructive testing for a wide variety of clients. Tests might range from stress tests on alloys to air quality. Many lab personnel become expert witnesses, especially in product liability cases. Your client wants feedback from quality control engineers representing a broad range of manufacturing in which testing is both routine and regular. Further, suppose that you know nothing about how a materials testing laboratory operates. How can you shape appropriate questions to a sample of quality control engineers? Don't try until you've done one or more focus group interviews. You should then have enough insights to put together a group of unambiguous questions that get the information you need.

Survey   The second means of getting information from people is the survey, which is a research workhorse. Drafting a questionnaire for a survey is difficult, however, and requires training and experience. Several simple questions are sometimes necessary to get a single piece of information.

It can be difficult to ask a question so that the respondent knows exactly what you mean by it. For example, a national survey once asked a question about "consumer movement leaders." Another researcher, attempting to replicate part of the study, used the same expression with different audiences and was asked by one respondent for a definition of "consumer leader." Did the researcher want to know about movement activists, government appointees or civil servants involved in consumer information, or corporate employees charged with responding to consumers? The question was invalid because it was being interpreted in different ways. One technique that helps to safeguard against this is to pretest the questions with focus groups before actually using the questionnaire and make changes as indicated by the interviews.

All questions should be phrased in such a way that they are bias-free. Consider this question: Do you still drink too much? Even a negative response signifies that the respondent drank too much at some previous time, though in fact the respondent may have never indulged in liquor at all. Questions asked in this fashion are not only ineffective but also unethical.

One survey that this author conducted was for a multinational company that had employees around the globe. It was necessary to ask questions in Chinese, English, French and Malay. While software is available to provide the same questions in each of numerous languages, the results are not always what you expect. For example, "some cultures don't recognize a difference between blue and green, at least in their speech: They have one word that covers both." In English, *time* is linear. "Time moves ahead, we put things behind us. In India, it's circular—the word for *tomorrow* and *yesterday* is the same: *kal*. To Mandarin speakers, time is vertical—next week is beneath you, last week is above you." And in some cultures, there is no word for *minute*.[6]

To develop a questionnaire, begin by simply listing all the information you want to know. Then begin to draft questions that will get at the information. Next, consider your respondents. Who will be responding to these questions and under what circumstances? Some people get impatient with long telephone questionnaires, especially if the questions are on a topic that is personally uninteresting. An online questionnaire or one that can be returned by mail gives the respondent the choice of answering on his or her own schedule. However, because you cannot control who responds, problems may arise regarding the representativeness of the sample.

The age and educational level of respondents may also be factors in how questions should be phrased. Familiarity with the subject is another possible factor. The less familiar respondents are with the topic, the simpler the questions and the longer the response times need to be. It is also important to arrange questions in logical sequence so that answers develop naturally in the respondent's mind.

In writing the questions, it is also important to consider how the questionnaire will be administered and scored. If a questionnaire is on the Internet, responses will be tabulated automatically, and results can be graphed, "sliced and diced" with a minimum of human involvement. But if questionnaires are to be used in a busy shopping mall, for example, or in a phone call, the respondent may not want to take time to answer long or involved questions. Open-ended questions are difficult to evaluate and score. How you ask a question affects the response, and that determines whether the information you get from the questionnaire will be valid and useful. And if responding to the questions requires more than a few minutes, you may be unable to collect completed responses from the number of people needed to provide a statistically valid sample.

Some open-ended questions and some interview responses are later subjected to content analysis. This means that words are counted to see how often they appear, and in what context. At least two national research agencies use in-depth interviewing and content analysis extensively. The system involves transcribing oral interviews and entering these in the computer, as you would for other open-ended responses. The computer can rank the words by their frequency of usage, and a social science software program can be used to analyze each word in relation to others. Subtle themes often emerge from such analyses, making it possible for researchers to determine accurately what people *mean* by what they say. Table 6.4 presents some of the pros and cons of surveys and focus group interviews.

T A B L E 6 . 4	*Pros and Cons of Surveys and Focus Group Interviews*
Pros	**Cons**
Surveys	
Good when definitive numbers are needed	Can be expensive and time-consuming
Recognized (that is, by management) as solid research technique	Usually do not uncover new information
Can disclose source and scope of problem	Data can be easily misinterpreted
Excellent way to track *trends*	Results are not necessarily indicative of the "truth" but do reflect *perceptions*
Focus Group Interviews	
Provide the possibility of learning completely new information	Information obtained is subjective
Can be modified as needed during process	Results cannot be charted and graphed
Facilitate obtaining information on "WHY?"	Management may not accept results as well as they would survey data
Can be relatively inexpensive	Good results depend heavily upon experience and objectivity of person conducting the focus groups

Caveats   Much of the information you get from secondary and primary sources will be in simple statistical form that relies on your understanding of concepts like sum, mean (average), median and mode. If you are not familiar with these terms now, get a mathematics book and study it until you are. Otherwise, you run the risk of misinterpreting factual information, drawing poor conclusions and eventually misleading your public.

Research information that infers cause–effect relationships usually entails more sophisticated statistics and research methodologies. There are several good books you can consult for help in these areas. One is Frederick Williams and Peter Monge's *Reasoning with Statistics,* a paperback designed for people who lack a statistical background but who need to know how to interpret and use information that is available only in statistical form.

Another tool to use in working with statistics or "stats" is the "Best Practices Guide for Use of Statistics in Public Relations," prepared by PRSA and the American Statistical Association. It is available on PRSA's website, http://www.prsa.org/intelligence/business case/measurementresources/statistics/#.U6CzqWdOW1s.

Online resources include Survey Monkey (www.surveymonkey.com) where you can get free online survey software and questionnaire tools. A user's manual is available for a fee. Templates for online surveys with examples of various types of questions—including multiple choice, rank order scaling, rating scale and semantic differential—are available from QuestionPro (www.questionpro.com).

Whether you are using secondary or primary data, be skeptical about its meaning, especially if the compilers claim that it is based on a random sample. The term *random* has a very strict scientific meaning when applied to survey research and is a *probability sampling* technique.

Probability sampling means that every person in your public should have an equal and known statistical probability of being included in the sample. The key point to remember here is that only when the sample is truly random can the findings be generalized to the total public being researched. For example, if you were conducting a survey of employees in an organization, a valid random sample of all the employees could be obtained by selecting every "Xth" (perhaps every third or fourth) employee. Using this simple random sampling technique, each member of the population has an equal chance of being included in the sample.

In *nonprobability sampling,* there is an assumption that there is an even distribution of characteristics within the population being surveyed. Since samples are chosen arbitrarily, there is no way to estimate the probability of any one element being included in the sample. An example of nonprobability sampling is the "shopper-intercept survey" in which shoppers in a mall or store are asked to participate in a survey. Using this technique, sometimes called "convenience sampling," samples are selected only if they can be accessed easily. The obvious advantage is that the method is easy to use, but that advantage is greatly offset by the presence of bias. Although useful applications of the technique are limited, it can deliver accurate results when the population is homogeneous.

You should look for certain research protocols in every piece of research data you use. These are listed in the form of questions in Table 6.5. If answers to these questions are missing from the research report or if they are so vague, you can't get a clear view of how the information was gathered, and you should be wary of the data and of any conclusions

T A B L E 6 . 5	*Checklist of Research Protocols*

1. What is the name of the person(s) or organization that did the research? What was the date on which it was done? For whom and why was it done?

2. If a sample was used, what steps were taken to ensure randomness?

3. What steps were taken to validate the questions before they were asked of respondents?

4. What steps were taken to ensure the reliability of the research methods?

5. Is a copy of the questionnaire (or measuring instrument) included in the research report?

6. How will this material help you or your organization to make a decision?

© Cengage Learning

based on it. It is possible, of course, that the information is reliable, but you should still use it with caution.

Verifying

When you start putting information together from all your sources, you will want to cross-check your sources. Check primary sources against each other. If you find areas of conflict, look for more primary sources so that the weight of information will clearly support your conclusions.

In addition, check primary sources against secondary sources. People have fallible memories. In attempting to check out information, you'll often find conflicts among secondary sources. Historians, for example, sometimes spend years tracking down an elusive date for an event. Most PR researchers don't do that type of research, nor do they have the time for it, but it pays to be careful, especially now that so much information is highly specialized and technical. If authorities disagree, you need to know it and to find out why. Check and keep checking until a pattern emerges.

Communication Audits

A special kind of research is the communication audit, sometimes called a *customer satisfaction study*. It's an analysis of how well information flows from one place to another in an organization and, sometimes, to special external publics such as selected financial analysts and media representatives. A great deal of emphasis also is placed on the credibility of sources. When an organization takes stock of its communication functions, it must rely on a wide range of research approaches, including individual interviews, focus group interviews, surveys and content analyses.

A lot of information can be gleaned from simply reading, analyzing and systematically evaluating newsletters, employee publications, intranets, emails, memos, letters, announcements, websites and other sources. An audit also produces a lot of empirical evidence. For example, it may involve focus group interviews with representatives of employee groups at various organizational levels. Several surveys may be used, with the questionnaires posted on intranet or Internet sites, sent through the mail, or distributed in person at meetings.

The reason for using a variety of research devices is one of the maxims of research: People sometimes are guilty of telling you what they think you want to hear rather than what they really think. This can be a significant problem when employees believe their responses may be monitored, even if that is not possible. Personal in-depth interviews also are necessary, especially when you're looking for blockages in information flow.

A well-executed communication audit can yield a wealth of information that can help you as a PR writer and also help all levels of management. Its results usually cause an extensive review of communication policies and would investigate the following:

- Management's communications philosophy
- Management's goals and objectives
- Communications goals and objectives compared with communications staff's goals and objectives
- Identification of internal constituencies
- Flow of information from management to communications staff and from communications staff to various internal constituencies
- Existing communications programs and vehicles
- Employee attitudes toward existing communications
- Employee needs and preferences in the area of communications

Research Using Social Media

Attitudinal research involves *listening to people*. Interviews, focus group interviews and surveys have made listening more efficient in gathering information, but they're not particularly good at gaining insights into what people are really thinking. Social media offer some new opportunities to do just that. Here are two examples:

Trudy Hardy, head of marketing for MINI USA, the American arm of BMW's MINI Cooper brand, set out to make the MINI more competitive. She had confidence in "her little car," and she knew that MINI owners loved their vehicles. "But what did they love, and how could the MINI take advantage of that? To understand and answer this question, MINI decided to monitor online chatter about its cars."[7]

MINI and its agency hired MotiveQuest, "one of half a dozen companies, including Nielsen's BuzzMetrics and TNS's Cymfony, that offer brand-monitoring services." All of these companies use automated monitoring of not only blogs but "of the entire online chatter associated with a brand: discussion groups, forums, MySpace pages, and so on."[8]

What they learned totally changed MINI's communications strategy. Other car owners talked about their *cars*—the power, the styling, the comfort, the speed. But MINI owners talked about the *culture* of people who owned MINIs. "As the first buyers of this odd little car, they bonded with each other. They identified themselves—and each other—*as* MINI owners. This insight led Trudy and her agency to a radical conclusion: it was time to market to MINI *owners,* not prospective *buyers.*" A typical activity in their new program included a series of MINI rallies across the country that resulted in more than 2,100 photos posted on Flickr and eight YouTube videos. In a year, they sold 38,000 cars.

Setting up a social media *private community* is another approach. Communispace, a rapidly growing "listening" company, "has set up hundreds of private communities for its clients, which include over 75 companies, ranging from hair care and breakfast cereal to financial service and IT advice. The company recruits 300–500 people in the client's target market. …" These "form a community that looks like any other online social network … but this is a *research* network. No one can see it except the members, the moderators from Communispace, and the clients." It's a listening machine that generates insight. Usually thanked with inexpensive Amazon certificates, the members "look" and act like social media participants, but they pledge to spend an hour a week on a site, interacting with others.

It's not inexpensive. But a group of 21 cancer centers across the country came together to share expenses, since they all needed the same information, and recruited more than 300 cancer patients to join the community. Interacting with this community changed the way New York's Memorial Sloan-Kettering Cancer Center approached its communications. Previously, the center had been focusing on touting its excellent worldwide reputation, believing that patients made decisions on where to seek treatment based on the best chance for a successful outcome. But they learned that when a patient hears a diagnosis of cancer, they become quite anxious. They want as much information as they can get, but they rely on their doctor to make a recommendation on a treatment center. With this insight, Memorial Sloan-Kettering switched the definition of its main target audience from cancer patients to primary care physicians.

Skepticism—A Requisite for All Research

Research involves digging, thinking, verifying and analyzing. It is the act of deciding between the probable and the improbable, the true and the false, the likely and the doubtful, the acceptable and the unacceptable and the right and the wrong. These acts are vital decisions in any PR situation. They call for sustained reasoning, a dedication to knowing the truth and a determination to be satisfied with nothing less.

Questions to Ask

Every writer should be from the "Show Me" state, because skepticism is the hallmark of all successful writers, including those in public relations. Skepticism should not be confused with cynicism. The former is a mind-set that says, "I will believe you, but you have to prove it to me." The cynic often rejects proof without considering it.

This skeptical approach is especially important for you to adopt as a public relations writer, as it is for other writers in mass communication, even when presenting your side of the story, because you are legally accountable for false information. You simply can't afford to take the word of any one person as "the truth." You should always insist on documentation and then cross-check the documentation just to be safe, even if the information comes from your senior management.

Even résumés are not exempt from careful scrutiny. A CareerBuilder.com survey of hiring managers uncovered tall tales and even bold lies that job seekers have constructed on their résumés. One candidate listed military experience dating back to before he was born. The CEO of Yahoo! Inc. resigned in May 2012 when a shareholder called attention to "inflated" academic credentials on his résumé.

Probe with questions such as these: Who says this is true? What documentation is available? Where is the evidence? Is there any outside authority to substantiate this? What is the experience within the industry? Can I test this myself? What does other research suggest might be the case? What is my instinctive reaction to the credibility of each source? Just remember that the only dumb question is the one not asked.

Answers Prompt Questions

When you begin researching secondary and primary sources, you'll discover that answers to your questions suggest more questions. These questions become an agenda for future research. The point is that, if you expect to make it in PR, you'll need to dedicate yourself to being a good researcher who is always pursuing new questions.

A good model is to use focus group interviews to frame questions for a survey, prepare the questionnaire, test and revise it (perhaps using focus groups), launch the survey and tabulate the results, then use post-survey focus groups to gain insight into why questions were answered the way they were.

Position Papers

As the name signifies, a position paper is designed to state an organization's position on an issue. (See Figure 6.1.) The issue may be local, regional, national or international in scope. Suppose your company opposes a national health insurance plan under consideration in Congress. The position paper should tell why. Your company may also take a positive position regarding a substitute proposal authored by a representative from the local district. The position paper should explain why it supports the substitute plan.

The position paper requires extensive research. Much of the information you need will be found in the backgrounder, so new research requirements may be minimal. (See Chapter 8 for information on backgrounders.) At this stage, however, you will need to solicit the input of management, which must scrutinize salient information, sort out the pros and cons of alternative positions and then make a policy decision. Research on a problem may produce a backgrounder that results in a management decision to offer or support a solution. Then you may be asked to write a position paper.

Once that decision has been made, you can write a thorough position paper representing the organization's point of view. If PR professionals in the company are held in high esteem, management may ask that a proposed position statement be written and used as a basis for discussion. A draft position paper is written with the expectation that it will be approved in principle, modified or rejected. After modifications are completed and approved, a final version is prepared for distribution to management and other publics.

Whenever a new issue surfaces, the public relations department should alert management to the need for a position paper. Recognizing an issue constitutes the first step in writing a position paper.

FIGURE 6.1

Position Paper: Condoms   *A position paper is a close relative of the backgrounder. However, the position paper is intended to clearly present an organization's position on a specific issue. This one presents the World Health Organization (WHO), UNAIDS and UNFPA's position on the use of condoms to prevent HIV and other sexually transmitted infections. It is clear and straightforward—hallmarks of a good position paper.*

POSITION STATEMENT   09

[Originally published in 2004 updated in 2009]

Condoms and HIV prevention

Condom use is a critical element in a comprehensive, effective and sustainable approach to HIV prevention and treatment

Prevention is the mainstay of the response to AIDS. Condoms are an integral and essential part of comprehensive prevention and care programmes, and their promotion must be accelerated. In 2007, an estimated 2.7 million people became newly infected with HIV. About 45% of them were young people from 15 to 24 years old, with young girls at greater risk of infection than boys.

The male latex condom is the single, most efficient, available technology to reduce the sexual transmission of HIV and other sexually transmitted infections.

The search for new preventive technologies such as HIV vaccines and microbicides continues to make progress, but condoms will remain the key preventive tool for many, many years to come. Condoms are a key component of combination prevention strategies individuals can choose at different times in their lives to reduce their risks of sexual exposure to HIV. These include delay of sexual initiation, abstinence, being safer by being faithful to one's partner when both partners are uninfected and consistently faithful, reducing the number of sexual partners, correct and consistent use of condoms[1], and male circumcision.

Conclusive evidence from extensive research among heterosexual couples in which one partner is infected with HIV shows that correct and consistent condom use significantly reduces the risk of HIV transmission from both men to women, and also from women to men[2]. Laboratory studies show that male latex condoms are impermeable to infectious agents contained in genital secretions[3]. To ensure safety and efficacy, condoms must be manufactured to the highest international standards. They must be procured according to the quality assurance procedures established by the WHO, UNFPA and UNAIDS and they should be stored away from direct heat sources. Prevention programmes need to ensure that high-quality condoms are accessible to those who need them, when they need them, and that people have the knowledge and skills to use them correctly.

Condoms must be readily available universally, either free or at low cost, and promoted in ways that help overcome social and personal obstacles to their use.
Condom use is more likely when people can access them at no cost or at greatly subsidized prices. Effective condom promotion targets not only the general population, but also people at higher risk of HIV exposure, especially women, young people, sex workers and their clients, injecting drug users and men who have sex with men. UNFPA estimates that the current supply of condoms in low- and middle-income countries falls well short of the number required (the condom 'gap')[4]. Despite the gap, international funding for condom procurement has not increased in recent years. Collective actions at all levels are needed to support efforts of countries, especially those that depend on external assistance for condom procurement, promotion and distribution.

FIGURE 6.1 (continued)

HIV prevention education and condom promotion must overcome the challenges of complex gender and cultural factors.

Young girls and women are regularly and repeatedly denied information about, and access to, condoms. Often they do not have the power to negotiate the use of condoms. In many social contexts, men are resistant to the use of condoms. This needs to be recognized in designing condom promotion programmes. Female condoms can provide women with more control in protecting themselves. However, women will remain highly vulnerable to HIV exposure, until men and women share equal decision-making powers in their interpersonal relationships.

Condoms have played a decisive role in HIV prevention efforts in many countries. Condoms have helped to reduce HIV infection rates where AIDS has already taken hold, curtailing the broader spread of HIV in settings where the epidemic is still concentrated in specific populations.

Condoms have also encouraged safer sexual behaviour more generally. Recent analysis of the AIDS epidemic in Uganda has confirmed that increased condom use, in conjunction with delay in age of first sexual intercourse and reduction of sexual partners was an important factor in the decline of HIV prevalence in the 1990s[5]. Thailand's efforts to de-stigmatize condoms and its targeted condom promotion for sex workers and their clients dramatically reduced HIV infections in these populations and helped reduce the spread of the epidemic to the general population. A similar policy in Cambodia has helped stabilize national prevalence, while substantially decreasing prevalence among sex workers. In addition, Brazil's early and vigorous condom promotion among the general population and vulnerable groups has successfully contributed to sustained control of the epidemic.

Increased access to antiretroviral treatment creates the need and the opportunity for accelerated condom promotion.

The success of antiretroviral therapy in industrialized countries in reducing illness and prolonging life can alter the perception of risk associated with HIV[6]. A perception of low-risk and a sense of complacency can lead to unprotected sex through reduced or non-consistent condom use. Promotion of correct and consistent condom use within antiretroviral treatment programmes, and within reproductive health and family planning services, is essential to reduce further opportunities for HIV transmission. Rapid scale-up of HIV testing and counselling is needed to meet the prevention needs of all people, whether they are HIV-positive or negative.

[1] UNAIDS. 2004 Report on the global AIDS epidemic, page.72.
[2] Holmes K, Levine R, Weaver M. Effectiveness of condoms in preventing sexually transmitted infections. *Bulletin of the World Health Organization. Geneva. June 2004.*
[3] WHO/UNAIDS. Information note on Effectiveness of Condoms in Preventing Sexually Transmitted Infections including HIV. Geneva. August 2001.
[4] UNFPA. 2007 report on donor support for contraceptives and condoms for STI/HIV prevention 2007.
[5] Singh S, Darroch J.E, Bankole A. A,B, and C in Uganda: The Roles of Abstinence, Monogamy and Condom Use in HIV Decline. *The Alan Guttmacher Institute. Washington DC. 2003.*
[6] Gremy I, Beltzer N. HIV risk and condom use in the adult heterosexual population in France between 1992 and 2001: return to the starting point? *AIDS 2004;18:805-9.*

Source: http://www.who.int/hiv/pub/condoms/20090318_position_condoms.pdf

Stating the Issue   No position paper will have much value if it fails to state the issue clearly. Your job as PR writer demands that you describe the issue fairly and honestly. *Don't distort the issue to suit your purposes or to make it easier to form—or defend—an opinion. The purpose of a position paper is to address an issue squarely, not evade it.*

If you are in the natural gas industry, your position statement will support the use of natural gas vehicles (NGVs) and would argue that these provide the most desirable solution to reducing emissions. However, a good position paper would acknowledge that success of NGVs depends on recognition in the marketplace and by state and local governments that society benefits from clean, domestic fuels to the extent that there is continued financial support for private sector initiatives. Furthermore, the NGV position paper would have to recognize current limitations for NGVs, especially such critical ones as fueling and servicing.

Don't dance around an issue; meet it squarely near the beginning of the position paper. One of the most obvious ways of doing this is by providing relevant background information.

Background   If you want your position paper to be comprehensible, you must provide pertinent background information. But remember that a position paper is not a historical analysis; leave that to the backgrounder. Give just enough background to provide a context for your position and to help your readers understand why the subject under discussion has become an issue. The nature of the issue often obviates the need for extensive background information, but be sure to give enough to make the basis for your position intelligible.

Position   Don't keep your readers in suspense. Come to the point immediately. Don't try to build suspense by including elaborate recitations of facts and flashy figures, and don't culminate the paper with an eloquent conclusion.

Begin by stating your position, so readers know where you stand. Then support it with facts and figures, logically organized and clearly written. Use examples or metaphors that readers can understand. Use statistics sparingly but include enough of them to support and reinforce your points.

Long lists of numbers might be appropriate in a backgrounder, but in a position paper, they will only clutter up your argument and cloud its sense. Make your point in clear, plain language; then select just the right statistic to support it. If you feel that a lot of statistics should be included as support material, put them in an appendix so they don't overpower the paper. Always provide the sources of your statistics. Readers who spend time with such information place a lot of weight on the authority behind the numbers.

Consider Both Sides   Although a position paper should come down strongly on your side of an issue, don't ignore opposing sides. You are expected to amass as much information as you can in support of your point of view, but don't stack the cards.

"Card-stacking" is a propaganda device whereby all the supporting arguments are given but no opposing points are mentioned. This gives the impression that the favorable evidence is more compelling than it really is. Such a position paper may seem impressive at first glance, but when readers discover other points of view, they will distrust not only this message but also others you send them later.

It is far better to state opposing points of view and try to refute them than to ignore them. This is especially important when the opposition has some good points. Acknowledge the cons, but show why you think these points are outweighed by objective evidence. With this tactic, you will gain respect, even among your foes.

Consider the Public   Although most position papers are written for internal use by management, some are written for distribution to other publics. Even when writing a position paper you believe will only be used internally, you must keep in mind other potential publics.

For example, a position paper may be written for presentation to the board of directors by management in an attempt to explain company policies to stockholders. But Wall Street analysts may ask to see the company's position too. And what about the media's business editors? They may ask for and should be given copies.

This can pose a serious problem for you as a PR writer, because information that makes sense to your management may not make sense to the external publics or to stockholders. It would be ideal, of course, to write one version of the position paper for use by all possible publics, but the nature of the issue may make this impractical. You may have to write more than one version of the same paper. You should not tell a different story in each version; rather, you should tell the same story differently and appropriately. Remember too that different publics may be more concerned with some questions than with others. Alter the emphasis of each version of your position paper accordingly.

Recommendations   It is generally perceived as bad form to be against something without offering an alternative solution. Taking a position means being both against one thing and for something else. If you omit your alternative proposals from your position paper, you will inevitably be asked what you recommend as a suitable substitute for something you oppose.

For example, on the NGV situation, currently there are stringent regulations on the conversion of vehicles from gasoline to alternate fuels (except pure battery electric vehicles). If a bill to reduce these regulations is being proposed and you want to support it, how do you address concerns about safety? Supporting the proposal carries an implicit obligation to help arrive at a resolution of issues posed by opponents.

Sometimes position papers suggest new policy on an issue or support a recommended but not yet implemented policy. Position papers also can support existing policy in the face of proposed change.

Format   When the writing is completed, determine its format and method of distribution. A position paper intended for internal use may exist only in digital form on the organization's intranet or in the computers of specific spokespersons after being distributed as email attachments.

Special Uses   Although position papers have many uses, especially as frames of reference when questions come from journalists and to orient spokespeople and management personnel, they also have some special uses. An organization that wants to exploit all the avenues for advocating its point of view can use a position paper as the basis for an essay or a commentary to be submitted to the op-ed page in the local newspaper. The position paper should have enough documentation in it to stand alone as the basis of an op-ed piece. If it doesn't, go back to the backgrounder on which the position paper was based. That should give you more than enough information with which to work. Other kinds of documents also can be used as you prepare the op-ed piece, but if a position paper is executed well, there should not be much need to seek and use other information.

Another special area is the use of position papers as the locus for image ads and public service announcements (PSAs) for an organization. Position papers can be of enormous help in positioning or repositioning an organization as it tries to shape and project a consistent image.

Plans for action, as in lobbying for or against something, can spring directly from position papers. If, for example, there's a proposal to cut all government support for AFVs and place the determination totally in the marketplace, the position statement against that policy represents your first line of offense in furthering the cause. Backgrounders may also be of use, but it is the position paper that sets the direction and highlights the major points of contention.

Testing Readability

Readability is the ease with which text can be read and understood. Research in readability goes back at least to the 1920s. Early work identified various factors—like sentence length, word length and prepositional phrases—that affected the readability of prose.

In *What Makes a Book Readable,* published in 1935, William Gray and Bernice Leary discussed 64 different aspects of prose that seemed to affect reading difficulty. It would have been nearly impossible to devise a usable formula covering that many variables, so when readability formulas were developed, most emphasized two of the most important factors: sentence length and word length. The book's full text is online at https://archive .org/details/whatmakesabookre028092mbp.

Since then many formulas have been designed to measure readability, but only a handful of these are in general use. The three best-known formulas are those devised by Rudolf Flesch, by Robert Gunning and by Edgar Dale and Jeanne Chall.

Both Microsoft Word™ and Corel's WordPerfect™ word-processing software programs include grammar, spelling and readability checking capabilities. Grammatik, an early computer program, added word, sentence and paragraph statistics as well as the Flesch Readability Formula, Gunning's Fog Index measuring years of education and the Flesch-Kincaid Reading Grade Level. Grammatik was purchased by Corel and is integrated into WordPerfect.[9] Microsoft Word provides Flesch Reading East and Flesch-Kincaid Grade Level testing.[10] (Also see information about readability formulas in Chapter 3.)

In addition to a qualitative assessment of the writing, *StyleWriter™,* a plain-English editorial program, provides word and sentence statistics with an index that gives the percentage of passive verbs plus a count of words in such categories as jargon, legal, abstract, complex and such.

Monitoring and Evaluation   Public relations programs have to prove their worth. This means that one of your tasks as a writer is to evaluate the cost-effectiveness of the program. You will need to know what worked well, what did not and why. Most of the techniques discussed earlier are used in this phase too. It is simply a matter of employing surveys, interviews and secondary sources to evaluate what has been accomplished. Of course, such common pieces of physical evidence as how many people attended an event, how many people were exposed to your message and how many people responded to a special coupon offer are critical in basic program evaluation.

Monitoring a program is essential. Functional strategies collectively define what is expected to happen to achieve stated goals. One of the primary functions of supervisors at all levels in every area is to monitor progress. This is a routine part of their jobs, but their efforts are mostly focused inside the organization. What about monitoring things that go on outside? That's a different situation. Certainly, the leadership of the communication program should routinely and regularly scan the environment for problems, issues, developments, trends, opportunities and other things that may affect the organization or the campaign in progress.

How can we tell whether the program is working? Do we go by intuition, or do we set some routine procedures to take the pulse of our target publics at regular intervals? One measure we might consider is to review progressive reports on the number of inquiries. If there is an increase in inquiries, how can we be sure the increase is a result of the campaign? Another measure might be to count the house at special events to gauge how well people are responding to the campaign. It may be that an overflow crowd attended a concert simply because of the quality of the singer but they will soon forget the sponsor, even if they ever realized who the sponsor was. If we are selling a product or service, weekly sales reports can give us some insights. But are contributions, sales or the number of orders a clear indication of how effectively we are communicating with our audience? Lots of variables—in addition to messages—affect those actions. If we are promoting a candidate or a political issue, telephone canvassing can tell us a lot, but can we predict with great accuracy a victory at the polling booth?

Although those indicators, as well as many others, may be prominent parts of many campaign plans, the information they yield is ambiguous about what the target public knows about us or whether there have been any shifts in attitudes toward us because of the campaign. These two issues deal exclusively with the communication function. The only way they can be evaluated objectively is to do systematic research on relevant publics at regular intervals. This means that we need incremental research on our relevant publics to get a clear picture of how the campaign is doing. Such information may help us spot problems that can be corrected during the remainder of a campaign.

The monitoring process results in an assortment of writing tasks. Prominent among them are emails, memos, letters and social media interaction. Analytical reports may also be written, along with cover letters. If something is awry in the campaign and ways of righting it are found, then recommendations or proposals for specific actions will need to be written. Monitoring should be, of course, a part of every functional plan.

When a program is completed, it is necessary to evaluate its productivity. The most effective evaluations are those with known benchmarks in place at the time the campaign begins. For example, pertinent data gathered in support of the strategic plan would ordinarily contain a good bit of benchmark information. The idea is to determine "where we are" when the program begins with a benchmark study, then measure "where we are now" periodically or at the end of the program. Comparing the two findings will provide information on results. Depending on the nature of the organization, this information might be found in measures of attitudes and behavior, brand shares, market shares, sales volumes, unit sales, contributions and pledges received, aided and unaided recall scores and others.

Particular measures should be selected that are uniquely appropriate to the campaign and its parent organization. In the case of APEX, a critical measure is the dollar volume of contributions and pledges. The sources can be identified fairly accurately and compared to the levels from the preceding year. It is easy to see whether the organization met its goal. If it did not, efforts must be made to determine why, so that those mistakes will not be made in future campaigns. If the goal was exceeded, we need to know why. Is the greater-than-expected increase due to the campaign, or is it attributable to some influence beyond the scope of the campaign? Is the awareness of APEX higher now than when the campaign began? Do people have more appreciation for APEX now than before the campaign? Clearly, many of these questions, and many like them, can be answered only if we expand the systematic research program that we used during the monitoring phase. Both monitoring and campaign evaluation cost money. This needs to be provided in the campaign budget. If there is not enough money for good monitoring and effective evaluation, then we can't really do these tasks correctly. An absence of evaluation cripples strategic planning for future campaigns.

Although many messages will be written as part of a campaign's final evaluation, the most daunting writing task is likely to be a thorough, lengthy report that summarizes the results of the campaign. Such reports must be highly persuasive, yet be careful not to mislead management as you try to marshal your arguments in support of conclusions. Much of the information in these reports is complex. That may make it useful to break out some pieces of information and recast them into backgrounders, position papers, letters and memos in support of forthcoming planning efforts. The reason for doing that, of course, is to make sure that the responsible managers get information that is in its most usable form without having to wade through a lengthy report.

Writing for the Institute for Public Relations, David Geddes outlined a framework for the measurement of the total value of public relations activities:

> *Activities*—Actions directly taken and under the control of public relations
> *Outputs*—Communications generated that may reach target audience members
> *Engagement*—How target audience members engage, manipulate or are involved with communications
> *Outtakes*—Cognitive changes in target audience awareness, knowledge, understanding, perceiving, intending, believing, etc.
> *Outcomes*—Actions target audience members take (or do not take) due to communications
> *Business value*—Contribution to building organizational value[11]

The eighth biennial Communication and Public Relations Generally Accepted Practices (GAP VIII) Study conducted by the USC Annenberg Strategic Communication and Public Relations Center (SCPRC) concluded, "Measurement and evaluation are still works in progress."

The GAP VIII report indicated, "as in all seven previous GAP studies no individual measurement tool earned a usage score significantly greater than five on a scale of 1 (no usage) to 7 (extensive usage), suggesting a lack of faith in currently available tools, and a need for new tools that do a better job of measuring actual outcomes and actions, rather than outputs. The five most commonly used measurement tools are:

#1—influence on reputation (5.01);
#2—social or online media metrics (4.87);
#3—content analysis of clips (4.65);
#4—total number of clips (4.35), and,
#5—total impressions (4.3)."[12]

T A B L E 6 . 6	*Typical Output, Outtake and Outcome Metrics*			
Goal	**Action**	**Output Metric**	**Outtake Metric**	**Outcome Metric Has To Answer "So What?"**
Sales Leads	Place product reviews Initiate speakers program Proactive blogger outreach	Number of meetings Number of speaking engagements Number of blog mentions Number of reviews Number of news releases sent Number of media contacts made	% awareness of your brand % considering your brand % preferring your brand	Number of requests for information
Employee Engagement	Conversations Meetings with management Intranet page Email blast	How many emails went out? % emails opened Unique visits to intranet page Attendance at meetings	% hearing engagement messages % believing engagement messages	Lower recruitment costs Lower turnover rates
Favorable Positioning as the Most Trusted, Reliable Source	White paper program, speakers program, blogger outreach	Number of meetings Number of speaking engagements Number of blog mentions Number of reviews Number of views of online articles	% believing message % agreeing with positioning	Number of downloads of white paper Number of referrals from blog to unique URL landing page

Source: Katharine Delahaye Paine, Pauline Draper and Angela C. Jeffrey, "Using Public Relations Research to Drive Business Results," Copyright © 2008, Institute for Public Relations, used with permission.

Forty-nine percent of respondents utilize measurement techniques developed in-house, 26 percent use techniques recommended by professional/industry groups and 20 percent use proprietary methods developed by their outside agencies. Twenty-two percent are making increasing use of audience research in planning and evaluating campaigns, while 31 percent are measuring online conversations; 71.4 percent strongly agree that there is a need for Communication and public relations who can interpret data and use it to plan and evaluate programs. Coupled with the increases in percentage of total budget allocated to evaluation seen over multiple GAP studies, these data reflect the growing importance of analytics and accountability in the practice.[13]

Barcelona Declaration of Measurement Principles   How to monitor and measure the effects and value of public relations provides fodder for an ongoing discussion among the world's experts. In June 2010, delegates attending the second European Summit on Measurement in Barcelona, Spain, adopted a Declaration of Measurement Principles intended to "address the need for clear standards and common approaches to measuring and evaluating public relations results."

Here are the basics of the Barcelona principles:

1. Goals are fundamentally important and should be as quantitative as possible, addressing who, what, when and how much impact is expected from a public relations campaign.
2. Media measurement should account for impressions among stakeholder audiences and quality (tone, credibility of the source and media outlet), message delivery, inclusion of third party spokespersons, prominence and visual dimension.
3. Advertising Value Equivalents (AVEs) do not measure the value of public relations and do not inform future activity; they measure the cost of media space and are rejected as a concept to value public relations.
4. Social media can and should be measured.
5. Measuring outcomes is preferred to measuring media results.
6. Business (read: organizational) results can and should be measured where possible.
7. PR measurement should be done in a manner that is transparent and replicable for all steps in the process.[14]

The Melbourne Mandate   Delegates from 29 countries meeting in Melbourne in November 2012 endorsed the Melbourne Mandate, which is "a call to action of new areas of value for public relations and communication management."

The mandate said, "Public relations and communication professionals have a mandate to:

- "define and maintain an organisation's character and values;
- "build a culture of listening and engagement; and
- "instill responsible behaviours by individuals and organisations."

The mandate continues:

1. "Develop research methodologies to measure an organisation's capacity to listen, and apply these metrics before and after the pursuit of strategy and during any major action.
2. "Identify and activate channels to enable organisational listening.
3. "Identify all stakeholder groups affected by the pursuit of an organisation's strategy, both now and in the future.
4. "Identify all stakeholder groups that affect the pursuit of the organisation's strategy, both now and in the future.
5. "Identify these stakeholder groups' expectations and consider them both in the organisation's strategy and before taking any action.
6. "Ensure sound reasons are communicated to stakeholders in cases where their expectations cannot be met.
7. "Prove that the organisation is genuinely listening as it takes actions in pursuit of its strategy.
8. "Evaluate the effectiveness of the organisation's listening."[15]

   Complete statements related to the Melbourne Mandate are available at http://melbournemandate.globalalliancepr.org/.

Measuring Public Relations' Return on Investment   Measuring *business value* is akin to measuring the *return on investment (ROI)* of public relations.

Writing in PRSA's magazine *The Public Relations Strategist,* Mark Weiner, CEO of Prime Research in North America, said, "For a given budget in an organization, the return on investment, or ROI, indicates how much profit or cost-saving is realized. While profits are not the goal of every PR program, organizations apply an ROI calculation along with other approaches to develop a business case for a given proposition. This includes the pursuit of memberships, donations or contributions, votes or loyalty. In cases where the immediate objectives include gaining market share, building infrastructure or positioning oneself for a public offering, for example, ROI might be measured in terms of meeting these objectives rather than the immediate bottom line. However, ROI is objective and quantifiable in terms of revenues generated, savings achieved or costs avoided—in other words, ROI relates strictly to monetization."

How is ROI calculated? Angela Sinickas, president of Sinickas Communications, Inc., has been measuring the effectiveness of communications since 1981. She explained, "To calculate a return on investment, you need to connect the communication you did with a change in audience behavior, because virtually all behaviors have a financial impact for an organization. If employees or customers or reporters do something differently, it will result in either an increase in revenues or a decrease in costs. This means you will not be able to calculate ROI based on an increase in awareness or knowledge or an improved opinion. Until knowledge and attitudes result in a behavior change, you have nothing to attach a monetary value to." Once that's done, she said, you have to decide how much of the behavior change you can take credit for. You may have to conduct a survey to get this information.

"Then," she said, "calculating ROI is easy":

Gross return: Start with the financial value of the behavior change for which you can take credit. **Subtract** the cost of your communications.

Net return: The difference between one and two is the amount of financial value to use in the ROI calculation.

Divide the result by the cost of your communications to end up with a percentage return on investment.[15]

Exercises

1. You are employed by a small company that recently moved to its present location. The owner of the business asks you to locate a form that she can use to assign legal authority to her son, who lives near the company's previous location. You know that the form is called "Power of Attorney." Explain how you would determine which form is appropriate and legal in the state and how you would evaluate the source.
2. After doing necessary research, draft a questionnaire for a survey to probe attitudes toward physical fitness. The target audience is young men and women, ages 21–35, upwardly mobile in their professions, with college degrees or some college experience, living in metropolitan areas. They lead very active social lives, but their careers are generally stressful.

3. Analyze the bias in the following questions. Rewrite them as necessary to eliminate bias.
   a. What did you like about the product you just tried?
   b. How good a job do you believe the USA president is doing?
   c. Do you believe that jogging does serious damage to the bone structures of the foot and joint?
   (See Chapter 3 for more information on eliminating bias in writing.)
4. Locate 10 websites for reliable reference material.
5. Compile a bibliography of at least 10 publications whose primary emphasis is on public relations.
6. Imagine that you are the public relations director for a city's transportation system, which includes, along with an electric subway system, fleets of gasoline-powered vehicles such as buses as well as special vans for the disabled. The city frequently has air-quality alerts that keep people who are at risk inside. Also, exhaust fumes are killing trees and other vegetation along the freeways. To help reduce emissions, the company has decided to use natural gas-fueled fleet vehicles. Prepare the opening paragraphs of a position paper to support that opinion and, in outline form, indicate what you would include in the rest of the document.
7. The position paper in Figure 6.1 will be subjected to criticism from various publics. List these publics and suggest which areas are open to dispute and/or skepticism.

Writing to Persuade

When you identify yourself as a public relations writer, some people may regard you with skepticism because they think of what you do as manipulation. Be prepared for that, but there's no need to apologize for it. Persuasion is implicit, if not explicit, every time a person tries to communicate with another.

It is just that public relations is widely known for trying to persuade publics to a particular point of view. Perhaps that is even more a reality, not just a perception as the formerly clear lines between public relations and advertising have blurred due to the integration of messaging in so many formats.

Persuasion is explicitly part of the public relations fabric. If it is done ethically and legally, it logically is no more objectionable than most other human activities. Persuasive efforts now may seem more focused than in the past, primarily because of the *integrated* approach used in planning and implementation. Integration simply means that a single communication strategy undergirds all messages from an organization. The intent is to give unity and consistency to all communications so the perception of the organizations is more unified and identifiable.

The literature labels this approach variously as *integrated marketing communication, marketing communication* or simply *integrated communication*. We prefer integrated communication because it seems to encompass a range of activities not often central to the selling emphasis of marketing. The most significant change is the embrace of social media by organizations, including news media. The term used is not important, but it is important that you recognize that public relations efforts by many companies now seem to have a sharper focus than in the past. That tends to sensitize people to the persuasive role of public relations.

More organizations of all kinds, profit and nonprofit, use social media for both helping to brand their organization, and to provide feedback that can be analyzed to give more guidance to strategies.

This integrated approach affects every public relations writer in at least three ways. Primarily, writers will be expected to tell stories about the organization and present images that will reflect what the organization is and does. Stories are the content for messages. Second, writers will be expected to adapt any message to any tactic in any medium—from white papers to news releases to posters to ads to Twitter feeds, to Facebook, YouTube postings and so on. That certainly is not a new development, but an integrated communication philosophy makes it far more common. Finally, writers who can think about persuasion at the strategic level will be at a premium. It is clear that a writer who knows how will always have a job. But the writer who knows why will always be the boss. That piece of wisdom is the focus of this chapter. Although persuasion has always been important in public relations, now it is critical that you understand the why, as well as the how, of persuasion. To begin, consider the following scenario.

A nuclear engineer especially good at explaining technical matters once gave a talk to a civic club in a small town. He used PowerPoint slides, charts and graphs to describe the operation of nuclear power plants and to explain how safe they were.

At the end of his talk, an elderly lady thanked the engineer for his presentation. "I don't understand anything you said," she told him, "but I agree with you a hundred percent." The point: People rely on information and logic in forming their opinions, but only up to a degree.

It is true that people are rational. But that only means they can think. People are also emotional. Were people driven only by logic, there would never be a need to persuade. The fact is, however, that people in economically advanced societies such as the USA base most of their decisions and behaviors on emotion rather than on logic. Most of us don't have to spend every waking hour just getting enough food, clothing and shelter to sustain life. As these things are easier to attain, we spend more and more time on improving their quality. That's where emotion comes in. And it is the context in which persuasion is most often used.

As we pursue our enlightened self-interest, we are often motivated more by emotions than by logic. Nevertheless, we place great value on information. It is the stuff of which good public relations is made. But a lot of public relations writing also attempts to persuade people to adopt a particular point of view.

To be a persuasive writer, you need to have some idea of the arguments—both factual and emotional—that will work best with your target publics. Common sense can give you some clues, but you'll do a much better job if you know something about the science of persuasion. Common sense is no substitute for what decades of research has revealed about how and why people form their opinions. As public relations pioneer Edward L. Bernays put it, "Like Columbus, you can sail west and reach new land by accident. But if you have charts, you can do better; you can arrive at a destination decided upon in advance."[1]

When engineers design bridges or buildings, Bernays pointed out, they apply a knowledge of physics, chemistry and other sciences. Doctors treat patients using a knowledge of biochemistry and medical research. In the same way, public relations people should apply the relevant findings of social sciences such as psychology, sociology and communication when they embark on efforts to persuade.

Persuasive writing focuses attention on these message areas: *recipients* of the message, intended and unintended; message *construction* with the emphasis on what consequences are intended—increased knowledge, attitude or behavior change; *source* for the message—who the source is and the credibility of that source with the intended recipients and the credibility of the organization identified with the source. Decisions have to be made at every level.

Primary, though, are the recipients: Who are they? What do they know or think they know? What do they believe about the issue/the organizations involved? You can't construct a message until you know that. The message construction then has to have a purpose: What do you want to happen as a result of communicating that message? What effect is it likely to have on each of the intended recipients? What about unintended recipients such as competitors, activists or other critics? What about people in other parts of the world who have a stakeholder interest in the issue, and through the Internet are exposed to messages not necessarily intended for them? Then there's the choice of a source: who is the most credible, overall, with particular publics? In a crisis, there is another consideration of source because there will be many message sources from all parties involved. You know from personal experience that coverage of an apartment fire means you're likely to see and hear statements from fire officials, police, hospitals, owners of the apartment complex, residents as well as their friends and relatives.

The intent of maintaining credibility is to be sure there is consistency in the message statements. Many questions come up time and again in persuasive writing. Should you give both sides of the story or only your side? If you give both, which side should you give first? Should you draw an explicit conclusion, or is it better to let the audience figure it out for itself? Which should you give first, the good news or the bad news? How effective are fear techniques? Should you make a point once or repeat it several times to make sure it sinks in? These are the sorts of questions that social scientists can *help* you answer. You need to keep up with recent studies too. For example, several opinion reports in 2011 noted that so much skepticism about messages exists because of widespread distrust of institutions that people had to get the same or a consonant message about an issue or situation from six independent sources before accepting its validity.

The use of social media has enhanced opportunities not only to tell the organization's story, but also to get instant feedback on reactions of various publics. For example, the nature of some social media is a "personal" space for interaction with friends, but organizations that are highly interactive with respondents in social media are accepted better that others that may be seen as invasive.[2] Nonprofit organizations that use social media for promotional as well as informational messages are likely to have their one-way messages shared in social media, with the respondents' own comments, of course.[3]

All organizations can improve their acceptance if they have a reputation for being candid and honest even when the organization is having a problem. Not owning up to the truth of a bad situation is likely to encourage critics, whereas, friends are more encouraged to add their support if they have experienced trusted messages and experiences.

Figuring out how to keep up with respondents is critical. For example, the Ritz-Carlton Hotel Company began a campaign on Facebook not because they were not receiving "likes" or being "friended," but because the company decided content of the responses was more important than the numbers. What careful analysis of the responses told them was what people liked and didn't like about their hotel stays. Popularity chasing was abandoned as a strategy to find out how to improve the experience of their customers and looked for ways to attract more people who had not stayed in hotels and were worried about the cost.[4]

Research into feedback, though, can be done in ethical ways and some that are ethically questionable. For example, analysis of feedback from messages that have not been manipulated is accepted. However, experiments need careful consideration.

Research using human subjects is usually carefully reviewed by organizations where the research is generated. Universities have review committees to which research proposals from its faculty and students must be submitted for review. Facebook has its own Data Science team that got undesirable exposure for a lack of oversight in 2014 when news of its researchers with Cornell University done in 2012 came to light.

Apparently the newsfeed to approximately 700,000 Facebook users for a week included an experiment to see if emotions could be manipulated on social media. The study was to see if negative responses resulted in negative responses and if positive responses encouraged others to respond positively. The study attracted attention when it was published in the Proceedings of the National Academy of Sciences.[5] The resulting furor caused Facebook to say it has revised its guidelines, but didn't dampen the concern of the potential for unethical practice of using large active databases for ethically questionable research.[6]

Of course, research findings can only help you answer questions about message strategy. Although research results can be valuable guides in planning persuasive communication, they are not laws of nature. In many cases, the findings collected are inconclusive. At times, you have to rely on personal experience and knowledge of your message recipients. Even then, messages are often pretested, especially promotional messages of all types for their appeal, the positioning of the organization's service or product, and the behavior of the message recipients in different parts of society and in different parts of the world.

Nevertheless, social science has found out a lot about the nature of persuasion, and it would be foolish not to put that knowledge to use. Research data is better than off-the-top-of-the-head speculation about the how and why of opinion formation.

Opinion Formation and Change

The first thing you need to know as a persuasive writer is that you are not going to gain many converts to your point of view, at least not immediately. The reason is simple. The few minutes a person gives to reading, viewing or listening to your message are not likely to change attitudes built up over a lifetime. If you're going to make headway at all, you need to know something about what attitudes and opinions are and how they are formed.

Opinion, Attitude and Belief

Some authorities see little or no need to distinguish among opinions, attitudes and beliefs, at least in theory. On the practical level of trying to understand how and why people behave as they do, however, it may be useful to you to make such a distinction. (See Table 7.1.)

In this context, opinions are temporal, fleeting and unstable. They can change on a whim. Attitudes are a little more stable and are less likely to change immediately. Beliefs, however, are very stable, and they are very resistant to change. To illustrate the different

T A B L E 7 . 1	*From Opinions to Attitudes to Beliefs*

Accumulation of information and experiences = Opinions (conditional, temporal, fleeting and unstable)

Clusters of opinions relevant to a specific way of thinking about something compared with personal experience = Attitudes (relatively stable)

Attitudes currently held measured against values = Beliefs (less flexible or subject to change, except over time)

© Cengage Learning

levels involved, suppose we get in a time machine and travel back to 1950. At that time, products made in Japan were generally believed to be of poor quality. Opinions in the USA of products with the "Made in Japan" label were not charitable. With the introduction of imported cars, a variety of electronic gear and camera systems of high quality, however, attitudes began to change. Now we believe that many brands of products made in Japan in these categories set the standards of quality against which all others are judged.

How did this change come about? As people in the USA began to experience products of higher quality from Japan, opinions shifted to the extent that favorable attitudes began to be common, and these eventually came together in support of a belief that the label "Made in Japan" deserved respect.

When we accumulate information and experiences, we form opinions. Some of these opinions tend to cluster as especially relevant to a specific attitude. Attitude clusters then tend to gather in support of a specific belief. As used here, belief is the same thing as *engaged attitude* in Table 7.1 because the emphasis is on the effects. The point is that opinions can change with the wind. Beliefs can change, too, but they are slow to do so. Attitudes fall somewhere between these extremes. In many respects, opinions, attitudes and beliefs are closely linked, so it makes sense for us to discuss them as one, using the term *attitude* to signify all three.

Models of Attitude Formation and Message Recipients

To begin with, an individual's personal background or historical setting plays an important role in his or her behavior. Where was the person born? Where did he or she grow up? What were the social and economic conditions of the day? What is that person's cultural background? These and similar factors help to shape personality. Historical factors also shape the issues that persuasive writers deal with—not only those of their audience, but their own as well.

All of these considerations are part of the social environment in which communication and persuasion take place. Individuals belong to groups with social norms that affect their opinions. A person's life experiences also play a large part in attitude formation. And naturally, the characteristics of the issue at hand are important.

One other major element of the social environment influences attitudes: available information. Here is the one door open to the persuasive writer. The writer has no power to change a person's personal history or the norms of social groups, although persuasive messages may be woven into those fabrics of experience. You can't expect to change someone's life situation or provide a significant new experience with your message. As a writer, however, you can hope to add to the information on which attitudes may be based.

If you look at the situation objectively, it does not appear to be encouraging. Why spend all the effort and resources necessary to shape and send persuasive messages if there isn't much hope for change? The fact is that providing information is your only chance of making an impact. Even if the impact is minimal, you have to try. That's why you need to understand the nature of persuasion.

The Influence of Social Media

As social media became more pervasive globally, communicators whose job it is to be persuasive began to consider social media just another way to get the message out and to get real time reactions. However, the personal tone of social media puts a burden on communicators. How do you gain the trust of these broader, more heterogeneous publics? Soon it became apparent that useful research had to focus on "feelings," the emotional reactions of people to actions and products.

Good content, commanding stories, get attention, but to establish a relationship that is trusted involves fulfilling expectations stimulated by conversation with actions. Then experiences with actions become the stories online audiences post. Think of the "reviews" you read of hotels, restaurants, performances, films and products.

The Nature of Persuasion

As a writer, you can look at persuasion in three basic ways. One is as a learning process, whereby you impart information and members of your audience seek information because they want to know something. The second way of looking at persuasion is as a power process, whereby you attempt to "force" information on someone. The third broad view is that persuasion is simply an emotional process. No single perspective of persuasion is likely to be adequate, because the formation of attitudes is a complex process. But we can outline some aspects of the process that, when taken together, offer some useful insights.

Aspects of Persuasion

One of the best outlines of this process appears in Otto Lerbinger's *Designs for Persuasive Communication*. Lerbinger describes five "designs" of persuasion: (1) stimulus-response, (2) cognitive, (3) motivational, (4) social and (5) personality.[7]

Stimulus-Response   The concept of stimulus-response (S-R) is the simplest approach to persuasion and, perhaps, the least useful. It is based on the idea of association. If two things are seen together many times, people tend to think of one when they see the other. Clearly, S-R behavior does not involve any intricate thought on the part of the audience. It is useful only when a low level of response is acceptable. It seems to work as well with animals as it does with people, or perhaps even better. The classic illustration of this approach is Pavlov's experiments with dogs, in which a tuning fork was struck each time meat powder was fed to the dogs. Soon, whenever the tuning fork was struck, the dogs began to drool in antici-pation of food. Similarly, a cat owner (a nonscientist) discovered that she could call her cats from any hiding place by starting up the electric can opener. The cats associated the sound of the can opener with food and thus with dinner.

All of that said, S-R is the foundation of branding. When a logo is seen the expectation is the product/company is immediately identified and the association drives selection. The effectiveness of S-R in branding is clear when you see the trademark sign (™), legal protec-tion of a brand. If you simply want to establish an "association" between an idea and your organization in the public mind, S-R may provide an adequate model to follow.

When a personality or an organization's founder becomes the "brand" for an institu-tion or a product that can be positive until the personality gets into trouble, leaves, dies or is fired. Apple had some problems when its founder and icon died. If the personality is fired, the situation can be worse. Men's Warehouse discovered that in 2013 when the company fired its founder and spokesman for almost 30 years, George Zimmer. The day after the announcement, social media reaction was mostly negative, according to *The New York Times*. The company's Facebook page had more than 200 negative comments about the firing, and the action was one of Google's top searches.[8]

Obviously, this design is not a very good way to persuade someone regarding a complex issue. Nor does it seem to be effective with internal publics/stakeholders. The reason appears to be that internal publics usually have much more cognitive information about the organization, so they tend to regard such low-level messages as fluff.

Cognitive   The concept behind the cognitive design is that people can think and reason about what they read, see or hear. And they will come to the right conclusion if they are given the right information in an understandable way. The "right conclusion" is not neces-sarily the one you advocate, but it is the one that is "right" by the standards of individual members of the audience.

The cognitive approach can be effective in many situations. If a person has no personal stake in an issue, for example, or has no preconceived notions about it, the simple presenta-tion of information may be effective. Also, if you have a complex story to tell, a cognitive approach may be your best choice. People like to think of themselves as fair and reason-able, and if you provide reasonable arguments, they are likely to agree with you—other things being equal.

Of course, other things seldom are equal. You can't expect to dump your message (whether S-R or cognitive) into people's heads without considering what is already in them. To persuade someone to take a certain position, you have to know what will motivate the person to take that position. This idea is the basis of the motivational design of persuasion.

Motivational   Generally, the motivational design is based on the idea that a person will change an attitude to fulfill a need. In essence, your message to the audience will offer some kind of emotional reward for accepting your message and responding to it as you suggest.

What are some needs that motivate people? A convenient outline of human needs was devised by the psychologist Abraham Maslow, who grouped human needs into a hier-archy ranging from the most basic to the least tangible. At the bottom of the hierarchy are physical needs such as food, water, air and sleep. One step up is the general need for safety, or the need to be free from fear of harm. Then come social needs: the need to belong to groups, the need to associate with others and the need for love. Next come personal needs, such as the desire for self-respect, the desire to feel important and the need for status. At the top of the scale are the self-actualizing needs: to fulfill potential, to be creative and to have a rewarding life.

Whether these needs are being fulfilled—and in what measure—may play a major role in an individual's response to your attempts at persuasion. Persuasion that ignores these needs in order to concentrate on reason and logic is not likely to get very far. It is also important for you, as a writer, to identify the relevant needs of the members of the public/stakeholders you are trying to reach. If your priority publics are mostly at the social needs level and you're appealing to them at the ego level, your chances of success are diminished. Attempts at persuasion that do not meet individuals' needs will fail.

Social   Closely related to the motivational design is the social design of persuasion. This design takes into account an individual's background, social class and group norms. Often, group membership is the most important element in determining attitudes. On issues in which attitudes are closely tied to social conditions, persuasion must be designed to address the social factors that influence the individual.

Essential to this design is the idea that we learn from society which values are best and worst and which patterns of behavior are most acceptable. The key point here is that if you are trying to persuade across major regional, ethnic, cultural or national boundaries, the same message is unlikely to be appropriate in every case. You'll have to prepare separate messages, based on different social influences.

Continuous monitoring of program effectiveness is recommended for all of these designs, but it is especially important with the social design because norms change. They are dynamic. It is necessary, then, that you continue to take the pulse of your public. The norm today may not be the norm tomorrow. You'll need to know when, why and how the norm changes so that you can adjust your messages to the new conditions.

Personality   Finally, you can't ignore the fact that each individual is unique. Personality characteristics can determine which arguments will work best with a given person or public. Of course, a persuasive message is frequently directed at a large group containing a number of different personality types, so the personality design cannot be used effectively in many instances. Even if your message is directed at a large group—that is, it is designed for the masses—you should always remember that it will be received separately by individuals. As a writer, you need to remain aware of how personality characteristics affect persuasibility.[9]

Rokeach's Value Hierarchy

Values are a major contribution to the way recipients of messages respond to them. A hierarchy of values developed by the late Milton Rokeach complements, rather than competes, with the Maslow hierarchy.[10] Rokeach said that values are more important than attitudes and beliefs as primary influencers of our behavior. His values system, however, is based on attitudes and beliefs that cluster together to form values that are even more resistant to change than needs in the Maslow construct.

Rokeach thought of values as specific clusters of attitudes and beliefs that act as long-term goals. He went further, asserting that values fall into two categories: *terminal* and *instrumental*. Terminal values represent ultimate life goals, but instrumental values are the tools we use to achieve terminal goals. Rokeach divided his values system into five levels.

Primitive values exist on two levels. At the first level are those core beliefs that are seldom challenged such as expectations that the sun will rise in the east. Writers are wise not to challenge messages that contradict basic beliefs because these disturb people who will dismiss them. At another level of primitive beliefs are values that are somewhat idiosyncratic and personal and for which there is no consensus. We may feel undervalued by our employer and/or family, for instance, but we seldom articulate these beliefs. Instead we hold them internally, but seldom do we change them very much. Such values are difficult to change, and the most effective messages are those that reinforce these values rather than contradict them.

Authority values depend upon our interaction with others, parents, friends or colleagues. An example may be the parental advice not to lie because then you don't have to remember the fiction you created. While beliefs on which these values are founded can change, the values may not change much. The writer may challenge the beliefs with persuasive messages but doesn't directly challenge authority values.

Derived values are ones we develop from our vicarious interaction with trusted sources such as books we read, Internet sites we have bookmarked, television or radio shows we listen to regularly and the social networks in which we participate. These derived values are better targets for persuasive messages because they are more easily influenced.

Inconsequential values are those based on individual preferences and tastes. These are more easily changed because they express a personal preference, such as preferring to live in a warm, dry climate, but they are not so substantive as to be self-defining.

Taken together these values, beliefs and attitudes define our self-concept—the way we see ourselves. If something arises that challenges our self-concept, we move quickly to reestablish our sense of well-being. Shifts in beliefs or attitudes ordinarily result in short-term changes in behavior, but the values on which they are based seem to control our lifelong set of behaviors.

Steps in the Persuasion Process

Once you have considered all the different designs for the art of persuasion, how do you actually go about persuading someone?

To answer that, we must first identify the steps in the persuasion process. Social psychologist William McGuire lists six such steps: presenting, attending, comprehending, yielding, retaining the new position and acting.[11]

Presenting   You can't persuade anyone of anything unless he or she is in the right place at the right time to perceive a message. A person who does not watch television probably will not see your public service announcement on TV. If he or she does get news and/or programs online, it's not likely that your PSA will be there. In both cases, it will not matter how beautifully you have written the announcement. The same is true of the story in the newspaper about the benefit concert to help the hospital. If a person does not subscribe to the paper in print or at the online site and does not buy one at the newsstand, your message is not going to penetrate and persuade that individual at all. What you can do is to use social media effectively by putting the information on your organization's website, Facebook page and send emails to your list of members/benefactors.

Attending   The non-TV viewer's next-door neighbor may have a TV and might see your announcement, but not pay the least attention to it. He might be looking straight at the screen but thinking about who's going to win the upcoming football game. If so, he's not getting your message either. He must attend to the message—that is, pay attention—if you're to have any hope of persuading him.

Comprehending   Suppose this neighbor's wife is paying attention. She is watching the screen and listening intently to the sounds. But she's Romanian and does not speak a word of English. She likes to watch football games even though she can't understand the announcers. But she can't understand the public service announcements either, so there isn't much chance that you'll persuade her. The point is, you have to use message symbols that your audience can comprehend. If you don't, your message, even if delivered and technically defined as sent, will fail to communicate.

Yielding   In the house next door is another woman who sees the same message. She understands English, so she comprehends what your announcement says about the concert and its benefit to the hospital. And she happens to work at the hospital. But her reaction is somewhat neutral because she isn't very fond of the musical group. "They just try to make up for a lack of talent by playing and yelling louder," she says to herself. She got your message, but she did not yield to it. Although communication occurred, persuasion did not.

Retaining the New Position   Let's assume that the first woman's husband isn't daydreaming about football scores after all, but sees the commercial and is impressed. "That looks like a great idea," he says. "I think we should go to the concert because it will not only be fun, it will help the hospital." But the concert does not happen for another month. By that time, he may have forgotten about the concert and the benefit to the hospital. Your attempt at persuasion has been successful in getting the viewer to accept it. But because the viewer didn't retain his new attitude, for all practical purposes this attempt at persuasion has failed.

This element, of course, represents one of the main arguments for sustained public relations programming. It is not enough to get the message through. The message has to be retained by the audience long enough for the desired action to occur. Frequent repetition of the message and in different media is necessary to reinforce the adopted position until a person can act on it.

Acting   Now let's assume that the viewer didn't forget your message. Perhaps he saw the same announcement again and once more expressed a desire to go to the benefit concert. He may even have gone online with the intention of buying tickets, discovering though, to his surprise, ads that told him his favorite pop singer was scheduled for a concert on the next weekend. So rather than buying the benefit concert tickets, he opted for the pop concert. Your announcement, then, did persuade him to a new attitude, but the persuasion was not strong enough to get him to act on it.

To be successful, persuasion must accomplish all six of these steps. McGuire calls the relationship between the steps in the persuasion process and those in the communication process the "matrix of persuasive communication." You must get your message to the audience. More important, you must get someone to pay attention to it. And the message must be understandable; people are more likely to read things that are easy to understand. In any event, they aren't likely to come over to your side if they don't understand what your side is. But understanding isn't enough. Your arguments must be convincing. The audience must be willing to give in, or yield. Then they must remember that they gave in, and then they must act.

You'll need to consider all these steps when designing persuasive messages. Techniques that work well for some steps might be useless for others. Some persuasive writing gets people to pay attention, but it might not be memorable. Messages designed only to produce yielding might not get the audience to act. For example, one research study tried to decide which persuasive methods were best for getting new mothers to go to the maternity ward for examinations. As it turned out, the best method depended on how the results were measured. One method got the most mothers to say they would come back a month later, but another method produced the most mothers who actually did go back a month later.[12] Obviously, one method was good at inducing yielding, but the other was better for retention and action.

Typology of Steps in Persuasion

A typology of steps in the persuasion process by David Therkelsen relates each step to the content areas of social science, communication, psychology and marketing and to such root functional areas as segmentation and writing. For example, his typology shows demographics, for instance, as relevant primarily to the first four steps in the persuasion process.[13] But writing relates mostly to the attention, comprehension and memorability steps.

A persuasion model with which you are probably familiar is a list of steps in the adoption process—adoption of a product, practice or idea. The first step is awareness, followed by interest, then some evaluation of the new information. If it is a product or a practice, this is followed by a trial, and if that works to the benefit of the experimenter, adoption follows. The model attracted more attention in public relations where it became known as the diffusion model.[14] This model indicates some elements that affect steps along the way as well as the personality of individuals taking those steps.

Persuasion and Logic

Although strategies and the steps in the persuasion process are easy to grasp, another element is often ignored. This element often makes people uncomfortable, because in its purest form, it demands rigorous thought. We're talking about *logic*, specifically *applied logic*. To understand the idea, consider this scene. A grandfather standing on the porch of his country home remarks to an adult grandson, as they peer into a cloudless sky, that a storm is coming. The grandson says that it is amazing how older people can predict weather. "How do you do it, Gramps?" he asks, adding, "Is your arthritis acting up?" To which the grandfather replies, "Nope. The TV just went out."

Although fiction, the scene symbolizes what applied logic is all about. Look again at how the characters interact. If you analyze them closely, you'll see that several major principles are illustrated.

Expectations

The elder character may be a little flighty, especially in the eyes of the grandson. The young man *expects* his grandfather to behave in certain ways. His expectations seemed to influence his view of his grandfather's behavior. Like this young man, publics—audiences for your message—have expectations. If these expectations are met, your message clears one major hurdle toward effective persuasion. If these expectations aren't met, or if messages tend to contradict expectations and experience, the opportunity to persuade may be nil or, at least, quite limited.

This means that you must know the expectations of your audience. You have expectations, too, so don't let them blind you to what a public wants. These expectations are formed from applied logic—that is, thinking about experiences and observations of life around us.

Experience

Perhaps the TV system failed often at the grandfather's house and he'd noticed that this failure was sometimes followed by a storm. Therefore, he concluded that the failure of the TV system was the result of a distant storm that would soon come his way. Never mind that it is not fully logical for him to conclude this cause-effect relationship. His experience tells him that it is a fact of life. Applied logic tells him that it is the way the world works.

You'll find that the quirkiness of the applied logic of your public may keep you from a real understanding of them. That means that you must work hard to grasp what goes on in that public's collective head. One key to this understanding is to recognize how perceptions influence reality for publics.

Perceptions

Perceptions are tricky. Both grandfather and grandson looked out on a cloudless sky. One saw nothing but an aging grandparent, the other, saw a storm coming. Perceptions are like that. They are individual, not collective, visions of the world around us. What we perceive may have little or no basis in reality, because our perceptions are our realities. Therefore, when the TV system goes down, it is perfectly clear, from the grandfather's perspective, that a storm is approaching. Because he had not had the same experience or concluded that there was cause and effect involved, the grandson could not perceive what his grandparent perceived. Grandson, used to relying on information from a weather app, is somewhat puzzled by his grandfather's reaction.

One reason we can't fully perceive what others perceive is that we think in abstractions. We use verbal language as a tool inside our heads to give meaning and value to the reality around us. Because words merely represent reality, our understanding of reality is limited by our command of language. As a writer, you can only be as successful as your ability to select words that represent basically the same thing to your audience as they do to you.

If you don't, you'll see a sky that has no hint of a storm. Therefore, you may fail to see the connections between things that your public sees. A semanticist will tell you that words are symbols with dictionary definitions, often more than one, but have value-laden meanings to individuals, based on experience, education, culture and beliefs. These associations are connections.

Connections

The principle of connectivity is simple, although vexing at times. The concept of connection is self-descriptive—that is, it refers to the way people see relationships between ideas, events, issues, processes and so on. Obviously, connectivity relates closely to perception. In fact, you can think of it as the next step after perception. It is the idea of "What does this mean?" or "How is this related to that?" or "What does this mean to me?" When the TV system went out, it meant to the grandfather that a storm was coming. That the system went out meant nothing to the grandson because he had not made a connection between the two events.

If strict rules of logic are applied, there may be no connection between the two events. Our experience is not that of the older man, so we can understand the grandson's skepticism. But if the grandfather is in your target public, you must make every effort to understand how he may have made that connection. Otherwise, you're not likely to frame a message that is meaningful to him. Meaningfulness suggests that you must also look at the values of your audience.

Values

Our personal values are always important to us. And they become even more important, and more rigid, as we age. The grandfather's observation that a storm was on the way may seem trivial to us. That may be because we tend to forget that he lives in a rural area where weather is an important part of his daily existence. Developments that reinforce our values are welcome. Those that contradict them, or call them into question, are often ignored as not worthy of consideration.

Values are at the core of our behavior. They are rooted in our basic beliefs, such as our convictions about what is right or wrong, important or unimportant, valuable or not valuable and so on. Value systems, once formed, remain pretty much unchanged throughout our lives; they are much like the leopard that can't change its spots. It is our value system that influences the way we apply logic to what we experience and perceive and the kinds of connections we make between our perceptions of reality.

Applied logic—the way we see relationships between developments, things or issues—often provides the motive behind our own efforts to persuade others to our points of view.

Persuasion and Communication

Persuasion is a special type of communication. To understand the persuasion process fully, then, we must understand something about communication. Like persuasion, the communication process can be divided into a number of elements.

As with persuasion, the communication process has many models. None of them is adequate in every situation. Some are clearly more relevant than others in certain situations. However, the principal paradigm of the communication process, as formulated by Harold Lasswell, is this: Who says what, through what channel, to whom, with what effect?[15] By using this paradigm, we can say that communication involves a source, a message, a medium (channel), a public and an effect. Changes in the characteristics of any of these elements can cause differences in the communication's persuasiveness.

Source

At first, it does not seem likely that you can change the "who"—the source of the message. You're stuck with who you are or who employs you. But then again, it is sometimes possible to change some of your characteristics (or some characteristics of your organization or client). At the very least, you can design your messages to take advantage of any helpful qualities that your organization has. Redefining an organization is a fundamental element in "rebranding."

What qualities of the source of the message influence the effectiveness of persuasion? One of the most important is credibility. Usually, the more credible a source, the more persuasive it is.[16] This means that your organization must constantly strive to remain believable if your message is to be effective. And the best way to remain credible is to tell the truth—even when it hurts. Thus, even if you are trying to persuade, you must remember to be honest and accurate. What you write must correspond to your company's actions. If the organization is not acting the part of a good member of the community, it does not really matter much what you say, because your message won't be believed. As Lerbinger puts it, "The communicator realizes that what he says must correspond to the realities of a given situation. The management he represents cannot be doing one thing while he is saying something else."[17]

Credibility can be viewed as having two major elements: *expertise* and *objectivity*. The audience is more likely to believe you if its members think you know what you're talking about. But to believe you completely, they must also think you are telling the truth. If you have a vested interest in an issue, your objectivity will be suspect. McGuire says, "For maximum believability, the source must be perceived as not only knowing the truth but being objective enough to be motivated to tell it as he sees it."[18] Research indicates that people tend to rate expertise higher in writers who use big words and longer, more involved sentences, compared to those who use common words and simpler syntax, especially when dealing with complex issues. The same study also indicates that people who already have a fairly clear understanding of an issue are more critical of what they read and who writes it.[19] This contradicts what PR writers have to do in simplifying the complex. So what's going on here? It's simple. Those who know the material expect the words they recognize, including some scientific jargon familiar to them. The solution is different messages for different publics. Another puzzle might be the fact that several research studies confirm that disinterestedness makes a source more persuasive to audiences. In fact, a source is most persuasive of all when arguing *against* his or her best interests.

Credibility isn't the only source characteristic that can aid persuasion. Your audiences are likely to be persuaded, too, by sources they like. Often that means someone "like them" or someone they want to be like. Of course, a public's feelings about the source aren't always clear. Is an audience persuaded by a source because it feels something in common with and likes the source, or does it like the source because it agrees with the message? In any event, being liked helps make persuasion more successful. So does *being similar* to the audience members in some way, especially when the similarity is ideological and not merely physical or social. Your persuasion, then, is more likely to be effective if you can establish some *ideological similarities* between yourself and your audience.

A third source characteristic that leads to effective persuasion is perceived power. Put simply, this means that your boss is more likely to persuade you than your neighbor is. Your boss has power over you; your neighbor does not.

Because many different source qualities affect persuasive success, it isn't always possible to predict what will happen when one of these qualities is changed. For example, if you work hard to appear to be an expert, your audience may very well perceive your expertise but may not agree with you as much as they would otherwise. By becoming more of an expert, you have become less similar to your nonexpert public. The increase in agreement produced by greater expertise can be more than offset by the loss of agreement caused by the decrease in similarity. In many cases, then, some intermediate level of expertise is probably best. Audiences tend to believe people who know more than they do, but not too much more.

Although these points are all supported by contemporary research findings, it is worth noting that the value of a reputation for personal truthfulness and expert experience was treated long ago by Aristotle under the general term *ethos.*[20]

Most of the time, you can choose your sources for expertise and credibility. However, in a crisis, that may not be the case. Others involved in the situation will be speaking out, and still others may be sought for their views. The proactive public relations practitioner gets those others involved in the situation to help tell the story and goes forward with the first news of the crisis, incident or situation in order to frame the issue in the minds of those hearing the news either through mass or specialized media or interpersonal communication.

Message

From the standpoint of the persuasive writer, the message element in the process is often the most important. At least, the message is the one element of communication over which the writer has complete control. In writing the message, you have to decide what things to say and how and when to say them. In doing this, you will be faced with many difficult decisions. Here is what communication research says about some of the questions surrounding those decisions.

Should You Give One Side or Both Sides?

In general, studies show that it is better to give both sides of the story. One-sided arguments are frequently dismissed, especially if a public is highly sophisticated or tends to oppose your point of view at the beginning. If the public does not like you, or if the public does not already agree with you on the issue at hand, it's usually best to give both sides. It's also better to give both sides if the public is likely to hear the other side of the story.

Is there any time when stressing your side of the story *only* is a good idea? Possibly, if circumstances include *all three* of the following conditions: the public is poorly educated, the public is friendly to you, and the public probably will not hear any arguments from the other side. Only rarely, however, are all of these requirements met. Generally that means you must introduce and refute other points of view.

A related question is occasionally faced by public relations writers: Should an issue be raised at all? Sometimes people (especially corporate executives) prefer to "let sleeping dogs lie" and not bring up a potentially controversial subject until somebody else does it first. This is usually a mistake. If there is any chance at all that someone will bring up an issue in the future, you should strike first with your side of the story. In fact, most research indicates that the first communicator has a significant advantage in winning over public opinion because of the inoculation effect. That is, you can try to "inoculate" an audience against the opponent's views, just as a person can be inoculated against a disease by an injection of a weakened form of the same disease. Thus, it is generally more effective to raise the issues yourself, before your opponent does, but don't expect "inoculation" to work miracles. In fact, many scholars question its value.

Nonetheless, a smart public relations writer will supply a weakened form of the opposition arguments and then refute them before the opposition can present its case. The public will resist persuasion by the opposition at a later date. This strategy, studies show, works better than providing the public with large amounts of propaganda designed merely to promote the persuader's point of view while ignoring the existence of conflicting opinions.

Which Side Should You Give First?
If, as in most cases, you use both sides of the story, whose side should you give first? Unfortunately, the evidence on this question is not conclusive. Giving the opposition arguments first is apparently better when dealing with controversial issues but not when dealing with noncontroversial ones.

Which Should Come First, the Good News or the Bad News?
In general, give the good news first. This approach will probably get you the widest overall agreement with your message.

Should You Make Conclusions Explicit or Let the Target Public Draw Its Own Conclusions?
In essence, this question asks whether it's better to tell people what to think or to offer the facts and let them figure it out. It's true that a person drawing his or her own conclusions is likely to hold the new opinion more strongly. The problem is that the conclusion might not be the one you are after. Generally, then, it is safer to make the conclusion explicit, especially when the issue under consideration is complex.

There are exceptions to this general guideline, however. A highly intelligent public can probably be trusted to form an obvious conclusion, based on the weight of evidence presented to it. In fact, such a public may consider an explicit conclusion in such situations insulting. Sometimes, an initially hostile public reacts negatively to explicit conclusions. And when the issues are very personal and members of the target public have a high ego involvement with your conclusions, it's definitely wiser not to make the conclusions explicit.

Do Fear Techniques Work?
Research on this question seems to indicate that fear appeals do enhance persuasion, but only up to a point. Mild fear appeals seem to be more effective than strong fear appeals. Even then, you need to offer a resolution to the fear.

McGuire offers an explanation for this. Fear may be effective in passing the yielding step of persuasion. But high fear levels may work against other steps in the process, such as comprehension or remembering. If you scare people too much, they won't get the substance of your message, they will put it out of their minds and forget it or they will modify it to a less threatening form. Thus, as with expertise, some medium level of fear is probably the best approach. Keep in mind, though, McGuire's observation that the more complex the message, the less fear arousal is desirable.[21]

Is It Better to Use Emotional or Factual Arguments?

Evidence on this question is simply not conclusive. Sometimes emotional appeals are the most persuasive, and sometimes factual ones are. It all depends on the issue involved and the composition of the public. There are no good general guidelines to follow.

It is probably safe to say, however, that the best persuasive writing employs both factual and emotional arguments. Because information by itself seldom changes attitudes, some writers tend to rely on emotional presentations. But information is also important to persuasion, if only to provide people with a rational basis for justifying attitudes that are primarily based on emotions. Information can strengthen or weaken attitudes. It can blunt the criticism of a public opposed to your position. It can strengthen the opinions of those already on your side. Furthermore, providing information to supporters of your view gives them a way to verbalize their feelings—and to defend them. This reduces the chances that subsequent persuasion from the opposition will undo what your message has accomplished.

Medium

Although it may be a bit of an exaggeration, Marshall McLuhan's contention that "the medium is the message" certainly responds to the question of how the channel, or medium, can influence a persuasive outcome.

It should be obvious that the medium is important in both the presentation and the attention steps of persuasion. As a writer, you must use a medium that will get your message to your priority public, and the medium has to be one that the audience will pay attention to. But research studies indicate that the medium is also important for other steps of persuasion.

One finding is that spoken communication is usually more likely than written communication to bring about yielding.[22] This does not mean that you should spend all your time writing speeches while ignoring other media. But it is useful to keep in mind that speech has more power to change minds than writing. The pen might be mightier than the sword, but the tongue can outdo both.

This is not an endorsement of "fiery oration," either. In fact, studies have been unable to show much difference between the persuasive effects of intense, enthusiastic speeches and more subdued ones. In both cases, however, the spoken word wins over the written word in persuasive power.

On the other hand, studies also show that the written word achieves better comprehension. But complete understanding is not always needed for successful persuasion. The spoken word diminishes understanding a little, but it increases yielding a lot.

These findings seem to recommend audible media for carrying your message. But though the evidence shows that oral persuasion is more effective than written persuasion, it also shows that face-to-face encounters are more persuasive than messages in traditional/legacy media, especially in attempts to influence voting behavior.[23] Such evidence suggests that spending a lot of money on traditional media time and space may not be worth the price. But if traditional media messages aren't effective, then the nation's businesses are wasting billions of dollars annually to promote their products, services and ideas in them. And there are reasons to believe that the media can play a role in persuasion, though perhaps an indirect one such as reinforcement. Some of the debate on this issue may simply reflect the fact that the effects of traditional media are too difficult to isolate and to measure. The ongoing process of convergence in traditional media is making it even more difficult to tease out effects peculiar to a specific medium. The fact that advertising messages are gravitating to online, especially social media, suggests that effectiveness has changed.

Advertising in social media has not been as effective as the comments of influencers in blogs and consumer reviews.

Studies show that legacy media can successfully convey information to people, though not in all cases, and not always to the extent that the communicator would like. And though information alone is usually not enough to get people to change their attitudes, it does play a part. Even if most people are not persuaded much by legacy media, opinion leaders—those who influence others in face-to-face contacts—do pay attention to legacy news media and base their opinions at least in part on media messages. The messages that are most successful, though, are electronic ones.

The idea that opinion leaders transmit social and legacy media messages to others is usually described as the "two-step flow" of mass communication. More recent research has cast some doubt on some of the details of this idea. For example, many people do receive input from the media, but they turn to opinion leaders for interpretations of facts more than for the facts themselves. Furthermore, the opinion leaders receive information from many sources other than legacy or social media.[24] Nevertheless, opinion leaders do provide a possible avenue for legacy media to influence public opinion. Bloggers, in general, are in the category of opinion leaders particularly in certain topics, and many of them are considered major influencers of public opinion.

Another important influence of the media has been described as "agenda setting." Research seems to show that issues considered important by the population often are also issues that the media devote much time and space to. Thus, it has been suggested that even if the media don't tell people what to think, they do tell them what to think about. Of course, it is possible that the situation is the other way around—that people decide what's important first, and then the media begin to run stories on those subjects. The more recent studies of agenda setting do indicate that media do influence what people think. So if your intention is to raise an issue to public consciousness, you must first get the attention of the media.

The question, though, is what media? It's not all news media. Social media provide instant, unmediated (not edited) delivery to particular groups that cluster around certain social media sites. Twitter seems to have the broadest network; others have particular audiences and special uses, such as for video, music, etc.

Given that all media can be used as channels for your messages, which media are best to use? That's a difficult question to answer. Because the media's measurable effects on attitudes are small, it isn't easy to tell if one medium is more effective than another. Looking at the credibility for traditional media separately, the evidence suggests that people are most likely to believe what they see and hear. People go to online media sites, so they are more likely to get both. Television news offers not only its broadcast information, but also websites that give more information, such as a complete interview or more video. For traditional media, television is generally given the strongest believability ratings. However, members of higher socioeconomic groups usually rate newspapers and magazines higher for accuracy and truthfulness.[25] Looking at the question from the standpoint of complexity of message, highly complex messages are generally more understandable and believable in print media. Messages charged with emotion appear to work best in broadcast media.

The problem with such a simplification is that familiarity with technology has made skeptics of consumers of most media messages. People know how to use Photoshop, how to record video and sound and how to transmit messages. People are carrying around a versatile message generator in their mobile devices. As experienced creators and editors of content, they are aware of how messages can be transformed and are thus somewhat skeptical of any information from untrusted sources. People who rely on business news to make financial decisions may question Associated Press business stories if they know that in 2014, the AP decided to use automated technology for its stories about earning reports. Data for the stories will come from Zacks Investment Research thus labeled "as being produced automatically with material from Zacks," according to AP Managing Editor Lou Ferrara.[26]

Public

The greatest lesson of social science research on the question of persuasion is one that all good writers should already understand: know your public. Techniques that will work wonders persuading a football team may flop with a group of engineers. Most of the guidelines for preparing a message or choosing a channel depend on the characteristics of the public. Publics that always have been fragmented are even more so. Any connectivity among them comes not from exposure to traditional media, but from conversations with family and friends, online and face to face.

Any public is made up of individuals. And all individuals, as receivers of your message, possess a common characteristic: they tend to forget things. This fact usually works to your disadvantage, because you must repeat messages often to combat forgetfulness. But attitudes built up over a long period of time are hard to forget. If your organization has a long history of exploiting employees or making a poor product, and if the company is perceived this way by your audience, you will have a difficult job writing credible messages. Before you can ever hope to be believed and accepted, your company will have to clean up its act. And you will have to tell the "good news" often over a long period of time before the new truth about the company will replace the old perceptions.

On the other hand, if your organization is generally perceived as a good place that is sensitive to employee and customer needs, you'll be able to weather a lawsuit filed by an employee or a customer with only moderate and temporary damage. A major part of that recovery is each individual member of a public's direct interaction with the organization.

That means organizations have to be involved with individual members of all of its publics. The one-line conversations may be one-on-one with members of a public, but are posted for all others to see and react to. Listening is more important than talking. Listening means paying attention to offline and informal discussions as well as online ones. You can learn whether or not your message was received and retained.

The point is that the "retention" step in the persuasion process is a particularly difficult one.

The human tendency to forget can sometimes be helpful, especially to communicators with low credibility, perhaps because of real or perceived bias. Messages from low-credibility sources may not induce any immediate change, but months later, a public may show some agreement with that same source's point of view. It is possible that they will remember the message but forget where it came from. Thus the message, no longer associated with the low-credibility source, may now be believed. It just takes a while for it to happen.

This is sometimes called the *sleeper effect,* and whether it actually exists is a matter of some debate. Nevertheless, it's useful to know that even a low-credibility source can be effective in persuasion under some circumstances.

Forgetfulness probably carries no such benefits for high-credibility sources who want the target public to remember everything. High-credibility sources often repeat their messages over and over to make sure the point is retained. Research on this issue indicates that repetition (as with a commercial announcement presented many times) may indeed achieve greater effects, but mostly because it increases the likelihood that more people will hear the message.

On this point, however, it is wise to remember that people tend to forget information at about the same rate as they learn it. Hence, if you stop the flow of messages about your organization, you can expect awareness of your company to drop, though it apparently never goes back to zero. This point, viewed from the stance of economy, supports the idea of sustained programming, because it is more efficient to sustain awareness than to build it in the first place.

Effect

When you begin writing a message about your company to its publics, you have some objective in mind. You want those publics to think about an issue in a certain way, or you want them to do something. In other words, there is a motive, or intent, not only behind the message you want to convey but also behind the way you will formulate and deliver it. Thus the overall "effect" question is: Did the message do what you wanted it to do?

You begin the process of writing with an intended effect in mind. It has to be "intended" because you don't know what the actual effect will be ahead of time. You can only guess—and hope. Nevertheless, you must ask yourself how your intended effect influences your success in persuasion.

The most obvious intention of any persuasive speaker or writer is to persuade. If the audience knows it is being persuaded, its resistance may increase. If, however, people merely overhear a message, without knowing that the message is intended for their ears, they might be more susceptible to the argument.

This fact suggests that it might be helpful to disguise your persuasive intent. Some evidence supports this view, but some does not. At times, the opposite effect can be seen.

Although there is little doubt that disguising the intent to persuade enhances yielding, such a disguise may hinder presentation, attention and comprehension. The benefits of making sure your audience gets the message may outweigh the disadvantages of letting your intent be clearly seen.[27]

A companion issue regarding intent is the matter of how extreme your appeal should be. Should you try to persuade people to change their minds just a little or a lot? This question has been the focus of many research studies. It seems, generally, that increasing the level of intended change helps to increase persuasion, but only up to a point. If you ask for too much attitude change, effectiveness decreases.[28]

An Alternative Theory

Because of conceptual problems with certain methods by which some of the foregoing ideas have been tested, you will be wise as a writer to use them simply as guidelines, not as gospels. Some research findings are contradictory or, at least, inconclusive. James E. Grunig has introduced yet another perspective that may help us to better understand the effects of persuasion.

Put simply, Grunig proposes a situational theory asserting that "how a person perceives a situation explains whether he will communicate about the situation, how he will communicate, and whether he will have an attitude relevant to the situation."[29] This perspective involves six key concepts: problem recognition, constraint recognition, referent criterion, involvement, information seeking and information processing.

Problem Recognition   A person must perceive that something is missing or indefinite in a situation in order to stop and think about it. The importance of this to the public relations writer is that recognition of a problem or issue increases the chances that a person will respond to a situation or express a need for more information about it. This idea is closely related to the *attending* and *comprehending* functions cited earlier.

Constraint Recognition   If the receiver of a public relations message thinks his or her options to respond to the situation are limited by group, institutional, legal, economic or other external constraints, there is less need for information about the situation. These constraints may be perceived as so compelling that people simply ignore the information because they feel impotent to use it or, perhaps, to do anything about it. Therefore, even if your message is loaded with relevant material, it may have little impact because the receiver is resigned to a limited response or no response at all. This idea is related to the *retaining* and *acting* functions discussed earlier.

Referent Criterion   A person brings to a situation some prior information that is relevant to the situation. If the situation is common, the prior information tends to lessen the person's need for additional information. This suggests that the person probably won't be very open to new information from a public relations writer. On the other hand, if the situation is new, related prior experience tends to serve initially as a guide to seeking information about behavior pertinent to the situation. This referent concept suggests that a public relations writer should be prepared to provide extensive information in new situations. This concept is related to Lerbinger's designs of persuasion, especially cognitive, motivational and social.

Involvement   The more salient or important the issue is perceived to be, the more likely a person will be to respond to it. Involvement seems to suggest not only if a person will respond but also *how*. Remember to attempt in every message to make its importance clear to the public.

Information Seeking   Deliberate acts by a person to get more information about the situation are characterized as information-seeking behavior. A need is perceived and behavior is directed at fulfilling the need. The concept of information seeking tends to suggest behavior that has risen to a higher level of involvement. Persons with these higher levels of involvement are much more eager to receive and accept your persuasive messages. As a public relations writer, you won't have to work as hard to communicate with these persons, but they will probably demand a lot more salient material.

Information Processing   Information processing implies a much lower level of involvement because some—maybe a lot of—information is encountered and processed incidentally, if not accidentally, about the situation. A large proportion of information acquisition is unplanned. It arises in the context of other behavior. For example, if there's nothing else to do, a person may switch on the television set and watch whatever appears on it, including your public service announcement on your community's blood drive. To reach this segment of your public, you will have to work especially hard to make your persuasive messages relevant. That's why we emphasize repeatedly in this book how important it is to know the public you are trying to influence. If you don't know your audience intimately, you probably will not be successful as a persuasive writer.

Five Ideas to Keep in Mind

1. Images have persuasive impact because they are faster and easier than text for the human brain to process. Used to complement text, visuals aid memory.
2. Consider the findings of social psychologists when you are crafting messages. Challenge values to initiate change. (Consider various tactics applied in civil rights arguments, healthy diet benefits, smoking and so on.)
3. Remember that the immediacy of social media is most likely to stimulate action.
4. In persuading, watch legal restrictions on promotion and follow guidelines from the Federal Trade Commission (FTC) on disclosure of source in social media. Disclosures must be easily seen, understandable, obvious and in a location that would normally get attention.
5. An organization's identity is its "brand." The ways people remember an organization may be any number of things, its logo (American Red Cross), a picture such as one of a character or a founder (Col. Sanders/Kentucky Fried Chicken) or its geographic location (Vermont Country Store). The association of a public to that point of recognition is, for that person, the organization's reputation.

Exercises

1. You came to college, with a laptop and an iPad, both with the latest technology. Now, you find that your laptop needs upgrading and the iPad too with some apps included. These changes are important for you to manage your classes and get your assignments done. You've been thinking about this for quite a while, and now you've decided to ask your parents to underwrite the costs. Although the style of your letter can be fairly informal, it needs to be persuasive enough for you to get the money to buy what you need. You have all of the information, including the prices; now you must apply persuasive writing.

2. You have been working as an intern this semester for a small public relations firm that has given you a great deal of responsibility. However, two of their clients are in the retail business, and you know that their busy months are going to be exactly the same ones as just before your final exams. You are concerned that if you devote the time the clients need, your grades will suffer and you may lose a scholarship. You want to write your employer a letter that will persuade your boss to give you a week off before exams. You know that others who have asked for favors have been told they are "not professional," and one was even fired. How can you write your letter so you won't suffer such consequences? This needs to be fairly formal.

3. Write a persuasive piece on any topic you know a great deal about but something that is fairly controversial. This will be an opinion piece for the student newspaper. Consider the time frame and analyze how you will construct your argument. Explain the rationale for your choices based on some of the theories in this chapter.

PART 4

Writing for Select Audiences

Select publics/stakeholders are groups of people who belong to an organization—employees or volunteers—or those who closely identify with an organization because of special relationships, whether business or personal. The organization controls what, when and how messages are delivered to these groups.

Media Kits, Media Pitches, Backgrounders and Columns

What does a media kit look like? That used to be easy to describe: it was a stiff-paper folder with a pocket or pockets containing printed-on-paper information for the media.

Not so today. Now many media kits are on the organizations' websites and are sometimes called online newsrooms. Others come on thumb drives that look like animals, vehicles and cartoon characters. Jersey City's USB drive looks like an airplane, and the USB connection pops out from under the cockpit. SeaWorld Orlando's media kit flash drive is a fanciful version of Shamu's tail. Disneyland's Cars Land flash drive is a cheerful, rubberized version of Lightning McQueen, and Disney's Dream media kit is on a toy version of the ship it promotes. Others are in leather sheaths, and some are in sleek wood or bamboo cases. The one from Royal Caribbean's Oasis of the Seas looks like a thick business card, but it unfolds, origami-style, to reveal the USB plug.[1] (See photos at http://jasoncochran .com/blog/cool-usb-flash-drive-press-kit-designs/.)

More traditional media kit formats have ranged from basic folders from the office supply shelf with a letterhead sticker on the cover to elaborate four-color packages with pockets for videos. Some—especially those introducing new consumer products—are three-dimensional.

Yes, they are "media" kits, not "press" kits. The difference is that public relations practitioners prepare packages of information for all media to use, not just the "dead tree press."

Traditionally, the contents of the kits have varied based on their use, but the contents are always prepared with the medium in mind. For example, black-and-white glossy photographs (printed or digital) that might be useful to print media are not included in broadcast media kits. Sound recordings that might be in radio news kits are not included in television news kits, which might have videos.

A 2015 TEKgroup International, Inc. survey found that 97 percent of the journalists responding said it's "very important" or "important" for a company to have an online newsroom. Ninety-eight percent said it's "very important" to find PR contact information there. Results of the survey included the following: "Most journalists visit company newsrooms regularly. 45% of journalists visit an online newsroom at least once a week; 54% visit at least once a month. Email distribution is far and away the best method to reach journalists. 92% prefer to receive company information by email; 94% prefer to receive story ideas and pitches by email."[2]

The survey indicated that the top 12 elements to have in an online newsroom included the following:

1. Search Functionality
2. PR Contacts
3. News Releases
4. Photos
5. Breaking News
6. Email Alerts
7. Product Information
8. Crisis Communications
9. Event Calendars
10. Social Media
11. Executive Bios
12. Information Requests[3]

In a study of online corporate websites, QSI Group, Inc. found that various companies offer as many as 65 features on their websites. Some of the more popular contents for both Web-based and printed media kits include:

- *Fact Sheet*—gives information about the organization: officers, offices with addresses and phone numbers and a description of what the organization is or makes or does. The fact sheet is the basic "building block" for a media kit. The "standard" fact sheet presents fundamental facts about the organization. These should be readily available, either on a single sheet or in folder form. You probably need more than one kind of fact sheet. A second one would be a historical fact sheet covering landmarks in the organization's development. Special-event fact sheets not only tell others what's going on, but they'll also help you preserve your sanity by organizing information in an easy-to-find-and-use format.
- *About Us*—summary or overview of the organization
- *Annual Report(s)*—most recent year(s)
- *Executives' Biographies*—principals of the organization: officers, founders and others with pictures (head shots); downloadable or reproducible ones for print media–small ones for identification for broadcast media and high-quality ones for magazine use
- *Board of Directors*—names, affiliations and addresses
- *Calendar of Events*—information on coming teleconferences, webcasts and executives' speeches
- *Community Service Programs*—information on charitable and civic activities and policies on contributions

- *Contact Information*—who to contact for media inquiries, customer service and investor relations
- *Downloadable Logos and Photos*—various sizes and forms of organization's logo and photos of typical operations
- *FAQs*—frequently asked questions and answers
- *Financial Information*—earnings releases, financial highlights, stock charts and dividend history
- *History*—background on the organization and historical milestones in its development—when it was founded and where, when new activities began and so on
- *News Releases*—usually headlines with hyperlinks to the entire release
- *Position Papers*—selected copies of any position papers the organization has prepared on current issues
- *Profile or Backgrounder*—tells about the character of the organization and the nature of what it does, including board committee charters and corporate code of ethics
- *SEC Filings*—information on filings with the Securities and Exchange Commission
- *Publications*—selected copies of the organization's serial publications such as magazines or newsletters.

(See Figures 8.1 and 8.2 for examples of media kit content.)

If you are using hard-copy media kits, then you need to think about how much material to include and how to make it appealing. The most conservative choice is to use a *shell*. The shell for media kits is usually a basic folder that has the name and logo of the organization on its cover. You can have these made up in bulk, so they are available when you need them. The only time you would want to have a different shell printed would be for a special event. Then you'll want the theme of the special event to dominate, although not at the expense of losing the identification of the organization.

The advantage of using an organization's website for a media kit/online newsroom is that it can offer news media not only much more material but also much more flexibility. When information becomes outdated, changing the information on the website is fast and quite inexpensive, compared to trashing a supply of printed materials and reprinting.

Media Kit Use

Media kits are used by organizations for basic information about the organization, special events (preliminary and on-site), news conferences and crises. Usually the kit has a letter to the user identifying the contents and the people to contact for more information. When kits are mailed, the kit letter is replaced by a cover letter explaining why the kit is being sent, its contents and any other particulars that would be important such as important dates or people who may be contacted.

The key to developing useful media kits is to think of who is going to use them and what that person is likely to need. (See Table 8.1.)

Media kits are not intended to be sent to new members of the board of directors, for example. They are not packages of information for general use by someone who wants to know something about the organization, although selected kit contents might be useful for that purpose. They are for hands-on use by working members of the news media: reporters, editors, news directors and producers. Remember that before you begin stuffing one with copies of ads or sales materials.

T A B L E 8 . 1	*Preparing a Media Kit*

1. Define the purpose for the media kit.

2. Identify the publics you need to reach.

3. Identify the media reaching those publics.

4. Determine which media will receive the kits.

5. Consider how each item in the media kit relates to the purpose for the kit.

6. Consider how the news media recipients will use each item in the kit.

7. For every item included in the kit, ask these questions:

   a. How do you expect the audience of each news medium to use the information?

   b. How does what you are providing the news medium convey that expectation to the medium's audience?

   c. What do you expect audiences of these media to do as a result of receiving this information? How will you measure that? (This question is significantly different from asking if the news media used the media kit or how much of it was used and when. That is easily measured. It's their audience's response that you need to know to determine if the kit is effective.)

Media Kits for Special Events

The use of the kit is particularly important when you are preparing one for a special event. Special-event kits are somewhat different in their contents, which are as follows:

- A *basic fact sheet about the newsmaking event* should detail the event and explain its significance in strictly factual terms. This should be a "stand-alone" sheet that gives a contact's phone and address, because it may become separated from the rest of the material. You need to include all important dates, times, participants and their relationship to the organization and to each other, such as those who work for wholly owned subsidiaries.

- A *historical fact sheet about the event* that tells when it was first held, where, who attended and how many if that is significant. You need to give milestones in the event's history, being sure to make clear why each is significant.

- A *program of events or schedule of activities* should have detailed time data, as that is especially significant to broadcasters. Provide a script if you have one. This is especially useful for the broadcast media but can be important for print photographers too.

- A *complete list of all participants* should explain their relationship to the organization and why they are a part of the event.

- *Biographical information on the principals as well as head shots* of them should be included. The black-and-white prints for newspapers and magazines should be of reproduction quality, and you should indicate when color pictures are available.

- A *straight news story* should give the basic information about the event in an announcement news approach. This should be about a page and a half, double-spaced on a 60-space line for print media and one or two short paragraphs triple-spaced for broadcast media. Be sure to give broadcast media both print and broadcast stories so they have the benefit of the additional information in the longer story. The print media need only the print version.

FIGURE 8.1

U.S. President's Emergency Plan for AIDS Relief (PEPFAR)   *Launched in 2003 by President George W. Bush, PEPFAR holds a place in history as the largest effort by any nation to combat a single disease. During its first phase, PEPFAR supported the provision of treatment to more than 2 million people, care to more than 10 million people, including more than 4 million orphans and vulnerable children, and prevention of mother-to-child treatment services during nearly 16 million pregnancies. PEPFAR's digital press kit provides an overview of the program's strategy as well as numerous fact sheets and information on various topics.*

U.S. President's Emergency Plan for AIDS Relief (PEPFAR)

FIGURE 8.2

PEPFAR Supporting Country Ownership, Key to a Sustainable Response.   *This is an*
example of the sheets in the digital kit that deal with the following topics:

- *Using Science to Save Lives: Latest PEPFAR Results*
- *PEPFAR Funding: Using Science to Save Lives*
- *US Support for the Global Fund: A Key Vehicle for Meeting Shared Responsibility*
- *Making Smart Investments to Increase Impact and Efficiency and Save More Lives*
- *Orphans and Vulnerable Children: Saving Children, Investing in Our Future*
- *Partnering in the Fight against HIV/AIDS*

Source: http://www.pepfar.gov/press/

U.S. President's Emergency Plan for AIDS Relief

PEPFAR Supporting Country Ownership, Key to a Sustainable Response

"To us, country ownership in health is the end state where a nation's efforts are led, implemented, and eventually paid for by its government, communities, civil society and private sector. To get there, a country's political leaders must set priorities and develop national plans to accomplish them in concert with their citizens, which means including women as well as men in the planning process. And these plans must be effectively carried out primarily by the country's own institutions, and then these groups must be able to hold each other accountable."

Secretary of State Hillary Rodham Clinton, June 1, 2012

In its second phase, PEPFAR has transitioned from an emergency response to a focus on supporting country ownership in the AIDS response – a key to long-term sustainability. PEPFAR fosters country ownership by investing in high-impact and evidence-based country-led priorities, plans and systems. Through U.S. investments in AIDS, systems of care have been established that countries are further leveraging to improve their citizens' overall health. As PEPFAR prioritizes country ownership, it works to advance programs based on science, support the development of capable leadership, and promote good governance, accountability and supportive economic and social policies.

Four Dimensions of Country Ownership

Political Ownership and Stewardship

Institutional and Community Ownership

Capabilities

Mutual Accountability, including Finance

To date, PEPFAR has signed over 20 Partnership Frameworks, and developed accompanying implementation plans with in-country stakeholders led by government. Partnership Frameworks provide a five-year joint strategic framework for objectives, contributions, targets and cooperation on AIDS among the U.S., the partner government, and other partners. They are a key tool for ensuring that PEPFAR activities support country ownership.

In evolving the Partnership Framework process to achieve sustainable HIV/AIDS programs, PEPFAR defines country ownership through 4 dimensions, promoted along with the necessary organizational change within PEPFAR to support success. This approach prioritizes joint planning; a facilitation role for the U.S.; building technical and managerial capacity in country; country stewardship; and responsible partnerships, including a shared responsibility for co-financing the national response in countries.

WWW.PEPFAR.GOV

The United States President's Emergency Plan for Aids Relief

- A *longer general news story* that ties in the background information may be as long as three double-spaced pages for print media and one full page for broadcast media.
- A *feature story* or two should be included to offer some insight into the more interesting aspects of the special event. There need be no broadcast version of these, but these features should be included in the broadcast kits for information.
- A *page of isolated facts* about the special event and others in the past, if this is an annual event, should be included. These facts often are picked up by broadcasters to use if they cover the event, and sometimes they are incorporated in print copy written by reporters covering the event.
- *Visual materials* can be included, or you can include small images with URLs that can be used to download the images, along with suggested captions. If the event is a first-time affair, shoot digital images and post them on your Internet site immediately following the event and let media representatives know where they will be. If the event is conducted annually, you can include pictures from the past, but be sure these are properly labeled so they are not misleading. *Do not include any pictures that have been used in advertising.* Also don't include any pictures of participants if they can be identified unless you have written permission. If you include paper photos, attach information to the pictures so it can be removed without marring the photos, and be sure you have permission to use them from owners of the copyrights, regardless of the content.
- *Information on cooperating organizations* is important for their recognition and support as well as for the news medium. However, you don't just stuff the kit with what cooperating organizations give you. You get the information about the organizations, then prepare information sheets explaining their contribution to the event and their relationship to your organization. For example, an organization may be supplying picnic lunches for volunteers who are taking children on an outing. You need to tell how much food and something about the supplier as well as why that organization is participating in your special event. Use quotes from people in the cooperating organization. If the contribution is significant enough, you may want to do a special news release on one or more of the cooperating organizations. This is especially important for them if your organization is organized as a nonprofit, and you have called on profit-making organizations for help in making the event a success. It may be easier for you to get media attention than it is for them, and if you see that they get credit for their support, they will be more willing to participate in the future. Be certain that you clear the information you have prepared with them to be sure it is factually accurate. You don't want your credibility undermined by some participant saying that what you have said about them is inaccurate.

Cover letters for special-event kits should tell the news media why you think the event deserves the attention of each medium, in terms of the interest of that medium's audience in the event. You want to be sure you make coverage easy for them too. Let them know what arrangements are being made, such as the facilities of the media room, and how to schedule an interview with celebrities or other participants.

You'll need to include information about how they gain access to the event, such as how to apply for badges and vehicle passes. You might even want to include information about transportation or eating facilities in the area of the event, if this is important.

You could save the information about the immediate area in which the event is held—such as food facilities and so on—for the cover letter that goes with on-site media kits.

On-site cover letters are different. You will need to let the news media know who to contact at all hours of the day and night in case they have problems or questions, and you'll need to let them know how to get others from their news medium in (such as technical crew) and what to do about personal and vehicle passes.

On-site media kits are different too. If you use a hard-copy kit, you'll need a sheet of changes in the front, and you must replace every piece of paper where a change has created an error. Keeping dates on your news releases and all other information elsewhere, such as on fact sheets, makes this easier for you to do. Things get so hectic in a special event though that some people use different-colored paper for different days so there's not a mistake. But this can be a problem with materials like news releases. Obviously, this is why online kits and news releases are less troublesome and also less expensive.

Your on-site kits should have materials arranged in order of importance and have a story for each day of the event or each feature of the event if it is a one-day affair. An example of the latter would be a story on a speaker, a feature on the food for the luncheon or the chef, and perhaps a feature on the planning for the event if there are unusual aspects to that. You can include in on-site kits any promotional brochures about the event that have been used. These often have dates and times that can be a quick reference for the person covering the event. *Facts must be absolutely up to date, so double-check to determine if any have changed since they were produced.*

Media Kits for News Conferences   When you are preparing a media kit for a news conference, it makes a difference what the occasion for the conference is. News conferences should be called for only two reasons: (1) to provide media access to a celebrity or expert whose time is limited and (2) to offer face-to-face access to a spokesperson for the organization when there is a controversy. The latter will be covered later in this chapter in the section on crisis kits. So if you are preparing a media kit for a news conference in which you are providing access to a celebrity, you need the following materials:

- A *biographical sketch of the celebrity* that is up to date and a recent photo. If there are any restrictions on the use of the photo, you should not include it, because you probably won't be able to control its use.
- *Information about the relationship of the celebrity to your organization,* such as providing entertainment or being a spokesperson in promotions, on issues or on new developments. You need to think of "celebrity" in very broad terms here. The "celebrity" may be a researcher who has done breakthrough research that your organization is able to take advantage of through serving clients in a medical facility or through providing medication or medical procedures. You can provide this information either in a fact sheet or as a backgrounder.
- A *general news story* that is the kind of story someone covering the news conference would write. To do that, of course, you will need to have interviewed the person and asked the kind of questions the news media attending are likely to ask and incorporated the responses in the story.
- A *basic fact sheet about the organization.* (See Figure 8.3.)

"Just the Facts" Format   *Fact sheets take various formats, depending upon their purpose. One typical format, which is a listing of "just the facts" from the USA Social Security Administration, is shown here.*

Fact Sheet

SOCIAL SECURITY

➢ **In 2009, nearly 51 million Americans will receive $650 billion in Social Security benefits.**

<u>December 2008 Beneficiary Data</u>

o Retired workers	32 million	$37.2 billion	$1,153 average monthly benefit
dependents	2.9 million	$ 1.6 billion	
o Disabled workers	7.4 million	$ 7.9 billion	$1,063 average monthly benefit
dependents	1.8 million	$ .6 billion	
o Survivors	6.5 million	$ 6.3 billion	$1,112 average monthly benefit

➢ **Social Security is the major source of income for most of the elderly.**
   o Nine out of ten individuals age 65 and older receive Social Security benefits.
   o Social Security benefits represent about 40% of the income of the elderly.
   o Among elderly Social Security beneficiaries, 52% of married couples and 72% of unmarried persons receive 50% or more of their income from Social Security.
   o Among elderly Social Security beneficiaries, 20% of married couples and about 41% of unmarried persons rely on Social Security for 90% or more of their income.

➢ **Social Security provides more than just retirement benefits.**
   o Retired workers and their dependents account for 69% of total benefits paid.
   o Disabled workers and their dependents account for 18% of total benefits paid.
     • About 91 percent of workers age 21-64 in covered employment and their families have protection in the event of a long-term disability.
     • Almost 1 in 4 of today's 20 year-olds will become disabled before reaching age 67.
     • 69% of the private sector workforce has no long-term disability insurance.
   o Survivors of deceased workers account for about 13% of total benefits paid.
     • About one in eight of today's 20-year-olds will die before reaching age 67.
     • About 97% of persons aged 20-49 who worked in covered employment in 2008 have survivors insurance protection for their young children and the surviving spouse caring for the children.

➢ **An estimated 162 million workers, 94% of all workers, are covered under Social Security.**
   o 52% of the workforce has no private pension coverage.
   o 31% of the workforce has no savings set aside specifically for retirement.

➢ **In 1935, the life expectancy of a 65-year-old was about 12½ years, today it's 18 years.**

➢ **By 2034, there will be almost twice as many older Americans as today – from 38.6 million today to 74 million.**

➢ **There are currently 3.3 workers for each Social Security beneficiary. By 2034, there will be 2.1 workers for each beneficiary.**

SSA Press Office   440 Altmeyer Bldg   6401 Security Blvd.   Baltimore, MD 21235   410-965-8904   FAX 410-966-9973

Promotional Media Kits   Promotional media kits are made up differently. These kits often include advertising used in the promotion, quotes from critics or reviewers when appropriate or even reprints of entire newspaper stories (reprinted with permission). It may be that the promotion is part of a larger event such as a national touring performance or exhibit. In that case, many of the materials will be provided by those planning and sponsoring the event, but you will need to add your organization's information to the materials and tailor news and advertising for the media you'll be using.

Depending on the organization, it's possible that you could have a basic digital media kit made for the organization. However, such material is easily dated so you need to be sure to provide for periodic updates. It's more likely that you'd create a media kit for a special event or a special observation like a 50-year anniversary.

Some of the materials needed are the same:

- Basic fact sheet
- Historical fact sheet
- Backgrounder
- Biographies of all principals (company officers, speakers, celebrities and others)
- Facts about the situation that can be used as column items, fillers or a story idea
- Visuals that include photos of the principals, pictures of the company or the event or whatever is appropriate to illustrate the purpose of the kit, but carefully chosen and edited with accompanying identification
- News stories
- Features
- Information on any cooperating organizations or perhaps on the site if the event is being held in an unusual place
- A source information directory so reporters or editors can locate names of people to call or to send faxes or email messages.

These suggestions for creating an effective digital media kit are offered by Tony Harrison, owner/publicist/copywriter at COMMposition of Boise, Idaho:

- Make the kit as interactive as possible with a wealth of information
- Make it easy to use by creating easy interfaces with big buttons, large type and readable fonts providing easy navigation from point to point so the users don't get lost offering mini-indexes for different locations so users know what's there without having to go into the location
- Arrange your images in an easy-to-use order by
  - Scanning photos (or copying digital images) onto digital media if you have a lot of still photography
  - Organizing the images well, so using and choosing the images is easy
  - Creating an image-placement database so that, if a photo or illustration is needed in several places in the kit or needs to be replaced, the change can easily be made
  - Saving (archiving) each step in the process of graphic images so that you can make changes without having to start the process over (for example, if there is a typo in an image created in Illustrator, touched up in Photoshop, then saved as a .jpg file)
- Update periodically to keep contents current.[4]

Media Kit for a Crisis   You may find that you are using your crisis media kit at a news conference because the confusion caused by crises generally means that at least one news conference is necessary. In the event of a severe, ongoing crisis such as effects of a natural disaster like an earthquake or hurricane, you may be giving daily briefings as well.

With information changing so quickly in a crisis, you will need to keep updating your website. This keeps down the number of direct media contacts you have to handle. It does mean, though, that in addition to your computer at the media center for the crisis communications, you must have a printer and a copier available.

Because crises are largely unpredictable, you need to have a supply of basic materials set aside for quick assembly. There won't be time to locate and print these items. You will have the media kit shell, which is a basic folder for the organization. You also should have on hand:

- Basic fact sheet about the organization, with names and titles; addresses of the home office and all branches or subsidiaries (if any); phone numbers, including the numbers of security people and night numbers that override the main control and put the caller through to the person on duty
- Backgrounder on the organization itself—what it is and what it does
- Biographical information on the principals of the organization—officers and board, including long in-depth pieces on the principals, often called "current biographical summaries," which are used for speeches and introductions but in this case may become "standing obits" (material ready for use in case of death)
- Detailed description of all facilities, giving layouts and square footage in each area as well as the number of people who work there and at what times. Some of these may be involved in the crisis
- Information on all the activities of the organization, including products, services, research funded or ongoing, and equipment
- Visual material, including pictures of facilities and principals
- Historical fact sheet on the institution, giving important milestones in its development
- Statistics on the facilities and the institution, including number of people employed; annual financial statements; major contracts with unions or suppliers; details of lawsuits pending against the institution; information on regulatory or accrediting agencies with some sort of oversight authority over the institution, its products and its services (for instance, the Food and Drug Administration or a hospital's accreditation bureau)

Keeping these materials updated for hasty assembly may be demanding for some organizations, but most have this material available on a fairly current basis from their annual report.

Material to be added includes the following:

- A statement from the crisis spokesperson about the crisis (provided in audio for the broadcast media)
- Information about whom to contact for information about the crisis as it continues or moves toward resolution

(Also see Chapter 14 for information on crisis communication.)

Media Credentials

For many events, having media personnel register and receive credentials—usually badges—is essential to maintain security and allow media personnel access where they need it. It's important to define who's eligible to receive media credentials. *The New York Times* reported, "Increasingly, bloggers are penetrating the preserves of the mainstream news media. They have secured seats on campaign planes, at political conventions and in presidential debates, and have become a driving force in news events themselves."[5]

The American Society of Plastic Surgery (ASPS) developed the following guidelines for media eligibility at its annual scientific meeting:

MEDIA ELIGIBILITY

Media credentials are available to working journalists whose attendance at the meeting may result in print, broadcast or electronic coverage of the ASPS, PSEF or ASMS and its individual members.

ASPS does not issue media credentials to the following: a publication's advertising, marketing, public relations or sales representatives; publishers, editors or reporters from manufacturers; "house organs" or promotional publications; public relations staff of exhibitors or educational institutions; writers creating analyses or reports sold as a commodity to customers; or other individuals who are not actually reporting on the meeting.

Working media representatives may not register as exhibitors.

To obtain media credentials, identification certifying that you are a working member of the news media on assignment to cover the meeting is required. Business cards from established news organizations are sufficient to establish eligibility.[6]

ASPS provided an online form for media registration and provided on-site registration for media representatives in its "press room" at the meeting.

Materials for Media Rooms—Crises and Special Events

The media room in any crisis or special event is an information hub. You need to be sure it is that and not a hubbub. So that staff and reporters are not frustrated, you need to have racks of information available that include all of the materials listed for the kits. In summary, you need:

- Fact sheets, informational and historical
- Backgrounders on the organization and situation
- Annual reports and informational brochures
- Biographical data and photos of organizational principals
- Special facts, such as information on the site, if it's a crisis, or on the event
- Statistics on the organization and/or event
- News releases, dated and numbered
- Quotes from principals, dated and numbered, and any actualities you have of these
- Visuals, with information and identifications attached

What you will be adding to these are *news briefs* on breaking or developing news. You should have a daily summary of new information, something that might be given at a crisis news conference or news briefing, and something usually put out each day of a special event to let reporters know what's going on and what has happened that day. Like news releases, these should be dated and numbered so you have a reference later. Unfortunately, some references aren't useful for quick retrieval later. Sometimes, in crisis situations, news releases and news briefs are part of the documentation in a court case. If you have a crisis, you must assume that your organization will be sued. Keep that in mind as you prepare materials. Stick to the facts. Think in advance about what reporters will want to know.

In case of crises, here are some facts reporters are going to want to know (and will find out from other sources if you don't provide the information):

- Numbers of dead and/or injured
- What was damaged and how (descriptive, not dollar amounts)
- Time of crisis events
- Location of all crisis events
- Names of dead and injured (released only after the next of kin are notified)
- Relationship of the casualties to the organization
- Number of people within your organization who were involved and who they are
- Who the spokesperson is and how to get in touch with that person
- What the effects of the crisis are on the organization

This last item is the troublesome question. Don't speculate; just provide facts. Don't sound too upbeat, because you'll appear to be insensitive. Don't be too negative, because your words will affect the morale of employees and the responses of other publics, such as investors and regulators, to the crisis. Keep a written account of everything released, to whom and on what date.

Having basic information on your organization loaded on a "dark" website can be extremely helpful in the event of a crisis. Such a site is developed, but the URL of the site is not made public. As information becomes available, it can be quickly loaded on the site and the URL can be made available to media representatives. This assures that information provided to media is always consistent. (See Chapter 14 on crisis communication.)

Special-event news briefs are generally on more positive news than a crisis, but you need to be sure you have good stories every day for print and broadcast media. Think in advance and plan in advance for good print stories and broadcast coverage. You will need to move around the event interviewing people and getting story material to provide to various media representatives as tip sheets or story ideas. This is your job, not theirs. If you want the event covered, you will have to do the fact-finding and initial story preparation. Again, keep copies and dates and names of the people you've given a story idea to. Remember, feature ideas are given to only one medium at a time. If a journalist seems interested but doesn't use the story in a reasonable period of time, you are free to give the same information to another medium after confirming that the first medium is not likely to use it.

At news conferences for crises and special events, you need to be sure you cover the news conference and capture audio and video of what occurs so you can write a follow-up release afterward. That story will incorporate what actually occurred at the news conference. You send the news conference media kit with this story as a substitute for the earlier news story to news media who were unable to attend the conference. You have to be careful about doing this because in writing the coverage story you don't want to take advantage of good questions asked by media people who were energetic enough to cover the news conference. Nevertheless, you want to get as much mileage as you can out of the news conference.

Media Pitches

A *media pitch* is just what it sounds like—a proposal to a media outlet. It's intended to "sell" a story idea on a specific topic. The media pitch can be in the form of an email, a phone call, a fax or a letter, depending in large measure on how well you know the person for whom the pitch is intended. (See Figure 8.4 for an example of an email pitch.)

The pitch can be for a new product or service, a new use for an existing product, an event or a movie—in other words, just about anything. The media pitch is the accepted way to make media representatives aware of a story idea in a clear and concise format. Each pitch should be targeted to a specific medium and should contain specific, unusual story angles.

Perhaps the most important part of a pitch is to present enough information to demonstrate that the story idea is of interest to their readers, listeners or viewers.

(See Tables 8.2 and 8.3 for more information on media pitches.)

Be Prepared and Be Persistent

Before you send your pitch email or letter, be sure you know the publication or station. Check a media directory, and check with PRSA members or others in the market where it's located.

Todd Brabender, president of Spread the News PR, says that one media pitch isn't enough and that your opportunity for placements "increases with meticulous, media follow-ups and re-pitches." "Based on my professional experience as a PR/Publicity specialist," he said "I would estimate that media placements occur in the following manner:

25% occur after the 1st–2nd pitch,
50% occur after the 3rd–5th pitch,
25% occur after the 6th–8th pitch."[7]

The California Association for Health Services at Home (CAHSAH) encourages its home care provider members to use a series of media "hits" in selling a story idea. It recommends that "Media Hit #1" be made by email, mail or fax. And it says, "… Craft your pitch letter to stand out from the crowd." It advises opening with an interesting statement "that motivates the reader to read on. Next, explain why the media should be interested in the pitch. Finally, address your proposal to a particular person, not just 'editor,' in the form of a standard, one-page professional letter."

CAHSAH says the second contact should be by telephone and should focus on how the story will appeal to the reporter's audience. The third contact, it says, should be by mail and should include your organization's media kit. Finally, it recommends following up by telephone to be sure the media contact has all of the information needed to develop the story.[8]

FIGURE 8.4

Media "Pitch" *One way to let media representatives know about an event or other newsworthy activity is to use a "media pitch." This is an example of a pitch that could be sent by snail mail or email. Telephone contact also can be effective in "pitching"—making media people aware of what you have to offer.*

Dear **(Insert Name):**

Although significant progress has been made in increasing awareness among women that heart disease is their #1 killer, most women fail to make the connection between heart disease risk factors and their personal risk of developing the disease. Join *The Heart Truth*® program on Friday, February **(insert day)**—National Wear Red Day®—to help spread the message that "Heart Disease Doesn't Care What You Wear—It's the #1 Killer of Women.®"

To help raise awareness about women and heart disease on National Wear Red Day, **(insert organization name)** is asking you to consider producing a three-part series on women's heart health. Your broadcast will send a clear message and go a long way in raising awareness and prompting action among your viewers.

The requested series could explore the following themes:

Part I: The Problem - An overview of the impact of heart disease on women

Part II: The Risk Factors - A look at heart disease risk factors and how they affect women

Part III: The Solution - A practical action plan women can follow to find out their heart disease risk and steps to lower it

The Heart Truth created and introduced the *Red Dress*® as the national symbol for women and heart disease awareness in 2002 to deliver an urgent wake-up call to American women. *The Red Dress*® reminds women of the need to protect their heart health, and inspires them to take action. National Wear Red Day embraces this symbol and prompts Americans to wear red in support of women's heart health.

We urge you to embrace this issue and help us alert women to *The Heart Truth*. Media coverage has proven to help raise awareness among its audiences and motivate change. Please consider including a series on women's heart health to your news programming to raise awareness about this critical issue.

For more information on *The Heart Truth* program visit http://www.hearttruth.gov.

Please contact **(insert contact name and information)** to discuss the proposed series. Thank you in advance for your consideration.

Sincerely,
(Insert Your Name/Signature)

Source: U.S. Department of Health & Human Services, National Institutes of Health,
http://www.nhlbi.nih.gov/health/educational/hearttruth/materials
/sample-pitch-nwrd.htm

T A B L E 8 . 2	*7 Tips for Writing a Media Pitch*

7 Tips for Writing a Media Pitch

1. **Be Brief** Limit the letter to one page. Make the letter easy to read and appealing by writing succinct sentences, short paragraphs, and using bullet points.

2. **Start with the Story Lead** Many effective letters provide the right frame-work or slant for the story. Put that information in the first paragraph.

3. **Provoke the Reader** One way to accomplish this is to begin the pitch letter with an intriguing question or startling statistic.

4. **Don't Oversell** Remember, you're not writing an ad. The letter must spell out why the story should be covered and the resources you can provide to formulate the piece.

5. **Tie the Pitch to a Journalist's Interest** Research the kind of stories the targeted journalist covers and reflect this knowledge in the pitch letter. This will make you appear "involved" in the journalist's activities. Even if the journalist declines your pitch this time, the person may be more amenable the next time.

6. **Attach Support Materials** A brochure, news release, photo, or even an article published in a non-competing media outlet (for example, you can send a trade magazine story if you are pitching to a newspaper) may be enclosed to provide additional background, if appropriate.

7. **Wrap up with a Promise to Call** State that you will call to discuss the story idea and any additional information you can provide.

Source: Centers for Disease Control & Prevention, *http://www.cdc.gov/injury/anniversary/media-pitch.html*

A national study by Cision and The George Washington University, Graduate Study of Political Management, found that editors and journalists "agreed that email pitches should be more relevant to their beat/area of interest, less promotional, should state benefits for their audiences, have stronger story ideas, cover the five Ws in leads, be better written and have less boilerplate."[9]

Keep It Short and Use Email

"Remember, journalists receive a ton of story pitches," said Holley (Julie Holley of Vocus Media Research Group). "They don't have time or the mental energy to make the leap and figure out how your pitch is relevant to them and their viewers. You need to make the case very clearly or you should not expect more than 10 seconds of their time and attention."

How do journalists prefer to receive pitches? The Vocus State of the Media Report 2014 provides some answers: "It's clear social media is increasingly being embraced by journalists, although email is still the preferred method to receive pitches. Similar to last year's response of 89 percent, 90.7 percent of respondents said they still prefer to be pitched by email, while only 2.7 percent chose social media as their top preference."

| **T A B L E   8 . 3** | *How to Pitch to the Press: The 8 No-Fail Strategies* |

How to Pitch to the Press: The 8 No-Fail Strategies

By Cheryl Conner, Snap Conner PR

Pitching the press may be easier than you think. Here are a few golden rules:

1. **Choose a target.** And make sure the target will actually fit. For example, thousands of companies through the years have attempted to pitch Walt Mossberg on writing about products such as network traffic management tools. Yet he specializes in covering products consumers would use. A good fit? Not at all.

2. **Read the writer's prior articles.** Thoroughly. Read them with an eye for their interests, their themes, and the way your idea would help extend their subject matter further. (Not "I see you wrote about XX, so how about you write about it again?") When you make your pitch, let the writer know how and where your idea might fit. Think through the idea through the reporter's eyes—how will this piece be of interest and need to the reader? How will it meet the criteria the publication and the writer's section and assignments must meet?

3. **Pitch a story—don't pitch your company.** Believe it or not, your company and product, by themselves, are not an interesting topic. But as part of a broader story or an example of a pervasive need or a message—now they can shine. Think of what that story might be and imagine what it might look like in the hands of the reporter you've chosen. From that point of view, prepare your pitch. Make your pitch by email first. Let it gel for at least an afternoon, or preferably for a day. If the idea is a good one, the reporter may respond right away. If you don't hear back, perhaps the next step is a call. When you call, refer to the earlier message. Regardless of whether the reporter has seen it or not, re-forward as a courtesy as you are talking to allow the individual to scan the high points of the message and preliminarily respond.

4. **Be respectful of the reporter's right to make the decision.** As tempting as it is to ply the reporter with a strong armed pitch, you will be more successful by respecting the reporter's right to say yes or no, while providing them with as many meaningful reasons as possible to have the desire to say yes. Is the story an exclusive? An idea or a slant that hasn't been offered to anybody else? Will it be of broad need and interest to the reporter's readers or viewers, and does it give them strong news or an angle on the information that hasn't been presented before? All of these ideas will help.

5. **When you speak to the reporter, get straight to the point.** The whole idea of buttering a reporter up to the topic you called for is a bad one. Clearly you phoned because you wanted something. With the first words out of your mouth, let them know what it is, and what your reasons are for thinking it's a good idea. If it's yes, follow through quickly with the next steps. If not, why not? For another person or with another approach could it be a better idea? With the business of the call handled, you can then visit with the reporter for a bit and catch up if they have the time and the willingness. And at that point, they'll know the personal interest is sincere.

6. **Be honest and transparent about your desire for the interview or the meeting.** For example, I was extremely annoyed to get an urgent message from a vendor needing my next available time to discuss their public relations only to find out their one and only reason for the appointment was to give me a demonstration of a product they were hoping I would cover for Forbes. And it was a product that didn't fit my area of coverage, at that. The executives wasted an hour and a half of their time and mine. Not only will they not see coverage, but the company they represent will now find it highly difficult to get a return appointment with me when they genuinely do want to meet to discuss their PR.

(Continued)

TABLE 8.3	(Continued)

7. **If you can't reach the reporter, avoid the temptation to call repeatedly.** Listen to the reporter's voice mail—it will often provide you with clues. For example, the reporter may be on vacation this week—out sick—moved to another beat (or even another publication) or may be so adamantly opposed to voice messages that you should be aware the message will likely never be heard (or may even offend them). If you do leave a message, one message in a day is ample. If the reporter has left a cell number on the message, refrain from using it unless the matter is genuinely urgent. They'll appreciate the courtesy you use in reaching out in the ways they most like to be contacted.

8. **Consider the strengths of Twitter.** Twitter can often be a clue as to where the reporter is and what they are doing on that day. For example, if they Tweet they just arrived at the World trade show, it's no wonder they didn't answer the office phone. Now you know. Time your next call for after the event. Also, many reporters will respond to direct messages through Twitter faster than any other mechanism. Use that advantage, when you can take it, with skill.

Source: Cheryl Snapp Connor, "How to Pitch to the Press: The 8 No-Fail Strategies," copyright 2013 by Cheryl Connor; used with permission, http://www.forbes.com/sites/cherylsnappconner/2013/10/13/how-to-pitch-the-prefcss-the-8-no-fail-strategies/ (accessed June 27, 2014) Snapp Conner PR, 1258 W 104th S Suite 301, South Jordan, UT 84095

A regional online business reporter responding to the survey said, "I get ideas from Facebook and Twitter, but I prefer pitches by email with more information. I don't want a 'marketing' pitch that sounds like an ad. In fact, that is usually a turn off. I need to be able to quickly figure out if it is a story that will interest my readers. And my readers let me know in the comment section of my stories if they think what I wrote sounds more like an ad than a story. I just want a short, clear press release with some facts so I can see if I want to follow up."[10]

Backgrounders

Writing of another kind is critical to public relations planning—the preparation of *back-grounders*. Outside academia, these often are called *white papers*.

The backgrounder is similar to a historical research paper that looks at a situation or problem in the present by considering its origins and its implications for the future. The position paper more closely resembles a research paper that takes a point of view or perspective on a situation and marshals evidence in support of the position taken. (See Chapter 6 for information on position papers.)

Both can be critical in media relations, particularly in responding to reporters' inquiries. Reporters may ask questions like: "What's your position on [name of act] now before Congress in Washington?" "What's your company's stand on the cause of the pollution in [name of river or area]?" "What does your company believe will be the impact of the new EPA rules?" "I'm doing a story on declining innovation in your industry. Can you give me some information?"

Your organization's executives and spokespeople must be able to respond quickly and knowledgeably to such questions. A "No comment" response is not acceptable. And if an executive promises to call the reporter back, this must be done faithfully. If such queries are not handled with skill and dispatch, the company loses credibility in a hurry. A company's credibility is hard won and easily lost. A thoughtless response can do unlimited damage.

The role of the public relations writer in such instances is to provide either in-depth information on the topic (in the form of a backgrounder) or a clear, definitive company point of view (in the form of a position paper). As the public relations writer, you are the eyes and ears of company spokespeople. You have to arm them with facts—solidly researched and documented, organized in logical fashion, clearly written and easily understandable.

Good public relations departments do not wait until a reporter calls to begin developing basic information for backgrounders. PR staffers routinely comb media of all types, searching for salient bits of information affecting their company or industry. These bits of information are accumulated and filed for reference. When the task of writing a backgrounder is assigned, they already have a head start on research.

It's common for backgrounders to be written and filed away—sometimes on a private intranet—for later use. The hope is that they will not be needed. But if they are, public relations personnel can respond quickly and appropriately to queries from any source.

Preparing backgrounders is often the first stage in planning a new public relations program. For example, assume that an electric utility is considering a new way of charging for the use of its electricity. The proposal calls for higher rates during the day but very low rates at night and on weekends. The PR department should prepare a backgrounder that describes the history of this time-of-day pricing structure, where such methods have been tried and with what success, the availability and cost of "time" meters and related points. Of course, the backgrounder should also compare this method to the one currently in use and to other methods.

At some point, company management will decide to stay with the present system or go with the time-of-day system. The backgrounder will help management make this decision. If the decision is to adopt the time-of-day system, the backgrounder will be used as the basis for developing and writing a company position paper on the new system. Both the backgrounder and the position paper will contain the information necessary to write news releases, ads, brochures and speeches, as well as articles for the company magazine, newsletter, intranet and Internet sites of all kinds.

Backgrounders tend to be heavy on facts and light on opinion and tend to deal with general topics, whereas position papers tend to treat specific issues.

For example, a backgrounder might deal with alternate fuel vehicles (AFVs) to reduce emissions that contribute to global warming, whereas a position paper would argue for the use of natural gas-fueled vehicles (NGVs) as a solution.

Backgrounders have many purposes. They serve as an information base for company executives and employees. They provide source materials to copywriters preparing ads, news releases, brochures, speeches or articles for the company magazine, intranets and websites. They may also be used as documents to distribute to reporters or members of the public who inquire about a certain topic. And company executives on the speakers' circuit

FIGURE 8.5

Backgrounder: Rotary International's PolioPlus Effort   *With 35,000 service clubs around the world, Rotary International brings together business and professional leaders to provide humanitarian service, encourage high ethical standards in all vocations, and help build goodwill and peace in the world. The organization's PolioPlus Effort is one of Rotary's many service activities.*

Backgrounder on Rotary International's PolioPlus Effort

World Polio Day, widely recognized on 24 October, is part of Rotary's 26-year mission to eradicate the highly infectious disease that causes paralysis and is sometimes fatal.

What is polio (poll-lee-oh)? Poliomyelitis is a disease caused by any of three viruses, one of which is most likely to cause epidemics. Vaccines are a protection. Two vaccines are used worldwide—the injection from the dead polio virus developed by Jonas Salk and first tested in 1952 then announced for world use in 1955 and the oral vaccine developed by Albert Sabin using attenuated poliovirus licensed in 1962.

Although polio usually strikes children, unprotected adults are not immune. Rotary International took on the challenge to eliminate polio worldwide by launching its 1988 Global Polio Eradication Initiative. Although new polio cases in the USA ended in 1979, that year Rotary International joined with the Republic of Philippines government to immunize six million children in a five-year period. That was the Rotary Foundation's first Health, Hunger and Humanity Grant program and led Rotary to launch the PolioPlus program in 1985 then the worldwide initiative in 1988. Since 1985, Rotary has contributed more than $8 billion and countless hours from 20 million volunteers to the protection of more than two billion children in 200 countries.

Three nations remain polio-endemic: Nigeria, Pakistan and Afghanistan.
Three nations remain polio-endemic: Nigeria, Pakistan and Afghanistan. These are the intensive focus for the PolioPlus campaign. However, new cases are appearing in nations with a previous low or polio-free record. One third (111) of all polio cases reported so far in 2011 (333) have occurred in endemic countries while two thirds (222) have taken place in re-established or importation countries. Over 50 percent (175) of all cases come from just two countries: Chad and the Democratic Republic of the Congo. Vaccines cost money and so does the administration of them. The global financial crisis has created problems for support within countries and from outside sources such as the World Health Organization (WHO). For as little as US 60 cents worth of vaccine, a child can be protected against this crippling disease for life.

Global travel creates an opportunity for contracting a virus and bringing it into a polio-free environment, which is why the Center for Disease Control (CDC) in the USA urges booster shots for travel abroad where the virus might be encountered. As of August 25, 2011, 52 countries were on that list. A polio virus lives in the throat and intestinal tract of those infected with the disease and generally enters through the mouth even from food in contaminated vessels. *There is no cure for the disease, only prevention.*

(Continued)

F I G U R E   8 . 5   *(Continued)*

2-Backgrounder on Rotary International's PolioPlus Effort

Bill & Melinda Gates Foundation, source of matching grant for Rotary Foundation, gives donations to GAVI Alliance, a partnership to get vaccines to children in developing countries.

Rotary International, the world's first service organization, has 34,000 clubs worldwide. All Rotary club members are volunteers working locally, regionally and internationally to combat hunger, improve health and sanitation, provide education and job training, promote peace and eradicate polio under the motto Service Above Self. (Adapted from Rotary International website.)

As part of Rotary's most recent campaign to match a US$355 million challenge grant from the Bill & Melinda Gates Foundation with $200 million by June 2012, the humanitarian service organization is close to reaching its goal, with more than US$180 million raised to date. The funding will provide critical support to polio eradication activities in parts of Africa and South Asia.

Rotary invites the public to support the polio eradication initiative by visiting www.rotary.org/endpolio.

For further information visit, www.rotary.org or www.polioeradication.org

Media note: High-resolution photography is available from www.rotary.org. Search: polio.

Rotary Polio Information Contact
District 5790 Polio Chair Conrad Heede at ccheede@aol.com
Or call: 817.235.8110
Or: email Doug Newsom at d.newsom@tcu.edu; call: 817.732.2901

Background Source Contacts/Resources:
The Rotarian, Rotary's Magazine, "Polio and the Culture of Fear," June 2010, p. 48–36.
Rotary International's Public Relations Division: email pr@rotary.org
World Health Organization
Global Polio Eradication Initiative for information on Rotary, CDC, Unicef
        www.polioeradication.org/casecount.asp
Center for Disease Control (CDC) for information on travel and polio
        wwwnc.cdc.gov/travel/content/in-th-news/polio-outbreaks.aspx
Directors of Health Protection and Education:
        www.dhpe.org/infect/polio.html
        For types and kinds of polio (three types of polio virus)
Wall Street Journal, World News, May 22-23, 2010 p. A8 for UN budget (World Health
        Organization) expecting shortfall (UN is a Rotary partner in effort to end polio
        worldwide.)
Bill & Melinda Gates Foundation and GAVI, Smithsonian Magazine, July/August 2010
        "Melinda French Gates Saving Lives," pp. 84–86, executive editor Terence
        Monmany's email exchange

can use them to bone up on a subject so they can field questions from the audience. Rarely does a backgrounder serve only one of these purposes; keep all of them in mind.

The hallmarks of a good backgrounder are accuracy and comprehensiveness. This means that the topic must be thoroughly researched.

Research   Doing research for a backgrounder often involves using all the research skills, techniques and sources discussed in Chapter 6. You are not being professionally responsible if you leave one bit of salient information unread or ignored in your evaluation. It just might contain the germ of an idea or the fact that makes all of your other material inconsequential or misleading. This can be fatal to the company, because company spokespeople have to rely on you for the information they convey to members of the media or to the public.

Research is a never-ending process. Once a backgrounder is completed, it may become less useful with each passing day because of new information. You should establish the practice of accumulating pertinent information, filing it and updating the backgrounder at regular intervals. Backgrounders that do not include the very latest important information are worthless.

Writing   Writing a backgrounder begins first with a simple statement of the subject and why it is important. Including such a statement may appear trite, but it is necessary to focus your research and writing. It keeps you on the right track. This opening statement should be both precise and concise. Besides helping you in the writing, it tells the reader what to expect in the document.

Once your opening statement is honed to perfection, write the body of the backgrounder. Be sure to provide an adequate, clear history of the issue, a thorough discussion of the current situation and implications for the future.

Background   As the name implies, a backgrounder supplies background and/or helpful information on a topic or issue. (See Figure 8.5.) It often provides a fairly complete historical overview so a reader unfamiliar with the topic can understand how the current situation evolved. You have to answer the question "Why are things the way they are today?" And you can't answer this question without giving details about how things were, and how and why they have changed.

The typical backgrounder includes such details as significant historical events, legislative enactments, changes in government and company policy and applicable social conditions. It specifies names, books, documents, articles and reports that played an important part in the development of the issue. In sum, this section of the backgrounder should describe the evolution of the current situation.

Current Situation   Having built a foundation on the past, you should now examine the current situation, including reviewing current public and company policies. Perhaps these points could be extended to include a discussion of alternative policies now under consideration.

The purpose of a backgrounder is to assemble and convey information, not to judge it. Any discussions of policy or alternatives should be presented from an objective, neutral position. Stick to facts. Describe policy options, discuss their good and bad points, but don't judge them.

If the issue is the high cost of home heating and its effects on poor people, one policy to consider might be the use of energy stamps to help poor people pay their utility bills. This idea has its good and bad points. One writer might say:

> Using energy stamps is a poor way to solve the problem because stamps require a massive, wasteful bureaucracy and excessive government funding.

Another writer might say:

> Using energy stamps is an excellent solution to the problem because stamps could be easily administered by existing government organizations.

Both writers may be justified in their points of view, but this is a backgrounder, not a position paper. Instead of taking a position, write to inform, saying:

> Use of energy stamps is one solution to this problem. An energy stamp program would require government funding and a system for administering these funds. Such a program might be administered by existing organizations.

Implications   To this point, we have considered the historical background and the current situation. The next step in writing the backgrounder is to examine the consequences of selecting one policy over another. If the backgrounder does not address such future implications directly, it should at least highlight points that must be considered.

A backgrounder on another aspect of energy policy might deal with state and federal policies that support AFVs. An expectation is that such a paper would put the whole issue into historical perspective by giving first the rationale for needing such policies, second the enactment of various federal policies, primarily by the EPA, and third the policy initiatives by various states. The backgrounder would also be expected to document which policies seem to be most effective, such as the EPA's clean air standards for ozone and fine particulates. The document would bring the situation up to date by explaining the current focus on market-based fuel incentives such as legislative actions that would offer tax incentives.

Identifying the implications of a certain policy includes anticipating developments. The public relations writer has to be aware of the flux of ideas about the issue and which of these may gain or lose support over time. Perhaps a public policy change is being debated now in Washington. Perhaps an extensive government study is under way, the results of which won't be released for a year. Perhaps the topic will be the focus of a convention this year. In all these cases, the issue and its implications are likely to be in the news now and in the future. As a public relations writer, you must be ahead of these developments.

Documentation   You must present full documentation of the information you use in the backgrounder. Before you try to write, as suggested in report writing, get a reliable style manual and study it carefully.

Although a backgrounder does not require the same rigorous scholarship and style required of reports and proposals, a style manual can help you properly cite the material you use in the backgrounder. Use a footnote or endnote system for citations, and include a complete bibliography at the end.

It is important to cite your sources carefully, because people using the backgrounder, whether inside or outside your organization, may want to pursue a specific point more fully. Or if they find a discrepancy between the facts in the backgrounder and those in some other source, they may want to evaluate the sources you have cited. This is especially important when a backgrounder provides the foundation for a position paper.

Format

When the writing is completed, determine its format and method of distribution. A backgrounder intended for internal use may exist only in digital form on the organization's intranet or in the computers of specific spokespersons after being distributed as email attachments. If printed copies are needed, the backgrounder usually is printed on plain or letterhead paper, copied, assembled, stapled and then distributed. Those distributed outside the company may be produced the same way, or they may be published as a printed booklet or monograph, embellished with art, color, design and typography and printed on expensive paper or published on the organization's website.

Some organizations prepare backgrounders for public consumption on special forms. These forms contain a company heading with the word *backgrounder* prominent. Others, particularly those in heavily regulated industries that require a large number of backgrounders or position papers each year, may produce punched versions suitable for inclusion in loose-leaf notebooks or—much less expensive and more accessible—put them on their websites.

Many backgrounders include charts and illustrations to help explain topics. For formal reports, preparing graphics for either printing or Web use is usually done using computer software, sometimes by a graphic artist. However, you should be fully aware of their content, how they look and where they will appear in the finished report. Placing these visuals close to appropriate text segments makes the information easier to understand.

Columns

There are good reasons for you to consider submitting content for what's usually called *opinion pages* in newspapers, magazines and even some Internet-based publications.

Why? The Earth Institute at Columbia University submits some good arguments: "The opinion pages are among the best-read sections of any publication—often on par with the front page itself. In addition to the general public, some of the most attentive readers of these pages are decision makers in government, corporations, and nonprofit institutions."[11]

"Three basic kinds of items appear in opinion pages: editorials, written by newspaper staff; letters to the editor, written by readers; and op-eds (OPposite the EDitorials on the page), generally written by people with special expertise or credibility in a certain field," according to The Earth Institute.[12]

The shortest of these—perhaps 50–150 words—are letters to the editor. These usually comment on a recent public issue or article in the publication. A major daily newspaper receives many of these every day, but only a few—usually those that represent each side of an issue—are published. Still, it's worth your time and trouble to submit such letters to briefly present your opinion or that of your organization.

Op-ed pieces are longer, presenting many more facts and analyses than letters to the editor. Well-known people who write op-ed articles receive payment for their submissions that are published. Many of them are syndicated, which means that their articles are regularly distributed to numerous publications. More important than fame in getting articles published are the credentials of the author. If you have specialized training or extensive experience related to the topic and are able to back up what your article says, your chance of getting published is better. Of course, you can "ghost-write" articles for a CEO, scientist or another person in your organization with specialized knowledge on an issue. You have a much better chance of having an op-ed article published in a local—perhaps weekly—newspaper than a big daily. Smaller newspapers often accept regular submissions of columns from people who represent organizations important to a community. Chambers of commerce, school districts, government agencies and large employers are examples.

If you decide to go for a regular column, work out an agreement with the editor and follow these guidelines:

- **Do your research;** be sure your facts are correct.
- **Be concise,** timely and to the point. State a strong argument both in the introduction and in the conclusion to keep the reader focused on the issue you are discussing.
- **Be clear on your position.**
- **Be specific.** Write about one specific policy issue at a time.
- **Provide a recommendation** but include suggestions of other possible solutions.
- **Use facts** to support your opinion—well-documented and well-researched statistics.
- **Get local.** When writing about global issues think about how your local community is tied to and affected by the issue you are raising.
- **Write in first person.** Don't be afraid to use "I."
- **Format.** Consider mixing long and short sentences to maintain the reader's attention.
- **Proofread.** Be sure your piece is organized in a logical manner. Of course, check for spelling, grammar and punctuation errors.
- **Provide contact information.**
- **Always meet deadlines!**[13]

Although editorials are—no surprise—written by the publication's editorial staff, your input and that of your organization can influence what editorials are written and, to some extent, the content of an editorial concerning an issue of importance to you and your organization. Because editorials can influence public opinion and decision makers, having a newspaper's support through an editorial can be important to your organization.

Each larger newspaper has an editorial board, and it's not hard to find. For example, if you go to WashingtonPost.com and search that site for "editorial board," you'll find that the *The Washington Post* editorial board has eight members. The website has photos and links to each person's biography.

Members of each editorial board schedule meetings during which a person or a group of people can meet briefly with them to present their position on an issue. The issue might be a potential zoning change, an ordinance that's to come before the city council, environmental concerns or anything else that is of significant interest to readers of that particular newspaper. "Significant interest to readers" is the editorial board's main interest in deciding whether or not to meet with a person or group requesting a meeting.

To set up a meeting with an editorial board, you must contact the person at the newspaper responsible for scheduling meetings weeks ahead of time. That person, usually the editor of the editorial page, will be aware that your purpose is to influence the editorial board to support your position on an issue and write an editorial supporting the issue. Keep in mind that the meeting with your group is not the only input the board will seek and that their final decision might not be in accord with your wishes.

You need to prepare thoroughly. You and your associates will have a very limited amount of time, maybe as little as five minutes, to make your presentation. So rehearse— perhaps more than once—and be sure you can "put on the table" your most important points when the meeting occurs. Depending on the issue, you might meet with the entire board or one member of the board who's responsible for that issue.

Public Service Announcements

Many media kits—especially those of nonprofit organizations—contain a collection of public service announcements (PSAs) for potential use by either print or broadcast media. Public service announcements are advertising messages from IRS 501(c)(3) nonprofit organizations that appear in media-donated time or space. Occasionally, a medium will give the nonprofit organization a "statement" that shows the commercial value of the donation. PSAs are different from situations where a commercial institution surrenders some of its contracted for time or space to a message from a nonprofit organization. When that occurs, the ad usually has a line in it that indicates the donor of the time or space.

PSAs for print media usually appear in the back of magazines or in "fill spaces" of newspapers where a paid-for ad didn't fit or the space, always small, simply was unsold and not desirable for an "in-house" ad. In broadcast media, the traffic manager for the station logs PSAs into unsold time that is not desirable for the station's own promos, promotional announcements.

What that means for the copywriter is that you must prepare public service ads of all shapes and sizes in a digital format so these are available for any open space, vertical or horizontal, color or black and white—usually color that fits just as well if seen only in black and white. Online spaces are less likely to be available, but occasionally are. If you, as a public relations writer, prepare much advertising for broadcast media, it is likely to consist mostly of PSAs.

Whatever the medium, there are some constants to consider. To do PSAs well, you must decide first whether your primary purpose is to *inform* or to *persuade*. If it is mostly to inform, you'll need to amass lots of information, sift it wisely and use it selectively. You must be able to say a lot in a little time or space. If the purpose is to persuade, you'll still need information, but you'll put more emphasis on its interpretation. And you'll arrange it, so it has the maximum persuasive impact.

A variation on these two purposes is a "positioning" PSA. A positioning PSA seeks to position an idea in some unique way against all other related ideas. Effective positioning can have a significant impact on what people understand, accept, reject or feel about something. It also may influence what they recall and how they associate it with other relevant information.

Whatever your purpose, PSAs for nonprofit organizations can be created on elaborately produced thumb drives (or DVDs, if the media kit is printed). These are included in the media kit. Both print and broadcast PSAs must be digital with scripts also included in the package. Many organizations' national headquarters provide their own PSAs in these forms, and they usually leave room for a tag line to be added at the local level.

More often, however, PSAs are produced locally for local agencies. PSA scriptwriters try to keep things simple. For television PSAs, you'll need video footage to be edited as the visual for the PSA. A station announcer or a local personality may volunteer services to do the audio. If the volunteer is a local personality, you should write the script to match as closely as possible that personality's style of speaking. Because all of this is recorded, there is some assurance of quality control, and it must be presented in broadcast quality. On radio, it is possible, although unlikely, that your PSA script given to a local station will be read live by an announcer. You should realize how little control you really have over whether or not your message will be broadcast at all and no control over its presentation. Your best assurance is to write an infallible script and it is always safer to *under*write—that is, use fewer words. Most radio stations, though, prefer to use a digital version provided in the media kit.

Online PSAs

Large nonprofit organizations maintain a selection of PSAs for print, television and radio on their websites, available for use. These PSAs may be uploaded to social network sites, and can be converted to a TinyURL to save space.

The American Kennel Club (www.akc.org/press_center/psa.cfm) offers a selection of TV PSAs and Print PSAs, using different approaches or themes. The organization also ties in with commercial organizations, such as films. The site shows color photos representing the theme and offers downloads of the PSA in different formats and lengths. The site also has some AKC TV commercials listed, but not all of them are available for downloading.

Government organizations at all levels are nonprofit and depend on free time or space. To make access easy, the nonprofits put print, television and radio announcements on a website. The USA Department of Defense launched a campaign to combat an increasingly bad image from news reports about harassment of women in uniform—Sexual Assault Prevention and Response Office (SAPRO) website. DoD representatives called attention to the campaign with news releases about it and with appearances on talk shows. (Go to their home page where you can see the campaign and all materials at http://www.sapr.mil/.)

Exercises

1. You have been given the responsibility of developing an online media kit for your university's PRSSA chapter. Prepare an outline of the contents and explain to whom and how you will promote the kit.
2. Choose a topic that concerns your school, such as the increasing use of drugs, getting term papers off the Internet, other forms of cheating or lack of diversity in the student or faculty population. Do your research and write a backgrounder on the topic.
3. Imagine that you are the public relations director for a city's transportation system, which includes, along with an electric subway system, fleets of gasoline-powered vehicles such as buses as well as special vans for the disabled. The city frequently has air-quality alerts that keep people who are at risk inside. Also, exhaust fumes are killing trees and other vegetation along the freeways. To help reduce emissions, the company has decided to use natural gas-fueled fleet vehicles. Prepare an outline of a backgrounder, indicating what you would include in the document.

CHAPTER NINE

Writing for Public Media

W hat used to be referred to as "mass media," then traditional media and most recently legacy media now include social media, so we are using the term *public media*. To coincide with public media experience, this chapter embraces news and information as well as advertising and incorporates experiences for both in social media.

Opportunities for News and Information

Public media are in transition embracing social media for their own organizations and for news gathering and presenting as well. Both national and local media maintain interactive Web pages; ask to be friended on their Facebook site; and invite participation by requesting information, photos and video be sent directly to them.

Television, in particular, has found that information gathered for a story that won't fit newscasts' time constraints can overflow into their program's online presence. Radio incorporates brief news summaries on the hour within daily programming.

Reporters for print and broadcast go about their news coverage with mobile devices to capture video and sound 24/7. Editors and news personalities also invite submissions from people present as events occur anywhere in the world. Global coverage and immediacy improve the delivery of information worldwide. A "2014 State of the Media Report" by *Vocus* predicted news media will continue to take digital implementation to new heights and to expect continuing experimentation especially in advertising.[1]

Although news content may be richer, that doesn't mean confidence in news media has improved.[2] News from the Internet as a source has increased. However, the increasing presence of traditional media on the Internet needs to be considered in such measurements. One trend, in the USA, at least, is the pursuit of news that resonates with an individual's own set of beliefs. Audience confidence in a medium is tied to the news that reinforces preexisting attitudes based on those beliefs. (See Chapter 7 on persuasion.) In some ways, that is even more of an incentive for public relation information to be sent to public media. Here are some other reasons.

- Public media reach vast audiences. That's why many stories that originate online take off only after traditional media talk about them.
- Public media are instantly recognizable—more than the most popular blog in your area of interest.
- Public media give instant status and credibility.
- Public media outlets also have an Internet presence, an online news source, sometimes streaming and usually offering "overflow" for information that there was not space or time to present. Audiences are encouraged to follow them on Facebook, Twitter and Instagram and offer analyses and opinions in blogs. Media with websites usually get more traffic than even the most popular personal blogs.[3]
- As a result, mass media (public media/traditional media/legacy media) have figured out a way to stay in business by setting up paywalls for content and offering online access to regular subscribers.[4]
- Advertisers too are using social media for "real-time" marketing, as you may know from experience of receiving emails, alerting you to one-day-only sale, and from fund-raisers using "crowd-sourcing" experiences.[5]

Let's examine how public relations practitioners provide information for public media.

News Releases

News releases and other information provided by public relations professionals remain a major source of content for journalists.

News releases differ for newspapers, television and radio. The writing is different, as well as the format.

In terms of length, news releases for newspapers can be longer; those for TV shorter and those for radio usually the shortest. For all three media, the organization originating the release must be identified, along with information on a person or persons who can be contacted for additional information. The date and location where the release originated need to be identified. The main parts of the news release are the lead, supporting information and, sometimes, a summary description of the originating organization. (See Figure 9.1.)

For your release to be noticed, you need a good story. Compelling content well told with good illustrations has a good chance of being noticed. You have to do research in your organization to find good stories and develop a news editor's sense of what will capture attention in the flood of information. You also have to consider how illustrations will back up your information. Yes, even for radio, you can use creative language to trigger images in

Traditional News Release Format   *News releases sent to news media traditionally have been double-spaced. This one is single-spaced, as are most releases that are posted to websites.*

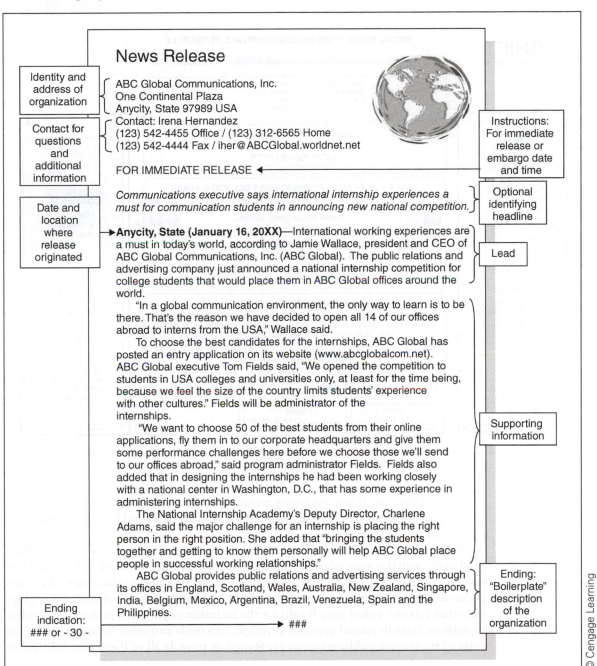

Identity and address of organization

Contact for questions and additional information

Date and location where release originated

Ending indication: ### or - 30 -

News Release

ABC Global Communications, Inc.
One Continental Plaza
Anycity, State 97989 USA
Contact: Irena Hernandez
(123) 542-4455 Office / (123) 312-6565 Home
(123) 542-4444 Fax / iher@ABCGlobal.worldnet.net

FOR IMMEDIATE RELEASE ◄

Communications executive says international internship experiences a must for communication students in announcing new national competition.

►**Anycity, State (January 16, 20XX)**—International working experiences are a must in today's world, according to Jamie Wallace, president and CEO of ABC Global Communications, Inc. (ABC Global). The public relations and advertising company just announced a national internship competition for college students that would place them in ABC Global offices around the world.

"In a global communication environment, the only way to learn is to be there. That's the reason we have decided to open all 14 of our offices abroad to interns from the USA," Wallace said.

To choose the best candidates for the internships, ABC Global has posted an entry application on its website (www.abcglobalcom.net). ABC Global executive Tom Fields said, "We opened the competition to students in USA colleges and universities only, at least for the time being, because we feel the size of the country limits students' experience with other cultures." Fields will be administrator of the internships.

"We want to choose 50 of the best students from their online applications, fly them in to our corporate headquarters and give them some performance challenges here before we choose those we'll send to our offices abroad," said program administrator Fields. Fields also added that in designing the internships he had been working closely with a national center in Washington, D.C., that has some experience in administering internships.

The National Internship Academy's Deputy Director, Charlene Adams, said the major challenge for an internship is placing the right person in the right position. She added that "bringing the students together and getting to know them personally will help ABC Global place people in successful working relationships."

ABC Global provides public relations and advertising services through its offices in England, Scotland, Wales, Australia, New Zealand, Singapore, India, Belgium, Mexico, Argentina, Brazil, Venezuela, Spain and the Philippines.

###

Instructions: For immediate release or embargo date and time

Optional identifying headline

Lead

Supporting information

Ending: "Boilerplate" description of the organization

Social Media Press Release Template   *This template illustrates how a basic news release can be supported by graphics, video, RSS feeds and links to additional information.*

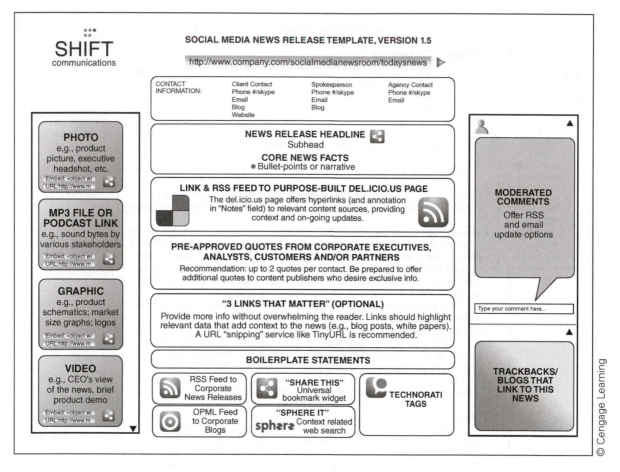

the heads of listeners. If you can supply audio, send it. For television you need audio and video, and for print media you need to send some sample photos and let editors know what else is available to tell the story.

Most journalists prefer email to get story tips. When they respond, be quick to follow up digitally with the news release and illustrations. Send video with sound too when you have it. (See Figure 9.2.) Figure 9.2 provides a guide for a release that meets the needs of journalists and citizen journalists representing newspapers, television, radio, blogs and other Internet-based sites. It calls for the inclusion of photos, a podcast link, video, quotations, links to related previous coverage, RSS feeds and other information. When those of us who are public relations professionals provide all of these possibilities, we offer media representatives a veritable "cafeteria" of information from which they can choose what they need.

If something occurs that needs instant communication and you want wide coverage, such as a comment from a speaker at a program, use Twitter and include a link. Make the tweet as provoking as a headline. Save the shortcut spelling for personal tweets, UR2 and such.

Who Gets News Releases?

Regardless of what your employer or client might think, not everyone wants your story. If you are sending a story by email and not using a distribution service, you might be tempted to send it to a large number of recipients. This is "spamming" and not regarded charitably by most newspeople.

Not only does the Internet make getting the release to the media easier and faster, but there's also more of an opportunity for media exposure, because many media have online sites that are treated and edited differently than their related, traditional sites. Nevertheless, although the news release is probably the most frequently used tool for getting publicity, it also is the most misused. The result is that many news releases are not used at all by media people.

What Is News?

Definitions for news abound, especially in textbooks on beginning reporting and articles about the mass media in society. But for public relations people, a practical definition will do: news is what newspapers and magazines publish and what radio and TV stations broadcast on their news shows. News is *not* what *you* think it is or what the company president thinks it is. Realizing this will take you a long way toward writing effective news releases.

Writing News Releases and Structure

How do you write legitimate news? The answer is simple: if you're writing for print media, prepare the material as you would if you were a reporter working for a newspaper. A news release should be written in the same form and style, following the same punctuation and spelling rules, that the publication you want it to appear in uses.

If you've ever been a reporter, writing a news release should be as easy as writing a straight news story. If you haven't, you need to know something about the methods of writing news.

Approach

Every reporter has a personal method for approaching a story. But all methods should have the same first step: identify the most important thing about the story. In writing a news release, the first step is identical. You must answer the question: what's the most important thing I have to say? Your answer will determine what you should say in the lead.

Lead   The lead (sometimes spelled leed)—the first paragraph or perhaps the first two—is the most important part of the release. You can't write a good release without a good lead, and you can't write a good lead until you've answered the question about what's important.

Deciding what's important sometimes takes a little judgment. *Important* must be construed broadly. What you really want to isolate is the most significant and most interesting aspect of your subject. And you have to keep in mind that news is what is happening now.

For example, if the release is about the opening of a new plant, the most important thing is the fact that the plant is *opening*. The action is the news. But is there something especially interesting about the plant itself? Is it the largest plant of its kind? The first? Will it provide a lot of jobs for the local economy? Once you've decided what's important and also what's interesting, you can write a lead.

The most important thing—in this case, the action—should form the main part of the lead: "The plant is opening." The interesting thing about the story provides an "angle" for the lead: "The first plant of its kind is opening," according to *X* authority.

Sometimes you don't have to look for the most important aspect of the story. For example, it may be the appearance of someone noteworthy. That's your lead. Of course, that might explain why public relations people planning special events always try to get celebrities to attend. The appearance of a well-known person becomes the focus for the news release.

Using the most interesting angle in the first sentence may cause you some problems in constructing the traditional newspaper lead, in which the who-what-when-where-why-how all appear in the first paragraph. Traditional leads are still the rule for most wire-service stories, because the first paragraph is all some newspapers will use. However, that first sentence can get very long if you try to jam in all the essential elements. The rule is often relaxed, so that only two or three of the traditional elements appear in the first sentence, with the others following in the next sentence or two.

If you're writing a release for a newswire service, try to get all of the elements in the first paragraph or, at most, the first two. When writing for newspapers in your area, study the papers' styles. Are all the basic questions usually answered in the first paragraph? Or do a paper's staff writers tend more toward the attention-grabbing lead, with the details of time and place following in the next few paragraphs? The style of the papers you write for should determine the style for your releases. You may find it worthwhile to have several versions of a release to accommodate different media. Some newspapers prefer fact sheets rather than news releases. (See Chapter 8 for information on fact sheets.)

Naturally, if your lead sentence contains the most important and most interesting elements of your story, it probably already gives the who and the what. You can sneak in the when, where and why later—but not too much later. The how usually comes last.

Once you've written a lead, read it over to make sure that it states clearly what the release is about and that it grabs the reader's interest. In other words, the lead must give a quick indication of what the story is about and why it is important. And it must be interesting—both to catch the eye of the editor and to get the attention of the newspaper reader.

Angling the Lead   One lead will not suit all of your needs. The news business is not a situation where "one size fits all," not if you expect your copy to be used. Think about the medium and how the news is going to be used. For an online site, immediacy and significance are the emphasis. Think about the time delay for the daily newspaper. The story may have been online and perhaps in the broadcast news before it can be printed. You need a fresh emphasis for the lead for the daily newspaper that picks up the story. If you are giving the story to a weekly publication, then there's even more to consider about the emphasis.

What will still be "fresh" when the story is published? You must consider that. Think too about the audience. *The Wall Street Journal*'s audience is not the same as that for *USA TODAY* and for local newspapers. What would each publication's audience be most interested in about your story? That's what the editor is thinking about, and so should you.

A local angle is essential in capturing the local newspaper editor's attention. Most newspapers rely on the wire services for nonlocal news, and a release without a local angle is usually dumped. In fact, some editors cite the lack of a local angle as the single most important reason releases aren't used. Be sure to identify the local angle. Make it clear and get it high in the story, preferably in the lead. If you have no local angle to interest a given newspaper, don't bother sending the release.

Timing is critical if your news is going to a newsletter or to a magazine. You must think not only of the audience and that particular audience's interest in your story, but also when the audience is going to be exposed to the story and what that audience may have learned about the news by then. The way you write the story depends on the editor's perception of its newsworthiness. You have to make it timely and interesting even if, in the case of some publications, there is a long delay—perhaps a month or more.

Amplifying the Lead   Once you have a lead that meets all these tests, writing the rest of the release should be easy. Simply amplify each of the elements introduced in the lead, giving all the details. Anticipate the questions that an interested individual might ask about your subject, and answer them in the body of the release.

Use short, concise sentences; short paragraphs; and common, concrete words. Avoid the jargon of your profession. If you must use a technical term, be sure to explain it fully. Above all, avoid editorial comment. Don't try to "sell" something in a news release. A release is not an ad. If a comment is necessary, enclose it in quotation marks and attribute it to a company executive.

Quotations   In using direct quotations, PR news release writers have a great advantage over reporters: they can *create* quotes. A reporter using quotation marks must report exactly what was said. You, however, can take what you've written to the executive you're supposed to be quoting and ask for approval of the words you've attributed to him or her. Write for time-sensitive use. (See Table 9.1.)

Sometimes you won't know what to create for the quote and will have to go directly to the person to see what he or she wants to say. Often the person will scrawl something quickly on a memo pad or ask you to take something from an official statement already prepared on the subject. Such quotes are almost always awkward and lifeless. You will need to recast the words to make them sound like someone said them in conversation.

Length   Knowing how to write a release is important. But knowing when to end the release is equally important. If a release is too long, an editor may decide there isn't time to read it, and into the trash (digital or physical) it will go.

The essential points usually can be covered in one page. Sometimes an important event will call for two or three pages, however, so if you need that much space to cover the subject, use it. But even then write the release so an editor can chop a few paragraphs off the bottom without damaging the story. That's especially important for releases going to news wire services.

Long releases with pages of generally irrelevant material are annoying to journalists. A common example is the release on an executive's promotion, a subject worth only two or three paragraphs. Frequently, however, such releases give pages of company history and information on the company's chief executive, who did nothing more than announce the promotion.

Keep the release brief, at least in most cases. If you believe more information might be needed—statistics or background, for example—attach a fact sheet to the release. A fact sheet lists the basic elements of the institution and the event. (See Chapter 8 for information on fact sheets.)

Ending   It's common practice to use a paragraph summarizing the organization and its operations. Essentials are as follows:

- The company's name
- Location of its headquarters

T A B L E 9 . 1	*News Release Checklist*

1. Is the lead direct and to the point? Does it contain the most important and most interesting aspects of the story?

2. Has the local angle been emphasized?

3. Have who, what, when, where, why and how been answered in the first few paragraphs?

4. Are sentences short, concise? Paragraphs short? Words common and concrete?

5. Has editorial comment been placed in quotation marks and attributed to the appropriate person?

6. Are quotations natural? That is, do they sound as though they could have been spoken?

7. Has newspaper style (AP or other) been followed faithfully throughout the release?

8. Are spelling and punctuation correct?

9. Have all statements of fact been double-checked for accuracy?

10. Has the release been properly prepared in the correct format?

11. Is the release dated? Is the release time indicated?

12. Are names, phone numbers, fax numbers and email addresses for further information included?

13. Has the release been cleared internally?

- Its stock symbol on its listed exchange
- The number and geographic scope of locations
- Information on its commitment to corporate responsibility and giving
- Its website's URL.

News Writing Style

Your most important concern in writing a news release is not length, of course, but getting your message across. To be understood, you must write clearly.

Unfortunately, the writing in most releases is more complex than that in the news stories of a typical daily newspaper. If you write news releases, write as a journalist and write for the editor; *don't* write for your boss. That doesn't mean you should present the facts in such a way that your story makes your company look bad. But it does mean that you leave out *no* pertinent facts, however embarrassing they might be.

When you write a story, it's not enough to conform to newspaper style in level of complexity and in basic story structure. You must follow newspaper style to the finest detail, making sure that every comma and period is in the proper place.

For newspapers, this generally means adhering to the *AP Stylebook*. Most newspapers follow AP style, but many have special style rules that you should know. It's a good practice to ask editors for copies of their stylebooks. You can get a copy of an *AP Stylebook* at a college bookstore, at Amazon.com or by going to the AP online bookstore http://www.apstylebook.com.web. Remember, there are two AP Stylebooks, one for print and the other for broadcast. PR writers need both.

A stylebook will guide you on such matters as when to capitalize, how to abbreviate and what titles to use for specific people. It also describes certain punctuation rules that may differ from common usage. In AP style, for example, there is no comma between a name and Jr. or Sr., as in "Joe Zilch Jr." Some changes are made each year.

AP has adopted *Webster's New World College Dictionary* as the standard guide for spelling. Use the first spelling listed, or the spelling given with a complete definition if a word has more than one entry (like *T-shirt* and *tee shirt*). The *AP Stylebook* lists some exceptions to the dictionary spelling. If a word isn't in *Webster's New World,* check in *Webster's Third New International Dictionary* (and think again about whether you should use the word).

What about grammar? Some writers worry about grammar above all else, combing every line for a possible split infinitive or a *who* that should be a *whom*. Certainly good grammar is important, and awkward, obvious errors like subject-verb disagreements should not be tolerated. But don't worry more about grammar than about communication. Your first concern must be the clarity of the message. If your sentences are clear and understandable, the grammar will take care of itself. (See Chapter 4.)

One more word about style. If you plan to send releases to newspapers other than local dailies—releases about financial news, for example, might go to *The Wall Street Journal*—you should know that these newspapers sometimes have completely different style rules. Some public relations people send the same release to all newspapers, using the style applicable to the majority. You can get away with this, but it never hurts to tailor releases to individual publications.

Electronic Transmission of Releases and Distribution

Having the correct style is particularly important now that many public relations practitioners are emailing draft releases, art and video clips to services that prepare the releases for the media distribution ordered by the client. The advantage of computer transmission is the ability to send the video attachments, pictures and clips with sound/motion, as well as the release targeted by medium and location.

One difficulty with too much reliance on a commercial wire service for public relations news releases is response time when reporters find a story that affects your organization on social media, particularly Twitter. You have to be prepared for immediate, even instant, responses with facts, video and sound bytes.

Numerous companies offer Internet-based services for an organization's use in distributing news releases automatically. Two of the best known national services are PR Newswire and Business Wire.

Types of Releases

Once you know how to write a release, the next question is: Why and when should you write one? The reason for writing releases depends on the type of organization you write for and what its goals are. Frequently the release is just one of many tools a company uses to get publicity.

So when do you write releases? The rule is simple: when you have news, release it. Certain things call for news releases. Generally these fall into one of several basic categories—announcements, created news, spot news, response situations, features, bad news and special matters.

Announcement Releases   These releases can announce the marketing of a new product, the opening of a new plant, the company's latest financial results or a new company policy.

"Created News" Releases   Often, a mere announcement isn't enough to attract much media attention. A company may therefore try to "dress up" the announcement release by making sure something newsworthy is going on. The company might bring a well-known speaker to a company function, for example, or stage a formal ceremony or other event such as a concert or rally. This gives the news release writer something more interesting or newsworthy to say and an opportunity to draw positive attention to the company.

Spot News Releases   Announcement releases can usually be planned. But sometimes things happen without warning. An electric utility's main power plant can be damaged by a storm, for example, raising the prospect of power shortages or higher costs for replacement power. An explosion can occur in a munitions factory; an airplane can be hijacked. Such occurrences are spot news, and when they happen, a news release is in order. You must fill in the facts as they become available, issue news bulletins and follow with a release incorporating as much information as you can provide. (See Chapter 14, Crisis Communication.) A spot news release often has to be followed quickly with a second release, explaining how the initial events were resolved.

Response Releases   Often news about a company reaches the media from sources other than the public relations department. A consumer group may issue a report critical of the company, for instance. The government may announce an investigation into company pricing practices. A research group may publish a major study on your company's industry. When these things happen, reporters call for a response. Companies with good public relations organizations anticipate these calls and have position papers for reference and response releases ready. (See Chapter 6.)

Feature Releases   Not every story in a newspaper or on television involves events that happened yesterday or today. Feature stories about topics of special interest occupy an increasing amount of media time and space. All public relations people can find feature material somewhere in their organizations—something going on in research and development, for example, like a new production process that improves efficiency or helps reduce pollution. Such feature stories can be prepared as ordinary news releases. An alternative, if the publication typically uses it, is a narrative style. The feature lends itself well to a "story-telling" approach. For television, it might even be used in sequences over several days, each telling a different part of the story.

Bad-News Releases   Sometimes events occur that a company would like to keep quiet. The natural tendency in such cases is to issue no news releases at all and hope that the problem will go unnoticed. But more often than not, attempts to keep bad news out of the media backfire. Such stories often involve a company's regulatory agency. Because regulatory agencies are supposed to act in the public's interest, you can be sure the agency will release a report.

Op-ed Articles, Columns, Letters and Photos   Sometimes the information you'd like to see in the newspaper doesn't fit the form of an ordinary news story. That doesn't mean you should forget about it. Most newspapers have special columns or sections that print unusual items, and these are often among the best-read parts of the publication. Individual columnists might make use of readers' information. Or readers might want to write a "guest column" or op-ed piece. (You might want to write one under the byline of your company's chief executive.) Here are some suggestions for writing an op-ed (for the page opposite the editorial page) article:

- **Jump at opportunities.** Link your issue to something happening in the news.
- **Limit the length** to 750 words.
- **Make a single point,** and put it at the top.
- **Use short sentences and paragraphs.**
- **Don't be afraid to use the personal voice.**
- **Avoid jargon.** When in doubt, leave it out.
- **Use the active voice.**

- **Acknowledge the ways in which the opponents are right.**
- **Entertain the reader.**
- **Summarize your argument** in a strong final paragraph.
- **Submit the article to regional and local papers,** not *The New York Times.*[6]

Such items don't always follow the form of an ordinary news release, but they can accomplish much the same thing. Study the newspapers your organization deals with so you'll know what outlets are available.

Photos are among the most effective publicity tools. Photos must tell a story to be worth using. They can accompany a release as an illustration, or they can stand alone. In either case, they must interest the audience. Sometimes single photos and their captions even qualify as what editors call "wild art"—photos that add reader interest to the page. Captions for photos that illustrate a story carry information that relieves the story of some detail. A caption for "wild art" only tells readers what they are looking at and points out the picture's significance, if any.

Some organizations use digitalized photo databases for images that they may want to use for internal or external distribution on their websites or intranets. This makes images—photos and graphics—available to print and broadcast media.

News for Broadcasting

There's something to the adage, "Seeing is believing." Seeing and hearing are influential experiences, even when the information they convey clashes with earlier experiences. As a result, credibility is always at risk in a broadcast world, especially if not much is known about an organization or an individual in the news.

Therefore, the technical aspects of providing information to news media dominate writing for broadcast. You must think of the information in a different way. What portion of the story can you get a person with authority and credibility to say so you can capture at least the audio, if not the video too? What quote from the story makes a good "sound byte"? Radio stations are interested in the sounds of an event: the voice of the mayor reading a proclamation, the president of the electric company explaining a power outage, the hospital director telling about medical care for tornado victims.

On the other hand, if it wiggles, it's TV news, or so the saying goes. And the remark is only half facetious. What in your story "wiggles" or offers movement and color? How can you capture that video in digital format?

Audio and video are far more likely to be used on radio and TV than is a news release telling what happened and what was said. Postings on a website can capture words, photos and sound. Many news stations encourage audience participation by asking for news with instructions on how to send it onsite by mobile devices. For more standard transmission, CDs and DVDs *can* be used but aren't favored because compatibility can be a problem. If a station refers viewers to its website for additional information on a story it is broadcasting, the digital format makes the information you send more accessible.

Consider your competition. Broadcast stations subscribe to news services that provide written broadcast-style stories and ready-to-air, satellite-fed audio and video for the stories.

Additionally, there are packages of whole segments that come ready to air. What chance do you have with your news release unless you take into consideration the elements—audio and video—that constitute broadcast news?

Opportunities for broadcast news releases began improving in 2009 with the economic downturn that caused broadcast media, like print, to lose staffing. Citizen "journalists" often respond, so remember that you need to be there when possible with your input if any breaking news or a special event concerns your organization. Even in a crisis, get on the scene as quickly as possible with your own video production crew. Citizen journalists are already there and sending in "in-time" reports. Expectations of quality and accuracy from the news media are different, though, for professionals such as public relations people.

Facts, Sights and Sounds

Facts are the vital elements of any news story, whether for print media or for broadcast media. Sometimes a formal news release isn't really necessary; the public relations writer can provide the media with a fact sheet, and the reporters can write the story. But with electronic media, facts alone are not enough. Whether you're planning a special event, holding a news conference or dealing with a crisis situation, you must also be aware of sights and sounds. These sights and sounds recorded at a news event are called "actualities."

Announcements

For TV, you'll have to stage some activity to record for an advance announcement of your special event. Thus, after holding the first of what is to be an annual event, you'll need visuals for the next year shot during this year's event—video and digital still photos for the news media to see and for your website. One word of caution: when you use last year's pictures as an advance story, be sure you label the pictures carefully. Sometimes editors get too busy to realize that you are sending a picture of something that already happened—and will inadvertently label last year's pictures as this year's. Protect yourself by labeling the pictures clearly and appropriately.

In preparing for an advance story, you should use previous digital documents of the event, preferably with sound. Radio can pull off the sound for its use. For an annual special event, it is a good idea to have some charts and graphs on PowerPoint that show attendance figures and such from the previous year. Be sure to show dates for the upcoming event. Place and dates for the next event of course will be on your website, and you may have some digitized images from the previous year's event there too. Remember that the quality of these is not always suitable for high-definition television, but TV news directors seeing the pictures on your Web page may want that same image, or one close to it, for their own stories. The moral to this is to shoot events with the idea of capturing close to the same images in multiple formats—expensive, but usually worth it.

When you stage an activity to photograph, don't *simulate* the event. You wouldn't want to perpetrate a hoax. Nor would you want to be wrongly accused of doing so. But feel free to shoot preparations for the event; they qualify as legitimate news. For audio, you can use the people involved—dignitaries, if possible—to make the announcements. Have these announcements recorded by technically qualified people, so they will be of broadcast quality. As the event gets closer, use interviews with some of the participants. Supply radio and television stations with your audiotapes and videotapes. Don't forget media tours. You can have experts appear on broadcast talk shows too in order to generate interest in an upcoming event.

So much for the advance. For actual coverage of your special event by the news media, find out at least three to six weeks in advance what mechanical equipment you will need to supply. You'll have to check out lighting and sound systems and prepare a list of what activities (of news value) will be available for coverage. When the news media arrive, you should be able to offer (again) all the materials prepared in advance, plus an update of what is happening that day and the next. Mention any changes in or corrections of materials sent previously. Supply these in writing when possible. Table 9.2 illustrates a special-event broadcast news release. Give reporters a copy of a brief story in broadcast style. Attach this release to a copy of the longer story prepared for the print media. In reworking the story or in writing their own to fit the coverage, broadcasters will find the longer release helpful.

It's important at special events to have someone at a central location to answer the telephone and respond intelligently to queries from the news media. That person also needs a complete set of materials on the event, a copy of your itinerary and a mobile with pager. In any case, you need to check in every hour or so regardless.

Remember that you will get only a few seconds, maybe a minute, of coverage. Use that time to direct competing media to different facets of the event. That way they will get better stories and you will get better coverage. Be absolutely sure of all your facts, because there will be no time for correction. The news media are not very forgiving of a public relations source that causes them to broadcast an inaccuracy.

Special Events are occasions for announcements and some speeches or presentations by officials or celebrities. The coverage is unpredictable, so some invited audience is part of the planning. Be sure you have news releases prepared as well as special media badges and an abundance of facts sheets.

News Conferences

News conferences are called by public relations directors where some interaction with the news media needs to take place. The situation may be when a major announcement needs to be made by management, or an explanation for an event given, or when a person's time in the area is limited, such as a visiting dignitary or celebrity. The whole point of a news conference is to allow as many questions to be asked as possible. The opportunity to ask questions is especially important if there is a controversy. Remember that members of the audience may be tweeting as the conference is going on. Prepare the presenter at the conference for that probability. It is easy for a presenter to be distracted, and that may cause unfortunate language, facial expressions or gestures.

There are many ways to hold a news conference. The most obvious one is a live news conference where the news media come to a specific site chosen for convenience or for significance, such as the dedication of a building or memorial of national significance. Often news conferences are held by satellite. A live videoconference involves considerable planning and expense, but is worth it because of increased participation from media as it doesn't require travel and does allow instant transmission. This is especially important in situations of global significance. A more low-key news conference is one only by telephone, something

T A B L E 9 . 2	*Format for Broadcast Release for a Special Event*

SPECIAL EVENT LETTERHEAD

Address for Event Sponsor
Phone Number for Event Sponsor
Fax Number for Event Sponsor

Your name, title, phone landline and mobile, fax and email address

Date (and number of release if many are being sent)*

Slug Line (for story identification instead of print release's suggested head)   Time: (in seconds, i.e., :00)

Set story for 60-space line 12-point font (Times
or Times Roman) so copy can be counted and time
estimated. That setting will give about four seconds a
line. For printout use triple space so copy can be easily
marked and read, although few releases will be read "as
is." Keep release to a single page, triple-spaced. Most
releases will be sent electronically, though, so use double
space because the receiver can convert it to triple space.

Give announcers a "lead-in" to your release before
the lead. Tell people what the special event is. Get them
ready for the news.

Keep your lead to between 16 and 20 words so it will
be easy to read. Make the next sentence short to vary the
pattern. Think of the listeners trying to follow the story
they are only hearing. Think of the announcer and show
how to pronounce unusual words or names. Indicate the
ending of the story by ###, 30 or End. To be sure about
timing, read copy and time reading with a stopwatch.

*Most large organizations number their releases, indicating purposes. For a special event, you need to develop
a special series with some reference alpha that tells what the event is or was, like A for Anniversary Celebration;
something that incorporates the date, such as 07 for year; and something that separates the media formats, such as
B for Broadcast. The number might look like A-1B08. The last release in the series might be A-10B08.

Because broadcasters will be rewriting news scripts frequently during the day, include a print release on the
event too so other versions can be created by the station's newswriters. That release would carry a number like A-1P01,
with the P for Print. Of course, a cover letter to the news director will explain why the longer release is being sent.

If the release is going to a television station, be sure that you include information about visuals that are
available, such as videotape with or without sound.

often done by investor relations people to hook up the CEO with a number of securities analysts and economics journalists all at the same time while simultaneously offering listener access to nonparticipants such as shareholders. However, a webinar can be arranged, so participants can see the PowerPoint presentation and ask questions from their computers.

However the conference is held, considerable advance planning is necessary. Ordinarily you'll prepare an announcement, giving the reason for the conference, identifying the person (giving background if he or she is a celebrity) and detailing the time, date and place and who to contact (by name, address and phone number) if there are any questions. Most of these announcements are sent to the broadcast media via email. You may use a distribution service or you may have a news conference about financial matters carried by financial wire services. Occasionally your news conference is significant enough that information about it will be carried on general news broadcast wire services.

If you are calling the conference to give information on a problem or to make an unexpected announcement, be sure you have prepared background materials to give to the media people who attend. A package should contain a printed copy of the announcement, biographical material on the person (if appropriate) and background materials addressing the most significant questions. You should also have prepared a "shooting schedule" for pictures. Be sure to have photographers shooting still images and capturing video and sound. You will need these records for your own reference and might also need to supply them to a medium that had mechanical problems.

Remember too that news conferences are not parties for the media. You might want to have coffee or soft drinks on hand, but save the rest for a festive occasion that's not a working situation. Table 9.3 lists logistical considerations for coverage. Table 9.4 illustrates a representative set of news conference materials.

T A B L E   9 . 3   *Logistical Needs of News Media at News Conferences and Speeches*
Broadcasters come with their own equipment bag, but what they need on site are the following:
A good microphone for the speakers and a reliable sound system in a room with good acoustics and lighting.
A mult box with enough sound system connections for the reporters to plug into to capture the audio.
Additional multi-extension cords so reporters can connect their recorders and keep them with them instead of having to leave them near the podium.
Industrial extension cords for extra lights and sufficient electrical outlets.
A public address mike on a podium that is large enough to accommodate reporters' mikes.
Telephones with jacks for reporters to file from the scene. (The reporter can feed audio from an audio recorder directly into the phone circuits.)
Internet connections would help those using digital/computer gear.
Plenty of duct tape to tape down all of the wires to keep people from tripping over them. Tape your own wires before the event, but have tape and scissors available for reporters who need to tape their own connections in a hurry.
Pens, pencils and pads of paper are always useful, even though most will be using laptops.
Be sure the doors to the room open wide enough for larger pieces of equipment to be brought in easily, and have technical staff of your own available to help with blown fuses, fuzzy sound systems, contrary mikes and such.
Crews need a place to park, especially if they are bringing a live truck and will broadcast or transmit from the scene.
Easily accessible water fountains and restrooms are always appreciated.

TABLE 9.4	*Reference Materials for Broadcast Media*

- **News release giving basic messages or statements of conference as anticipated.**
  Generally announcements are made at news conferences, but there are responses to questions that of course can't be anticipated.

- **Biographies of all principals involved in news conference.**
  Usually only one or two people are involved in the newsmaking part of the news conference. For example, it may be a major appointment by a government official like the president, governor or mayor, or a university announcement of a new athletic coach.

- **Background information on the situation or the event.**
  For example, the news conference may be to announce an agreement that resolves a conflict. Be sure that the presentation materials are balanced and fair. This might even be a joint news conference, so materials must be shared and coordinated.

- **Who to call for additional information if it is needed when the story is prepared in the newsroom.**
  Be sure email addresses are available, as well as the website address.

- **Fact sheet on the event or situation.**
  For events, the details of the event can be given; for appointments, the names and dates of previous holders of the office can be useful to a reporter.

Broadcast News Releases

Like those for print media, news releases for broadcast media are either advance stories about something soon to occur or stories explaining what has occurred or what is going on. Although no news media personnel will get excited about doing your promotion for you, many will use well-prepared advance stories if the event has enough news value. News releases on upcoming events should be extremely brief for the broadcast media—no more than two or three short paragraphs. However, you should send along your longer print-media version, a fact sheet and (when appropriate) a brochure or printed program. If the event is likely to have regional interest, send a courtesy copy of the news release to the broadcast wire services, just to alert them to an event their reporters might be interested in. Be sure to identify the courtesy copy as such when the release is sent electronically.

When you are sending your materials by email, remember to send contact information in your message with the releases, fact sheets, graphics and video clips each as separate attachments because the receiver may encounter problems opening the files or downloading them.

Electronic transmission of messages, images and sound has changed and continues to change the delivery of information to broadcast media. Direct feeds from satellites are common. Stations can take broadcast-quality interviews by phone. However, the broadcast medium, be it a network or a station, has to want to receive your information. The way you accomplish that is by building a history of credibility and reliability for providing timely and accurate material of broadcast quality.

For stations in your immediate area, it's a good idea to build your reputation through direct in-person contact. You want to develop working professional relationships with

FIGURE 9.3

Model Broadcast News Tip Sheet

A Compelling Headline

What: Don't just tell what is happening; give some descriptions of irresistible visual and/or audio possibilities.

When: Broadcasters live by the clock. Tell precisely when something is occurring, the date, day of the week, time of day for openings/closings and best time to catch the action.

Where: Be very specific about location and access. Give tested directions so no one is confused or lost. Give your mobile phone contact number should someone get lost *en route*.

Who: Who is sponsoring this event and why and how significant this is to the broadcast audience because that's who matters, not you and your organization.

Contact Information: Your name, email address, organization's physical address and phone numbers including your office, mobile (cell) and home numbers.

© Cengage Learning

broadcast people so they know who you are when you contact them. That's very important now that broadcast stations, especially in metropolitan areas, are security conscious and not open to "drop-in" visits from strangers. Otherwise you literally can't get past the front door. Media advisories and tip sheets help build relationships and pique media interest. (See Figure 9.3.)

Timeliness is a problem for stories about events that have already happened. Nevertheless, the broadcast media and freelancers who supply stories to them will cover most events of any significance—even news on past events. If you are supplying audio and visual materials, be sure you prepare all materials to meet media deadlines and mechanical requirements. The quickest is digital. If for some reason, perhaps a crisis, you are delivering material directly to local stations, call the news directors to let them know that the material is coming, and hand-deliver the package. If the event was a speech/announcement, attach a complete copy to the brief release. You can file a courtesy copy with the wire service if the speech has regional interest—though, again, the wire services often provide their own coverage or get it from media subscribers.

For television, you can offer graphs and charts to help explain the event; for radio, you can offer broadcasters a phone interview to flesh out their story and give it a sense of immediacy. In the latter instance, be sure you have all the facts and figures within easy reach for the phone interview. Be aware that your interview will be edited. Still, if you are prepared, editors won't have to cut out dead air—gaps of silence—while you search for a fact.

Broadcast News Writing Style

The basic difference between writing for broadcast media and writing for print media is that copy for the former must appeal to the ear. (In television and video, of course, the visuals must capture the eye.) Copy must command attention through sound and word symbolism. The words must be clear enough to be understandable the first time through. The listener will not have a chance to review what is said. In radio, the listener can't reread a sentence to understand what it meant and can't go back to the one preceding it to figure out the sequence of ideas. Each offering is a one-time-only presentation. To compensate for the lack of review opportunity, broadcast writers first tell listeners (and viewers) what they are going to tell them, alerting them to the content by calling up frames of reference. Then they present the content. Finally, in the summary, they again tell the listener what the message was. It takes a skillful writer to prepare material in this way without sounding redundant. As the writer follows this sequence, keep the time element in mind. Clarity and brevity are both important.

Because broadcast media are intimate, their style is conversational. Each listener or viewer experiences the broadcast media as an individual and responds personally. The relaxed style means that the leads, or first paragraphs, in broadcast stories, including news stories, are "soft." That is, the listener is introduced to the story before hearing it.

One type of soft lead is called a "throwaway": "Vacationers driving around the country this summer are likely to find lots of detours. The American Automobile Association says road repairs and construction are going on all over the nation." Another soft lead is the "angle" lead that hooks your attention: "Planning to drive your car on your vacation this year? Get ready for lots of detours. The American Automobile Association says road repairs and construction are going on all over the nation." If one news story is related to another, a soft lead may be used to introduce both of them: "Vacationers planning to drive their cars this summer are likely to have some unexpected problems. Road repairs and construction have put detour signs up all over the nation. The longer routes may cause motorists to run out of gas because many small service stations in outlying areas have closed during the last year. New highways bypassing towns have closed stations, and storms are the cause of the road repairs." (The story goes on to say that the American Automobile Association will help car travelers plan trips to find out about detours in advance, and that the major oil companies are offering credit card holders lists of service stations open along interstate, state and rural roads.)

We can make some other generalizations about broadcast writing. Because the tone is conversational, for instance, sentences are sometimes incomplete. We talk that way, so in broadcast journalism, it's acceptable to write that way. Sentence length and structure are also governed by special rules. In broadcast writing, sentences are kept short in defer-ence to both the announcer (who has a limited amount of breath) and the listener (whose attention span shouldn't be taxed). For the same reason, subjects and verbs are kept close together. Normally, sentences should not begin with prepositional phrases; the basic infor-mation should be conveyed first. "According to a report from the Mason County Sheriff's office today, vacationers driving through are likely to find fewer service stations than last year." By the time listeners decide that fewer service stations might be important to them, the "Mason County" is lost to all but the most attentive among them.

Broadcast writers should avoid two peculiarities of newspaper style—sometimes called "journalese"—in preparing broadcast copy. One is inverted sentence structure, where the statement precedes the attribution: " 'Victims of the Mississippi tornado are all back in permanent housing,' said Scott Smith, director of emergency disaster relief."

This sentence illustrates what not to do in writing broadcast copy. Because broadcast audiences may not be attending to the first part of the sentence, information should be presented as it would probably be spoken in conversation: "The director of emergency disaster relief said that all victims of the Mississippi tornado are now back in permanent housing." The name of the director is not important to the story, so his title alone is used. If the story were a long one in which Smith was quoted, his name would be used, but he would be identified in a separate sentence: "Scott Smith is the director of emergency disaster relief."

The second newspaper-style characteristic to avoid in broadcast writing is the identification of subjects by age, job title and such. In newspapers, this information usually follows the name and is set off by commas. But what is efficient in newspaper copy becomes cumbersome when read on the air. Again, the name of an individual is often unimportant; title identification is enough.

Here is a typical print story:

> Vacationers traveling by car may be encountering an unusual number of detours this summer, according to James R. Ragland, manager of the Dixon American Automobile Association office.
>
> Storm damage all over the nation has resulted in more than the usual amount of road repair, and the severe winter also put a number of highway projects behind schedule, Ragland said. The result is detours in almost every state.
>
> AAA offices are trying to help motorists plan trips to at least be able to predict delays, Ragland said.
>
> The service is free to AAA members, and there's a nominal charge for nonmembers, according to Ragland. The Dixon AAA office is in the Chamber of Commerce Building at Fifth and Ledbetter.

Here is a broadcast version (30 seconds long) of the same story:

> That severe winter the nation had is going to make summer vacations by car more difficult than usual, the American Automobile Association says.
>
> Triple A is offering travelers plans marked with all of the detours for road repairs and construction. Triple A's Dixon manager says the plans are free to members, but available to nonmembers for a nominal fee.

An admonition to keep it short but clear comes from broadcaster and academician Dr. Suzanne Huffman: "Most radio news stories on commercial stations are *very* short. As a writer, think in terms of 30 seconds for each story; that's about five sentences long. A story that runs 35 seconds will raise an eyebrow at the editor's desk. Write the bare minimum you need. You have to be clear, but you have to be concise and short."[7]

Physical Preparation

Unlike copy for print media, all broadcast copy is triple spaced and written on one side of the page. Some broadcast news departments prefer that copy be typed in all caps (capital letters); others prefer the standard combination of uppercase and lowercase letters. Most public relations people supplying information to the broadcast news media use caps and lowercase. For radio, select font size and margins to produce a 60-space line, to give an average of 10 words per line. Most announcers read at a rate of about 15 of these lines per minute. So in radio news, one typed line takes about four seconds to read. A 30-second story is seven to eight lines long. (See the AAA story.)

The audio copy for a TV script goes on the right side of the page, opposite the video instructions. When you are writing for television and using only half the page (the audio side), set your margins to yield about six words to the line, or about 21 lines per minute at an average reading speed—the equivalent of about two seconds per line. Thus, a 30-second TV story is about 15 of these lines.

Much of the format for a broadcast release is similar to that of print copy. Appearing in the upper-left corner of the first page of each story is a slug line—the words identifying the story—the date, the name of the organization submitting the information, your name and phone numbers where you can be reached day or night. On the following pages, all you need are the page number, slug line (story identification) and your last name. The story's end is marked by the traditional "30," and "more" goes at the bottom of each page in the story except the last. Never break a paragraph at the bottom of a page.

To facilitate reading by announcers, don't break words at the end of lines either and don't split sentences between pages. If a word or name is difficult to pronounce, give the proper pronunciation in parentheses beside it *each* time it appears. The announcer should not have to go back and look for your previous instructions. Do not use diacritical markings you find in dictionaries to indicate the proper pronunciation. Use popular phonetics like those the newsmagazines employ (SHEE-fur for Schieffer, for example).

Remember, the audience can't see punctuation marks. These exist only to help the announcer interpret the copy. Don't use them unless they serve this purpose. And don't use colons, semicolons, percentage signs, dollar signs, fractions, ampersands and other exotica. Just use commas, periods, question marks, dots, dashes and quotation marks. Use quotation marks only when repeating the exact words is essential. It is better to rephrase a quote into indirect statements. If you feel that a quote is necessary, precede it with something like, "In his words," or "What she asked for was" or "The statement read."

Use hyphens only when you want the letters to be spelled out individually, as in Y-W-C-A, as opposed to being read as a word, as in *NASA*. Don't use abbreviations unless you want them read on the air as abbreviations. Exceptions are such titles as Dr. and parts of names like *St.* Louis. If you don't know whether to write a word out or abbreviate it, write it out.

Numbers are difficult to follow when they're heard but not seen, so avoid using them as much as possible. Throughout this book, we preach the importance of using AP style. Here is where we'll vary somewhat. If the reporter is used to getting copy from you, then use the *AP Broadcast Manual's* instructions for numerals. It's a bit different from the AP print in that the rule of spelling out numbers one to ten is now one through eleven. AP broadcast style calls for using Arabic numerals for 12 through 999. Above that AP broadcast style calls for using what is more conversational, such as two thousand dollars but 12-hundred dollars. However, if you are sending copy to broadcasters unfamiliar with you as a news source, use the AP broadcast style, but in parenthesis spell out the numbers. Announcers don't read anything in parenthesis, and it can be marked through in the copy during the editing process or deleted if the copy is going electronically. You must be absolutely sure there is no error in delivering numbers to the news media. It's seldom a risk in print, but can be a real hazard in broadcast copy. Also, to prevent errors, don't use a.m. or p.m. with times of the day; announcers wouldn't read the letters anyway.

Write, for example, "this morning" or "tomorrow night." However, because your copy is going to the news media for handling, put dates in parentheses beside the weekday designation—Monday (May 1). When the copy is processed for reading on the air, that information will be omitted. But writing it in will prevent errors. Another expression to avoid when reading numbers is per, as in "miles per hour." Instead, use "miles an hour."

In reporting names and titles, use the title before the name, and avoid beginning a sentence with a name, especially if it is unfamiliar. If the title is long and cumbersome, break it up or shorten it. You generally do not use a person's middle initial in speech, so avoid using middle initials in broadcast copy unless they are important for clarification and identification or unless they are commonly used with the names in question. On second reference use the surname only, except when you are referring to the president of the USA or a member of the clergy. Clergy retains their titles on second reference—Rabbi Brown, for instance.

> *Print version*: Madison A. Clark, bishop coadjutor for the Episcopal Diocese of Dixon, today announced that $50,000 had been raised for the World Famine Relief project. The funds will be sent to agencies designated to purchase and distribute food in Africa, Bishop Clark said. There are three such agencies—the American Red Cross, the National Council of Churches and CARE.
>
> *Rewritten:* Dixon's Episcopal Diocese has raised $50,000 (fifty thousand dollars) for the World Famine Relief project. The announcement came today from Bishop Madison Clark. Bishop Clark said the money will be sent to three agencies designated to purchase and distribute food in Africa.

Watch for and clarify obscurities. Be very careful about using pronouns. Listeners have trouble following the references. If you are dealing with specialized jargon, translate it. Use words and terms the audience will understand and relate to. If you are writing about little-known groups, explain who they are and what they do. Don't assume the audience will know or understand. And do use contractions, like don't, just as you do in speech. Use the active voice. It gives life and movement to your writing. Keep your verbs in the present tense when possible because broadcast media expect to offer timely information. When your audience's language is not English, provide a translated version of your information. (See Figure 9.4 and a still photo of the use of a wedding chapel at Texas Christian University.)

Structural Considerations

Broadcast story leads differ from print leads, in which the who, what, when, where, why and how are often all crammed into the first paragraph. This burst of information can be confusing for the listener and difficult for the announcer to read. When you are preparing your broadcast story, first alert listeners to what you are going to discuss, getting their attention with something that is important to them. Using a summary statement is a good way to get into the story. Then you can give the essentials. Make your sentences simple; don't use long clauses at the beginning or end or between the subject and verb. As you develop the story, look for ways to connect paragraphs with transitions that allow the story to emerge and flow logically. Keep the listener and the announcer in mind, and think about how each will be able to handle the words you write.

FIGURE 9.4

Script Template

TCU NEWS NOW

SLUG:	*0307_CB_RobertCarr*
LENGTH:	1:30
REPORTER:	Caressa Bateman

Anchor intro	TCU's Robert Carr Chapel is being recognized for hosting weddings. Caressa Bateman explains why this venue is so popular.
NAT/S OPEN	Nats
VO: Flowers, dresses, chapel Super: Caressa Bateman REPORTING TCU News Now	Flower arrangements, wedding dresses, cakes and venues are all features of a wedding. One venue, Robert Carr Chapel, was nominated as the best ceremony venue in Dallas-Fort Worth.
SOT: *Brittney Luby, Robert Carr Chapel Events Coordinator*	"It was very special for us."
VO: Luby	Brittney Luby said the nomination came from the American Association of Certified Wedding Planners. Area wedding planners chose the nominees.
SOT: *Brittney Luby, Robert Carr Chapel Events Coordinator*	"I have a lot of staff and so the nomination is a testament to just the hard work and motivation that I think they all have to put on really good weddings here."
VO: Aisle	Luby said Robert Carr's long aisle draws a lot of couples to the Chapel to host their weddings because brides can experience the traditional long walk down the aisle with their fathers.
VO: Kendall Decorations	For bride-to-be Kendall Worn, TCU's holiday spirit led her and her future husband to pick Robert Carr Chapel to host their wedding.
SOT: *Kendall Worn, Bride-to-be at RCC*	"We're getting married in the winter time so everything is going to be lit up through TCU's campus and we just thought this met our needs and was a perfect place for a winter wedding."
SOT: *Stand Up* *Caressa Bateman* *TCU News Now*	"Robert Carr Chapel has been hosting weddings for nearly six decades and with occupancy set at about 300 people, Luby said it's the perfect place for both small and large parties to host weddings. I'm Caressa Bateman, TCU News Now."
ANCHOR TAG	For more information about weddings at Robert Carr Chapel, you can check out their website online at www.chapel.tcu.edu.

FIGURE 9.4   (*Continued*)

The Schieffer School of Journalism

Broadcast wire stories undergo much more reworking than newspaper wire stories, because the broadcast wire serves stations that use news directly from the wire on an hourly basis. One story, repeated hour after hour, can get dull if the audience remains the same—as in offices that have piped-in radio. Research can flesh out a breaking story both to give it depth and to keep the sparse facts from getting monotonous. Broadcast leads vary dramatically from print leads. The lead-in sentence is designed to capture attention. The listener needs to know what the story is about because if it is something that is important to them, they may want to pay more careful attention. Broadcast stories more often follow a narrative format because that's the way we are accustomed to talking and sharing information. Use of the active voice conveys immediacy and importance to the story. Personalizing the story helps too, and more and more newspapers are using this format. Find a person as an example of the issue or effect and start with his or her perspective. Follow with expert information and understandable statistics. Then close with a summary that goes back to the individual used as an illustration, showing the consequences or choices for that person. Remember this when you furnish actualities.

Supplying Pictures and Sound

When you supply actualities in any way other than digitally, you also need to furnish a script. Attach it firmly to the CD/DVD or Video news releases (VNR). Identify the script with exactly the same title that appears on the disk, and add your name, your institution's name and the address and phone numbers where you can be reached day and night. Also give an email address. Broadcasters don't have time to play every submission they get to see what is there. Of course, if they decide the story might be used, they will preview the story, and they are also likely to edit it if they schedule it to run. The station will also write a lead-in to the tape, so it's a good idea to supply additional information—for example, a copy of the news release covering the occasion for making the tape. Lead-ins identify speakers and action without detailing the content of the tape.

As evidence mounts that most people depend primarily on the broadcast media for news, organizations must focus their attention on getting their information into the broadcast media. If one reporter picks up on a story that is broadcast, the chances of its being used by other broadcast media is good.

News Features

The best thing that can happen to you is that a news station decides to do a feature story on your organization because of something special about it. Perhaps it is an employee who has an unusual job in the organization or does something in his or her own time that is creative and contributes to the community—one who makes quilts for a homeless shelter, for example. Or perhaps someone whose hobby has won national or international attention, such as someone who trains dogs for rescue or health support by identifying the onset of a medical problem. Your organization is not the focus of the story, but gains attention not only through the individual but also for what that person working there says about the organization. Maybe it's not an employee, but a volunteer who is a professional chef but volunteers to give food preparation sessions for low-income families.

Study the media for reporters who cover these sorts of stories. Remember that print and broadcast reporters look for good stories in what is called in the trade "enterprise journalism." Some reporters are free-lancers, so look beyond staff bylines.

An innovative PR person pitches stories to writers who consistently get placement in media. They are looking for stories and you are looking for exposure.

Digital Delivery and Use

Video content is generally delivered to newsrooms digitally. This includes VNRs and other public relations materials such as Satellite Media Tours (SMTs). All of the materials can be sent digitally, including scripts, videos, graphics and supplemental story content as well as advisories. The delivery is not over the Internet because the results may or may not be of broadcast quality. But other digital news delivery systems do work. Reporters can take the digitally delivered material directly from the station's server to an edit system or video recorder.

Advantages of digital delivery are the speed of the system and the ability of the reporters to edit in supplementary material such as "B" roll and more information to update a story and make it unique to the station's newscast. With SMT delivery, much more in-depth material is available to the reporters to flesh out stories they are working on, or for them to develop a feature from the material sent.

Digital material can also be sent to special publics. "Broadcast public relations has only recently surfaced as a regularly used term … but it has yet to achieve a universal understanding or recognized definition," says Kelli B. Newman. She notes that the varied menu of distribution outlets generated by technology, such as the video iPod, "places a greater priority on content and the strategies used to create it. So, whether webcasting, podcasting, vodcasting, blogging or televising, broadcast public relations delivers the greatest value when defined as a subspecialty of our profession that applies multidimensional content strategies to its productions."[8]

PR As Broadcast News Suppliers

VNRs

Video news releases (VNRs) are increasingly accepted by news directors, especially in the areas of science stories and health and medical news. This may be the only way the broadcast media can get access to the story because of proprietary information in the case of drug companies, the complexity of the material in science research presentations or the need to protect patients' rights in some medical stories.

Writing a VNR means writing a script, just as a news team might write it if the news team had access to the information in advance of the event. Of course, what can happen is that broadcast news teams cover an event with reporters, photographers and technical crews. Then they go back to the station, look at and listen to what they were able to capture and write a script describing what is usable from the audio and video that they got. With staff reductions at both TV and radio, what you may have is a reporter with equipment who will get visuals and sound, add information then send the material directly to the station for broadcast and for the station's website use.

In writing a VNR, the public relations writer has control of the situation. The script is written with the information in place and the visuals and sound indicated. Then the video is photographed and recorded. It is edited to a usable news segment, usually 30 seconds, but it may be longer. The outtakes are kept, and additional footage or a "B" roll usually is shot, as well as some additional actualities as long as the production studio is leased for the VNR.

Remember that your VNRs are likely to be 30 seconds, maybe a minute. A long piece is 3 minutes. If the VNR is a news feature, it could run between 5 and 20 minutes. Although you will be using professional producers, some things you need to watch for in viewing the final piece are suggested by videotape editor Eric Alkire (alkire@worldnet.att.net). Look for useless cutaways and sound breaks, because these interrupt the flow of the story. The story should flow and any break, audio or video, should contribute to, not distract from, the story. Watch for flash frames or muddy audio cuts. Most importantly, Alkire advises, watch objectively and ask if the story gets told and the video is watchable.[9]

Additional suggestions come from Canadian public relations professional David Eisenstadt who warns about being sure that the VNR is really news and not commercial, that the production is simple, not glitzy, so that it fits most stations' formats and that you use sound. Additionally, you need to know whether to send VHS or BETA. Although stations have both, one is usually preferred, usually BETA.[10]

Most broadcasters indicate that they prefer to get the VNR by satellite and want to be notified that it is coming by fax or phone.[11]

Although some news directors still worry about lack of flexibility in adjusting the story to their format, time frame and audience, most have figured out a way to let audiences know that the information comes from a public relations source by a simple credit line. Some VNR productions help by superimposing the words "footage supplied by XXX" over footage of a new product or over a simulation of a scientific breakthrough.

The acknowledgment of the source for VNRs has posed an ethical problem. (See Chapter 2.) However, many VNR producers, other producers and distributors now subscribe to a VNR Code of Practice developed in 1992 by the Public Relations Service Council.[12]

News on Call

Some organizations offer broadcast-quality information and actualities (visual or audio) on call either through a special number or a toll-free line.

The information is changed frequently during the day so that broadcast news stories can be updated with fresh actualities.

Although websites continue to be an excellent source of information updates and certainly a good place for gathering background information, the audio, when there is any, like the pictures, may not be of broadcast quality. However, in designing your Web pages, don't forget that broadcast media will be using them, so give phone contact numbers on your news pages and on your home page. The assumption of many website designers is that the contact will be made by computer. With broadcast media, that is less likely if what is needed is an actuality, not just information, although the show's producers can go directly to the site if the broadcast quality for sound and video in news clips is there.

Talk Shows

At the national level, public relations people may work directly through the radio or television show's producers, or they may use a national placement agency. These agencies have the contacts, and the reputation with the television producers, for "delivering." What producers don't want is a "no-show," or someone who appears in the studio but really is not prepared to give an interview that pulls audience response, either in ratings or phone calls and emails, if it is a call-in show.

If the show is local, occasionally the public relations person is the talk-show guest, but this really is not greeted with much enthusiasm by the broadcasters. Try to find someone who will capture the attention of not only the broadcaster but also the audience. Shows of this nature are not as fluid as they appear. Generally, they are structured by the host in a brief period before the show is aired.

You'll need to prepare certain materials for such an event. The show's host needs to have a backgrounder or fact sheet on the institution that the individual represents, the event or occasion for the attention and biographical information on the person being interviewed. All of this information must be very brief and in a form the show's host can take on the air—triple spaced on sheets of paper heavy enough not to rattle or preferably in digital form so it can be displayed for the host to read on a screen. You can take it on a thumb drive. The guest should have in mind all the information he or she is going to present. To prepare mentally and to keep facts and figures fresh, the guest usually requires briefing sessions the day before and again just before airtime. The guest needs to alert the host to information that should be presented for the benefit of the listening audience. If the talk show is on television, take along materials that can be shown physically, if not on a video. Remember the wiggle.

Handling Messages During Crises

A crisis, such as a plant fire or hostage situation, is a disorganized combination of a special event and a news conference. The media will need information that even you as an insider will have difficulty getting. Nevertheless, getting and supplying that information is the most important service you can perform. (See Chapter 14.) Crises involve considerable use of social media on the organization's part and on that of reporters covering the event. As speakers will be offering information, reporters will be tweeting. Think in terms of "tweets" in the coverage and offer your own. (See Chapter 14.)

Advertising Now in the Mix

Contrary to what you might suppose, one of the greatest challenges you might have as a PR writer is crafting advertising messages. You will have more rigid constraints on time, space and images. A close parallel is writing poetry, but that doesn't have to be goal-oriented to achieve measurable results. Writing advertising copy does, and ad copy is one kind of writing you will be doing.

What kind of messages might these be? Ads that PR people prepare are different from the direct sales advertising for products and services generally prepared by advertising agencies. You may be called on to create copy for catalogs, especially promotional ones, usually seasonal. Most promotional materials, though, may be prepared by PR firms or ad agencies. As a PR writer you are in charge of selling ideas and managing public perception of an organization, its image and reputation.

Advertising involves both electronic and print media. Electronic ads include promotional commercials, public policy ads that are often called infomercials and entire sponsored programs offering cooking, financial or other problem-solving advice. Electronic ads may also appear in space controlled by the organization such as its website or its blogs. It also may be placement in social media, the "pop-up" ads that appear when you get your email, for example, although some of these may be product or sales oriented.

Ads for print media include billboards, posters, public policy ads about issues of concern to the organization (advertorials), corporate image/institutional identity ads and house ads—ads that appear in publications an organization prints and distributes. Some ads look like editorial features except for the identifying "paid advertising." These are covered in Chapter 12 in information on brochures, which they closely resemble.

You will be writing Public Service Announcements (PSAs). Although these are written like advertising, PSAs are not in paid for time or space. While you can control the content, you have no control over their use, either in electronic or print media. (See Chapter 8 on Media Kits for PSAs.)

Three types of ads that PR writers are likely to be called on to write are house ads, issue ads, program ads and a mix of information and advertising—the special section.

FIGURE 9.5

Image ad for real estate prepared for program copy in the Cliburn Concert Series at Bass Hall in Fort Worth, Texas.

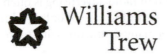

B sharp when selling your flat.

Williams Trew | Sotheby's
INTERNATIONAL REALTY

3707 Camp Bowie Blvd.   Possum Kingdom   2821 S.Hulen Street
www.williamstrew.com | **817.732.8400** | www.wtlakefront.com

Advertising as a Persuasive Force

Many people believe that advertising can make people do something or think something. If that were true, public relations professionals could make publics accept ideas they might otherwise reject. But advertising does not work that way. The power of advertising is limited to persuasion. It cannot coerce. Used skillfully, advertising may stimulate in an audience a predisposition to buy a product, use a service or accept an idea.

Appeal

The key element in a successful ad is the relevance of the appeal it has for the receiver of the message. This appeal should be as direct as possible. In writing ads, don't leave the appeal to inference. Spell it out. An appeal can be emotional, rational or a combination of the two. For example, mobile apps may alert you to come into a store, movie house, restaurant or other enterprise as you walk by. That appeal is based on a programmed knowledge of who you are and what you usually do.

Emotional appeals tug at the heart. They suggest that the receiver can benefit—become happier, healthier, sexier, more attractive, more successful or richer in any number of other qualities if he or she behaves in a specific way. The number of emotional appeals open to the ad writer seems to be infinite. See the catalog ads in Figure 9.6. This company is known for its copy appeals and its art.

Rational appeals, on the other hand, appeal to the receiver's reason. Such appeals are likely to be based on economy, durability, profit, efficiency and performance, among others.

Combination appeals use emotion first to get people to pay attention and then use rational appeals once the receivers are interested in the copy. The copy will usually close by returning to an appeal to the heart.

One reason to use a media mix is the quality of attention these appeals get in various media. A television or magazine ad is likely to get undivided attention, once it captures attention. This is usually the case too with other print media, including newspapers, but less true of radio advertising because attention to radio advertising is often divided by driving demands, passengers or mobile phone use. In the case of online advertising, whether it be websites or social media, there are too many distractions due to moving images and a crowded competitive field.

Positioning

A particular appeal works in concert with the marketing idea of "positioning the product." The writer expresses the appeal creatively in an attempt to differentiate a product from direct competitor by carving out a special niche for the advertiser in the minds of the potential customers.

This principle of positioning was aptly applied when a major city wanted to pass an enormous bond program to rebuild and improve an extensive portion of one of its oldest freeways. Each time they were asked, voters denied the bonds. On its last try, the city launched a "safety bond" program to finance the project. Positioning it as a safety project focused attention on its benefit rather than on its cost. The issue passed by a comfortable margin. Cause-related nonprofit organizations can learn from this to focus on the solutions, not on the problems.

Slogans matter. Slogans reinforce branding because they aid identification. One mistake often made is changing a slogan because the management is tired of it. A slogan encourages employees and keeps everyone in the organization focused on the mission. Slogans comfort customers and give them a reason to choose the product, service or organization. Even children recognize a slogan their parents, and probably grandparents, grew up with: "Melts in your mouth. Not in your hand." The two Ms "Melt and Mouth" reinforce the product's name: M&M.

Positioning is fundamental to **branding** for an institution. Branding is an effort to create instant identification of the organization and association with what it does and is. In that respect, the repetitive appearance of the brand in the news media appears to enhance brand value, more probably it is brand recognition. Media appearance, though, can be in news or advertising, and this complicates measurements of effect.

Advertising bought for the idea/product/institution presents a favorable perspective because the message is controlled, and it enforces recognition due to planned exposure—purchased time or space. Exposure in the news media on the editorial side can put the brand in a positive or negative light. Political advertising by opponents often is negative because the idea is to damage the other side's "brand."

Behavior

Understanding what people think and do in different parts of society is critical to developing credible advertising. Good advertising writers understand that there may be a little bit (and perhaps a lot) of snobbery in all of us, because we like to relate to others and have others relate to us.

Behaviorists spend a lot of time trying to understand our reference groups—organizations to which we belong or want to belong. We all want the comfort of belonging, of being accepted. For this reason, friends and family are important to us, and we seek their approval.

A proliferation of social media has resulted in an acceleration of the spread of information and the reinforcement of opinions, both positive and negative about an organization's products, services, actions, consumer experiences and such. The result is the emergence of unanticipated and previously unidentified leaders.

We are all influenced by opinion leaders, but not the same ones. Different segments of society have different opinion leaders, and each of us reacts to those leaders differently based on our experiences, education and our own personality. For example, authoritarian types are more vulnerable to leaders who have status and authority.

If you are getting the idea that people don't respond rationally to a lot of advertising copy, you are right. Most of the decisions we make are based on emotion, not reason. That is why good advertising copy is a complex blend of information (facts) and appeal (emotion).

One reason why you want to use visuals in media is that 90 percent of all the information our brain gets is visual. Furthermore, the brain processes visuals faster than text—60,000 times faster. Forty percent, almost half of your audience, in any medium, responds better to visuals than text.[13]

Special sections are a combination of ads from those connected to the theme and corresponding copy, usually feature stories, about the advertisers. Contacts for these special sections are usually based on the size of the ad purchased being the base for the amount of editorial copy. Most special sections have themes that allow for the maximum number of possible advertisers. For example, a boat show will include craft from different companies that sell them, and probably some from the companies that build the boats. You can think of all the other possible advertisers: motors, sails, interiors, safety equipment, related sporting gear and so on.

Special sections may be the creation of newspaper advertising departments that choose something like Community Health Suppliers and seek support from hospitals, physicians in specialist practices, pharmacies, health units that are stand-alone operations or units in grocery stores.

However a special section can be the idea of a mall, a single professional organization such as a bank or university or a prominent retailer, usually to celebrate an historic moment in its history or an imaginative creative conception. For example, on the front page of their special section, jeweler Bachendorf's used an invitation to what it called its "Golden Angel Event" for one Saturday afternoon. Captions on the three photos at the top pull a reader into the story: One caption praising the precision of Wellendorff products and their prestigious collaboration read: "The Long History of the Bock Family From Devastation in Dachau to Eminence in Dallas." Another caption picked up on the title of the event "The Tale of the Golden Angel," telling the dramatic story about what happened to a set of Wellendorff jewelry given as a present. A third was titled, "A Family Business Driven by Values," the secrets of Wellendorff, Germany's finest jeweler: Tragedy, Mystery and Family Values. The final piece of copy on the front page, next to a three-quarter page ad of one of its most recognizable products, a stack of rings, was the explanation for the occasion from the owner of the Dallas store. He tells of his conversation with two of the Wellendorff brothers from Germany who tell of a customer whose home burned and all that was left was a Wellendorff necklace with a golden angel. The Dallas Bachendorf store's owner, Lawrence Bock, said that on hearing the story he felt everyone needs a guardian angel. Page-turner copy and brilliant illustrations make for special section advertising that works.

Basic Guidelines for Writing Advertising Copy

Advertising copywriters are often believed to have a great deal more creative freedom than most other writers because they work under few artificial restraints. For example, you might view writing a news release as less creative than writing copy for an ad, because in the former case you must conform to newswriting style. But there are rules and restraints on ad copywriting too.

Purpose

To begin with, you must have a clear understanding of what you want to accomplish with the ad. What do you want to happen as a result of the ad? Do you want your public to support the bond issue? Do you want people to give to the organization's disaster relief fund? You must know the single (never multiple) specific purpose for the ad. And everything you put in the ad should contribute to that purpose. In editing the ad, delete as excess baggage any word, phrase, sentence, paragraph or visual that does not specifically further the purpose.

Objective Facts

You'll be able to select a specific purpose for the ad only after carefully and thoroughly reviewing all the pertinent facts about the issue. You should review these facts not only from your side's point of view but also from that of your opposition. In fact, the latter review is just as important as the former. And both reviews have to be done with objectivity. Only then can you make an informed judgment about the strengths and weaknesses of your position and those of your competition. And only then should you attempt to derive a purpose calculated to capitalize on one of your strengths or to attack one of the opposition's weaknesses.

Multiple publics always are involved in each effort, so you have to prioritize publics and evaluate desirable outcomes for each. Without a clear behavioral goal for each public involved, you have no way of evaluating the results of your effort. Writers can be sure that analytics will be used to measure the effectiveness of what they do.

The Publics

You should review the facts and select a purpose for the ad with a full awareness of the uniqueness of your publics. You need to know their wants, needs and values. This is where demographic and psychographic information assume great importance. Although no public is homogeneous, you must consider some basic characteristics.

Publics examine every message for how it may affect them personally. In a diverse society, you need to know the consistency and conflicts of value systems. Furthermore, many of these publics are interactive and share messages and opinions about them.

Emphasis matters in advertising messages. As an example, look at prescription drug advertising. A study of direct-to-consumer advertising shows that when a drug is not directly associated with risks, people tend to focus on the benefits and underestimate the side effects. Words like "may cause dizziness" or disattachment of effects blurs their understanding of choice. This may cause some legal challenges.[14]

One consideration often overlooked is how employees react to advertising from their employer. Remember employees are your PR front line because they interact with other publics and are seen as credible witnesses to an organization's reputation. If advertising conflicts with their realities, it damages their trust, their morale and the organization's credibility. You have to keep in mind that we have a global marketplace of ideas as well as products and services, including media that potentially reach across cultures, borders and time zones.

Media

Before you write the copy, you must know which medium or media you are writing for. One of your first concerns, of course, is to meet the technical requirements of the medium.

Beyond technical issues, you need to know a lot about the medium you will use. How credible is it? How evocative is it? How do people react to it? What audience does it reach? What audience does it seek? What is its editorial slant? What have other advertisers experienced who have used it in similar situations? These are important questions, and you must know—not guess at—the answers. In some cases, you may have to rely on word of mouth or social media, but in other cases, you will be able to gather a lot of information from the medium itself simply by writing or calling.

The Creative Approach

Never try to develop a creative approach or write a line of copy until after you have made the decisions specified earlier. These decision areas are parts of what advertising professionals call a *copy platform*. A copy platform is a succinct document that spells out pertinent information about the public and contains a simple statement of creative strategy.

A creative-strategy statement for a little-known candidate running for senator against an incumbent might read like this:

> To convince voters that Mr. X will represent the views of eastern Kentuckians better than Ms. Y.

This statement clearly expresses your purpose (strategy). The question then becomes: How will I do it? That's where creativity comes in.

Let's suppose that Ms. Y is noted for being absent from the Senate floor when important bills that may affect eastern Kentuckians are up for a vote. You could construct a series of ads in which Mr. X pledges to be in the Senate chamber during every important vote. The voters would probably want to hear this message, though they might consider the claim to be mere political rhetoric.

You could take the offensive and attack Ms. Y by showing an empty chair during a roll call. You could then support the point with a table, showing not only the bills on which Ms. Y did not cast votes but also the number and dates of her absences. In other words, you could provide a lot of solid, verifiable, convincing information that Ms. Y is not doing the job properly. Still another approach might be to show Mr. X, dressed in hunting garb and following some hunting hounds on the scent. Mr. X would look up and explain that he and his "dawgs" were looking for Ms. Y. An obvious close would be a superimposed message like this:

> Where *is* Ms. Y? Vote for Mr. X. You will always find him in the Senate.

Of these three approaches, the first is mundane. It is low on persuasiveness because there is nothing unique about its claim. The ad neither excites the emotions nor challenges the reason. The second ad is more creative, and it contains lots of convincing and damning information about Ms. Y. It is more likely to be persuasive. But the third approach, which is obviously best executed for television, is not only more creative but it is also dramatically persuasive. How could a voter see that ad and remain free of resentment toward Ms. Y? And as resentment builds, voters will be more easily persuaded to vote for Mr. X. Emotion is the essence of good creativity in advertising.

Another strategic consideration is what is called a "push" or "pull" tactic. Media selection generally is considered a "push" tactic—placing an ad where it will be exposed to the publics you want to reach. This is a downward message system to the consumer. Pull is an upward message from the consumer, stimulated by a number of tactics creating interest or demand from the consumer. The "pull" tactic is less direct in that you have to provide for ways for recipients to reach you and encourage that tug.

Prescription drug ads that invite people to ask their doctors about the product are the most obvious. Pull is most subtle in blog links and in social networks. Pull by mentions, promotions, product placement and such are more likely devices that involve public relations writers.

Visualization

As you read the discussion on creative approaches, it may have occurred to you that creative strategy in advertising involves visual as well as verbal thinking. If so, you caught on to an essential difference between writing news copy and writing advertising copy. A good advertising copywriter always thinks in visual as well as verbal terms. The reason the hunting scene just described is so dramatic is that the visual element graphically

FIGURE 9.6

Copy that entertains as well as informs and sketches that stimulate the reader's imagination.

Rebellious.

He was ahead of his time.

There had been actors before who were animals. There had been actors with brains. Actors who had heart. Actors who were "sensitive." Actors who had a body. Actors who looked like they might explode if you weren't careful.

What nobody remembered ever seeing before was an actor, or a person, who was born with all that.

John Garfield was born with all of it; none of it was an act. He didn't know he had any of it; if he did know, he never let it show.

Men liked him as well as women, maybe because he wasn't "pretty." He wasn't even good-looking.

People remembered him fondly for being in movies he was never in. This is because he had a quiet but very far-reaching effect on how people acted, talked, moved, argued, flirted, scratched, laughed, lit cigarettes, entered rooms, shook hands and dressed.

It was John Garfield who made wearing shirts like the one shown here OK. In fact, he wore a black silk shirt before gangsters did; before Mediterranean millionaires and Tunisian tycoons even thought of it.

JG Silk Shirt (N⁰. 1223). 25 mm silk. Smoked pearl buttons. Single-needle throughout. Imported.

Men's sizes: S, M, L, XL, XXL.

Colors: Original Black, Purple.

Price: $149.

(Don't be afraid of silk. It's about as fragile as a Mercedes-Benz. And will last as long.)

Pamplona.

A beret is probably the most universal hat of our time. Worn by Hemingway at the Running of the Bulls. Worn by Jean-Paul Sartre contemplating existence, or only another café au lait. Worn by Che Guevara, Tyrone Power, Groucho Marx, Picasso.

Authentic Basque Beret (N⁰. 1539). Water-resistant black wool, with faux leather band. Made in France.

You should have one around. It will grow on you.

Men's sizes: S (6 3/4"– 6 7/8"), M (7"– 7 1/8"), L (7 1/4"– 7 3/8"), XL (7 1/2"– 7 3/4").

Price: $75.

85

The J. Peterman Company

(Continued)

FIGURE 9.6   *(continued)*

Devil May Care.

Gin-soaked.

Freewheeling.

"Ain't Misbehavin'" by Fats Waller (at Zanzibar Room in LA).

Short bob haircuts, lacey corsets and high hemlines. Sometimes high ground was low ground (it became hard to tell). Hollywood darlings like Colleen Moore wore slinky little numbers like this while smiling in a way we haven't seen in a while.

"Don't worry, girls," she wrote in 1926. "No edict of fashion arbiters will ever swathe you in long and cumbersome skirts."

You may feel it first when you bounce down the stairs. Again when performing a jazzed up fox trot at neighbor's Christmas gala (he remembers some of the steps from class but mostly just watches you).

Will you be different?

Something more gilded?

Something More Dress (№. 5010). Rayon-silk blend with two tiers of black fringe, silver and black beading along neckline, and silver corded spaghetti straps. Straight hem. Left side invisible zipper with hook and eye closure. Knee length. Imported.

Women's sizes: 2 through 20.

Color: Black.

Price: $498.

Freewheeling Fascinator (№. 4368).

You might not know all the steps to the fox trot, but nobody's looking at your feet. Headpiece with black velvet edges, flower and feather plumes. Satin-covered headband. Guaranteed to make your old hats feel, well, old hat. Imported.

Color: Black.

Women's sizes: One size.

Price: $39.

 To order, call toll-free 888 647-2555 / visit jpeterman.com.
New: See photographic images of our stuff at jpeterman.com.

86

characterizes the verbal message. In the best advertising copy, verbal and visual content harmonize perfectly so that each complements and extends the message of the other.

Language

It is axiomatic that, if you want to communicate with someone, you must use language that the other person will understand. Language has certain rules, and if they are not generally observed, communication may be impossible or the result unwanted. Thus the common rules of grammar and syntax are the standard in advertising, as they are in other forms of writing. You can break a grammar rule for a purpose—to achieve a specific effect not possible with traditional rules—but doing so should be the exception, not the rule.

Always choose the simple over the complex word. Your public might be able to read and comprehend at the college-graduate level, but people generally prefer to read copy that is two to four grade levels below their ability. And if you have any doubt about the educational level of your audience, you should gear your writing to about three grade levels lower than you believe it to be.

With increasing numbers of Spanish speakers in the USA, decisions about using Spanish in advertising have copywriters in a quandary. Some attempts have been made to put the ad copy, whatever the medium, all in Spanish. Sometimes a mix of Spanish and English is used—Spanglish, it sometimes is called. People who speak and read Spanish only are more comfortable with Spanish, especially if the copy is dealing with a complex subject. However, many Spanish speakers are just as comfortable with a mix of English and Spanish. Knowing which your priority publics prefer, and in what circumstances, is essential.

Language choices always matter, even in English. Obviously, if you are writing an idea ad for your company that will appear in a highly specialized professional journal, you should use language appropriate to that public. This may mean using some professional jargon. If your ad is to appear in a general mass medium, however, simplify the language and avoid jargon.

Not only should you use simple words, you should also use short phrases, sentences and paragraphs. Sentences should average no longer than 12 to 15 words. Paragraphs should average about three to five sentences. Following these guidelines will improve your writing's readability.

Repetition

When the repetitions are plotted on a graph, a learning curve takes shape until the curve eventually levels. Thus repetition is an essential principle of learning. You can apply this principle to your message in two basic ways.

The repetition principle applies first to the actual writing of copy. The general rule is that you should repeat the essential point of your message at least three times in your ad. This does not mean that you have to repeat it verbatim, but only that you must repeat the idea. This is absolutely crucial in broadcast messages, because they are so fleeting.

The principle of repetition also applies to how frequently you repeat the message to your public and in what time frame. Generally, if you are introducing a new program or idea, you will have to present your message fairly frequently during the early stages of your program.

As your audience becomes familiar with what you are promoting, you can reduce the number of presentations and space them out, while still maintaining a reasonable level of awareness.

When your campaign ends, the public will begin to forget at approximately the same rate at which it learned. Still, the public's awareness about what you said will not drop back to zero. Hence, it will take less effort in a subsequent campaign to raise public awareness to former levels. This is a good argument for sustained programming, of course, because it suggests that sustaining awareness is more efficient than building it.

Although these general guidelines apply across all media and in all copywriting situations, you'll find them discussed separately as they relate to specific media and situations. Because electronic media are everywhere, starting with your mobile devices, advertising for these is discussed next.

Writing Advertising Copy for Electronic Media—Television, Radio, Online

Brevity, clear style and sharp technique are the hallmarks of good electronic copywriting. Because an audience's attention is easily distracted, your copy must be simple, direct and provocative. Avoid clichés and slang. Be careful to make smooth transitions from one point to the next. Personalize the message by emphasizing "you" at every opportunity. People are more likely to respond personally to a message if they think it is directed to them. So try to write your copy as if it were a personal conversation between you and a friend.

Avoid exaggerated claims. Your persuasive appeal must be distinctive so that your audience will remember it when they see or hear it again.

You must capture the attention of your audience in the first few seconds or you will lose it completely. Be sure to register the name of the company or organization, and let the audience know what you want it to do. A sense of urgency may help move the audience to action.

With broadcast media, TV and radio, time frames vary by medium and even among stations. Generally, though, you will usually write for periods lasting 10 seconds (25 words), 20 seconds (45 words), 30 seconds (65 words) or 60 seconds (125 words). Word count is approximate. Count it! The actual word limits may vary a little from radio to television to videos, but in any case, you have to tell a complete story in just a few well-chosen words. This is seldom easy.

Radio and television have different technical capabilities, of course, but some styles of message presentation are common to all three media. One is the "slice of life," which is a mini-drama that presents a situation anyone might experience. It provides the context for the message.

Another is the jingle approach, in which music and words are combined to make the message memorable, identifiable and entertaining. A humorous approach is appropriate in either of these media. This may include anything from a cartoon or a mini-sitcom (situation comedy), for television, or to a joke, usually radio only. The difficulty with humor is in finding universal themes that will not go stale quickly. And remember; never make your audience the victim of the humor.

Another technique is the interview. Here an announcer talks with representative members of your public. Still another approach is the testimonial. If you use a testimonial approach, however, be sure to establish the credibility of the people testifying. Otherwise, the audience will tune out your message.

You can use sound effects with any or all of these approaches. And you can combine the techniques themselves in some fashion.

Television and film have the additional benefit of permitting visual demonstration. This may be done through live action, animation or a combination of the two. In writing for television or film, consider the visual aspect carefully. Production involves someone responsible for coordinating all of the elements of the script—sound, including music, artists, maybe actors, lighting, filming and so on. Your job is to give clear instructions in the script so they can interpret your visualization. Be prepared for other interpretations that may not entirely resemble your concept.

Copywriting for TV Commercials or Public Service Announcements

When writing copy for television, imagine how your ad will look as well as how it will sound. This will help make the message stronger and more persuasive. Remember that you have to think visually and verbally.

Divide your paper down the middle so that you have two equal columns. Label the left column "description" and the right column "script." In the right column, begin to write the words you want your public to hear. Concentrate on the single, basic idea of the message, and remember to promise your public some reward—a benefit that is both explained and supported.

Now go back and polish what you have written. Pare away unneeded words, phrases and sentences. Get the verbal message into what you consider finished form. Then have someone read the script aloud to you. Make sure the reader doesn't study the message beforehand, but reads it "cold." Listening to your copy being read aloud by someone else will help you to spot parts that need to be corrected, eliminated or rearranged.

Now repeat the process, this time working down the left side and describing the visuals that are to accompany the verbal message. Make certain that the visual images match and interpret their verbal counterparts. In some cases, you may be working from a prepared television script sheet.

Remember that one of television's strengths is action. Avoid static scenes. If the image does not move, the audience will shift its attention to something more interesting. You must pay attention to the visual, but don't become so carried away with it that you forget the message you want to convey.

In television, it is common to carry the preparation process a step further and create a storyboard. A storyboard depicts graphically what you have described down the left side of your script sheet. Although an artist is often assigned the job of making a storyboard, many copywriters find it is helpful to make their own, using stick figures to properly sequence the visuals. They often write their copy under each frame so they can better judge its unity.

Copywriting for Radio Commercials or PSAs

Approach copywriting for radio as you would do that for television—by dividing your paper and labeling the columns to make a script sheet. That is simple enough, but writing really good radio copy is more difficult than writing for television. In television, you have visual images to help you convey your message. In radio, you have only the visual theater of the mind. Although this is a vast territory, it is one in which many copywriters get lost.

Begin your copy in the right-hand column. You'll have to search especially hard for just the right words to evoke the images you want to paint in the public's collective mind. That is, you'll have to imagine exactly what you want the public to see. Language can be your best ally or your worst enemy. It will be the latter if you use uncommon words, especially those that have regional or local usages. Be wary of these. Also be cautious about using dialects.

Once you have written the message in the right-hand column, have someone read it "cold" so you can listen for semantic traps. Verify that the mental images you evoke unfold in a logical, easy-to-follow sequence, or you'll lose your listeners. You'll need to build excitement and drama, but be sure to drive home the message by repeating it at least three times in the script.

With the verbal content completed, work in the left-hand column providing complete cues regarding music, volume changes, announcers, sound effects and similar production concerns. Check your descriptions against the verbal messages in the right-hand column to make sure they match.

Sometimes in small local markets, radio scripts are read live by announcers. If you distribute your copy to stations in script form to be read live, make sure the words are simple to pronounce and flow smoothly, so the announcers will not foul up the announcement with their mispronunciations or the wrong inflection. Placing the wrong inflection on a word or phrase can distort the message by giving copy elements the wrong emphasis. The safest step is to prerecord your spots.

Government Regulations

You need to be aware that the release of information—especially from a corporation whose stock is publicly traded—falls under federal and state regulations as well as the rules of the stock exchange where the company's stock is traded. The Securities and Exchange Commission (SEC) regulates what kind of information about a corporation and its financial affairs can—or *must*—be released and under what conditions.

In an effort to "level the playing field" for investors, the SEC issued its Regulation FD (Fair Disclosure) in October 2000. This regulation makes selective disclosure of information illegal.[15]

The Sarbanes-Oxley Act (SOX or SOA) was signed into law in 2002. It's designed to prevent financial malpractice and accounting scandals such as the Enron debacle and is known as SOX or SOA. It's also known as the Public Company Accounting Reform and Investor Protection Act and is considered one of the most significant changes to USA securities laws since the 1930s.[16]

To conform to these and other regulations, the rule of thumb is to "tell no one until you tell everyone." Once information on a significant transaction or event is disclosed to anyone, regulations require full disclosure, usually in the form of a news release that is widely distributed.

The Federal Trade Commission (FTC) watches out for all consumers of information. Writing for promotion or advertising means the public relations writer has to watch out for false claims by checking facts carefully and documenting their findings. The FTC has guidelines for Infomercials, which appear in purchased broadcast time. Furthermore, the FTC holds celebrities responsible for claims that they use or buy particular products or services. False endorsements have legal consequences. Using the Internet to mask a commercial effort as a "grassroots" response will not escape the FTC. In promotional copy of all kinds, the FTC requires disclosures for all sorts of contract-like promises such as warranties and giveaways.

In 2013, the FTC issued guidelines for disclosure in social media, so you need to watch out for all postings, including blogs and other seemingly "editorial" copy as well as commercial copy. Information has to be easy to locate, clear and accessible.[17]

Another watchdog for legal violations is the Food and Drug Administration (FDA). Drug advertising is particularly watched in commercials, ads, promotional brochures and articles. If you can't prove it, don't say it or write it. Food and drug companies have been fined. It's better to get clearance from the FDA before using any claims in labels, ads, commercials, promotions, newsletters or anything the FDA could consider "misleading."

Another government agency with considerable oversight is the United States Postal Service. All pieces that go through the mails have multiple regulations regarding size, weight, thickness, enclosures, design of where information may be placed and, of course, content that is prohibited. Violations will come from the office of the U.S. Postmaster General and can be responded to, and perhaps result even in a hearing. Compliance can be enforced through the U.S. Attorney General's office with a court order. Preapproval of materials going through the postal system will save time and money.

Plagiary is a very serious offense and can happen to public relations writers who get careless in using material discovered in Internet searches. Give credit. Material that appears in any source, including the Internet, is not free for the taking without credit, and sometimes without explicit permission. Occasionally small excerpts are considered "fair use," but don't guess. Read copyright rules carefully. You'll see in this textbook various places where an example or illustration has a line that reads "used with permission." That means there is a formal written permission granted, often with payment for use.

Exercises

1. Write a news release on a current campus event in both print and broadcast style.
2. Write a news release for a specialized publication for the topic, naming the publication and stating its purpose.
3. Write a "pitch" for each, cover letters telling each editor why the story has value for its audience.
4. Find an event from your campus calendar that you think would make an interesting news story. Get information about the event from the planners. Write a media

advisory for the event. Write a news release for the student newspaper and then a broadcast version for the student radio station. If you have a television station or stream news on the student publications website, prepare for that editor a revised media advisory that suggests videos for their coverage along with your advance news release on the event.

5. Most universities have visiting celebrities as guest speakers to the campus or to a particular department. Find out information about the appearance of a celebrity at your school and write a news conference announcement. Prepare all materials you would need to have on hand for the conference. Where would you plan to have the conference so the sound and light would be good for the media, the guest would be comfortable and the school would look good in the clips?

6. Universities generate a great deal of research. Look at your university's publication of ongoing research and choose a topic that would make a good video news release. Decide how you would make it timely. Do the necessary additional fact-finding for a video news release and write the script. If this is outside of your academic unit, be sure to tell those you contact that this is a classroom project.

7. Write a news release on a current campus event in both print and broadcast style.

8. Write a news release for a specialized publication for the topic, naming the publication and stating its purpose.

Email, Memos, Letters, Proposals and Reports

They're the front-line pieces in public relations: email, memos and letters. They help build and sustain professional relationships by maintaining a good, relevant and timely flow of information within an organization and with its external publics. Proposals and reports are important to the ongoing functions of the organization—especially those organizations like public relations and advertising firms that compete for the award of contracts. Additional opportunities for communicating with select publics are available through such specialized media as direct mail, out-of-home media and sales promotion.

It is exciting, of course, to write copy for a showpiece brochure that is a major part of a campaign. It is a professional fact of life, however, that more seasoned writers probably will be assigned such tasks. New writers are assigned what some consider more mundane tasks, such as writing emails, memos and letters. Public relations professionals write lots of emails, memos and letters in their everyday routine office work. They also write many such pieces for key officers in the organization, because these forms of writing frequently function to persuade in some way.

Email

Boring! That's email, right? Texting is more personal and immediate, and using social media is more fun. Perhaps! But as a public relations professional, you must use email frequently, because email is a required tool of the public relations professional.

The Cision 2013 Social Journalism Survey, which drew more than 3,000 responses from journalists from 11 countries, points that out. According to survey results, "The top three methods used by PR professionals to contact journalists were via email (84%), telephone (47%) and social media (19%). When asked how they would *prefer* to be contacted, email remained the most popular (82%), with telephone preferred by fewer journalists (33%) and social media the least preferred (25%)."[1]

In "PC Magazine," Michael Muchmore makes a good case for email: "Yes, you can send your pals a message in Facebook, and you can get to them more immediately with an SMS, iMessage, twitter DM, or instant message, but there are still plenty of usage cases that call for a good-old-fashioned email account. Just try signing up for any Web service without one. We scrutinized the five leading Web-based email services here. In descending order of U.S. popularity, they are: Yahoo Mail, Google Gmail, Hotmail (now in its new Outlook.com form), AOL Mail, and mail.com."[2]

Most public relations professionals use email extensively for all aspects of their work. Some receive and send hundreds of email messages each day. Email systems allow a person to send the same message and attachments to one, ten or even thousands of people. Many organizations have email systems that allow distribution of a message to selected groups by title—or even to all employees. But more than a few people have been embarrassed by selecting "All" by mistake.

Such a mistake was reported by the *Los Angeles Times*. An email message, saying, "'We're thrilled that you've been admitted to UC San Diego, and we're showcasing our beautiful campus on Admit Day,' was sent to the entire freshman applicant pool of more than 46,000 students, instead of just the 18,000 who had been admitted. All 28,000 applicants who had been rejected received an email congratulating them on their acceptance, only to receive another notification admitting there was a mistake."[3]

People seem to pay more attention to email messages and respond to them more quickly than to paper messages. It's easy to figure out why. It's easier and quicker.

Of course, email also has its problems. Some of the major ones are spam, malware and zombies. McAfee Labs is a leading source for threat research, threat intelligence and cyber-security thought leadership. In the first quarter of 2014, McAfee reported that its "total malware sample count broke the 200 million sample barrier. In just one year, the total number of mobile malware samples has grown by 167%. New threats attacking the master boot record increased by 49% this period, reaching an all-time high for a single quarter. The McAfee Labs count of new suspect URLs set a three-month record with more than 18 million, a 19% increase over Q4 and the fourth straight quarterly increase."[4]

Malicious codes can infect a computer through websites visited, in addition to email. Sophos, another leader in cyber threat prevention, reports, "The Web is now the primary route by which cybercriminals infect computers. … As a consequence, cybercriminals are planting malicious code on innocent websites. This code then simply lies in wait and silently infects visiting computers."[5]

Kaspersky Lab, one of the fastest growing IT security vendors in the world, detects and blocks more than 200,000 new malicious programs *every day,* a significant increase from the first half of 2012, when 125,000 malicious programs were detected and blocked each day on average.[6]

Another problem is email overload. The report of a Motorola employee communications study said, "On any given day, more than 30 percent of respondents had at least 30 unread emails, while more than 40 percent of respondents spent more than half their day on email. Some employees are satisfied with updates sent via mass distribution (email) as they appreciate the push, but there are those who find it too much to deal with in addition to all other communications with which they must contend."[7]

You need to understand that email is not private. Because email messages are owned by the organization where they are created, it's common for them to be subpoenaed in legal cases. If you don't want it on the front page of the newspaper, don't email it. Google "email lawsuit" and you'll get 34.4 *million* responses!

Interoffice or external postal systems can suffer from delays in delivery. But email is instantaneous. This can be an enormous advantage when a major development—especially one that was not anticipated—begins to unfold. Speed counts, and email meets that need.

Time management can be enhanced by email. If you're working and have a question for someone, you can send the query immediately (before you forget it) and that person can respond when convenient. Your message is kept in your "Sent" mailbox for reference. You can also leave messages for people when they are away from their desks—at meetings or on business trips or vacations. Then they can respond and you'll get the message even if this time you're the one who's not available.

Email is interactive—that is, two-way communication can occur. So a message may be superseded immediately by an exchange of information between senders and receivers. When they use interactive systems, people tend to feel they are listened to more carefully by their supervisors. And they can "talk back" without the risk of a face-to-face confrontation. Yes, it's slower than texting, but it provides information that you may need—the date and time the message was sent, and a digital, printable record of everything sent and received.

Notebook computers and handheld devices have increased the use of email. Suppose you're on deadline with a major writing task and you work at home until 3 a.m. to finish it. You write a short memo to the vice president for corporate communication explaining that, because you finished the project at 3 a.m., you won't be in the office at your regular time. You send the memo and your copy to the office and go to bed. The next morning, you find an email message from the VP saying that the copy looks great and that you should sleep tight.

And email makes it possible for you to be an integral part of your organization even though you may be working at home or in an airport lounge on the other side of the world. Wireless connections have made emailing from schools, airports and even entire towns more omnipresent and convenient.

With email you can attach digital images as well as text documents and database files. This makes working with news media representatives both fast and convenient, since you can send what the media folks want, and they can receive it immediately, whether they're across the street or on the other side of the world. High-quality images can be huge, so they should be transferred using file transfer protocol (FTP) with email messages to media representatives giving information on where to locate the images.

Companies in crisis situations have found email particularly useful because it allows for a timely interchange of information across not only geographic boundaries, but also those that separate customers and investors from management and even employees from management and each other.

Formats and Content

Instant messaging (IM) allows a person to interact instantly with people on a "buddy" or "contact" list, as long as all of the people involved are online. It allows a person to create a private chat room with another individual or group, if all are online.

Texting uses short-text messaging service (SMS) to send and receive brief messages. (Think Twitter.) *Encyclopedia Britannica* reported, "Worldwide, the number of text messages sent each year is approaching one trillion, and the major wireless companies report that users now do more texting than talking on their cell phones."[8]

The consumer research company Nielsen Mobile, which kept track of 50,000 individual customer accounts in the second quarter of 2014, found that Americans each sent or received 357 text messages a month, compared with just 204 phone calls. That was the second repeated quarter in which texting significantly surpassed the number of voice calls.[9]

Distracted driving is the term for texting and cell phone use and other activities while driving a vehicle. According to the National Highway Traffic Safety Administration (NHTSA), about 6,000 deaths and a half-million injuries are caused by distracted drivers every year. While teenagers are texting, they spend about 10 percent of the time outside the driving lane they're supposed to be in. But it's not only teens who drive while distracted. "The 30- to 39-year-old age group had the highest percentage of cell phone use in fatal crashes," according to the NHTSA.[10]

Responding to an email is simple; all you need to do to respond to one is click the reply button, type in your response and then click "send." The problem is what you say and how you say it. The ease of this technology often works against clarity and accuracy. People tend to write "stream of consciousness" messages and send them unedited. The consequences can be mystifying to the recipients, who try to figure out what you meant from what you sent. Other consequences, such as lawsuits, are more serious.

The spontaneity of the process often encourages intemperate remarks that can result in legal action. The system itself is regarded as a cross between a telephone message and a letter or interoffice memo, so it encourages people to put messages on the screen that they would never put on paper. The result has been some unpleasant legal battles over discrimination or sexual harassment, for example.

Like messages in other media, you need to know exactly what you want the receiver to think, know or do. That strategic approach sharpens the focus of your message. You also need to know how much the reader knows about the subject. If it is a lot, your message can be terse. If it is little or none, your message must be longer because you must provide enough background from which the reader can make a decision.

The process of emailing is so easy that some people tend to forget that it is also writing. That can be disastrous because writing demands a lot more precision than speaking. That fact alone should warn us away from being too casual in the way we write emails.

In the fourth annual Email Addiction Survey conducted by AOL, 68 percent of respondents said emails with spelling and punctuation errors annoyed them. Interestingly, 74 percent said they excuse errors when emails are sent from a mobile device like a BlackBerry® or iPhone®.[11]

Style

Remember that although the message is electronic, the recipient is human and you need to imagine how that person is likely to respond to your message. Begin with an appropriate greeting, one that you might use in face-to-face conversation or on the phone with that person.

You need to be conversational in tone because this is a more spontaneous type of communication, but avoid words that might be acceptable if spoken but sound too harsh or inflammatory in print. They will be in print, on the screen, even if a hard copy isn't made.

Let the person know right away what the message is about, so they can begin to follow your thought processes. In the subject line, use short but relevant information that will lead the reader into the message. Make it easy to read by using simple words, short sentences and very brief paragraphs.

Let the recipient know what you expect from them. Use something like, "Please let me know about *xyz*." Or "I'll expect to hear from you this afternoon [or a time and date] about the following: 1. *x*; 2. *y*; 3. *z*." This allows them to respond perhaps immediately by saying something like, "Thanks for your message this morning. I can tell you now about *x* and *y*. Before I answer you about *z*, I need to make some phone calls. I'll get back to you by [date and time]. Good to hear from you."

Used the right way, email can be a very satisfying means of communication. Excessive, inconsiderate or inappropriate use can elevate your blood pressure considerably. See Table 10.1 for some email dos and don'ts.

TABLE 10.1	*Dos and Don'ts of Email* Most people think of email as quick, casual, responsive and fun. It is so easy to use, it may be abused. These dos and don'ts may help you to better use business email.

1. Be sure the email address is correct. If incorrect, it may not return to you for hours. The solution is to keep your online address book current.

2. Always write a subject line. This gives addressees an idea of the content in just a few words.

3. Verify frequently that the internal clock on your computer is correct. This helps you and receivers to sort through messages chronologically.

4. Keep the caps lock key in the off position. All caps in emails is the equivalent of shouting.

5. Avoid abbreviations. However, they're acceptable in personal emails.

6. You can express yourself informally in email. But remember that email demands good writing, a level of preciseness that speaking sometimes does not require. Your writing can't duplicate speech.

7. Formal greetings or closings don't work well in email. Be more personal, as in "Hi, Diana." Don't use "Sincerely" or "Respectfully" in closing. Use something like "Cheers" or "All the best."

8. Keep sentences short, averaging no more than about 12–15 words. Avoid run-on sentences and conditional clauses. These can be confusing.

(Continued)

T A B L E 1 0 . 1	(Continued)

9. Remember that email is instant. You don't get a second chance after clicking on the send button. Make sure the message is accurate in fact and correct in grammar, spelling and punctuation. If your email program has a spell checker, be sure it's turned on.

10. Attach only documents to your email that you know can be downloaded by the receiver.

11. Be sensitive to what you say and how it may be interpreted.

12. Email is not private. Don't say anything in email that you don't want your boss to see or that you would not want to see on the front page of a newspaper. Send it another way if your message is private or confidential.

13. Read your incoming email regularly, perhaps at set intervals during the workday.

14. When an email requires action by the receiver and you don't get a timely response, follow up. Don't delay.

15. When sending to a group, ask three questions of yourself: Does each group member need the message? Does each have sufficient background to understand the message? Does each member of the group have operating responsibilities that relate to the message? If no, modify the content or exclude them.

16. Don't use business email systems to send jokes and other nonbusiness matter.

© Cengage Learning

In the online article in theMuse.com, "Are Your Emails Too Long (Hint: Probably)," Elliott Bell reminds us, "The Gettysburg Address was 271 words long" and recommends that we work to shorten our emails. "Before you fire an email off," he writes, "take an extra 30 seconds and read it over. Ask yourself the following questions: (1) Is there a clear, easy-to-understand point to this email? (2) Is there anything I can take out that doesn't add to the main point? (3) Can anything be simplified? The more you train yourself to review your writing, the more you'll see that there are areas to improve. And, more importantly, the more you'll start to automatically make these changes in future emails."[12]

Memos

The word *memo* is the short form of *memorandum,* meaning an informal reminder of something important that has occurred or will occur. Memos are generally used to communicate within the organization. They should seldom be used to communicate with people outside the organization, with the exception of those sent to members of boards, committees and task forces. Messages sent by email and fax often are written in memo format.

Memo Formats

A good memo disseminates information simply. It should begin with a guide to its contents, as shown in Figure 10.1.

If the writer and receiver know each other, the memo style may be even less formal, containing neither last names nor titles. This is especially common when the memo is sent to someone in the same office or immediate area of operations.

FIGURE 10.1

Memo Format   *Formats for memos vary from organization to organization, but this one is typical. Memos are used when those addressed don't have email and when posting on bulletin boards is a good way to communicate—for example, with groups of employees who don't have computers in their workplaces.*

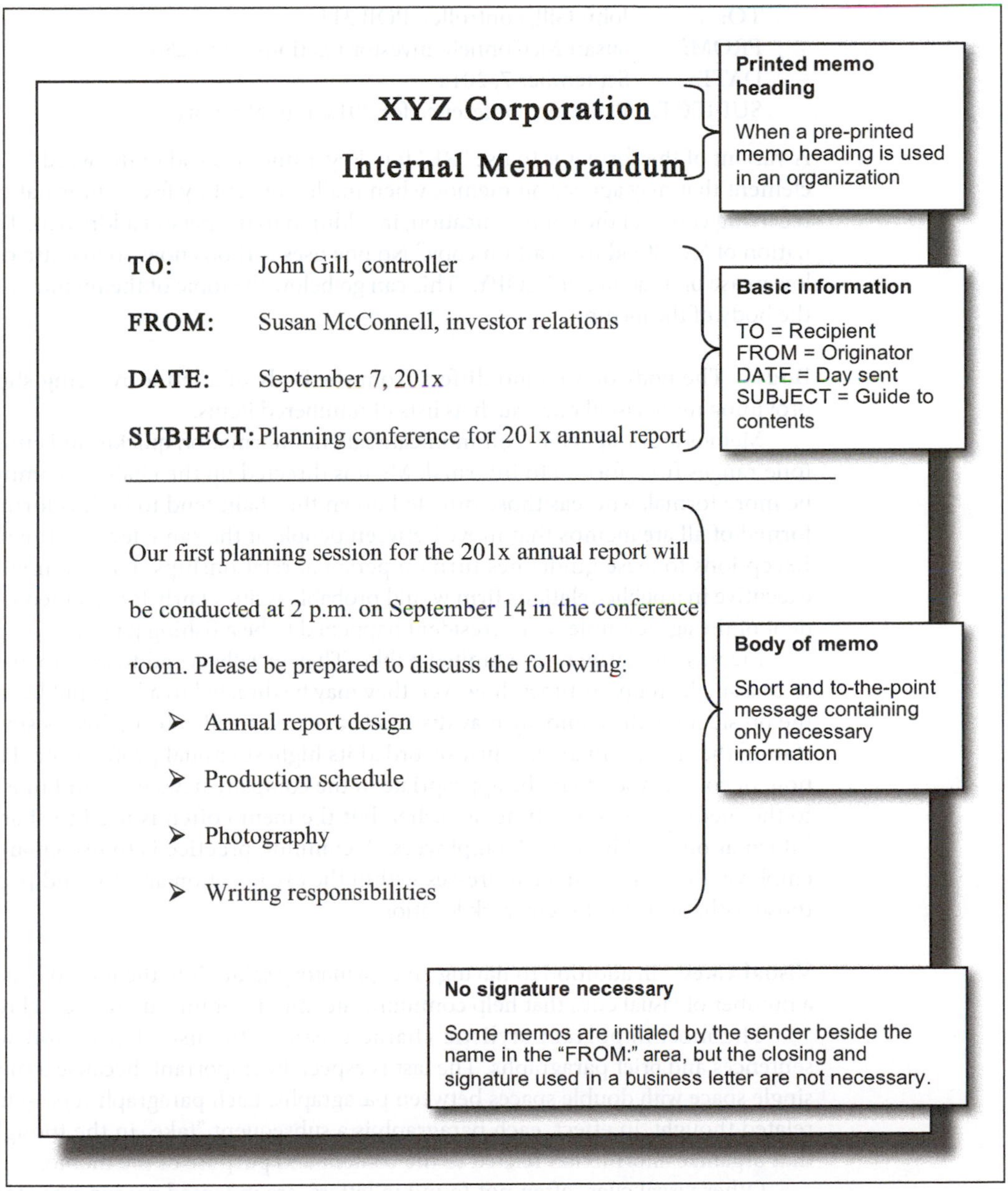

XYZ Corporation

Internal Memorandum

Printed memo heading

When a pre-printed memo heading is used in an organization

TO: John Gill, controller

FROM: Susan McConnell, investor relations

DATE: September 7, 201x

SUBJECT: Planning conference for 201x annual report

Basic information

TO = Recipient
FROM = Originator
DATE = Day sent
SUBJECT = Guide to contents

Our first planning session for the 201x annual report will

be conducted at 2 p.m. on September 14 in the conference

room. Please be prepared to discuss the following:

➢ Annual report design

➢ Production schedule

➢ Photography

➢ Writing responsibilities

Body of memo

Short and to-the-point message containing only necessary information

No signature necessary

Some memos are initialed by the sender beside the name in the "FROM:" area, but the closing and signature used in a business letter are not necessary.

When people have the same mailing address, it is unnecessary to use anything more than a departmental designation. Include addresses below the names if the addresses are different, such as different internal post office box numbers. Of course, if you're using digital or printed letterhead, there's no need to include your address below your name. If you don't use letterhead or if you have stationery that does not include phone numbers and addresses, include your address. The heading for the memo would then look like this:

TO: John Gill, controller, POB 311
FROM: Susan McConnell, investor relations, POB 286
DATE: September 7, 201x
SUBJECT: Planning conference for 201x annual report

A variant of this format is to use "RE" for "Regarding" instead of the word "SUBJECT." An element that may appear on memos when mailed or sent by fax is information on who is receiving copies of the communication, in addition to the person addressed. The old designation of "cc" stood for "carbon copy." No one uses carbons now, so just use one "c," either lowercase or a capital, or "COPY." This can go below the topic of the memo or at the end of the body of the memo.

Body   The body of a memo differs from the body of a letter by being shorter and by providing more visual cues, such as lists of numbered items.

Memos are designed to communicate salient information quickly and efficiently. Their tone ranges from formal to informal. Memos directed up the chain of command tend to be more formal, whereas those directed down the chain tend to be less formal. The least formal of all are memos that move between people at the same level in the organization. Exceptions to these guidelines turn on personal relationships. For example, an account executive in a public relations firm would probably write a fairly formal memo to the president of the agency, unless the president happened to be a fishing partner.

Memos ordinarily have a limited public. They usually are addressed to just one person or to a small group. At times, however, they may be directed to a large public. For example, the president of the company may distribute a memo to all 600 employees simultaneously, stating that the company has just recorded its highest annual profits ever. This information, of course, also would be appropriate in the company newsletter and must be released to the media at the same time or earlier, but the memo often is used to share important information quickly with all employees. A common practice is to use email to reach all employees who have email addresses within the organization and to send paper copies to those without email at their work location.

Visual Cues   In addition to having an explanatory salutation, the memo usually contains a number of visual cues that help communicate important information quickly.

The most important stylistic characteristic is the use of common words, short sentences and brief paragraphs. The last is especially important, because a memo is typed single space with double spaces between paragraphs. Each paragraph represents a new but related thought. In effect, each paragraph is a subsequent "take" in the thought processes that organize information related to the content and purpose of the memo.

Other visual cues, often not found in letters, are indented paragraphs (for emphasis), numbered or bulleted items (to accent important matter), fragmented sentences (for emphasis, but be cautious about using these often) and lists of items (often in vertical format rather than serially in a paragraph).

Context   Memo writers tend to assume that, because the person addressed in the memo is a member of the team, he or she knows all the pertinent background information related to the topic at hand. This often is a mistake. If you want to be understood, provide clarifying information that makes what you say comprehensible and leaves little room for misinterpretation. Do not, of course, provide superfluous information.

Establishing a context for your message is especially important if the memo is directed to people with whom you do not work regularly. When in doubt, always provide appropriate background materials. These may not be needed, but it is better to be safe than sorry. (See Table 10.2 for what *not* to do.)

When you do provide background materials, you need to say so. The way you do that is to put at the bottom of the memo the word "Attachments:" or "Enclosures:" followed by a list of everything you're including. List the items vertically and use bullets so it's easier to check them all. Sometimes not all of the enclosures make it into the envelope. The intended recipient needs to know what to expect.

The procedure is a bit different when you're sending a fax. You may need to use a cover page for the fax, which looks like the heading of the fax, but also tells the addressee how many pages to expect.

TO:	Alan Cooper Phone: 313-457-6733 Fax: 313-457-6734
FROM:	Susan Foster Phone: 623-535-6354 Fax: 623-535-7453
DATE:	October 1, 201x
RE:	Artwork for St. Louis Hospital Brochure
PAGES:	6 plus cover

Classifications of Memos

The tone and tempo of a memo depend on its purpose, style and public. There are six general categories of memos: bulletin, essay, informative, action, summary and file.

Bulletin Memo   The bulletin memo usually has a sense of urgency. It is generally brief and may be terse in style. It is the "telegram" of the memo world. The bulletin memo gets its name from the bulletins that appear on the wire services notifying editors that something important has happened or is about to happen. Given the nature of its content, such a memo may wind up being posted on a bulletin board, even if it is addressed to just one person.

Essay Memo   An essay memo is usually much more descriptive than a bulletin memo. It is used for "let's talk it over" material or situations. Its content may range from management philosophy to questions of how to get employees to clean up the coffee room after using it. The style is often conversational.

Informative Memo   The informative memo is usually a detailed descriptive piece of writing. An example might be a memo from the account executive to the account group

T A B L E 1 0 . 2	*How to Make Sure No One Reads Your Memo*

1. Hide the Message in a Block of Print

You want your reader to pick up your document, and put it down again. You can get this block effect in several ways.

- Make the document as long as possible. You see how forbidding the one-page memo is. Imagine seeing two pages of it. Imagine them printed on both sides of one sheet.

- Make your paragraphs long. Think of three inches as a minimum length. Write everything single-space.

- Don't leave a blank space between paragraphs. Announce a new paragraph by indenting the first line 1.4 of an inch. Add as many modifiers as you need to make sure the last line in a paragraph extends to the right margin.

- Justify the right margin.

Do this and you'll produce a formidable document. It's one most readers will glance at and immediately set aside.

2. Make the Message Appear Difficult and Irrelevant

Your goal is to lose the reader's interest.

- Send the message "To: File" or "To: Distribution." This is a strong barrier. It tells readers that the document has no relevance to them personally. The longer the distribution list at the end, the clearer the message.

- Use the "Subject" announcement to turn off the reader. It should make your topic seem dull or complex. (The word "theory" is especially useful here.)

  There must be no hint that the topic has any immediate importance.

- People who read beyond the subject-heading are a threat. You have to stop them with the first sentence of the text. This sentence *must* contain 30–50 words. It will help if a dozen of these words separate the subject and the verb.

  The first sentence should discuss a single detail of the report. There must be no suggestion of a summary or a conclusion.

- Use the second sentence as a fail-safe device. Hopefully, no one will do more than glance at it. But that glance must show it says nothing about the purpose of the document. It's a good idea if the second sentence starts with a long dependent clause. Let it begin with "If " or "Although."

Readers who go beyond the second sentence are intrepid and will be hard to stop. But they can be slowed down. You must take steps to frustrate them.

3. Make Individual Sentences Difficult to Read

Again, you should follow the example of the Fort Knox memo. It illustrates all the important techniques. Try them.

- Use a typeface that is hard to read.

  Write with a sans serif font. This is more difficult for many people to read. (A good word processing program will let you choose from scores of fonts, some of them pretty bizarre.)

  WRITE IN ALL CAPS. THIS SLOWS DOWN READING BY 10 PERCENT OR MORE.

  Use 8-point type. The tiny print puts so many words on a crowded page that your reader, on finishing one line, will have difficulty seeing where the next line begins.

(Continued)

T A B L E 1 0 . 2	(*Continued*)

- Write crowded sentences.

  Use long, compound-complex sentences. Begin with a participial phrase 15 words long, and end with a "which" clause that is 20 words long. Insert one or two parenthetical sentences in every paragraph. Keep your subject some distance from your verb. Stay with the passive voice.

- Use vague jargon that turns off the reader. Rely on abstractions, words ending in "ness," "ity," "tion," "ence," "ship," and "ment." Avoid anything specific, like proper names or sums of money.

  Devise difficult words, like "consortial," and challenging phrases, like "quantum signification." Introduce obscure acronyms, like "B.O.A. optimization." Sprinkle the message with high-sounding cliches, like "pursuant," "in lieu of," "per," "parameter," "closure," and "prioritize." These have deadened reading for years.

- Confuse readers with an unusual division of words. This is a subtle tactic, but quietly effective.

  It bothers most people to see merged forms like "problemsolver" and "costeffective." They are thrown off by words unexpectedly separated, like "fore men" and "counter indicated." They will be frustrated by unusual hyphens, as in "bi-nomial" and "di-agnostic." And you can unsettle them with slashed creations, like "enhance/monitor." Always justify your right margin. This leaves disturbing gaps between words throughout the text.

- Provide a dim copy. Make your readers work to recognize the words on the page.

By now you have the message. If you want your memo to remain unread, you can do wonders. You can offer a block of print, or introduce it with a deadly subject-head, or write awkward sentences full of strange acronyms. You won't need to do this often.

But you will see these forms every day. You'll see reports crowded with pages, and pages crowded with words, and paragraphs crowded with tiny print. You'll see messages written in all-caps or in italics or in the MosEisley font. You'll see dot-matrix print too faint to read and dittographed memos which have faded into obscurity. You'll throw away some important announcement because the subject-head read "Patterns of Supernumerary Clarification." And all these documents come from people who genuinely want to be read. Somehow they never learned that effective writing takes more than facts, vocabulary, and prose style. It takes readability.

Source: The above is excerpted from Daniel McDonald's "Achieving the Unreadable Memo" in *Et cetera* (Fall 1992): 280–284. Reprinted with permission of the International Society for General Semantics.

and client. This memo might document actions taken and their results. Or it might recommend programs and describe projected outcomes. The style and tone of these memos are usually fairly formal.

Action Memo   The action memo describes action taken or planned. Such memos, especially those dealing with future actions, often contain places for responses by recipients. For example, there might be a space for the receiver's initials on a section to indicate that he or she accepts responsibility for the initialed action. Or in the case of a supervisor, the initials might indicate approval or disapproval of the planned action.

Action memos sometimes include an element of coercion. This may be the case, for instance, when the author of the memo does not assign or suggest responsibility but seeks volunteers to assume responsibility. Coercion is at work when the implication of the memo is,

"If you don't select an area of responsibility, one will be assigned to you." If you're alert to this message, you'll quickly "volunteer" for the area of action that you will do best and enjoy most.

Summary Memo   This is a detailed descriptive memo in essay or outline form. Discussions and actions are collected under appropriate topical headings to facilitate progress during a meeting. The summary memo is used, too, in evaluating the progress of a program. In this case, it reflects an accumulation of information over time and often explains actions taken or planned.

File Memo   As its name implies, a file memo is addressed to the file—not to another person. It simply records information and is stored for reference. Memos of this type are used extensively when the program being planned is complex, when many people are involved in some ongoing action or program or when sharp divisions in points of view arise as to how or whether something should be done. In style and tone, it may be terse, almost cryptic. The purpose, remember, is merely to record information for internal use.

In a sense, a file memo is like a diary. It records names, dates, places and points of information. If serious debate arises over how or whether something should be done, the file memo should identify individuals with their respective points of view, even including verbatim accounts as necessary.

Factors Affecting the Use of Memos

Memos should be personalized. Involve the recipient with your memo by emphasizing "you." This is not only a pleasant way to write, it is also effective.

The way your memo is distributed may affect the attention it receives. Email distribution is the most common way.

Posting memos on bulletin boards is a common practice, but this can be an ineffective way to communicate. The company bulletin board often is filled with messages that remain unread by many people in the organization. If you intend your memo for posting, design it like a poster. Add graphics to gain attention, and treat the content like a bulletin to encourage easy, quick reading. One good reason to use bulletin boards is that in many organizations, employees—including flight crews of airlines—don't have access to email. One airline's PR staff prepares a daily newsletter that is emailed to each airport, where it is printed and posted for the information of flight crew members.

If your memo is to be distributed to a large number of people in the organization, you have several options. The best approach, of course, is to email the memo to each person. An alternative is to provide supervisors with stacks of copies and rely on them to pass a copy along to each employee. Many supervisors will be careful to distribute the information, but others will not, and communication breakdowns may result.

Some memos are best suited for special methods of distribution. For example, a memo about the company picnic might better be mailed to employees' homes, as you'll want other members of the employee's household to know about the event too.

The setting in which the memo is received may also influence its effectiveness. Obviously, the company picnic is a social event that involves the employee and the employee's family. Therefore, it is appropriate to send the memo announcing it to employees' home addresses. However, a memo calling a meeting of department heads should be emailed or sent to the recipients' respective offices, not to their homes. In general, if the memo is social, send it to the employee's home; if it is business, send it to the employee's work address.

Letters

Even though the use of texting and email has greatly increased, letters still play a significant role in business relationships. The problem is that some letter writers think that because they are going to the trouble to write a letter, it must be long. One solicitation letter from a university president to alumni was four full pages. Way too long. As a rule, try to keep your letters to one page in a readable size type. To give one-page letter writers more space, many letterhead designers put all addresses, including email, phone and fax information, in a single line along the bottom of the stationery.

Business Letter Format

The typical business letter has six parts: heading, salutation, body, close, signature and reference matter. (See Figure 10.2.)

Heading   The heading has two parts. The first is the identity of the sender. This material is usually printed on the letterhead. The second part is the date, plus the "inside address" containing the name, title and address of the recipient. The heading should always contain these elements, even when you know the person you're writing to quite well. Always document the sender and receiver completely and accurately.

Salutation   In the salutation you address the person to whom you're writing. This might appear to be simple, but it can cause some problems if you're insensitive to your receiver.

Suppose you're writing a letter from your CEO to Doug Newsom, one of the co-authors of this text, seeking names of people who might be used as public relations consultants. You might address Doug variously as "Dear Mr. Newsom," "Dear Dr. Newsom" or "Dear Doug." The first salutation would be incorrect because Doug's name is Douglas *Ann* Newsom, but she goes by Doug. The second form would be correct, because she has an earned doctorate. The last form would be correct only if your CEO knows her personally. Two points are illustrated here: avoid using a gender-specific title if you don't know the person's gender, and do not use a title if you don't know that it is correct.

If you're writing a promotional letter to send to hundreds of clients and it will not be computer personalized by name, use a salutation like "Dear Customer," "Dear Client" or "Dear Colleague." Even though these salutations are impersonal, they are better than ones that might be genuinely offensive.

Body   The level of formality in the tone depends on the relationship between the writer and the recipient of the letter. If a personal relationship exists, the letter may have a casual salutation and a conversational tone. In general, the tone of the body will be more formal if the letter is addressed to a person whose status is higher than that of the writer; it will be more informal if the writer's status is higher than the recipient's.

FIGURE 10.2

Letter Format *The parts of a typical business letter are shown here. When no letterhead is available, the sender's address; city, state and zip code; and the date are placed above the "inside address" of the recipient. This example shows a block format in which every line is flush with the left margin. Using an indented format, the date (and the sender's address; city, state and zip code when those are typed) appears indented halfway across the page, and the complimentary statement, signature and typed name and title are indented in the same way.*

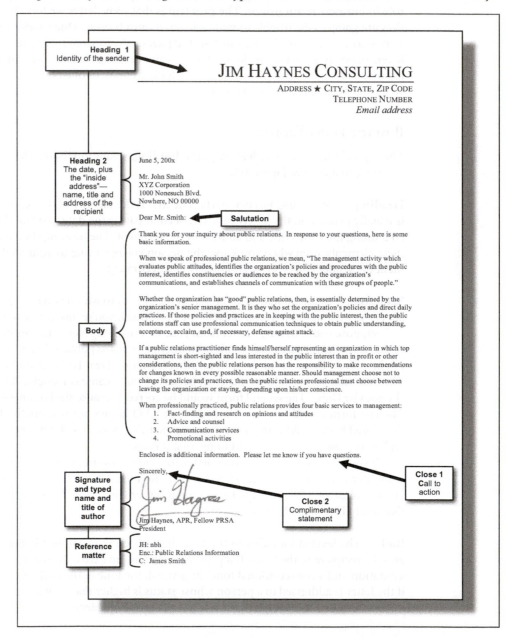

Close   The close of a business letter contains two elements. One is a call to action (if that is the purpose of the letter) or an offer of further help. The other is a complimentary statement that appears above the signature. Most business letters close with a simple "Sincerely" above the signature block. Business letters to and from friends outside the company sometimes close with "Best regards," "Cordially yours" or simply "Cordially." Letters between strangers are more likely to have a more formal close, such as "Respectfully yours" or "Respectfully." Whatever the form used, only the first letter of the close is capitalized.

Signature   The name of the writer should always be typed; the handwritten signature will appear just above it. The signer's title should also be typed immediately below the name if the title is not printed on the letterhead.

When the recipient is a friend, the signer might inscribe only his or her first name. If little or no personal relationship exists between the writer and the receiver, then the full signature is appropriate.

Reference Matter   All business letters prepared by a person other than the sender should contain symbols below the signature block that look like this:

BC: rlb

The capitalized letters are the initials of the writer and the small letters are the initials of the person who keyboarded the letter. If the writer also keyboards the letter, do not include any initials.

The next element in the reference material is a notation about enclosures, if any, that go with the letter. The notation reads like this:

Enc.: [name of enclosure(s)]

This note serves both as a form of documentation by the sender of the message and a flag to the receiver that material is enclosed.

The third element in the reference material designates other people (if any) who are to receive a copy of the letter. The designation reads like this:

C: [names of people who also receive copies]

You may use "bc," which stands for "blind copy." Use this when you want to share information with another without letting those who received official copies know about it. The "bc," should appear on your copy and on copies sent to recipients of the blind copies to alert them that they are being notified confidentially.

Types of Letters

Public relations writers generally find themselves writing six types of letters: information, solicitation, promotion, transmittal, cover and response (including apologies).

Information   Naturally, these letters inform. They let people know about an event coming up, a decision made or an action taken. A letter of recommendation for a person would also be of this type. They are straightforward and try to anticipate and respond to any questions the reader might have. Although these letters might require an acknowledgment, they seldom require a response.

Solicitation   Letters making any kind of request can be considered a solicitation. Nonprofit organizations often write letters asking for contributions or pledges of support of one kind or another. Politicians ask for your support and your vote. These letters should be careful to suggest some sort of reward, usually intrinsic, for that support. Letters from an environmental group may ask you to "Save the Rain Forest." The question is "Why?" The letter will probably tell you that many of the new medicines that could save your life are being discovered in the rain forest.

Promotion   Causes or events are promoted in letters that encourage your acceptance and participation. There should be an emotional appeal in the letter but also a specific call to action. By using subheads, italics, boldface, underlining and indents, you can help the reader to spot these two important elements in your message.

Transmittal   Use letters of transmittal when you're sending a number of materials to someone, like a client. The letter reminds the receiver of what's being sent and why. Sometimes it's appropriate to tell the person to call after receiving the materials, especially if there are any questions or concerns. This letter should have a paragraph that lists the contents, separating items with indented bullets, and with at least the titles in boldface. You want to make it easy for the person to look at the letter, see what should be included in the package and quickly determine if everything listed is indeed included.

Cover   Some people confuse cover letters with letters of transmittal. The cover letter is a very brief note in letter format that simply tells the recipient what is being sent, why and what the recipient might be interested in doing with it.

Response   The most important forms of response letters are the "Apology" and the "Thank You." You should thank people for doing or saying something to support you or your organization. It's amazing how many people think to ask but forget to thank. You can build strong relationships by being gracious and thoughtful.

Apologies   "Airlines apologize a lot to their customers," said an article in *The Wall Street Journal*. "They've made a science of saying sorry out of necessity: The Department of Transportation fines airlines for not responding to customers with 'substantive' answers to gripes." Wayne Shaw, Southwest Airline's director of customer relations, said, "Good apologies are direct: They identify what the transgressor did wrong, take responsibility and either say what will be different in the future or offer some compensation."

Interestingly, "Southwest uses software to perform triage on upset customers. Computers look for keywords that show up in the letters, then sort the notes into four personality categories: Feelers, Drivers, Entertainers and Thinkers. Customer relations agents then write to that type of personality," according to *The Wall Street Journal*. In the article, "Who Is the Sorriest Airline?" the Journal said, "United Airlines, which had the highest rate of complaints filed at the DOT among major airlines the past three years, has a team of about 450 customer-care agents handling general issues and refunds. Add to that 400 people handing frequent-flier program issues and about 100 answering baggage-related letters and emails."[13]

Responses can be intended for private or public use. Response letters usually are written to react to something that has occurred, which may be something said or written. *Private response* letters are written to *individuals* with the anticipation that the letter will not be made public. However, it's always possible that the recipient will make the letter public. Therefore, it's better to write all letters with the anticipation that the contents may be made public.

Some letters are written for public use, and often these are sent to news media to be published or broadcast. Some are written to correct or to put something in perspective. Others are observations or comments. You can find these in newspaper and magazine "letters to the editor" columns and hear them on radio and on television, where a brief version of the contents often is scrolled for the viewer. The important point to remember about public letters is to be direct and concise. The editor of the medium is not going to give you much time or space. Think in terms of sound bites even when you're writing for print.

Choose your words carefully, because the tone of the expression conveys both mood and character. Be persuasive in your choice, because you want to have an impact. You may be writing to change an opinion that a previous presentation in the media has created, or you may be attempting to correct an error that has been made by a medium. Be clear. These letters get a quick scan. You need to be sure your point is not missed.

Some broadcast media allow verbal responses called in to be recorded. If you plan to make such a call, write the response first. Read it into a recorder and play it back. You should say what you have to say in 15 seconds or maybe 20. No more. It won't be used if it isn't succinct. Try your response on some others who are hearing it for the first time without seeing the written piece. Test for tone and clarity. Many public relations writers must have response letters cleared by multiple levels of management. You will have to be persistent to prevent distortion of the message. Be cautious about using humor or sarcasm. These can be easily misunderstood or taken for arrogance.

Proposals and Reports

Remember those book reports from your high school English classes? The reports that public relations people write are not so different. The report author examines what might be a complex set of facts, then puts fingers to keyboard to distill the information into a one-of-a-kind summary.

And do you remember when you said you wanted to drive on public streets the first time? That was a proposal—a suggestion, stating something for consideration.

Proposals and Reports Compared

They may look alike, which can be confusing, but proposals and reports are very different. Their differences become apparent in their purposes. A proposal details a plan of action to be considered. A report summarizes information on some topic.

You might say that a report is a summary of the status of something. Suppose you're on the management team of a food-processing company and marketer. The company has endured a slight decline in market share and profitability the last two years because it has not adopted some new technologies that competitors are using to produce products at lower costs. The chief financial officer was asked to prepare a report that evaluates the economics of these new technologies. That report, contained in a 48-page booklet, is before the team now, having been distributed to members a week earlier so they could study it in detail.

After lengthy discussion, the team asked the director of manufacturing to prepare a proposal that describes in detail what the company must do to acquire these technologies, related costs and a timeline that projects when the new technologies could be put to use. It should be clear that when the report is presented it will deal with a planned, recommended course of action. It is then that the management team must make a go or no-go decision to take the proposal to its board of directors for approval and funding.

The requirements for organizing and writing reports and proposals are similar enough for both to be considered together. As used here, the terms *report* and *proposal* refer to extensive documents that are researched, written and presented much like a traditional scholarly research paper or the manuscript for a monograph or book.

In fact, if you must write a report or proposal of this type, the first thing you should do is get a copy of a style manual such as Kate L. Turabian's *A Manual for Writers of Term Papers, Theses and Dissertations*. A style manual will save you innumerable hours of research time by showing you, as you begin to research the project, what information you need to gather and how to credit it.

Organization of Proposals and Reports

After your research on the topic is completed, you're ready to begin organizing and writing your proposal or report. This requires special skills and attention to details, because a finished project often has as many as seven major sections: letter, front matter, executive summary, body, references, bibliography and appendixes. In a proposal there's also a proposed budget and timeline.

Letter   A letter of documentation should always accompany a report or a proposal. Sometimes a letter of transmittal should also be included if there are many enclosures.

A letter of documentation, often called a *cover letter,* addresses the person or people who will consider the report or proposal. It usually describes both the content of the report and the people who did the research, planning, writing and illustrating. The letter may close with a brief summary of findings or recommendations, and it may call attention to any conditions affecting adoption or rejection. Finally, it should indicate where to locate the person who signed the letter. A letter of documentation is sometimes made a part of the report, in which case it should be inserted immediately following the front matter.

A letter of transmittal is needed when a person or group has been authorized to write a report or proposal. It should seek to establish the credibility of the report or proposal. The letter should note who gave the authorization and when, as well as summarize results or recommendations. It may include a list of acknowledgments of special help or meritorious work by individuals who contributed to the project. Such a letter allows you to include information that may not belong in the body of the document but nonetheless provides additional insights into what is there.

Skillfully written letters of documentation and transmittal prepare readers of the document for what follows.

Front Matter   The front matter in a proposal or report is organized in the same general way as the front matter of this book. It consists of a cover page, a table of contents and a list of tables, figures and illustrations. These pages are numbered serially with small Roman numerals (i, ii, iii, iv, v and so on). Although the cover page is counted in this series of numbers, no number appears on the cover page.

Executive Summary   When an executive summary or synopsis is used, it appears at the end of the front matter and before the body of the proposal or report. Usually only a page or two long, it is a concisely written digest of the content of the document. Its purpose is to give the reader a clear picture of what is in the document. In the business world, *executive summary* is the term most often used, and you'll be expected to use it when your employer asks you to write a report or proposal.

Body   The body of the report or proposal follows the executive summary. It consists of three basic parts: introduction, body and conclusions.

The introduction should review the background of the problem being studied, the scope of the study and the methods used in the study. It should also explain why the study is important, what special problems (if any) were encountered in the course of research and how these were resolved. The last point is especially important because it prepares the reader for any limitations of the study. In a proposal, the introduction might review the activities that have preceded the submission of the proposal—meetings, the request for the proposal and, sometimes, the proposing organization's capabilities and competencies related to the work to be accomplished. Often a proposal is written in response to a request for proposal (RFP) and must follow the guidelines for content specified in the RFP.

The body of a proposal often focuses on the objective and goals to be met if the proposal is accepted, along with the activities to be undertaken and, sometimes, the assumptions made. A timeline for the activities, along with a budget and information on the people who will be undertaking the activities, also is common.

The body of a report should be built around a single, simple statement. Called a *thesis statement* or *hypothesis,* it unifies the entire report and helps you address the issue point by logical point. Develop each point and support it with pertinent facts. Use headings and subheads to guide the reader through the body of the report.

Conclusions should follow naturally from any summary findings in the report or proposal. Sometimes recommendations will stem from your conclusions. Conclusions and recommendations should be stated clearly. This may take courage, because you may conclude or recommend something that your readers would prefer to ignore. Clarity is necessary because a report or proposal that invites many interpretations is not very useful to anyone.

References   In a proposal or report of this type, you must properly cite the source of every piece of information that is not common knowledge to your public. This means using footnotes or endnotes, with complete bibliographic citations, so anyone can locate and read the original materials. In this respect, proposals and reports are exactly like scholarly research papers.

Bibliography   In addition to supplying footnotes or endnotes, you must include a full bibliography. The bibliography, of course, includes all of the basic sources cited in the footnotes or endnotes, but it also includes sources you reviewed but did not specifically cite in the body of the paper. Thus the bibliography identifies the full range of works you consulted, whether or not you eventually cited them.

Appendixes   An appendix contains any charts, tables, illustrations, maps, copies of questionnaires and other exhibits that could not be woven into the body of the paper. As a general rule, the only items of this type that should appear in the body are simple tables and charts illustrating specific points. More complex material goes in the appendixes. Be certain, however, that you interpret the complex materials sufficiently to make them understandable. Each appendix should be labeled separately—Appendix A, B and so on.

Readability and Applicability

A reader of your report or proposal should be able to conclude something from what you have written. Two factors will influence this outcome: readability and applicability.

Readability   If your report or proposal is in a specialized field, your reader expects to see jargon common to that field used in your document. But this is not a license to use jargon without restraint. On the contrary, you should write in plain English with just enough jargon to establish your credibility with the reader.

Jargon invariably makes your writing more difficult to understand. Try Gunning's Fog Index (see http://gunning-fog-index.com/) on some samples of writing in your report. Then go back and do some severe editing to make it clearer and easier to understand.

Unless you're an extraordinarily gifted and lucky writer, you will not be able to write a good proposal or report in the first draft. You will probably have to write the whole report at least twice. You may have to rewrite several times. In this sense, the art of good proposal and report writing is rewriting.

If time allows, you're sure to improve the readability of your report by writing a draft and then putting it aside for a week or more. When you pick up the document and read it cold, trouble spots will jump out at you. Fix them immediately and do the reorganizing and rewriting necessary to clarify the draft. And don't forget that headings, subheads, indented segments, underlining and other visuals, including tables, charts and graphs, can improve understanding.

All these points apply to both reports and proposals, but one consideration applies to proposals alone. In a sense, proposals resemble ad copy. They are meant to persuade—to sell ideas. So showmanship with words counts more in proposals than in reports.

Applicability   When you complete a report, you will want your readers to accept the document as meaningful and significant enough to prompt a course of action. You'll want your readers to say, "This is important. We should do something." When you submit a proposal, you'll be trying to evoke this response: "This is a really good idea. Let's go with it." You will elicit such judgments only if the reader finds what you have written to be clear, reliable and justified. Additionally, what you present should be singularly relevant to the situation. And any action you call for must appear easy to accomplish.

Annual Reports

First you need to know that a corporation whose stock is publicly traded is required to prepare not one but *two* annual reports. One is the SEC Form 10-K annual report to the Securities and Exchange Commission. This form is prepared in a format decreed by the SEC that is plain—no graphics, no photos, no color, just black type on white paper. Because it is a legal document, it usually is prepared by accountants and attorneys, and it must be transmitted electronically to the SEC. The other is the Annual Report to Shareholders.

As a result of corporate scandals involving fraud at companies, including Enron, WorldCom, Global Crossing, Arthur Andersen and others, President George W. Bush signed into law the Sarbanes-Oxley Act of 2002 ("SOX"). The Act mandated a number of reforms to enhance corporate and management responsibility, improve financial disclosures and combat corporate and accounting fraud.

Because SOX requires increased disclosure and reporting, public companies now must provide shareholders much of the information contained in a corporation's SEC Form 10-K. As a result, many companies now provide the Form 10-K to shareholders. Forty-five percent "wrap" their annual report to shareholders around the 10-K, according to Brad Allen in IR Magazine, reporting on a National Investor Relations Institute (NIRI) survey to which 133 companies responded.[14]

Some "wraps" are limited to the cover; others have pages devoted to explaining the company's operations and include four-color photos. The NIRI survey indicates that only 38 percent still use a traditional annual report format, and 95 percent bind the company's proxy statement into the printed report. That's true mainly because those procedures cut costs, since by doing so a company prepares and distributes one—not two—annual reports. And most corporations make their annual reports available on their corporate websites, cutting the cost of mailing paper copies to "information only" distribution lists. The survey indicated that in 77 percent of responding companies, the investor relations department is responsible for the annual report; corporate communications/public relations bears the responsibility in 38 percent and finance/treasury, public affairs and accounting are responsible for 25 percent. The remaining 7 percent said "other" departments handle the responsibility.[15]

The NIRI survey indicated that the most common content in corporate annual reports are: letter from the CEO, five-year financials, auditor's report, information on subsidiaries, objectives for future quarters, market segment information, plans for new products, research and development information, management's discussion and analysis, CSR (corporate social responsibility) information, list of directors and officers and a narrative section of about 15 pages.[16]

Since 2007 the Securities and Exchange Commission (SEC) has allowed companies to provide proxy materials, including annual reports, to shareholders through the Internet.[17]

Direct Response and Direct Advertising

The severest test of your ability as a persuasive copywriter is whether you can write effective direct-response or direct-advertising copy.

Copy that is designed to promote direct action by the audience is called *direct-response copy*. It is the type of message that urges people to take immediate action such as going to a website, mailing in a coupon, calling an 800 number, entering a sweepstakes or figuratively raising their hands and saying, "Hey, we're interested."

Direct-response copy can appear in most any medium. The key is not the type of medium in which the message appears, but the type of message conveyed. If it urges the audience to do something now, it is direct-response copy. For example, a commercial on television from Publishers Clearing House touts its subscriptions and provides an incentive by offering fabulous sweepstake prizes. All you have to do is to call a toll-free number, but you have to call *now*.

Direct-advertising copy appears in written, printed or processed form and is sent via a controlled method of circulation to individuals. There are three types of direct advertising: direct mail, mail order and unmailed direct advertising.

Direct Mail   This covers all forms of mailed direct advertising, except mail order. It includes letters, postcards, booklets, broadsides, brochures, circulars, catalogs and stuffers, among others.

Mail Order   Mail-order copy is responsible for the entire "selling" job. It may appear in a variety of forms, from catalogs such as L. L. Bean's to a letter urging the recipient to give to the Disabled American Veterans.

Unmailed Direct Advertising   Unmailed direct-advertising copy differs from direct mail and mail order only in its method of distribution. It includes promotional pieces that may be delivered to a person's home or may be picked up in a store, showroom, fair or exhibit or at any other site allowing promotional efforts.

All forms of direct-advertising copy are especially difficult to write effectively, because you have to create the medium as well as the message. You don't have the support of a preselected audience from the standard media.

Each message has to stand alone and produce results. In fact, success is carefully measured by the number of responses generated. These can be in any number of forms— for example, coupons, orders or queries—and the response rate measures precisely how much action you have generated with your writing. Once you have designed and written a successful ad that has proved itself, you are not likely to change it very much in the future.

Obviously, the overall design of coupons, order forms and related materials has to be very good, so that people can respond easily.

Out-of-Home Media

The term *out-of-home media* refers to a variety of media—outdoor, transit, skywriting and the like. The key feature they share is that readers go to them rather than the other way around. This characteristic imposes severe constraints on what you can say and how you can say it. The average reading time is about 5 seconds or less, so the number of words is usually 8 to 10 words. Each out-of-home medium is unique, but the general guidelines for outdoor media apply to all.

There are three basic kinds of outdoor billboards: the poster panel, the painted bulletin and the digital display. Poster panels, which are printed on large printing presses, are of two standard sizes: 8 sheets are 5 by 11 feet or 30 sheets, 12 by 25 feet. These are developed by an agency and shipped to the outdoor company that will be putting them up. Painted panels are created on-site, which could be a board, a building, a concrete wall or almost anything else, so the size depends on the site. However, most painted signs are 14 by 48 feet. Some of these have extensions, called cutouts, on the top or side. Digital displays have several advantages in that they can be changed easily and are visible even in bad weather.

Many advertisers use poster panels routinely, changing their messages monthly or several times a year, and advertising in many markets simultaneously. Once the cost of designing and producing the panel is absorbed, the costs become incrementally smaller as additional sites or markets are used.

An advertiser will use "paints" only when cultivating one or a very few markets and when the message will not be changed within a year. Usually an advertiser will not use more than two or three painted bulletins, or "paints," in a specific market, depending on the size of the market.

Digital outdoor signs are rapidly gaining popularity because of their ability to command attention and the fact that they can be changed much less expensively. Ads on digital boards often are rotated—using ads from several clients—so looking at a digital board is a bit like watching commercials on TV.

Outdoor advertising—called *outdoor* for short—is remarkably cost-effective when you need to saturate a market with an idea. The price of an outdoor campaign is based on what are called *showings*. A 100-show is a campaign in which enough signs, including some illuminated for night viewing, are set up to provide 100 percent coverage of the mobile market for a 30-day period. Studies show that it is not unusual for a 100-show to produce a high level of message repetitions—an average of 25 or more per month. A 50-show thus would involve half the coverage and repetition of a 100-show.

Copywriting is especially difficult for outdoor. Because your message usually can be seen for only a few seconds, it has to be especially simple and compelling to register with the viewer. As a general rule, you can't use more than about eight words, including the company's name, and expect the message to punch through. No more than three verbal and visual elements should appear in the message. So you must restrain yourself in both your verbal and visual thinking if you expect to write a good outdoor message.

Simplicity is the hallmark of good outdoor. If your message is complex, don't use outdoor. But if you can reduce your message to just a few words, and if you can employ bold, even garish, visuals, you will be able to do a lot with a little.

Although ads for subways, taxis and similar media have different size specifications, the same guidelines apply to them as to outdoor.

Sales Promotion

Point-of-purchase or point-of-sale advertising, samples, contests, advertising specialties and cooperative advertising are sales-promotion pieces, as are coupons, booklets, brochures and mailers. (See Chapter 12 for information on brochures.)

Point-of-purchase advertising is advertising displayed with a product, service or idea and specifically designed to inspire the customer to buy on impulse. Most point-of-purchase advertising is strong on emotional impact, particularly symbolism, and ties in with other existing promotional materials to create additional recognition. Another promotional device is the sample, a free product sent out along with descriptive literature.

The copy accompanying a sample often tries to inspire a sense of obligation in prospective customers by urging them to accept the "gift."

Contests are designed to offer customers something extra and to maintain their awareness of the idea through participation and anticipation. Advertising specialties can be anything with the corporate logo on it, but generally they are useful objects, like ice scrapers for windshields, or things with high visibility that will be remembered.

In cooperative advertising, the retail outlet appeals for direct sales while receiving support from the manufacturer. When the manufacturer's logo appears alongside the retailer's in a local company's advertising for a product or service, this is usually a tip-off that the ad is a cooperative one, with the retailer and manufacturer sharing in the cost of space, time or position.

Exercises

1. Write an email or a letter asking for money. The appeal could be directed to a family member who may be providing some assistance with the students' educational expenses, to the administrator of a trust fund who has the students on allowances, or to an employer who is paying them a wage. The message should be especially written to appeal to a specific individual. Also provide a description of that person and the rationale for the approach taken in the letter. The letter should be serious.

2. You are the vice president of communication at O. Joyitz Funn Manufacturing Systems. OJF is a major producer of plastic toys. The research and development department has recently created and successfully tested a new toy. Tests seem to suggest that the new toy, called "Rotzie," will be a huge seller. OJF is frantically working on a plant expansion to help accommodate the demand it expects when Rotzie is introduced. You are equally busy getting communication plans ready for a formal announcement two months from today. Although some employees are aware of Rotzie, most of them have no clue as to how its potential sales will affect them or OJF. You know that you must put together news releases for local and national media as well as trade journals, and prepare speeches, brochures, sales literature and other things. But right now, you're pondering how to write a memo or email to employees to make them aware of the importance of Rotzie to the future of the company. Discuss the content for the memo or email, then write the memo or email.

3. You are a public relations writer for The Pet Spa & Stuff, a major provider of pet supplies and grooming in large stores across the USA. The company president received a letter from an irate customer who brought her (expensive!) show dog to a Pet Spa & Staff near her home to be groomed for an upcoming show. According to her letter, the animal was "scalped" by a groomer who was "uncaring, untrained, unapologetic" and so on. "Before and after" photos accompanying the customer's letter confirm the accuracy of the letter. You checked and found that instructions to the groomer had been mixed up, with the result that the show dog got a very short "summer cut." As a result, the dog cannot appear at the show next week. The woman's letter mentions her attorney. Write the letter of apology for the signature of the CEO. If you believe you should confer with another person or persons as you write the letter, indicate who those people would be.

CHAPTER ELEVEN

Newsletters

Can putting together a newsletter really be *fun*? Well, if your newsletter is *The Moos-Paper,* it *is* fun! *The Moos-Paper* is published online by The Red Cow, a pub in Chrishall, Essex, 60 miles north of London. *The Moos-Paper* headlines include "Escaping the Herd?" and "Feeling Socia-Bull." The pub carries out the theme by listing its location as "7 miles west of Saffron Walden and 7 miles east of Royston … **but that's not as the cow flies**!" Their menu? "Amazing Grazing," of course, and they have an Annual Moosic Fest. Corny? Maybe, but certainly interesting! Check it out at http://www.theredcow.com/the-moos-paper.php.

What *is* a newsletter? Dictionary.com defines it as "A periodically published work containing news and announcements on some subject, typically with a small circulation."

Newsletters often are distributed by email or as an email attachment, while e-newsletters usually reside on websites. When a new edition of an e-newsletter is available, a link to it usually is distributed by email. Some organizations print their newsletters on paper and make them available to employees or members or mail them to homes. Other organizations, including Southwest Airlines, distribute brief daily newsletters that are sent to supervisors throughout their operating areas and are posted there on bulletin boards.

A newsletter or magazine often is rated as the single most important benefit of membership in an organization. At Public Relations Society of America (PRSA), a member survey indicated that the society's more than 21,000 members said PRSA's newspaper, *Public Relations Tactics,* and its magazine, *Public Relations Strategist,* rank high among products and services.

Subscriber newsletters that are operated as businesses carry valued information for which people are willing to pay, and pay substantially. These newsletters—trade, industry or professional—often are monitored by business reporters and bloggers for trends and other news. How has the Internet affected the value attributes of these print media? The answer seems to be *enhancement*.

Some subscriptions to newsletters and e-newsletters are free; it's just a matter of signing up to be included in the "distribution." Why would an organization do this? Obviously, whether the organization is commercial or nonprofit, access to extended audiences is seen as an opportunity.

Because these publications are being delivered both by the USA Postal Service and by the Internet, they pose new writing challenges. Writing for the two is not the same, as you discovered in Chapters 5 and 9. Nor can designs move entirely comfortably between the two.

Most newsletters now carry their website addresses on the printed versions. (And if the newsletter is membership-based or subscriber-based, the website likely has a home page with a requirement for the member/subscriber to enter a password to get to the information.)

As organizations began to downsize, many public relations people took advantage of their job losses to go into business for themselves. Early on, those were the people most comfortable with the journalistic tactics of public relations and the ones who had mastered desktop publishing. Now the emphasis is on people who are comfortable working in cyberspace and preparing newsletters that are unlikely to appear in a printed form.

The significance of this to public relations writers is that many college graduates find their first jobs in the newsletter industry. The opportunity usually comes because they understand how to gather information, write in a compelling and interesting way and know desktop publishing.

For organizations, the increasing number of professional newsletters requires an awareness of how their organization is being covered because the coverage is often more objective and critical than they may be comfortable with.

Criteria for Successful Newsletters

Several criteria affect the success of any newsletter:

- It must fill an unmet need.
- It must be able to do things for its audience other media can't and it must convey information in some unique way so people will pay attention to it.
- It must be distributed in a way that is efficient and regularly reaches its intended audience.
- There must be a person or a staff of people interested in it, skilled enough to produce it and with time committed solely to its production.
- It must be a serial publication (Vol. #, No. #) issued with enough frequency that its contents remain timely in the eyes of its readers.

(See Figure 11.1 for an example of a newsletter written in easy-to-understand language.)

FIGURE 11.1

England's Health & Safety Newsletter   *This newsletter from England's Health & Safety Executive (HSE), is part of the agency's work to prevent death, injury and ill health in Great Britain's workplaces. Information is presented in layperson's language, and the graphics add interesting touches.*

Health and Safety Executive

Filling Unmet Needs

Intranets, memos, letters, bulletin boards and staff meetings commonly are used to communicate inside an organization. But as an organization grows, these sometimes aren't sufficient to carry all the interesting and important information that should be shared. A newsletter can be as large and as frequent as necessary (within the budget) to carry important information.

It's important for you to understand that one medium just isn't adequate in reaching a large number of people. Within any organization, both demographics and psychographics vary tremendously. Trying to reach even hundreds of people—much less millions—is destined to fail.

AARP, previously known as the American Association of Retired Persons, has 40 million members and offices in all 50 states, the District of Columbia, Puerto Rico and the USA Virgin Islands. It tries to reach each segment of its membership in appropriate and appealing ways. To do that, it publishes the world's largest-circulation magazine, *AARP The Magazine.* Its newspaper, *AARP Bulletin,* is printed 10 times a year and published online daily. AARP also publishes *Segunda Juventud (Second Youth),* a bimonthly magazine and radio program in both Spanish and English; "Prime Time," a public affairs radio program; and two syndicated TV shows: "Inside E Street," a public affairs show; and "My Generation," a magazine-style show. Its award-winning website is aarp.org. This one huge nonprofit organization has a multitude of writing jobs! Preparation of news releases, speeches, marketing materials and other materials requires additional writers.

A newsletter can reach out and mobilize the self-interest of such vast audiences. Even if an organization has a magazine, it often emphasizes feature material, but a newsletter, as the first part of the name signifies, can focus on information that is current, thus making it more immediately useful to its readers. Other media, such as newspapers, magazines and television, provide data, but none of them provides the select, in-depth and sharply focused information found in newsletters.

Newsletter Developed in Response to Specific Need   Baycrest Health Sciences in Ontario, affiliated with the University of Toronto, needed to cut its staff and find new sources of revenue because of changes in Ontario's healthcare funding formula. Research found that only 64 percent of employees understood the budget issues. Only a third of the staff has dedicated computer access, so email, social media and intranet postings can't be relied upon to reach the majority of employees.

An employee survey showed that 83 percent of respondents indicated newsletters were their preferred communication. So a new publication, "Financial Focus," was created to focus on the financial strengthening process, using a plain-language, transparent approach that honestly presents the challenges, explains the decisions being made and takes an aspirational look at opportunities for investment and growth.

Each edition features a message from the Chief Financial Officer (CFO), providing context for the newsletter as well as a human face for the financial issues. Rather than sharing information in a third-person style, the CFO message personalizes each newsletter and adds accountability for the financial strengthening process.

In a December survey, 81 percent of respondents said they felt Informed or Very Informed about Baycrest's financial challenges, the budget process and the opportunities for the future—up from 64 percent in September. (See Figure 11.2.)

FIGURE 11.2

Newsletter Developed in Response to Specific Need

Financial Focus

Baycrest
Innovations in aging

October 2013 — Achieving financial strength—together.

By working together, we can achieve success

By Brian Mackie, Vice President, Finance and Support Services

Welcome to our first issue of *Financial Focus*, a monthly newsletter designed to share information with you about our budget and financial strengthening processes. It's important to know that the work we're currently undertaking looks well beyond our next year's budget, and aims to establish a much firmer financial footing for Baycrest in the years to come.

I think we all understand that the funding environment for hospitals in Ontario has changed significantly, and it's fair to assume that all healthcare organizations—including ours—need to find innovative solutions for ensuring fiscal accountability and sustainability. The infographic at the bottom of this page shows the hard reality the province is facing.

The good news is that we are in far better shape than many of our peers. We are projecting about a $6 million gap between our revenue and our expenses

next year, which on an overall budget of $156 million is not an insurmountable challenge. While it is never easy to find additional efficiencies, especially having already tightened our belts, there are a number of things we can do to help us achieve our target. As an organization we are looking at additional revenue generating and commercialization opportunities, as well as a new clinical services plan. We believe there could be some changes to Health System Funding Reform in Ontario that will positively benefit Baycrest and our unique slate of programs and services. And we have been working with our Foundation

to find Enhanced Programming Funds that can help us reduce our reliance on shrinking government funds.

Even in the face of some positive opportunities for 2014-15, though, we find ourselves with a one-time operating deficit for this year. To help manage this shortfall, we have implemented a temporary hiring and discretionary spending freeze. You can read more about these measures in this newsletter.

I believe that by working together, we can meet our financial objectives. It's important that you, our staff, physicians and volunteers, understand the environment we find ourselves in, and are able to contribute toward achieving success.

We will continue to keep you informed about our ongoing budget and financial strength initiatives, and I welcome your comments or questions at bmackie@baycrest.org.

Sub-groups strategize on 2014-15 budget opportunities

Three sub-groups of the Budget and Financial Strength Steering Committee have been formed to oversee specific pieces of the 2014-15 budget planning process and ongoing financial strengthening activities at Baycrest.

Efficiencies and Financial Reporting Sub-Group
This sub-group will focus on strengthening the financial sustainability of Baycrest by guiding the efficiencies component of the 2014-15 budget process through benchmarking against comparator institutions. As well, they will develop a sustainable process to better monitor financial results, control expenses, improve accountability, share best practices and create an ongoing forum for discussion and consideration of cost reduction and revenue enhancement initiatives.

Revenue and Corporate Expenses Sub-Group
The primary purpose of this group is to create a rigorous process to ensure all revenues are being captured and maximized, and to identify and implement strategies to reduce corporate expenditures.

Strategic Sub-Group
Members of the Strategic Sub-Group will guide the Strategic/Service Reduction component of the 2014-15 budget through zero-based budgeting principles, guided by Baycrest's 2013-18 Strategic Plan.

Membership of these sub-groups comprises Vice Presidents, Directors and Managers across the organization.

Q. Can we expect more program, service or staff reductions in the future?

A. Financial stability is a core competency of any organization, especially one that must respond to the changing nature of the healthcare funding environment. That means we must continually examine how we are doing things—for efficiencies, for strategic alignment and for effective-

ness. Change is a constant factor in our field, and for Baycrest we have never accepted the status quo.

It would simply not be possible—or honest—to promise no future reductions.

But it's not all doom and gloom.

In fact, we believe we have the opportunity to strengthen our financial position in order to ensure we can sustain and even invest in some of the programs and services that make Baycrest so special.

That may mean adjusting what we currently do to bring things into alignment with our strategic plan and our funding accountabilities, but it may also help us gain the much-needed stability we are seeking.

The cost of NOT curbing healthcare spending in Ontario

42¢   10   70¢

Last year, **42 cents** of every Ontario tax dollar was spent on healthcare. Without making changes to the way health services are funded, those costs could balloon to **70 cents** in just 12 years.

2012-13   2024-25

* Based on Ontario Ministry of Health and Long-Term Care projections

Source: http://www.hse.gov.uk/pubns/books/newsletter-winter13.pdf

Uniqueness

A successful newsletter is one that conveys information particularly useful and interesting to its audience. Of the two general types—organizational and subscription—the organizational goes to employees of an organization or members of an association. As an employee or as a member of an association, you have special interests related to that involvement. For example, if you fish for bass, you may become a member of a bass fishing club. That club will have a newsletter that informs you regularly about forthcoming fishing tournaments, who is the current leader in club points and related matters. No other medium provides you with such targeted information.

Subscription newsletters also address special interests, both personal and professional. Some of your interests or hobbies may lead you to subscribe to newsletters that give you "inside information." For example, if you invest in the stock market, you might subscribe to at least one market newsletter that keeps you abreast of news relating to the market. If your interest is in precious metals, you may even focus narrowly on a gold and silver market newsletter. As an avid booster of a professional or collegiate sports team, you may get a personal view of that team through a newsletter that goes only to its contributing boosters.

Note that in all these examples and others, although information about the organizations and interests is available from other sources, none can speak to your special interest as directly as a newsletter.

Writing

As we have said before, your writing should follow the pattern of the way you talk—better yet, the way your readers talk. It should be casual and should match the demographics of the people for whom it is written. If you work in a high-tech organization, and are responsible for an employee newsletter, keep in mind that a significant percentage of the staff may be scientists. You may need to plan a special online publication just for them, because their vocabularies and understanding of scientific terms is far above the average.

But how about average reading levels? "According to a study conducted in late April [2015] by the U.S. Department of Education and the National Institute of Literacy, 32 million adults in the U.S. can't read. That's 14 percent of the population. 21 percent of adults in the U.S. read below a 5th grade level, and 19 percent of high school graduates can't read."[1] Keep that in mind as you write for a newsletter intended for manufacturing plant employees, for example. In other words, keep it simple.

Distribution

All of the effort and expense of putting together a newsletter is wasted unless the newsletter reaches your intended public. If you work for a membership organization such as a professional society or trade association, that's not too difficult. The organization collects information about each member and typically stores the information in a database. Then the mail or email addresses can be used to send each edition of the newsletter to members as well as others whom the organization wants to receive the publication. Even so, you need to be aware that many people change their email addresses frequently.

The organization can ask its members to update profile information through its website, but that activity might not be high among your public's priorities. Because many societies and associations charge annual dues and send paper invoices each year, the dues billing provides an opportunity to update members' addresses, phone numbers and email addresses.

But suppose you're volunteering to help pass a clean-up-the-environment issue in your community. You may have to start "from scratch" to build an email database. Since you can't just pull information from a directory, it takes a lot of effort and attention to gather, file and maintain such a list.

If your newsletter is printed on paper, getting it into the hands of its target audience is a key element of success. And it can be quite expensive. If you can't create a mailing list with the right names and addresses and keep it up to date, you can't be successful. Of course, names of people and their addresses are easy to get when distributing a newsletter through interoffice mail. Some organizations save time and money by simply putting quantities of printed newsletters at central locations like lobbies and break rooms where employees can pick them up; others ask mail room personnel to deliver a newsletter to each employee.

If you must create your own list, be prepared to spend a lot of time and money building it. Maintaining its accuracy over the years also is expensive and time-consuming. So is delivery by the USA Postal Service, even if your newsletter qualifies for a second-class mail permit. Distribution sounds easy, but it often isn't. So be resourceful and persistent in creation and maintenance of an effective distribution system.

Knowledge and Skills

Producing a newsletter that earns the loyalty of its readers is time-consuming work. It also takes specialized knowledge and a combination of skills at writing, editing, designing and visualizing. Many who start newsletters are short on both knowledge and skills, but if they are long on commitment, they learn by doing. That's often the case in small organizations because there probably isn't someone on the staff who has the academic or professional training needed for the task. Small budgets also may preclude hiring someone with the knowledge and skills needed. Newsletters from big organizations usually aim for and achieve higher professional standards. But it is the restricted, focused coverage of news that makes readers look forward to the next issue.

Frequency

The frequency of a newsletter is governed by three primary issues—budget, timeliness and serialization. Your budget may restrict your frequency as well as the number of pages in your newsletter. There are trade-offs you can make. If you cut the number of pages, you may be able to publish more often and stay within a tight budget. If timeliness is critical, you must publish more often, even if with fewer pages. If the timeliness of newsletter content is not an issue, you may publish less often but with more pages.

Some guidelines are provided by Mark Brownlow in email-marketing-reports.com:

- Any email newsletter that comes out less frequently than once a month is unlikely to make an impression on its readers.
- Very frequent newsletters (more frequent than weekly) or very infrequent newsletters (less frequent than monthly) must offer exceptional value or impact. For infrequent

newsletters, exceptional value and impact can make up for infrequency. For frequent newsletters, exceptional value and impact justify the time the reader has to allocate to the emails.

- Your preferred frequency from the perspective of recognition and awareness also depends on how else you are communicating with these email addresses. Take into account other newsletters you may be sending them, or whether you already send them promotional emails. In other words, look at the bigger picture before settling on a frequency.[2]

Perhaps the least understood influence is serialization. For a printed publication to be classified as a newsletter by the USA Postal Service, it must be issued on a regular basis, and each issue must contain volume and issue numbers. A publication issued on an irregular schedule, although it may have every appearance of a newsletter, isn't one unless published at regular intervals. Also, the only way the USA Postal Service will grant a second-class mailing permit is for you to publish it on a regular schedule. If you distribute your newsletter through interoffice mail, there can be some variability in your schedule, but you still need volume and issue numbers. If you use the USA mail, you must keep a rigid publishing schedule. If your newsletter is distributed only by email, this restriction is not an issue.

Format

If your intention is to deliver your newsletter electronically, your format choices should relate to the readers' ability to access and read your content. Email is almost always a player. One of the better choices is to distribute an email message containing headlines and perhaps a brief summary of each article, with links to "Read more." This allows you to place the bulk of the content on a website where you can use graphics without affecting the size of the email messages. But remember that even within a technology-heavy organization, some employees don't have access to computers during their workdays. That might include drivers, heavy equipment operators, maintenance personnel and so on.

If the newsletter is to be delivered on paper, the best format for a specific newsletter often is a curious blend resulting from content, budget and readers' convenience. If the intent is, as in most newsletters, to write tight, edit tighter and present information in almost-bulletin form, an 8.5-by-11-inch page size may be perfectly suitable. Readers who keep backfiles of the newsletter in binders or in cabinets like the convenience of an 8.5-by-11-inch sheet size. Copies of newsletters that routinely get routed from office to office within an organization also seem to work better in an 8.5-by-11-inch page size. If your newsletter routinely runs longer pieces, especially feature material, a larger page size—such as 11-by-17 inches or tabloid—may be more appropriate. If pictures and graphs are important parts of each issue, larger sheet sizes may be needed.

Format also requires that you weigh the relative merits of vertical versus horizontal layout of content. Small sheet sizes can accommodate either vertical or horizontal displays, if they are done skillfully. Nevertheless, horizontal displays of content are usually more attractive in larger sheet sizes. That apparently is a function of the more pleasing proportions produced by the vertical length of a large sheet size, such as 11-by-17 inches.

Unless your budget is generous, money may restrict your choice of formats as well as the extent to which you can afford to use visual materials and color. Four-color printing can hit your budget hard, but is very important if your distribution is large. Of course that drives down the unit cost. It also, as noted previously, influences the frequency of your newsletter and the number of pages per issue.

Word processing programs like Word and WordPerfect provide templates that simplify and speed the production of newsletters. Some templates are part of the program installed on your computer; others are provided without charge online by the software company.

Although it is important to know about the criteria that can make a newsletter successful, it is equally important to know about the types and functions of newsletters.

Types and Functions of Newsletters

The main purpose of newsletters is to communicate regularly with members of a special public. Sharing information sustains the unity of those bound together only by a special interest.

Employee and Member Newsletters

Good managers know that the success of the company or institution rests on the cooperation and support of employees as much as on their own managerial skills. As an organization grows, however, it becomes increasingly difficult to communicate policy or other information on a personal basis. A newsletter may serve this purpose.

An organization's endurance depends on maintaining its membership base and attracting new members. Frequently a newsletter is a periodic reminder of the organization and invites or structures the member's participation in the organization's activities.

In the case of both employees and members, though, the timeliness of newsletter information may suffer from the production and delivery process. There's something to the term *snail mail*. For employees who use computers in their jobs, email systems may be a better delivery system for messages that need immediate attention, and members of organizations often turn to websites for news and updates.

Internal Communication   Newsletters nevertheless are an effective channel of internal communication. Their content is carefully selected, written and presented to convey a common experience and a feeling of belonging, and to promote identification and unity with the group. A newsletter shouldn't be the only means of communicating with employees or members. Interpersonal communication is the most preferred and most effective way to communicate. But as an organization grows, other techniques need to supplement the limited amount of time that senior executives can spend with individuals and small groups.

In many organizations, email is used extensively to communicate. If it's the main source for messages, people get turned off with the increased number of emails they receive. A newsletter can consolidate the messages and provide an outlet for announcements and changes.

Personal Touch   Newsletters are often expected to help humanize what may otherwise be viewed as an impersonal relationship. Because of this, a common thread of content runs through newsletters: a focus on accomplishments.

Employee newsletters often focus on work-related accomplishments. For example, an employee may be given special recognition in the company's newsletter for having developed a new materials-handling system that saves the company thousands of dollars annually. The company is obviously better because of the employee's contribution, which is acknowledged among his or her peers in the newsletter. Such recognition also implies that others can get the same kind of treatment if they contribute beyond the normal call of duty.

Employees often are recognized, too, as people worth knowing because of their dedication, skill or accomplishments in areas not related to their jobs. For example, Rose McKenna devotes many hours of volunteer service weekly to the Big Sisters program. Rose is someone you should know, not because she is one of three quality-control supervisors at the plant but because she is who she is. Companies and institutions routinely encourage employees to take an active interest in community affairs because they create goodwill toward the company or institution.

Newsletters for organizations also call attention to the accomplishments of the organization, primarily as achieved through its members. This kind of recognition encourages others. If it is a nonprofit organization that is primarily driven by volunteerism, the recognition may be critical not only to encourage other volunteers, but also to convince potential donors that the organization engages in worthwhile projects.

In their efforts to humanize the company or institution, newsletter writers sometimes use humor. Humor is, of course, a good method of conveying some information. However, unless you have a special gift for writing humor, avoid it, because poor humor can come across as trite. And it can be inadvertently offensive as well. If you use humor now and then, remember that you should never poke fun at anyone other than yourself or the company or institution.

Gary F. Grates, who leads the Corporate and Strategy practices at W2O Group Worldwide, says today's employees "are working with the volume off. People are inundated with so much information—most of it irrelevant and conflicting—that it overwhelms and confuses them. [It] creates cynicism instead of enthusiasm, like watching a sports event with the volume turned off. Employees determine *truth* and *reality* by watching behavior—they are watching but choosing not to listen."[3]

He added, "Just when organizations have made improving relationships with employees a priority, they've encountered an interesting, sobering reality—employees aren't engaged—they aren't listening." Robyn Reilly, in "Five Ways to Improve Employee Engagement Now," said "According to Gallup's State of the Global Workplace report, only 13% of employees worldwide are engaged at work. New Zealand has one of the highest levels of engaged employees among the countries surveyed, at 23%. Australia's engagement rate is similar, at 24%. But both countries fall short of the United States, where 30% of employed residents are engaged at work."[4]

The report described *engaged employees* as those who "work with passion and feel a profound connection to their company. They drive innovation and move the organization forward." *Not-engaged* employees, the report stated, "are essentially 'checked out.' They're sleepwalking through their workday, putting time—but not energy or passion—into their work." According to the report, "*actively disengaged* employees aren't just unhappy at work; they're busy acting out their unhappiness. Every day, these workers undermine what their engaged coworkers accomplish."[5]

Engagement affects the bottom line. "Every one percent increase in employee engagement indicates a 0.6 percent growth in sales, accordingly to Aon Hewitt's 2013 Trends in Global Employee Engagement report. Applying this logic to a $5 billion company with a gross margin of 55 percent and 15 percent operating margin, a one percent increase in engagement would be worth $20 million—hardly pocket change."[6]

"Companies that are highly effective at both communication and change management are 2.5 times as likely to be high-performing than those that are not, according to Towers Watson's 2011–2012 Change and Communication ROI Study Report."[7]

Special-Interest Subscriber Newsletters

The term *special interest* describes group relationships bound by a common interest other than as an employee or a member.

The purpose of these newsletters is to communicate information about the special interest that binds the group. Information is thus highly targeted and seldom presents anything not directly related to the interest of the group.

Writing style is often informal and, depending on the field of interest, may involve jargon. For example, a newsletter for personal computer hackers may be filled with computerese. If you are really interested in communicating fully, though, you'll minimize the jargon and stay with simple English. (See Figure 11.3.)

What's significant about special-interest subscriber newsletters is that the information has to be substantive enough that people feel they are getting value for their money. They

---

FIGURE 11.3

Subscription Newsletter *Many public relations professionals keep up with changes in the field by subscribing to newsletters that follow recent public relations research, trends and people. One such newsletter is PR Daily, one of several subscription newsletters published by Lawrence Ragan Communications, Inc. The publication is available only online because the company discontinued printing paper copies of the newsletters in the fall of 2013.*

Source: Lawrence Ragan Communications; used with permission.

are paying for information about lifestyles (traveling, health, economics); earning money or investing it; computers (new software and technology updates); hobbies (gardening, scuba diving); collecting (everything from antique glassware to baseball cards) or renovating old real estate (from houses to office buildings). Subscription newsletters offer a lifeline to important information for people concerned with these and other topics.

Technical and Content Considerations

There is no best way to prepare a newsletter. The writing style may range from informal to formal, but it is always keenly focused on the interest of the group at hand. Some newsletters are simply prepared on a computer, printed, photocopied, folded and mailed. Others are elaborately designed and printed on fine-quality paper. Budget, of course, is a key factor in determining the appearance and method of reproduction. The important point to remember is that the newsletter's content, not its appearance, counts most. If the content is perceived as important by readers, you have accomplished your purpose. (See Table 11.1.)

Reporting and Writing for Newsletters

Reporting and writing for newsletters are two very different tasks. Reporting deals with getting information. Writing deals with analyzing and packaging information.

Reporting   Getting useful information is the lifeblood of any newsletter. There is no reason for a newsletter if it doesn't have information that other media don't have. Otherwise, potential readers may simply yawn away its existence. So reporting is a key element of a good newsletter.

Relying on standard journalistic approaches to fact gathering won't do. You must have an angle that sets your search process apart from others. For example, the *White House Bulletin* began in 1990 with the idea that other media reporting on White House activities were overlooking many important details. Written by an editorial staff of former White House and congressional officials relying on inside sources and wire-service reports, the newsletter is a daily, Internet- and fax-delivered news service for subscribers. In a few years, it has become a mainstay of the Washington press corps as well as government leaders. As it sifts continually for overlooked details, the *White House Bulletin* has scooped national media several times on some major stories.

You can look for a newsletter angle by identifying a gap and trying to fill it. Examples of filling gaps show in these newsletter titles: *Underground Storage Tank Guide, Back Pain Monitor* and *Anesthesia Malpractice Protector*.

Get It Right or Get Out   Every reporter makes mistakes. But mistakes often are deadlier in newsletters than they are in the mass media, because you're dealing with an audience with specialized knowledge. Readers spot mistakes quickly, and they are not forgiving. Because of your mistake, they feel that you've broken faith with their trust. Your credibility and the future of your newsletter may go down the drain. That's especially the case if you're reporting for a commercial, profit-making newsletter. Even a decimal point out of place

T A B L E 1 1 . 1	*Newsletters*

Newsletters

What Do People Want to Know?

By Jeff Rubin, The Newsletter Guy

Guess what's the most frequent question I'm asked about publishing newsletters? OK. The second most. After people want to know how much it costs, the question I hear the most is "What should I put in my newsletter?" It's a good question. I know because I see a lot of bad newsletters that contain information I'm not interested in and don't pertain to my business. How do you get the right mix to keep your customers, potential customers and/or employees reading? Here are some of my thoughts.

External Newsletters

These are for your customers and potential customers. What are they interested in? Do you think they'd like to hear about who in your company got married, had a baby or celebrated a birthday, or about how your new product or service can save them time and money and make their businesses more efficient?

Give your readers useful information:

- A few ideas they can implement immediately.
- Updates on trends in your industry which may affect them.
- "How to" information so they can do things themselves (you can't expect your customers to buy EVERYTHING from you).
- General articles that help them save time and money and make their business and personal lives more meaningful.
- A great way to honor a customer is to highlight them in your newsletter. This not only creates good will between you and the customer you're writing about, but shows others that you value your business relationships.

Internal Newsletters

What do employees want to know? A survey conducted by the International Association of Business Communicators yielded the following results:

- Organizational plans for the future—company goals, expansion, etc.
- Job advancement opportunities.
- Job related "how to" information.
- How local, state, world events or changes in the business climate affect their job, their company and their customers.
- Productivity improvement.
- Human Resources policies and practices.
- Staff changes and promotions.
- Benefits information.
- How we're doing vs. the competition.
- Recognition of employees for achievements.
- Human interest stories about employees/customers.
- Personal news (birthdays, marriages, anniversaries, births, etc.).
- News of what's going on in departments/divisions.
- Financial results.
- How profits are used.
- Advertising and promotional plans.
- Company's community involvement.

Jeff Rubin, a former newspaper reporter and editor and instructor at The Learning Annex in San Francisco, is The Newsletter Guy, owner of the Pinole, California-based newsletter publishing firm of the same name (www .thenewsletterguy.com). He's written and designed more than 1,600 company newsletters since starting his business in 1981. He may be reached via e-mail at jeff@thenewsletterguy.com or by phone at (877) 588-1212.

can be disastrous for your readers. You must be right all the time. Impossible? No, it just means that you do what all reporters should do routinely, but often don't—check, double-check and check again.

No-Nonsense News   Commercial subscriber newsletters, especially, adhere to a hard-news policy. Fluff, features and humor have no place in these newsletters. However, employee and member newsletters may carry soft news, but if the news is all soft the news-letter loses its audience. Audiences read newsletters expecting to find current information that is important to them. So go light on soft stuff.

Writing Tips for Newsletters

Newsletter recipients are likely to be fairly cohesive groups. Those receiving a particular newsletter already belong to a club or are employees of a company, or are philosophically aligned with or at least inclined toward a group. Assume but also reinforce readers' areas of shared knowledge and commitment. Use acronyms and other abbreviations accordingly.

As their name implies, newsletters have much in common with newspapers. They are often read for their content and then discarded. The standard rules of grammar, punctuation and spelling apply to newsletters as they do to all other media. However, there are some different emphases.

Crisp, Clear Style   Sentences in newsletters are mostly bare bones—subject-verb-object. Adjectives and adverbs are scarce. Compound clauses and sentences are uncommon. In short, the writing style in newsletters is simply spartan. Much of it might even remind you of what you'd see in a news bulletin. There are three secrets to this type of writing. First, you must know the needs of your public and keep up with changes in those needs. Second, you must know the subject matter very well. That comes from good reporting as described previously. Third, write in your usual fashion but then edit out about half of what you've written. If you allow yourself to get enamored with your prose, you can't be a good newsletter writer. You have to cut and trim until only a polished diamond of information remains. In that sense, editing your copy properly is more difficult in newsletters than it is in most newspapers or magazines.

Five Ws and the H   The who, what, when, where, why and how of standard newswriting also is important in newsletters. But the angle chosen for the newsletter may put the emphasis on one of these in story after story after story. Angle not only influences the focus of your reporting, it also may shape the way you write a story. If you concentrate on enter-tainment celebrities, the "who" is paramount in your newsletter. If you focus on back pain, "what" gets emphasized throughout your newsletter.

You also should remember to avoid summary leads. Put the key point into the lead sentence and build the body of the story on that key point only. If there are several key points, make each one a separate story. Use the KISS method—Keep It Short, Simple. (See Table 11.2.)

Fitting Newsletter Copy and Design

Designing newsletters to display information attractively is important in gaining attention for your message.

TABLE 11.2	*Newsletters—15 tips on writing, editing* A newsletter is the paring knife of communication tools. It seems simple and is easy to take for granted. Handled well, however, it's a highly capable tool.

1. **Keep your strategic audiences in mind, always.**
   What is relevant to them? What is important?

2. **Effective management involves planning and influence.**
   Develop a publication structure, an editorial calendar and written writers guidelines.

3. **A newsletter must be sustainable.**
   Be realistic about the amount of content you can consistently produce.

4. **Begin with good basics and build on solid ground.**
   The most basic newsletter should have a few lead stories, shorter news items and a message from your leader. A more developed publication might include features, departments, columns, an editorial, cartoon, in-house news, news tidbits, regional round-ups, etc.

5. **Deadlines are sacred.**
   Build in a safety cushion to allow for unexpected delays.

6. **An editor, like a captain, needs to know where the ship is going.**
   When dealing with writers, negotiate topic, length, treatment and deadline before assigning an article. Include important sources and the key questions which the story will address.

7. **Offer feature writers a byline and an author's note.**
   Writers gain exposure and your publication gains credibility.

8. **Be concerned about how your newsletter *reads* before you worry about how it *looks*.**
   Attractive graphics can obscure important content needs. Relevant and well-written content should be able to stand on its own, even as plain text.

9. **If you're doing an emailed newsletter, "clean and simple" spells "effective."**
   Keep it to plain text. Be concise, and put an "in-this-issue" outline at the top. The footer should have complete "subscribe" and "unsubscribe" information. You should archive back issues, with an annotated index, on your website.

10. **Good writing and good editing require direction and hard work.**
    Your copy should sing rather than drone. It should ring when tapped. Write compact copy in the active voice. Edit for clarity, conciseness, jargon, length, correctness. The bottom line is your readership; give them top priority.

11. **Lead with strong items that have broad appeal.**
    Learn from the best daily newspapers—people decide *within seconds*, whether or not to read. Your editorial or a message from the CEO should have a regular spot after the lead items. In-house or more parochial news should have a regular spot much further in. This gives you the best chance of competing for attention, while those familiar with your newsletter know where to find what they want.

12. **Learn the distinction between simple information and a story.**
    Information comes to life as a story when someone talks about it. Try to cite sources as part of the way you do things.

13. **Any successful newsletter depends on plentiful and reliable sources.**
    Consider an acknowledgment box that lists everyone who contributed to an issue. This will reward people for helping and encourage others to participate.

14. **Look for reader feedback, always.**
    Watch to see how people scan your publication. Talk with a new sampling of readers after each issue. Do a formal readership survey on a regular basis. Track what's happening.

15. **The true test of performance is behavior.**
    You'll know you have an effective publication when your strategic audiences clip and save articles and when people are eager to write for it.

Some newsletters may have a great deal of room for copy, if they do not use many, if any, illustrations. The danger is in crowding the piece with too much copy. Headlines, indentations and generous paragraphing help break up the copy in a word-heavy piece. Others tend to use too many illustrations and look cluttered.

Use   The purpose of a newsletter is closely aligned with its use. When you are deciding how to communicate with an audience, you have to determine what you want to accomplish, and then you have to approach that goal in the way most likely to succeed. If you have a dive shop in the Virgin Islands, for example, you can excite the imagination and probably stimulate business better with a brochure that presents more pictures than words. On the other hand, if you want to keep in touch with all the Corvette owners in your state, you're better off with a newsletter full of copy about rallies and parts.

How you plan to distribute the newsletter also has a great deal to do with its design. If you intend the newsletter to be a self-mailer, one side will have to carry your return address and accommodate the postage and mailing label. Furthermore, the whole piece will have to meet the specifications of the USA Postal Service. Always check with the postmaster in the community where the newsletter will be mailed. Postal regulations may seem to be pretty clear, but in practice they are often subject to local interpretation. It is better to check first than to be sorry later.

With so many organizations becoming international in scope, you may be dealing with postal systems that you don't know anything about. For example, you might inadvertently use USA postage stamps that don't have the numerical value on them for newsletters going abroad. If you read the fine print carefully, those stamps say for USA use only. If you don't read the fine print, your newsletter will come back from or not even reach the destination country, which does not accept postage that doesn't have the value on it because they don't know whether or not the amount paid is appropriate.

What the receiver is likely to do with the newsletter also has a bearing on the design. Will it wind up on a bulletin board, for example? Some newsletters are designed with that purpose in mind. A copy is sent to the president of a group, who then posts it for others to read. Other newsletters may be designed for display in a rack or countertop display unit. In both cases, the display unit has to be designed to call attention to the newsletter, and the newsletter should call attention to itself.

Writing to Fit   When you are writing the copy, you have to prepare the message to say what you think needs to be said in an appropriate way. Then you have to decide how you are going to convey the information on hand in the space available. Some professionals are experienced enough to be able to "write to fit," but most prepare the message and then spend a lot of time trimming it to fit and generally tailoring the message to the medium. A newsletter is somewhat flexible because pages can be added, but that usually costs more money. A better solution is to determine your information hole first and then write the message to fit it.

Writing for Other Cultures   The USA is very culturally diversified, and you can get yourself into trouble within its borders by not being sensitive to mores and taboos. However, the difficulties you can create in the USA are nothing compared to the problems you can cause for yourself abroad if you don't know what is culturally acceptable. Because English has become an internationally accepted language, many newsletters are produced in English and distributed internationally. It is easy to forget that some contents—photographs, for example—are not accepted in some countries, especially those governed by religious and not secular laws. If you have any questions, it's best to ask. Most embassies and consulates are helpful on such matters.

Writing and Designing Newsletters on Computers

The rules of the game regarding newsletters remain imperative, even if you write, edit, design and produce camera-ready copy on a computer. That's a point you must understand fully; otherwise, you may wrongly assume that a computer is the answer to all your prayers, because:

1. It can speed up the process of getting verbal and nonverbal material into condition for many purposes.
2. It allows you to experiment at little cost (except for time) with formats, graphic treatments, typefaces, type sizes and the like.
3. It enables you to exert more direct control over how things fit and look before you release your work for duplication or printing.

But a computer can't make you a better writer or designer. Those are uniquely human qualities that no computer has yet been able to simulate. You should use your computer to its maximum advantage, but don't let it mesmerize you. It is a wonderful device that helps you do things you could only dream about without it. But it is still a dumb machine that can only move digitized information through electronic gates. Its behavior is controlled by which gates are open and closed. You open and close gates each time you enter a command. What comes out are your ideas, not your computer's. If your ideas aren't good, your computer can't make them better.

Designing

Although efficient word processing was fairly common by the mid-1970s, desktop publishing only began to emerge in the early 1980s. And it was not until the late 1980s that easy-to-use systems at affordable prices began to appear in substantial numbers. The term *desktop publishing* then came into vogue. It isn't publishing in the usual sense. A computer is used to assemble verbal and nonverbal material into a cohesive unit; and this, if produced on a laser printer, may be used as camera-ready copy for duplication or printing.

Here are some of the most popular publishing software programs:

1. QuarkXPress: "a formidable tool in the hands of professionals."
2. Adobe InDesign: "serious, feature-packed competition to QuarkXPress."
3. Serif PagePlus X6: "combines ease-of-use and professional output options, including PDF, with word processing, drawing, and advanced layout and typesetting."
4. Microsoft Publisher 2010: "primary desktop publishing application in the Office suite; popular with individuals, small businesses, and schools."
5. Adobe FrameMaker 10: "for corporations and others producing technical writing or complex documents for Web, print, and other distribution methods; for in-house, big business publishing it's a top choice."
6. Serif PagePlus: "combines ease-of-use and professional output options, including PDF, with word processing, drawing, and advanced layout and typesetting."[8]

Because publishing software is now easier to use, many people and organizations have been motivated to produce materials in-house that traditionally would have been done by professional designers, typesetters and printers. The results are a mixed bag. Some are superbly done; others are tawdry at best. The reasons for this rainbow of results are many, but a few are vital for you to know as you prepare for a career.

Format   A key production issue to settle about newsletters is the question of format. This simply refers to the visual frame within which verbal and nonverbal content is displayed. Is a vertical rectangle, a horizontal rectangle or a square most appropriate? Will the design elements be balanced, unbalanced, modular or free-flowing? One of the features of desktop systems is that you can quickly produce a seemingly endless variety of formats.

This cornucopia of formats can so dazzle the unwary that the next issue of a newsletter may not look at all like the present one or the one before that. Just because you *can* change the format instantly does not mean that you *should*. The best use of publishing software is to experiment with formats until you create the one that is right for your purpose. Once you have found it, use it consistently. Don't change just for the sake of change. You can create a template of the right format, store it and use it on demand. By using the same format for each issue, you create a visual identity for your newsletter, one your audience comes to recognize and to trust.

Fit   Publishing software can show you how a story fits into the space assigned to it. This feature simplifies the task of fitting copy to type, because the computer does it for you, instantly. But this does not mean that you should let the computer control how much you write. To avoid this trap, observe these steps:

1. Write for content first. Make sure you say what must be said.
2. Then try to fit the content to the space.
3. If it does not fit and you can't excise the surplus without affecting sense or add the deficit without being redundant, change the size of the type or the spacing to fit the content.
4. Never let space rule content.

Visuals   The very best systems can't improve the quality that a professional production artist or photographer can achieve. However, when these systems are used by people who have little or no visual sense or artistic skill, the results may be highly undesirable. If the finished product is to be four-color throughout, you can use a system to input information and to provide a basic design for initial approval, but you may want to turn to vendors for the finished work.

Much computer art is clip art. It is generic and general, not organization-specific, and it often is used as "wild art" to dress up a page. It contains little real information. Some software lets you modify clip art to your own needs, but unless you are remarkably deft, your efforts may well be in vain.

Scanners allow you to scan a photograph or printed visuals and create digital images. Digital cameras provide digital images directly to your computer. You also can modify this art, but often with the same results as with clip art. Also available are digital "pencils" you can use to draw on an electronic palette. If you can't draw well with pencil on paper, however, don't even try this alternative. No computer can overcome a lack of basic talent.

The mix of desktop publishing for print and for the Internet has created some serious design and content problems for both. It is possible to design a newsletter that can go on the Internet and be printed and mailed, but it requires a great deal of time and talent. Use the separate and different assets of each medium to their fullest.

Exercises

1. Find a newsletter for members or employees and another that goes to subscribers. Write an analysis that compares their purposes, content, writing styles and formats.
2. Select a newsletter of your choice. Review the focus of its content. Write an essay describing your perceptions of the readers of that newsletter.
3. Write a story for a newsletter of your choice assuming that the newsletter will be mailed as well as appear on the Internet. How does the dual delivery system affect your writing style, the timeliness of the copy and the number of words you use?

CHAPTER TWELVE

Magazines and Brochures

When you hear the word *magazine* you may conjure up an image of the magazines you see on supermarket and bookstore racks. But did you know that thousands and thousands of organizations of all kinds publish their own magazines—both online and in print?

Those magazines usually are published monthly or quarterly. They may be mainly for internal publics or for external publics and occasionally for a mix. An organization may publish a variety of magazines, but each should have a clear and distinct purpose that sets it apart from the others. Here we focus on the demands made on the writer of these significant tools of organizational communication.

Even though the contents of Internet and intranet sites have replaced printed publications in many organizations, magazines still can be powerful public relations tools, whether they're published in digital or printed form. They allow greater depth of treatment than most other media, permit more vivid and attractive display and enable writers to compose messages for specific target publics. Printed magazines have a longer life, and they have more "pass-along" readership.

Sometimes the public is internal—when a magazine is published for the employees or members of an organization, for example. Sometimes it is external, like that of *Methodist Health Talk,* published by Methodist Health System, which goes quarterly to 200,000 people in the system's north Texas service area.

By one estimate, more than 10,000 public relations magazines are published in the USA by corporations, government agencies, nonprofits and other organizations. Many such magazines now are published only on websites to increase their availability and eliminate printing and distribution costs. Want help with digital publishing? It's available from organizations like Issuu, which claims to be "the fastest growing digital publishing platform in the world," with "over 15 million publications" online. (See www.issuu.com.)

Methodist Health Talk is one of many nonprofit magazines that "represent a large and stable sector of the overall magazine industry, exceeding the number of for-profit publishers and accounting for more than 7% of advertising revenue. Roughly half of the advertising revenue is earned by 100 organizations. Nonprofit magazines are published by a wide range of organizations, including professional and trade associations, educational and cultural institutions, quasi-governmental agencies, labor unions and charitable groups."[1]

Some of the largest-circulation magazines published by nonprofit organizations are *IEEE Spectrum,* published by the Institute of Electrical and Electronics Engineers, *JAMA: Journal of the American Medical Association;* and *National Dragster,* published by the National Hot Rod Association. Other large nonprofit magazines include those of a diverse group of organizations: *Smithsonian Magazine,* published by the Smithsonian Institution; *Boy's Life,* published by the Boy Scouts of America National Council; *Eos,* published by the American Geophysical Union; and *American Rifleman,* published by the National Rifle Association of America. Some of the publications carry advertising from external sources and others have only house ads or no advertising at all.

The 10 largest USA consumer magazines, ranked in descending order by circulation are: *AARP The Magazine* (22.3 million), *Costco Connection* (8.7 million), *Game Informer* (7.6 million), *Better Homes and Gardens* (7.6 million), *Reader's Digest* (4.5 million), *Good Housekeeping* (4.4 million), *Family Circle* (4.0 million), *National Geographic* (4.0 million), *People* (3.5 million) and *Woman's Day* (3.3 million).[2]

The success of such publications is determined in part by format, illustrations, design, editing and proper distribution. But the most important element of any magazine is the writing—its quality, its relevance and its appropriateness for the target readers. The most beautifully designed, illustrated and printed magazine in the world cannot sustain success without well-written articles, because it won't communicate much.

Topics

When you are choosing topics, it pays to look again at the mission statement for this public relations tool. What is it supposed to do? Who are its readers?

Most magazines conduct readership studies and, for budget purposes, a magazine must show a cost-effective benefit as a public relations tool. Because organizational publications compete with mass media for the time and attention of their readers, even if they are "free," you must be sure of their appeal. That means you must give priority to developing good topics for articles. Sometimes your topics will be assigned to you by your superiors, but more than likely you will be left to your own devices most of the time. Although a good writer can usually make a mundane topic interesting, success can be assured only with a consistent inventory of good article ideas.

Finding Topics   If you know your readers well, certain topics will virtually suggest themselves. Your own flashes of insight may not be sufficient, however, to fill every issue of the magazine you work on. Fortunately, they don't have to be. There are other sources for article ideas.

First, however, let's talk more about knowing your readers. As a writer, you need to move about your organization and get to know people from all areas of the operation. You can't know everyone personally, of course, but you should get to know at least a few people in every area. Personnel can be good sources of ideas, and they also can help you gauge the value of your own ideas.

A growing concern these days among employees is the lack of information about where their organizations are headed and the reasons behind these and other decisions. They also want management to listen to them, not just talk down to them. They further believe that, despite claims to the contrary, management does not actually encourage free exchange of information. If this is a correct assessment, your task is greatly simplified. Simply talk to other employees throughout the company. Listen carefully. You'll turn up a wealth of topics your readers want to know more about. If you research and write the stories well, your magazine will be greeted with eagerness rather than a yawn.

But be prepared for the politics of getting some topics approved by management. Many of the things employees want to know are exactly what some managers don't want to talk about. The latter may support you, however, if you prepare them to look at story ideas from strategic points of view. (See Figure 12.1.)

Doing a story now may defuse a small problem before it becomes large. An organization may gain a lot more support in the long run if it sensitizes employees now to a delicate situation rather than issuing edicts about it later when it may be even more delicate. Yet another strategic consideration is that the pain caused by candor, especially in a crisis, is usually temporary. Candor clears the air quickly, so an organization can get on with its business.

Many companies perform what is called a *communication audit* or *customer satisfaction study*. This is a systematic evaluation of the effectiveness of the organization's communications program, including the magazine, if one is issued. The audit zeros in on strengths and weaknesses in the organization's communications program. Some of these findings become fodder for good magazine articles. Refer to Chapter 4 for more information about communication audits.

Survey results can be treasure troves for article ideas. Managements sometimes conduct organization-wide employee surveys. Survey participants may include readers of the magazine who are customers or who have more than a passing interest in what goes on at the organization. Communication is often one of the survey topics and can provide useful avenues to improvement if questions are posed professionally and results are interpreted objectively.

Public opinion surveys like those done by the worldwide Gallup Organization are common sources of ideas. They regularly take the pulse of the American public. You should make it a practice to read, study and save these polls for future reference. Even if the topic of the survey report seems unrelated to your company or industry, later analysis may show otherwise.

Additionally, you must regularly consult both local and national news sources and a variety of consumer magazines. Save items that strike your interest, even if a specific article idea does not leap out at you. Watch both network and local television news, public affairs broadcasts and special-events programs. Listen to a broad spectrum of local radio stations, and tune in some of the news and commentary programs on public radio.

101 Story Ideas   *There's an unlimited supply of possibilities for articles in your magazine or newsletter. Here are 101 of them. Some are "newsy" and more appropriate for a newsletter. Others offer feature story possibilities more suited for a magazine.*

101 STORY IDEAS

FOR YOUR PRINTED OR ONLINE PUBLICATION

HISTORIC

1. Anniversaries and other organizational milestones
2. Anniversaries of staff (especially after 15 years)
3. Anniversaries of volunteers with long service records
4. Individuals in the organization making outstanding contributions
5. New building planned
6. Cornerstone-laying
7. 25 or 50-year anniversaries of buildings
8. New achievements in client service
9. New products or services (and their anniversaries)
10. Meeting fundraising goals
11. State and national holidays that can be tied to organization
12. Service awards to the organization or personnel

RESEARCH & ACTIVITY

13. Reports on new experiments, studies, discoveries (or responses to others' experiments)
14. Grant announcements
15. Grant or project achievements or milestones
16. New facilities and programs
17. New research staff or special personnel
18. Response to others' research reports
19. Presentation of papers
20. Publication of books
21. Future programs and milestones
22. Improvements in operating efficiency
23. Patents acquired
24. Procedures developed
25. New uses for old products or services
26. Labor-saving discoveries
27. Employment and other statistics which indicate important trends

PRODUCTS & SERVICES

28. New products
29. New services
30. Improvements in products or services

31. Unusual uses of products
32. Unusual or efficient service use
33. New client groups
34. How, when and where to use organization's products or services
35. Demonstrations
36. Successful bids or awards
37. Efficiency records with clients
38. Comparative tests
39. Quality developments or controls

PROMOTION

40. New channels of distribution or promotion
41. Booths at exhibits, fairs, special showings
42. Speeches
43. Training programs
44. New media use (social media, etc.)
45. Contests
46. New premiums or special deals
47. Success stories (service, product use, employee effort, client success, etc.)
48. Cooperative arrangements with other organizations

(Continued)

FIGURE 12.1 (*Continued*)

SLOGANS & ENDORSEMENTS

49. Sponsoring a worthwhile non-profit cause
50. Using quotations from historic figures to "set the tone" in annual reports, product information or literature on services to clients and customers
51. Tie-in with another issue or organization
52. Endorsements by prominent individuals and organizations

PERSONALITIES

53. Interviews with executive staff on important issues or policies
54. Important speeches
55. Visits by famous persons (clients, media stars, noted educators, etc.)
56. New staff members with distinguished records
57. Election of Board members
58. Community service by staff

EMPLOYEES & ACTIVITIES

59. Number of employees on payroll
60. Number of volunteers
61. Personalities with interesting backgrounds, achievements, hobbies
62. Personal accomplishments of individuals within the organization

63. Professional accomplishments
64. Honors, awards, other recognitions
65. Board memberships by employees
66. Training, degrees completed
67. Scholarships to organization employees/families
68. Grants to employees or departments
69. Safety programs and records
70. Donations made as a group
71. Time donations to community groups
72. Retirements, transfers, deaths, etc.
73. Awards banquets, luncheons, parties, picnics

POLICIES

74. Change(s) in policies
75. Change(s) in contract terms
76. State and federal government policies (and responses to these)
77. Community, state and national problems and responses to these
78. Training programs or policies

ORGANIZATIONAL

79. Annual report issued
80. Annual meeting conducted

81. Board meetings, especially on important topics
82. Interim reports
83. Advisory council meetings
84. Forecasts
85. Fundraising events and activities

COMMUNITY ACTIVITIES

86. Participation in community or industry programs
87. Leadership by staff members in community/industry activities
88. Open houses, tours
89. Exhibits, displays
90. News that relates to the organization
91. Assistance to community groups
92. Awards to community or industry groups or individuals

CORPORATE IMAGE/IDENTIFICATION

93. New logo
94. Name for new program
95. New literature, brochure
96. Annual report
97. Information packet
98. Photo file
99. Guest relations program
100. Newsletter(s)
101. Survey findings, industry standing

Source: Copyright© Gladney Flatt, Medimarc, Medical Marketing Communications, 2012. Used with permission.

It should be obvious that you must read the appropriate professional, trade, industrial and scholarly journals. And you should go to meetings of all types. These can range from local service-club meetings to national professional conventions. The point is that you must go.

Any one or all of these may be the source of an idea. And an article idea may come into focus when you least expect it. But the idea you want won't come looking for you. You have to be on the alert all the time. If you're not tuned in, you may not recognize it. The clue may be a word or phrase, even out of context, or a major event. You have to pay attention to what goes on around you.

Form Versus Substance   This chapter began by saying that magazines are good communication tools for organizations. And they are. But are they as good as they can be? No. Who can make them better? Writers. Who are the writers? You. At least, you expect to be. So it is you—not "them"—who will improve company magazines and other publications.

That's not a small challenge, because it seems that everyone interested in the organization is more concerned with the substance of your writing than with your writing skills. That's no license to lessen your attention to proper grammar, syntax and other technical matters. Rather, it is an indication of the trap that some writers fall into: they substitute form for substance. You must strive for both good form *and* substance.

Good substance is defined as what interests readers. There is growing uneasiness among employees about how they relate to their organizations. Many don't have the depth of personal identification with or loyalty to their organizations that was characteristic some years ago. They sense they are interchangeable pieces in a chess game being played by management. They feel frozen out of decisions about which moves to make and why. If they get jumped, they are summarily removed from the game board.

As a writer, you can help. But you can do this only if you listen carefully to your readers and are sensitive to their information needs. When you identify those needs, meet them.

Just choosing the right word can make the difference in whether or not you convey your meaning and—if you do—what the emotional reaction might be. Two studies—one from Opinion Research Corporation (ORC) and another from Hill & Knowlton (H&K)— call attention to the different vocabularies of management and employees. In the ORC report, the findings show that employee-effective words satisfy three criteria:

1. Familiarity: Employees know the word well enough to define it.
2. Understandability: In workers' dictionaries, *capitalism* may be understood differently.
3. Emotional impact: Beyond familiarity and understanding, a word might trigger a different emotional reaction from employees than from management.

A current example might be the word *downsizing*, which management might see as positive (that is, becoming more efficient), but employees probably see as negative (that is, firing a lot of people). The H&K study cited identifies 30 words and 25 phrases that show how inflated language used by management during a steel strike made matters worse. For instance, instead of the word *accrue*, simpler words like *pile up* or *collect* would have been better understood. Similarly, the phrase *exclusive function* should have been translated *sole right.* Both study results came from talking to people to find out what worked for them. Such consultation is important if the publication is to be useful.[3]

Some people think that magazines and other employee publications are perhaps expected to carry too much of the communication load for organizations. That may be true. But it is certainly true that employees place more value on information they get from personal sources than from impersonal ones.

You can't change a magazine or other publication from its impersonal form, but that's no reason for you as a writer to treat your readers impersonally. Talk to them. Listen to them. See things through their eyes. Be them. Then write to them. Focus on the substantive information they want and need. If you do these things well, maybe you can make your magazine a lot better.

Employee Publications

Most organizations have a publication of some sort for employees. Often the employee publication is a full-fledged magazine; sometimes it looks more like a newspaper or newsletter. Often it's in digital form on an intranet or Internet website. But whatever the format, the writing in employee publications should follow most closely the style of magazine articles.

Why? Because whether an employee publication looks like a newsletter, a newspaper or a magazine, it rarely functions as a medium for hard news. Very few are published daily, so an employee publication cannot compete with other information sources available to employees. Informal communication networks among supervisors and secretaries can spread news faster in the organization than can the AP wire. And when important events occur or major decisions are made, they are generally announced at once rather than held for publication in the next month's employee magazine.

According to Carol Kinsey Goman, Ph.D., you can be successful in communicating with employees if you follow these guidelines:

- Emotion is more powerful than logic.
- What employees see is more powerful than what you say.
- Informal communication is more powerful than formal communication.
- Nonverbal communication is more powerful than verbal communication. Employee publications can be an extremely potent tool of internal public relations, and they should be used to accomplish more than telling of the shop foreman's new baby or the vice president's successful fishing trip. (This is known as the dead-fish-and-live-babies syndrome.) As experienced employee publication editor Don Fabun points out, employee publications today must appeal not only to a telephone operator, but "to an atomic physicist, a systems engineer, a market analyst, and an operations analyst. These latter are not likely to be interested in, or motivated by, bowling scores and a detailed account of the company picnic."[4]

Employee publications can help generate support among employees for corporate goals and objectives. Articles can build employee morale and enhance job satisfaction, thus boosting productivity. Publications can create a broader understanding among employees of the problems a company faces.

How can these goals be accomplished? Mainly by keeping such objectives in mind when you're writing articles for employees, and by following the principles of magazine writing outlined earlier in this chapter. Specifically, you must orient the writing to the reader. Explain the significance of events from the point of view of the employee—not from the point of view of the board of directors. In other words, don't relate verbatim a new company policy as handed down from on high. Explain the policy and tell what it means to the reader. But explain it in an interesting way: find a good angle, write a good lead and make the article as human and dramatic as possible.

If you take this approach, your organization's employee publication can be a valuable asset to the organization. Articles about achievements in research can generate pride among the employees, giving them a good feeling about being part of the organization. Articles about the need to save energy or improve safety can motivate employees to improve their performance in those areas. Articles about the relationship between your company's work and the well-being of the community can give employees a sense of involvement in a socially useful occupation. Articles about the accomplishments of individuals can be an incentive to other workers.

Some organizations set up networks of reporters for their publication. The idea is that one employee agrees to report "people" activities within their part of the organization before each issue of the magazine (or newsletter) is published. Names of reporters appear in the publication, and some organizations bring the group together each year for a luncheon or dinner to honor them.

If you write articles on such subjects skillfully, so that employees will read them, you can accomplish much more than you would with a publication written strictly to provide entertainment or to relate social fluff. This does not mean that an employee publication should be a propaganda engine for the views of management. Rather, such a publication should be mutually beneficial to the individual employees and to the organization as a whole. (See Figure 12.2.)

Association Publications

Members feel very involved in their associations and look forward to receiving the publication that their membership fees entitle them to. Even the government of the USA has associations with membership fees and publications such as the *Smithsonian* from the Smithsonian Institution.

What's important for a public relations writer to remember about them, though, is their high credibility and in-depth reading. Although these publications compete with commercial, newsstand magazines for their audience's attention, they are likely to get it.

(See Chapter 14 for information on the summer 2014 edition of *The Public Relations Strategist,* the magazine published by the Public Relations Society of America, that was devoted entirely to crises.)

Trade and Industry Publications

The "trade press" is composed of trade/professional magazines that provide information targeted to a specific industry or type of trade. In the PR field, there's *PR Week, PR News,*

CHAPTER

FIGURE 12.2

Code of Conduct

Source: Copyright © 2015 by WPX Energy. Used with permission.

This award-winning WXP Energy publication provides information on the company's Code of Business Conduct. Much of the text of the brochure, or booklet, is focused on a series of questions that employees ask about company values and business and include the following and numerous other topics:

- How to report an ethics violation or concern
- Equal opportunity, affirmative action and diversity and inclusion, including harassment and threats
- Alcohol and substance abuse
- Health, safety and the environment
- Confidential information
- Use of social media
- Commitment to our communities, including corporate contributions
- Political contributions
- Conflicts of interest

The brochure was prepared following the development of specific goals and the following key messages:

- Do what's right, report what's wrong
- Retaliation is not tolerated
- It is easy to make an anonymous report

The publication is available online at https://wpx-extranet-media.s3.amazonaws .com/237979/CodeofConduct_July2014.pdf.

Ragan's *PR Daily* (See Figure 12.3.), *Adweek, Bulldog Reporter, O'Dwyer's* and numerous others. Add "communication" and "marketing" and the list grows long.

If you work for a pipeline company that explores for, refines and transports petroleum products, for example, you'll find many opportunities to provide content for the numerous magazines in fields of interest to your employer. Because most of these publications are published monthly, they are not on the tight schedule that TV and daily newspaper staffers must meet, they are often more receptive to work with PR people. If your company has a major new pipeline or refinery under construction, some of the trade press editors could be interested in a media tour to learn about, visit, photograph and write about the project. Once the information is published and copyright approvals are received, reprints of the articles and photographs can be used for employee recruiting, investor relations and other purposes.

Major trade/professional magazines include *Interior Design, Communication Arts, Progressive Farmer, Aviation Week & Space Technology, Engineering News Record (ENR), Selling Power, Publishers Weekly, Successful Farming, U.S. Banker* and *E&P (Editor & Publisher)*.[5]

Most trade and industry publications are of little interest to anyone outside a particular area of business. But for people in the business, these magazines are major sources of information. You can find the *Cattleman* in most cattle raisers' homes or offices and the *Grocer* in most food store owners' and managers' offices.

If you want to get your story into a trade or professional magazine, check its editorial calendar. The editorial calendar is a tentative list of topics that the publication intends to cover during the next 12 months. By examining a publication's editorial calendar, you should be able to develop story "angles" that will give each magazine or newsletter editor reasons to include your organization in one or more issues. If you have questions about whether your story will "fit" into an issue, call the editor, briefly explain your idea and ask if it sounds as if it will work. A phone call may save both the editor and you considerable time developing a pitch that doesn't have a chance of success. Editorial calendars include submission deadlines, so you need to pitch your article concepts well in advance of those deadlines to allow time for developing the article before the deadline.

Although most of these trade and industry publications are the product of associations, they differ somewhat from the lifestyle or interest associations that produce such publications as *National Geographic*. If anything, though, their readers are even more dedicated and more avid. If you go to work for a trade or industry publication, you'll find that the smallest mistake will result in countless phone calls, faxes and letters to the editor.

FIGURE 12.3

Subscription Trade Publication   *Many public relations professionals keep up with changes in the field by subscribing to publications that provide information on news, analysis, features and jobs in the field. One such magazine is* PR Week, *published by Haymarket Media, Inc., in New York.*

Source: Copyright *PRWeek*/Haymarket Media, Inc., New York. Used with permission.

It's nice to be noticed, but it's better if the notice comes from some creative or inspired writing, rather than from a mistake.

Corporate Publications for the Public

More companies are producing magazines about their product line, offering advice and services. Health maintenance organizations (HMOs) publish magazines about their services. Manufacturers like Ford are likely to have more than one publication. Ford publishes *Ford, Ford Retro, Classic Ford* and other magazines.

Although these are published for customer convenience and information, their purpose is to establish brand loyalty.[6] Slick and expensive, these publications do have subscriptions, but the subscriber costs are generally low, intended to cover marketing and distribution costs. Subscribers also benefit from coupons in the publications and special prices to subscribers.

Another type of corporate magazine sells image. One of the most impressive magazines of this type is *Saudi Aramco World,* published by Aramco Services Company in Houston. The company uses its magazine to share information about the history, art and culture of the Middle East. There is no charge for this publication, which goes to a limited audience of appreciative readers. Another, a slick four-color magazine, *food & family,* is published by Kraft Foods North America, Inc., and includes feature articles, full-page ads and recipes touting its products while building its image.

Brochures

Brochures often look a lot like magazines and in fact you'll find some brochures tucked inside magazines.

Brochure is a term most people are familiar with. The problem is, it doesn't mean the same thing to everyone. This chapter will clarify usage, at least for this text. Public relations people write lots of copy for brochures. But if you ask them to tell you what a brochure is, you'll get a rainbow of explanations. That's because the term can mean booklets, fliers, circulars, leaflets, pamphlets or tracts. The difference between a brochure and these other pieces is sometimes a judgment call, so here are some quick guidelines for you to consider.

When the term *brochure* is used in its narrow sense, it signifies a printed piece of six or more pages, published only once and distributed to special publics for a single purpose. Brochures aren't serial publications like newsletters.

A *booklet* is basically a piece of at least eight pages, stitched (with staples) on the spine. Often it is small enough to fit into a pocket or small purse. *Fliers* and *circulars* usually are single-sheet pieces, printed on one side that may be mailed, often in bulk, or distributed directly, like those you may find stuck on your car's windshield in a parking lot.

A *leaflet* is similar but it is usually folded, although not stapled or trimmed. A *pamphlet* is also folded and usually has more pages. A *tract* is a pamphlet or booklet whose content promotes a political or religious point of view.

These differences are pretty nominal. What these pieces have in common is more important, including:

- Message statements are always singular.
- Their purposes are to persuade, inform and educate.
- They are published only once, but multiple printings of some are common, with or without updates.
- They must attract and hold the attention of their own publics.
- Because they aren't parts of other media, they are their own delivery systems.
- They must have clear writing and be visually attractive.

Although the term *brochure* will be used in the remainder of this chapter, the principles will apply to all the types of pieces discussed. The creation of a brochure is a complex process that includes six basic steps:

1. Clearly define its purpose.
2. Develop an organizing concept for it.
3. Write the content.
4. Design the presentation of information, including format and the use of type, visuals, paper, space and color.
5. Produce the brochure, including the selection of a method of reproduction.
6. Distribute the brochure. This might include posting a digital version on your organization's public Internet site or a private intranet site.

"What's a SIAST?" Glad you asked. It's the Saskatchewan Institute of Applied Science and Technology. (Now, perhaps more memorable, the name has been changed to Saskatchewan Polytechnic.) With 26,000 students and 180 credit course offerings, the university has four campuses—in Saskatoon, Moose Jaw, Regina and Prince Albert.

The SIAST Student Recruitment Preview is an easy-to-use 48-page reference of program options, and it directs readers to gosiast.com to learn more and apply for admission. (One two-page spread is shown below. (See Figure 12.4.) To view digital images, go to http://gosiast.com/programs-and-courses/resources/calendar.aspx.) It is a takeaway for high school visits, campus tours and career fairs. Annually, 17,000 printed Previews are distributed. Printed in four colors on slick paper, it's one of a "family" of printed pieces designed for the institute's target audience—high school students. To appeal to them, SIAST used personal pronouns throughout the copy. Photos of SIAST students, five of whom are shown below, provide a believable look. There's a brief testimonial with each of them representing the targets' age, ethnicity, gender and geography.

The pieces in the "family" are the Preview brochure, the Career Guide, seven 6" × 8" Smart Choice cards, and a big 38" × 27" Program Summary. The look of the printed pieces is reflected in the institute's website, and photos of the same students are used there, also.

Two of the objectives of producing the materials were (1) to increase visits to the application page on the website by 10 percent and (2) to increase the number of applicants by 10. The publications worked! Both of those percentages were exceeded.

Part of the "Family" of materials that successfully recruited students to the Saskatchewan Institute of Applied Science and Technology (SIAST), now renamed Saskatchewan Polytechnic.

(Continued)

FIGURE 12.4 (*Continued*)

(*Continued*)

FIGURE 12.4 *(Continued)*

(Continued)

FIGURE 12.4 (*Continued*)

SIAST programs are a smart choice and here are just a few reasons why. Don't take our word for it – read what SIAST students have to say.

Job-ready skills

Behind the scenes, program advisory committees ensure your curriculum is relevant and up-to-date. Innovative networking events connect you with potential employers. And, with many programs, the door is open to use your SIAST credentials as a stepping stone to a university degree, professional designation or advanced professional standing.

"I gained so much valuable knowledge. I accepted a job offer even before I was finished my program. SIAST was definitely the right choice for me."

JANA
Hometown: Moose Jaw SK
Program: Business Accountancy

Program choice

SIAST has more than 150 programs to choose from, with courses in aviation, engineering, health sciences, technology, trades and more.

And with smaller class sizes, instructors get to know students on a first-name basis. It makes for a more personal learning experience, and allows more one-on-one attention.

My SIAST experience has been fun and full of laughs, as well as interesting and informative.

JOLENE
Hometown: Perdue SK
Program: Parts Management Technician

Grads in demand

There's a reason almost 93% of surveyed SIAST grads said they'd found work. Our programs are career-focused and results-oriented.

That means our graduates are job ready. That's a big advantage in today's market. Top employers are competing to recruit quality employees – and they like the blend of knowledge, skills and experience SIAST grads demonstrate. A SIAST education gives you an edge in the job market.

Make the popular choice!
SIAST produces more undergrads each year than any Saskatchewan university.

2010–11 GRAD EMPLOYMENT SURVEY (AFTER 6 MONTHS)

98% graduate satisfaction

Source: Photos: SIAST Student Recruitment Preview Viewbook, 2014 international Gold Quill Award of Excellence winning entry in International Association of Business Communicators (IABC). See http://gosiast .com/programs-and-courses/resources/calendar.aspx. Small images: SIAST "Smart Choice" cards. Text: SIAST Work Plan for Preview View book. All Copyright © 2014 by Saskatchewan Institute of Applied Science and Technology (SIAST). Used with permission.

Purpose

The first step is to define the purpose of the brochure. What is it that you really want to accomplish? That sounds simple, and it is. But it can be tricky. That's because people often begin with a general rather than a specific idea of what they want to do. If you force yourself to write a single declarative sentence that describes the purpose, then you can move ahead with relative ease. If you can't reduce the purpose to a simple sentence, you need to think about it some more. You also can define purpose by developing a basic message strategy. A message strategy simply defines the key idea that you want to convey to your publics.

Real estate agents use brochures to show property and to describe the advantages of owning it. Sometimes realtors use a brochure to "sell" the services of the company, rather than specific properties offered by the company. Those reflect very different purposes. Many professional public relations people receive at least one brochure a week describing a seminar that has been designed to help improve their skills—yet a different purpose. Public relations professional groups publish brochures offering members as speakers to interested groups. "Selling" talent is selling a service from which others can benefit. Other brochures may promote membership, affiliation or participation. These serve all different purposes.

Still other brochures sell intangibles, by describing the worth of an idea—for example, those designed to get support (usually financial) for foundations. One mental health foundation sends out brochures "selling" its publications and audiovisual materials at prices that barely cover mailing costs. The foundation "sells" ideas for sound mental health but offers the materials to educate the public about its mission.

Brochures also can be informational and educational in the strict sense. The Hogg Foundation for Mental Health publishes on its website (hogg.utexas.edu) a list of publications and reports on mental health. Most are available online in PDF format, and others are available in print and can be ordered by email. A person seriously interested in the study of mental health issues would find this an invaluable resource.

Informational brochures about subjects like a suicide prevention hotline or accident or crime deterrence are often produced as a community service. A pharmacist may dispense, along with prescriptions, a brochure on how to prevent poisoning accidents and what to do if an accident occurs. Such informational brochures perform a service and generate goodwill for those who distribute them.

Persuade

Brochures always try to persuade. In that sense, brochures try to "sell" or publicize a product, service or idea. Your purpose, of course, influences not only the way you write copy for the brochure, but also the design you evolve, the visuals you include and, perhaps, the way you reproduce it. If your intent is mostly persuasive, your copy will lean heavily on adjectives, similes and metaphors intended to tug the emotional heartstrings of readers. Although factual information has its place in persuasive efforts, the copy appeal is mostly emotional.

Inform and Educate

If your purpose is primarily to inform or educate, the copy you write will contain lots of factual information, perhaps replete with tables and graphs. This kind of copy appeals to the cognitive behavior of readers. It is a good idea to review the basic persuasive strategies in Chapter 3, one of which is cognitive strategy. This does not suggest that you should use only cognitive strategy in brochures.

But writing copy that informs and educates is more fact-intensive and descriptive than writing copy intended only to persuade. You should remember, however, that even the purest of information can have a persuasive impact.

Concept

Once the purpose of a brochure is settled, you're ready to take the second step, which is to define a concept for it. An effective concept is one that helps you to organize words, visuals, color and space so they work well together to tell your story in a way that gets and holds the attention of your readers.

How does that work? First, you need a simple message statement. That statement becomes the basis for a creative concept. The concept has to include some symbolism for conveying the message. Then you need a headline that encapsulates the message. The visual must complement, not compete with, the message. The remaining pages should explain the offer, give the reader response options that are easy to complete and urge the reader to send or to call for further information or to take another action.

A good concept takes a key idea and interprets it, shapes it and, in turn, is shaped by it, and follows through with the production of a fully coordinated message that blends all the elements into a cohesive unit so that the whole is a sum greater than its parts.

Purpose and Object

Although the purpose is to persuade, inform or educate your readers, those broad purposes usually aren't enough to give you the firm direction you need for an effective brochure. You have to combine them with an object or application. Persuasion is usually the dominant purpose of a brochure, but some brochures educate or inform.

The guideline is: Begin with a general purpose—persuasion, information or education—and then extend it to the specific—an object or an application.

The Farmers Insurance Group (FIG), like most insurance companies, was very concerned about the rising number of young people killed or maimed annually in auto-mobile accidents because of driving and drinking. FIG wanted to educate young people about the risks they take when they drink and drive. The general purpose was primarily to educate. The object was to offer advice on how to break the drinking and driving cycle. So the concept evolved into "young drivers at risk." The six-page, 8-by-10-inch color brochure used a magazine design treatment to convey stories about how individuals can make a difference, comments about the rites of passage, the impact of fantasy and a first-person account of how "A Drunk Driver Changed My Life." The last page carried a signed statement from the chairman of the board and chief operating officer of FIG. Remember to proceed from the general to the specific.

Uniqueness   Not only must you have a well-refined concept for the brochure, but you also want it to stand out from all others that readers may see. You want it to be memorable. That means that you must be concerned with making your brochure different. The struggle to be unusual can lead you into some bad decisions, so be careful.

Cleverness   Inexperienced writers too often depend on cleverness to make a brochure stand out. Being clever is desirable, of course, but cleverness can be a slippery concept. Cleverness may turn out to be terribly trite, as in the case of a brochure for an electronics discount retailer that shouted "You've shopped the rest. Now shop the best."

Genuine cleverness takes something familiar to readers and gives it a *new and different twist*. Suppose you're creating a brochure to "sell" the idea that writing, designing and producing a brochure is really an exercise in packaging information. Talking about packaging information is fairly routine. So you might give it a different twist and call it giving shape to information. Giving shape to information also is more descriptive of what you're actually doing as you prepare a brochure.

Puffery   In their zeal to be unique, writers may stretch the truth. It is true that the FTC allows the use of puffery in language as an essential part of promoting goods, services and ideas. Even if puff words like *best, greatest, lowest, richest* and so on are sanctioned, they often are viewed skeptically by many readers. Readers usually recognize puffery for what it is: truth stretched to the point of unbelief. Puffery can help to create a memorable brochure, but it may be remembered for the wrong reasons.

Suppose the Rose Petal, a chain of 21 high-quality cleaners, has given you the job of developing a small brochure, claiming that the Rose Petal gives customers the cleanest clothes in town. The brochure will be clipped to the plastic bags that cover the cleaned clothing. The story can be told by describing the care Rose Petal's professional staff gives to clothing, including comments about special chemicals they use and so on, but it is best to avoid an exaggerated claim like "cleanest." In the absence of an objective measure, "cleanest" is a red flag that may inhibit credibility.

The guideline to use is: avoid puffery.

Validity   Puffery aside, you naturally want to put your best foot forward. But your best foot must stand firmly on the accuracy of what you say. You must be careful in collecting information about the subject of the brochure. If you're writing a brochure that encourages prospective clients to lease space in a new office building, make certain, for example, that each office indeed does have its own working thermostat control before you claim that in your copy. If a company rents space and installs computer components that need special temperature control—and there is no thermostat—you can be challenged for misrepresentation in the brochure you produced.

Brochures about financial matters are especially hazardous—investments in particular. You must carefully spell out all the financial considerations and review the copy with both an accountant and an attorney before going into production. The underlying reason in cases like this is the same as with the new office building. People should be assured of getting their money's worth.

A professional organization's foundation offered a brochure detailing for potential contributors the benefits of membership in the foundation. The group's attorney was adamant that the mechanism for providing these benefits be in place before the publication went to press. Colleges and universities now do more careful reviews of their catalogs and brochures after being told by counsel of cases in which institutions were taken to court for promising more than they could deliver. The same caution extends to college and university websites.

Suppose you're promoting contributions to a local philanthropic group and claim that "all your dollars remain in the community." Keeping contributions at home is a powerful appeal to many potential donors, but if you're using a professional fund-raiser, the claim might be perceived as misleading because of the sometimes-inflated commissions that go to fund-raisers.

Brochures that inform and educate are much easier to write than ones intended to create or sustain an image. Image is often nebulous. Informing and educating are more concrete. Accuracy is critical. So is completeness. Now, we're ready for the third step.

Giving Shape to Information

You may not realize it at first, but the overall task in producing a brochure simply is giving shape to information. You do that by what and how you write, and how you illustrate and display it.

Notice that writing is the third basic step in creating a brochure. And you should take that step only after you're thoroughly convinced that the purpose is clear and you have a well-understood concept that helps you to organize and shape the information that goes into the brochure.

Rules

The rules of good grammar, punctuation and spelling apply to all brochures as they do to other media. Fractured grammar wreaks havoc with the language in a brochure as it does in a news release or a feature story. Reader reaction also may be even more virulent to mistakes in brochures. That's because of the specialized publics of brochures.

Suppose you're 21 years old and in good physical condition, but you find yourself in the office of a urologist. You're there because in the last three days you've had some severe back pain. You wonder if you have a kidney infection or if something is wrong with your back. As you try to relax in the waiting room, you pick up a brochure on kidney diseases. You begin to read it carefully and in the third paragraph you discover a subject-verb disagreement that results in confusion about the number of causes of kidney infections. The earth doesn't open and swallow you, but your anxiety level does go up. You begin to wonder if you can really trust a physician who would produce such writing. Your skepticism may lead you to cancel the appointment and see another physician or, at least, to get a second opinion.

Accuracy

Accuracy is essential. Most brochures have lots of information. To be able to write good brochure copy, you must first be a good reporter. Gather, sort, evaluate and synthesize facts carefully. Check and double-check information you're unsure about. Learn as much about the topic as you can. This is necessary because it is when you are writing about something that stretches your knowledge to its limits that you make mistakes. If you aren't careful, you may not even realize you've made a mistake.

In a sense, when you produce a brochure, you're making a contract with readers. They expect to be able to depend on you. Accuracy is one of the key elements of good brochure copy.

Active Voice

Use the active voice almost always, but there will be times when passive voice seems to better fit the context of what you're saying. So it is permissible to use the passive voice, but a general guideline is to avoid it when you can.

Style

Every piece of writing should conform to a specific style. Your organization may have its own. Use it. If a client has a style that is unique to that organization, you should use that style. If neither your organization nor your client has a standard style, adopt one. If you must adopt one, consult the *Associated Press Stylebook and Briefing on Media Law* for help. AP style is widely used, but often with adaptations. The particular style you use or adopt is not an issue, but being consistent is. That's what style is all about—consistency. Don't use *Mr.* or *Ms.* in one place and not in other places. Such inconsistencies in style nag subconsciously at readers. They may not overtly recognize such glitches in your writing, but they "know" something is wrong. They just can't place it. Adopt a style and use it.

Tone

Good brochure copy has a clear, distinct tone. It may be light or heavy or formal or informal in treatment. The tone should be appropriate to the brochure's purpose and subject matter. It may have a lilting quality or it could be a dirge. It really depends on what you're trying to do. It may walk slowly or run across the reader's consciousness. It might jump, crawl or turn cartwheels. For example, think about writing brochure copy for a funeral home. Death is not easy to talk about. Getting people to *plan* for their own death is a special challenge. You walk slowly, carefully. You might begin by talking about consideration for others who must handle funeral arrangements—physical and financial. Few people want to inflict inconvenience or financial obligations on those they love. Your persuasive appeal and tone have to be personal but not too emotional or sentimental.

Visuals

Thinking visually as you write brochure copy is as important as it is when writing advertising copy. The *process* is exactly the same. Because of space limitations in an ad, however, you may be able to use only one visual. Brochures usually have more space than ads, so you can use more visuals. But it is a mistake to use visuals just because you can. The general rule for using visuals in brochures is: Use a visual to substitute for a paragraph or a section of copy. If you can say it visually, do it. If you can't, then write it.

That raises a question: Do you visualize, then write? No. Write first. Write as much as is necessary to tell the story. Then go back and examine each new idea to see if it can be conveyed visually—by photographic or drawn art. If it can be shown, use a visual. In effect, what you write governs the extent to which you use visuals. And don't forget to use charts and graphs. Done well, they can simplify complex information so it can be understood at a glance.

Unless reproduction is done using a xerography process (which might be used for a very limited number of copies), there are two types of visuals in printed brochures. One is *line art*. This is art with no gradations of tone. For example, a pen-and-ink drawing is all black and white. There are no grays. The other type is *screened* or *halftone art*. Art that must show gradations of tone must be screened. For example, a photograph must be screened before it can be printed. This is done by filtering the picture through a screen that breaks up the image into dots. Screens are designated by their relative coarseness. An 85-line screen means that the screen will break up an image into a dot pattern that has 85 rows of dots vertically and horizontally per square inch. That computes to 7,225 dots per square inch. By comparison, a 200-line screen has 40,000 dots per square inch. This is a much finer screen. Most of the art you'll use in a brochure will likely be screened at about 150 or higher, because coarser screens simply can't reproduce subtle gradations of tone.

Only your imagination and budget limit your sources of visuals. The most common source of visuals is clip art. Clip art can be literally clipped from any printed source (but you can't use it without permission). Clip art can also come from a variety of digital sources. There are many sources that provide clip art including websites, PC- and Macintosh-formatted disks and CDs. You are free to use this art without additional payment or permission. If you have a scanner, you may clip from a printed source, scan it to convert it to a digital format and then edit it to suit your needs, but you must get written permission from the owner of the copyright to use it.

The problem with clip art is that it is rare to find exactly the art needed to convey an idea quickly, precisely and accurately. That's because it was created for some other purpose or it is generic art. The alternative is to hire photographers and production artists to execute the unique art that you want. This is the most expensive method of getting visuals, but it usually is the most satisfactory. When you hire photographers and artists, even though your organization will pay them for their work, they probably will own the copyright for the photos and artwork.

You can save time, trouble and perhaps additional expense by negotiating—before the work is done—permission to use the art and photos for unlimited purposes. Let's say you were responsible for a brochure, and you hired a photographer who took excellent photos. The brochure was printed, and the results were great. Now your boss wants to have the brochure digitized and put on your organization's website. Can you do that without violating the photographer's copyright? The answer probably is no unless you have a signed contract that says your organization has the right to use the photos for purposes other than the printed brochure.

Writing brochure copy is, in a sense, an exercise in integrating words and visuals to their highest degree, more so than even in the best magazines. That's because magazines operate with fixed formats. The format of a brochure is controlled by you, so you have much more flexibility in creating a fully integrated message. In effect, you let the content of what you say dictate the format in which you say it. All of which brings us to the fourth step in producing brochures.

Designing Brochures

The fourth step in creating a brochure is designing. It includes several major elements: format, type, paper, space and color. Each of these elements may be worthy of a complete book. What follows are selected comments intended to give you a general sense of direction. They are not, and can't be, definitive in such limited space.

Format

First of all, a brochure format should complement the content and the method of distribution. Suppose the purpose of a new brochure you're assigned to write for a bank client is to promote the use of the bank's electronic (paperless) banking system. You learn that the brochure will be inserted with monthly statements to customers, so perhaps it's a flier or a folder. It's probably a good idea not to quibble about the technical definitions. In any event the content of the printed piece will not demand much space, and the brochure must fit into statement envelopes. With those two pieces of information, you can begin to shape the message to a complementary format.

Because an 8.5-by-11-inch sheet of paper will fold to fit easily into a regular business envelope, you can begin with that size of paper. Now you must decide whether it will be done in a flier format (one wide column printed on one side) or in a folded-page format. Because the sheet must be folded to fit into the statement envelope, it makes sense to design the format as a six-page folder where each page measures 3.667-by-8.5 inches.

Consult Figure 12.5 and look at 2A and 2B. The first folding option, 2A, is called a *gatefold*. When folding back page one so you can see the second page, it is much like opening a swinging gate—thus the name. *Accordion fold* is the name applied to 2B because it folds and unfolds like the bellows of an accordion. Folder options 1A and 1B, called four-page folds, do not work well for this project because its page dimensions don't fit into the statement envelope. Folder options 3A, 3B and 3C are referred to as eight-page folds. Folder options 4A and 4B represent standard 12-page folds. Folder options 5A and 5B represent 16-page folds. Folder options 3, 4 and 5 usually are used with much larger paper stocks, like 17-by-22 inches.

A different kind of project might call for something other than a folder-type brochure. For example, if you're doing a recruiting piece for your university, you may end up with a 36-page, 8.5-by-11-inch booklet in full color. If that's the case, you'll work with an

FIGURE 12.5

Brochure Folding Styles   *These are the most common folding options used when producing brochures.*

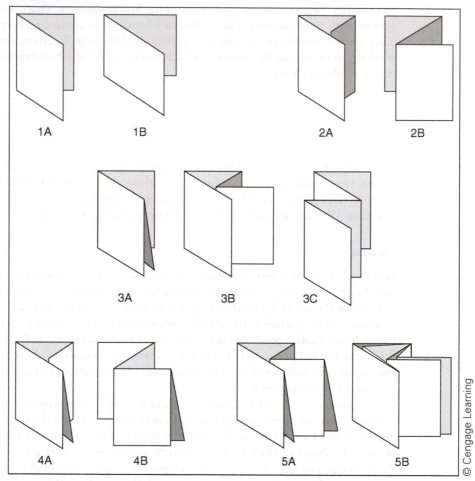

1A   1B   2A   2B

3A   3B   3C

4A   4B   5A   5B

© Cengage Learning

8.5-by-11-inch format and adjust the number of pages to those needed to display the content fully. The key thing to remember about these larger formats is that the number of pages must always be in multiples of 4-, 8-, 12- or 16-page flats. A *flat* is the number of pages on one side of a large uncut sheet of paper stock. Which one you use will depend on the press sizes available from your printer and the number of pages in the brochure. Look at Figure 12.6 for illustrations of the most common flats. Booklets like these usually are stapled along the spine, but some are pasted.

FIGURE 12.6

Most Common Page Flats for Large Paper Stock *The actual size of a brochure is determined by its content. Selection of a printing flat is based on the number of pages in a brochure and the size of the printing press on which it will be reproduced. Flats always are printed in multiples of 4, 8, 12 or 16 pages.*

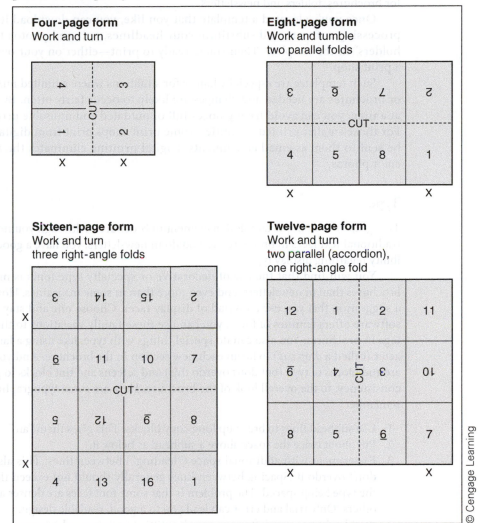

Using Computer Templates

Computer programs like Word and WordPerfect provide templates that simplify and speed the production of folders and brochures, as well as business cards, certificates, greeting cards, résumés, business letters and even basic annual reports. Some templates are provided online by the software publisher. Microsoft, for example, offers more than 100 templates for brochures, folders and newsletters.

Once you've located a template that you like, you can download it into the word processing software and substitute your headlines, text and photos for the "place-holders" in the template. Then you're ready to print—either on your own printer or at a print shop.

Such templates are especially handy for situations where a limited number of folders or brochures are needed and changes are likely to occur fairly often. By printing a few at a time, you can avoid having boxes full of outdated and unusable printed materials. For those smaller printed quantities, some print shops print from digital files that can be sent to them as email attachments. Digital printing eliminates the need to screen color photos.

Type

Typography is an important design element in brochures. Although you need to stay with traditional text faces in brochures, as you do in newsletters, you have a good bit more flexibility regarding display type.

You will find that the use of decorative or specialty type fonts is much greater in brochures than in newsletters, and even more than in some magazines. However, that isn't a suggestion that you use a myriad of display faces. Choose one and stay with it. If your software offers families of fonts, you can use these family variations to their best advantage in brochures. You also can do special things with type, like using a large initial character (called a *drop cap*) to begin each new section in the brochure. And you can use rules around blocks of type (but don't overdo this) and screens and tint blocks to give variety, yet consistency, to the overall look of the brochure. Here are some typographic guidelines to remember:

1. Use subhead lines to break up long copy blocks. This gives them "air."
2. Put about twice the space above a subhead as below it.
3. Experiment with additional space ("leading") between lines. This also gives air but don't overdo it. Spacing between lines generally should not exceed the point size of the type being spaced. The problem is that some font faces are denser and bolder than others. Only trial and error can lead you to a good, readable design.
4. Avoid using uneven left margins unless fitting copy around art.
5. Don't tilt type at odd angles. If you must tilt it, keep it to no greater than 15 degrees.
6. Don't run type vertically. It kills readability.
7. Select typefaces—text and display—that are legible and appropriate.
8. Avoid sans serif faces for text.
9. Generally, don't try to wrap text around odd shapes.

Paper

The paper stock on which your brochure is printed can add a lot to the impact of your message. If it is printed on inappropriate stock, your message loses some of its impact. Printing stock can be a baffling topic and one far too complex to explain fully here. The best advice is to work closely with a printing expert who can guide you properly. However, there are some basic things about paper that you should know before you talk to a paper authority.

Paper has a *grain*. That means that the fibers run in a specific direction. Knowing about grain is important because paper folds better and cleaner with the grain, and paper is stiffer in the direction of the grain. Paper is also designated by its *basis weight*. Seventy-pound paper is 500 sheets (a ream) of 25-by-38-inch paper. That size, by the way, is the standard for USA book papers, which include coated, text, offset, opaque and so on. The basis weight of typical business letterheads is 20 pounds, meaning 500 sheets of 17-by-22 inches. Cover stocks come from different sizes of basis weights.

Curl refers to the degree to which paper tends to buckle because it has excess moisture. This usually isn't a problem except when you use a cover stock that is coated on one side only. *Paper-ink affinity* refers to the speed with which ink dries on the printed stock. If the paper is very porous, as is newsprint, the ink is absorbed and dries quickly, but the images are not as sharply defined as on better stock that dries more slowly. Gas and electric dryers often are used on many paper stocks to speed the drying process.

Paper color can affect color reproduction of lighter tints. Type is generally easier to read on a soft (yellowish) white stock, but four-color process reproduces more accurately on neutral white stock. When you select a paper color, be aware that photos of people on some paper colors—green and blue, for example—are far from flattering. *Brightness* also can be a factor. It affects contrast, brilliance, snap and sparkle of the printed content. *Opacity* refers to the show-through of printing from the other side of the paper or from a sheet under it. Papers with higher basis weights usually are more opaque than those with lower basis weights. *Smoothness* is a very important quality. If you're printing using a letterpress or gravure process, you need a smooth surface for the best results. Smoothness seems not to matter as much when printing offset. The paper's *ink absorbency* also results in a color appearing to be different on various types of paper.

Paper also is *graded* by its primary uses. Although there are many grades, those that follow are the ones you'll most likely use:

- *Bond* paper is typical business correspondence paper.
- *Coated* stock is what you will likely use when you must have the highest-quality reproduction.
- *Text* paper is noted for its interesting textures and colors. You'll use it mostly for announcements, fliers and brochures.
- *Book* is a grade that is common for trade books and textbooks.
- *Offset* stock is similar to coated and text papers but it is less moisture absorbent to compensate for the extra moisture present in offset printing.
- *Cover* papers have heavier basis weights and are made to complement coated and text papers.

If all of this is baffling, remember the simple rule: when in doubt, consult an expert.

White Space

The term *white space* refers to the unused portion of the total space in your brochure. Good design includes a judicious use of white space because it is, indeed, a design element, just like a piece of art.

The most important decision about the use of white space is how much margin you will use at the top and bottom of a page and on the left and right sides. There are no fixed rules to follow. A rule of thumb you may find useful is that the smaller the page size the smaller the margins can (not must) be. The reverse is also true. For example, if you are working with a page size of 8.5-by-11 inches, you might use three-quarters of an inch margins at the top and left and right sides and one inch at the bottom. Should the bottom margin be wider? Yes, to compensate for the optical center (not the symmetrical center) of the page.

The next most important decision about white space is the line length of your text. Try for an optimal length that is plus or minus one to three picas from the result of the following formula: Text type point size × 1.5 = line length in picas.

If you're using 12-point type, then the best line length for that size would be from 15 to 21 picas. If you stay within that framework, you'll generally improve the readability of your brochure.

Another decision affecting the use of space is the space between columns of type, or gutter space. A space in points 1.5 times the point size of text type is about the minimum space to consider. For example, 12-point type should have no less than 18 points between columns.

The next consideration is the amount of space you'll use to separate text from artwork. This can vary a good bit, but a general rule is to use the point size of text type as the minimum.

The final major consideration is whether you'll bleed artwork. Bleeding refers to running artwork off the edge of the page. Always stop artwork at the margin or bleed it off the page. Never stop it between the margin and the edge. Bleeding often requires a larger paper size, because the paper must be trimmed into the artwork (and discarded) to provide a sharp edge.

One major rule to remember about white space is: Never trap white space inside the page design. The reader's eye tends to fall into these "white holes," and it is hard to escape them. Always arrange your visuals, heads and copy blocks so there is white space opening to the outside of the design. This avoids the "white holes."

Color

Color enhances the attractiveness of almost any publication. Even so, don't use color just to make things look better, because many messages don't need color at all. Using it in those situations is simply a waste of money. But other messages not only need but demand color. If you're creating a brochure for a new luxury hotel, you not only need color but also four-color process to show the decor of the hotel. The same is true if you're trying to raise funds to send underprivileged kids to summer camp in the mountains. How can you really show the thrill of a child catching a trout in the splendor of a mountain stream if you don't use color? So color can be an important element in the success of many brochures.

There are four basic components of color that you need to think about when working with electronic images. First is *pigment*—red, yellow and blue—the primary colors that mix to produce all other colors. The second is *light*—red, green and blue—the color that you see on your computer or TV screen that comes from beaming three light sources at triads of red, green and blue phosphor pixels, which then causes the pixels to glow at different intensities. The third component is *complementary colors*—cyan, magenta and yellow—created by mixing two light sources such as in theater lighting. The fourth component is *print colors*—cyan, magenta, yellow and black—also referred to as process colors or CMYK (the K stands for black), that are mixed in printing to create all other colors.[7]

For electronic colors, the brightness of each pixel is determined by *voltage*. The range is from zero voltage or black to equal voltage or white. The range of brightness is greater than for ink on paper because the brightness of the ink we see depends on the amount of light reflected from the image to our eyes. Different surfaces and different inks affect brightness, as does ambient light. Our eyes have rods that detect black and white, and cones that see color—but not well in low light.[8] You need to know how different colors will show up on the screen because this affects the balance of the design and readability.

There are two broad types of color usage. One is called *spot color*. That's where you use a second color to supplement a basic ink color—usually black. If you use still another color, it will be called the third color. Spot color is fairly inexpensive, and with the creative use of screens and tint blocks, you can get a rainbow of effects for a modest investment. Spot color also is not, in printing terms, close register—that is, it does not have to line up within thousandths of an inch.

The other kind of color is called *four-color process.* Photographic art is screened four separate times with special filters that sequentially block out all colors but yellow, red, blue and black (the primary colors). When they are printed properly one on top of the other, they produce the full range of colors visible to the human eye. Four-color process is close-register printing, meaning that the dot patterns must align precisely or the picture is fuzzy, requiring additional paper and press time for setup. That is why four-color process color is more expensive than spot color. So check your budget carefully.

Reproduction

Unless you are relying on a digital print shop or desktop publishing, you must prepare your brochure for reproduction, meaning you must choose between three types of printing: letterpress, offset or gravure. Each method has its own distinguishing quality and characteristics. Because of rapid technological improvements, differences in the final images produced by these methods are not as noticeable as they were just a few years ago. All three are capable of producing the same copy and art with satisfactory results.

Letterpress

Letterpress printing is the oldest of the three. It reproduces images from raised surfaces, working on the same principle as a rubber stamp. Letterpress is noted for its sharp, crisp printing and slight embossing (because paper is pressed into direct contact with the raised image to be printed).

Well-tooled letterpress printing plates are good for long pressruns into the hundreds of thousands. Quantities of a half million or more will likely require a second set of printing plates. Because there are so many press sizes, letterpress can be an efficient choice, even for small, short-run brochures.

Offset

Offset or offset lithography prints from a flat surface. It works on the principle that oil and water don't mix. The image to be printed is burned into a light-sensitive printing plate and developed with special chemicals. The developing process sensitizes the image so that it will accept ink. The unsensitized area rejects ink. The image is transferred to a rubber blanket that then offsets the image to paper. Thus the printing plate never comes into contact with the paper on which the image is offset or printed.

Offset printing is characterized by soft, smooth transitions of color and tones and slight differences in color balance throughout a pressrun. It is a good method for creating a mood piece, especially if soft contrast in tones is needed. Generally, offset printing is less expensive than letterpress and gravure. It is also easy to work with if you're using a desktop system to produce camera-ready pages.

Gravure

Gravure is a printing system that transfers an image from recessed images on printing plates—the opposite of the raised surface in letterpress. The image is etched into the printing plate so that ink fills the individual dots (wells). A device called a doctor blade moves across the surface and wipes away excess ink, leaving ink in the holes. When paper comes into contact with the printing plate, it lifts the ink from the wells, thus creating an image.

Gravure is known for the finest quality of color reproduction and is often used in high-fashion printed pieces, which many years ago got it mentioned in the old song "Easter Parade." It is also known for high-quality printing on a variety of surfaces like transparent and flexible films, cartons and even vinyl floor covering. If you use gravure, get ready for a budget shock, because it is more expensive than letterpress and offset.

Distribution

The way you distribute a brochure may influence its overall design. If it is to be mailed in an envelope, its finished form must conform to the size of the envelope chosen. If it is to be a self-mailer, the back page or panel must be designed with a return address in the upper left corner and a place in the center lower half for the mailing address.

If you're using a postage meter or stamps, postage must be affixed in the upper right corner. If you're using some sort of mail permit, this must be printed in the area where postage normally appears. It's important to check with the post office where the piece will be mailed to be sure that you know and conform to appropriate regulations. In fact, you'd be wise to create a dummy of the brochure and take it to the postmaster for inspection and guidance. It is a lot easier to prevent a mailing problem than to correct one.

Of course, if your brochure will be distributed from racks, as in waiting rooms of physicians, your concern is that the size will fit readily into such display racks and that the paper stock on which the brochure is printed is stiff enough to remain vertical when placed in racks.

Creating your brochure in digital form or converting your brochure into digital images is an additional option. Once in digital form, the brochure can be loaded onto a website or distributed via email. Here you have several options:

- If your computer has Adobe® Acrobat® software installed, you can produce a digital portable document format (PDF) file by selecting Adobe Acrobat (the complete program; not just the free PDF reader) as your "printer." Some word processing software allows the user to save a file in PDF format.
- If the brochure was designed by a vendor, that person probably can produce a PDF file, but don't expect that service to be done without charge. As you are preparing your budget before the work is done, ask your vendor to include in the quote preparation of a PDF file.
- Another option is to use a scanner with PDF capabilities to scan the printed brochure and produce a PDF file. The result will be digital images with the same colors as the printed brochure.

If you convert your brochure to a PDF format and distribute it via your website or email, you should provide a link to Adobe's website where a free download of Acrobat Reader® is available.

Keep in mind that if you convert a brochure, annual report or other printed materials to digital format, you must have copyright permission from the owner of artwork, photos and other images in the pieces. Your organization may have commissioned production of the art and photos, but posting digital images on a website may be considered an additional use not covered by the original agreement with the photographer and/or artist. You may be in a poor negotiating position if you failed to purchase the right to use the materials for additional uses with the initial agreements.

Exercises

1. You are a Public Relations Writer for a major PR agency in a large city on the East Coast. One of the agency's clients is a large jewelry company known for its middle-of-the-road products sold through stores in shopping malls throughout the USA. The company is trying to "upscale" its identity and has begun to move higher-quality (and of course, higher-priced) products into the stores. As a way to attract consumer attention, the company has acquired a large, rare blue diamond that will be sent around the country for special-event showings, delivered to each store accompanied by armed security guards and so on. Before the tour begins, the jewelry company wants to set up

special presentations for members of the trade/professional press. Much work is to be done preparing media packets, photos and so on. A network of small PR agencies has been retained to handle work with the media in each of the tour cities, so you will not be involved in that, at least initially. The task you have been assigned is to create a list of the trade publications to be invited. Search the Internet, and be creative in the types of publications for which you search. Jewelry design, of course. Manufacturing? The museum professions? What else?

2. You are the vice president of communication at O. Joyitz Funn Manufacturing Systems. OJF is a major producer of plastic toys. The research and development department has recently created and successfully tested a new toy. Tests seem to suggest that the new toy, called "Rotzie," will be a huge seller. OJF is frantically working on a plant expansion to help accommodate the demand it expects when Rotzie is introduced. You are equally busy getting communication plans ready for a formal announcement two months from today. Although some employees are aware of Rotzie, most of them have no clue as to how its potential sales will affect them or OJF. You know that you must put together news releases for local and national media as well as trade journals, and prepare speeches, brochures, sales literature and other things. But right now, you're pondering how to approach a feature story about Rotzie for the OJF employee magazine and the leading toy trade journal. Should the approach be the same for both? Why? Why not? Explain your decision.

3. Select brochures of your choice from a bank and a hospital (or two other dissimilar organizations). Analyze the two brochures in terms of purpose, concept, writing style, clarity of information and design. Evaluate whether these brochures are attuned to their publics and explain why you believe that is the case.

4. Get a copy of the recruiting brochure from your university. Do a readability analysis of the writing (refer to Chapter 6). Is the readability level appropriate for the intended public? Select three or four consecutive paragraphs and rewrite them to a ninth-grade level.

5. Develop a concept for a brochure to promote the department or field in which you are majoring.

CHAPTER THIRTEEN

Speeches, Presentations and Other Orally Delivered Messages

Speeches are presentations, but the presenter is one person who may or may not use any visuals. Other presentations involve multiple participants, such as panels, or more elaborate affairs with visuals and/or handouts for the audience and sometimes-complex productions with music and costumed performers. Other messages that public relations people deliver may be in the context of introductions of speakers, presenting awards, acceptance of recognition and recorded messages.

All of these are planned, but then there are the unplanned messages in response to media interviews by phone, by Skype or directly on camera. At a news conference, or in an arranged interview, most responses are to expected inquiries, but not always. Unexpected questions, though, should not mean unanticipated.

What speeches and all oral presentations have in common for public relations writers is the consideration of two critical elements—the impression the audience will take away from the experience and the information that the audience will retain. In some situations, a persuasive element is crucial because of what the audience is expected to do or to think as a result of the experience.

Speeches and presentations are strategic tools. Three strategies to consider are organizational, business and functional. Each poses some questions that must be answered by the public relations writer. Organizational strategies are closely tied to the mission and purpose of a particular organization. Business strategies are designed to achieve a particular outcome and the major consideration is return on investment (ROI). Functional strategies, for the most part, are part of a campaign to achieve a particular goal or objective. Launching the campaign, controlling and monitoring its progress and evaluating results are critical elements.

Speeches and other oral communications play a major role in all three strategies.

Regarding organizational strategies, what is the reality within the organization's mission, its goals and objectives, its resources? What strategic function does a speech or presentation serve in fulfilling a goal? How will that speech or presentation be accepted internally? How will the speech or presentation affect the organization's primary publics, those most closely identified with the organization?

In terms of business strategies, what does the organization expect as a result of the speech or presentation? Is direct action a needed consequence? Is delayed response not only anticipated but desired? What has to happen from the organization's investment in the time and trouble to give the speech or make the presentation?

The functional strategy is how the speech or presentation fits into the overall communication tactics. Is publicity a crucial factor? Or is a subtle, low-keyed persuasive approach needed? What effects are anticipated from the various publics who will have direct exposure to the speech or presentation? What about side effects from those who read or hear about the speech or presentation? How will these be measured?

As these descriptions suggest, speeches and any other oral presentations are part of strategic planning. A significant consideration is how close the audience is to the information being presented. If the speech or presentation is for internal audiences such as employees or related trade or professional groups, some allowances can be made for assumptions about familiarity with the topic. If the audiences are primarily external, nothing can be taken for granted, and some special care needs to be taken to eliminate misunderstandings or misinterpretations. Some speeches or presentations can have negative public relations consequences, often just because of one word or phrase.

Speeches

Delivering a speech is a hazardous undertaking. A speech takes place in real time—once. Although its delivery occurs once, that one presentation may be recorded and re-presented—out of context and without explanation. Another challenge is that members of the audience may be sending out—in real time by social media—points the speaker is making. It's not unlikely that the content will appear in a blog within minutes of the conclusion of the speech.

Often writing a speech is a collaborative effort, especially if the speech is one that a government official or corporate executive will be giving. Implications of words or phrases can have legal, historical, religious or discriminatory ramifications. Reactions can be immediate or delayed. Consequences of missteps can be long-term. Many nonwriters might be involved making the word crafting arduous. Speechwriters for high-profile personalities need patience and persuasion to get desired results that also fit the style of the person delivering the speech.

A speech first has to claim the audience. Without audience attention, no communication can occur. A speaker can only send messages, verbally and nonverbally, to an audience. It's the audience that gives those messages meaning. For this reason, writing speeches and scripts demands more attention and care from the public relations writer than almost any other writing task. You can't simply write your thoughts on a subject and expect them to be delivered successfully by any speaker.

Audiences react emotionally to the speaker's authority, trustworthiness, tolerance and friendliness, so the speechwriter must consider these factors when writing. In essence, this means the speech must be personalized. The words must go with the person. A speaker must sound natural and not like reading cue cards. A person who feels comfortable with the words being spoken will be a more credible speaker.

Direct interaction with an audience in either a speech or visuals/words presentation brings out the best in most of us. The person preparing the material must remember that, although the audience is the ultimate receiver of the information, the person presenting it is most important. The speaker is both medium and message.

Sometimes public relations writers deliver speeches themselves, and in these cases, it should be easy to write a natural-sounding speech. But there's more to consider than just the speaker. Whether writing for another person or for yourself, you must have an idea of what the audience will be like. What experiences do audience members bring with them? What do they expect from the speaker? What stereotypes do they hold? That is, what are the "pictures in their heads"? If you don't know these things, you won't be able to write an effective speech.

You need to know the language patterns of the audience as well as of the speaker, because certain words used in particular ways can send thoughts down familiar paths. Remember that the connotations of words are as important as the denotations. And keep in mind that meanings change with time and that the same words may mean different things in different contexts or in different parts of the country. This means you can't write like you talk (or like the speaker talks) without considering how the audience talks.

Words, important as they are, aren't the only thing to be considered. Nonverbal cues can help emphasize points or obscure them. Audiences are sensitive to body movements, gestures, facial expressions, physical appearance and displays of personality and emotion. Effective speakers use these nonverbal expressions to hold attention and to help get the message across. Most speakers video record rehearsals to perfect the blend of words and nonverbal expressions.

Visualizing the Setting as You Write

Many speechwriters get stalled at the beginning because they don't ask some important questions: Why was the speaker invited to address this particular group? What do the group members expect to hear? What does the speaker want to accomplish by giving a speech to this particular group? What particular topic will meet the speaker's needs and the group's expectations? You have to answer these questions before you start writing.

The next two questions have to be considered together: How long should the speech be, and what is the physical setting? A luncheon group won't tolerate as long an address as a dinner group, for example. People attending luncheons usually have other obligations; people who go to dinner are making an evening of it. Are there other speakers? Who are they and what are their topics? (These last questions are especially important if the speech is part of a seminar.)

Types of Speeches

Public relations people usually deal with four basic types of speeches: informative, persuasive, entertaining and technical. A fifth, less formal type of speech, is termed brief remarks.

Informative   The informative speech generally—but not always—makes use of visuals. The subject matter is information that can be understood readily by audiences with little or no background in the subject matter. Thus it is an educational opportunity for the organization. Such a speech may consist of telling a civic organization what the speaker's organization does, or it may involve telling an advisory body or an internal public what the organization is planning to do or has done. The speech given by the head of an organization at the annual meeting falls in this category. A caution in using numbers is to be very simple and straightforward. Don't mix percentages with fractions, for example, two thirds of X and 20 percent of Y. People, especially those who don't deal with numbers on a daily basis, are distracted from what you are trying to tell them by attempting to work the math in their minds.

Persuasive   The persuasive speech attempts to sell an audience on an idea, a person or a course of action. It could also be used to promote a specific product—anything from T-shirts to season tickets to the opera. More likely, though, the subject is something more abstract and, therefore, more difficult to sell. The speech might be aimed at convincing employees to take an early retirement opportunity or to contribute to a political action committee. It could be intended to convince a union of the desirability of accepting management's proposal or to favorably impress investor-rating agencies with the state of the organization. Presentations like these may also make use of graphs and even handouts or booklets of charts and supporting documentation.

Entertaining   The presentation may be designed primarily to entertain, such as an after-dinner talk or a luncheon speech. In some cases, a keynote address may be classified as chiefly entertaining, although such addresses are generally more purposeful. Even when emphasis is placed on giving the audience an enjoyable experience, information about the organization is presented, and the speaker tries to leave the audience with a favorable impression not only of herself or himself, but also of the organization. A principal risk here is the use of humor. Self-depreciating humor is the safest. To make a point memorable by humor means that what is said has to relevant and, where possible, timely. Jokes often don't work because there is a "victim," the target of the ridicule or teasing.

Technical   The technical presentation almost always involves visuals, usually PowerPoint slides and/or videos, and printed handouts. A problem with technical presentations is that the technology often fails. Memory sticks (thumb drives) are easy to carry but are not always compatible with the available equipment. PowerPoint presentations on disks are particularly vulnerable to incompatible components or unfavorable lighting. Videos, especially those with audio tracks, sometimes don't work as well as planned either, for a variety of reasons. Computers may have compatibility problems and so disks may be used in stand-alone projection units. If your speaker will be using a Teleprompter, be sure the speaker is well trained and rehearsed in delivery. The Teleprompter needs a good technical support team standing by, and a backup system.

Technical presentations are usually for peers at trade or professional meetings, or an official presentation to a regulatory body or a board of directors. The audience is likely to be less forgiving since it wants and needs the information. Be sure to have a backup plan for a verbal-only presentation with handouts. A consideration is when to make the handouts available: at first for the audience to follow as you speak, or at the end so they won't just accept the handouts and either not listen or simply leave.

Brief Remarks   Other speeches fall into the category of brief remarks, which are given on special occasions as introductions, expressions of thanks, welcome, acceptance, recognitions, or as an expert respondent in a program about issues, situations or problems. The respondent can only prepare for discussion of possible subject matter, and may do that with index cards and lists of references. The other occasions, although certainly important, need not be entirely scripted unless the person speaking is uncomfortable without a script. What works best for these occasions is to develop the gist or content of the remarks and have the speaker put them in his or her own words. If it is a highly official function, it may be better to use a script and rehearse the speaker a number of times until she or he is comfortable with the brief remarks. A major problem encountered with these is that the speaker may not be familiar with the pronunciation of names or terms. Be sure that these are spelled in easy-to-read phonetic terms, such as those used by broadcasters. (See *AP Broadcast News Handbook* by Brad Kalbfeld, p. 475). Another help is a website www .pronouncenames.com.

Planning   Once you have the date, prospective audience—including number, location and the setting, then you can begin to consider the topic. Even if it is an assigned one, the particular emphasis may be something you need to decide after you have done some research.

First look at the proposed speech subject in general. Search for new information about it, particular aspects or recent findings will give currency to the speech. This means using a search engine to discover recent news, speeches, publications, and people involved in particular activities associated with the topic. Once you have discovered what facets are possible topics, consult with people in the organization to understand their focus. Now you can make a list of topics to research.

With a narrow list, examine the possible audience, its demographics in particular. You want to challenge the audience, not bore them. You don't want to overwhelm them either by assuming backgrounds they may not have. If the audience is a general one, the best place to begin is to use a search engine to find what has been said about a topic. Another resource is the *Readers' Guide to Periodical Literature*. You need to find out what the audience might have been exposed to recently. If the audience is a specialized group, consult the publications that group members receive and find out what is being written. You'll learn their current concerns and get an idea of what the group is like.

Most speeches written for public relations purposes are informative speeches. After you have determined what the audience has already been exposed to, then you can turn your attention to new ideas about the topic or new relationships of the topic to other public issues or concerns. If you work for the organization for which you are writing, as an "insider" you may feel you already know the material well enough to write a speech in your sleep, still do some secondary research. When you are doing a computer search, remember institutions such as libraries provide access to materials that contain needed information even if you are not a subscriber. Because all your knowledge of the topic is likely to be from an insider's point of view, you should find out what others are saying and thinking about the topic. You probably have seen some materials that come from competitors and critics, but you should look at what has appeared in other media as well, particularly popular blogs and prestige publications such as indexes for *The New York Times, Forbes, The Economist* and *The Wall Street Journal*. Most public libraries in metropolitan areas and in cities with universities have electronic research capabilities if yours are limited. Select your topic and have the literature searched for sources. Keep a detailed record of your research findings. Although speeches don't usually come with footnotes, create a resource list so you can respond to questions, challenges.

Remember that, in writing an informative speech, you are charged with offering members of the audience new and valuable information and then helping them understand and retain it. When you are writing a speech for someone else to deliver, you need to meet with the speaker after this initial research to get an idea of what he or she thinks is most important and to determine the slant or approach for the presentation.

Paring and Timing

If you have done your research well, you will have many more ideas than you can or should introduce in a single speech. Begin paring. Cut away until you have no more than three items you want to communicate.

Select the three most important ideas you want people in the audience to carry away with them, and then present the ideas as something fresh and meaningful. (It helps if the ideas are startling in themselves, but don't fake it.) Give the listeners some way to associate these ideas with others they hold. You'll have to repeat the ideas often to make sure they are retained, but don't be redundant. You don't want the audience thinking, "You just said that a few minutes ago." You also have to introduce the ideas in a logical sequence, using relationships that aid retention. It helps if you can break the pace of the presentation, adding some visuals when appropriate. Injecting humor helps people retain information, but problems can arise with this if the speechwriter and the speaker are not the same person. Humor is very personal. It's difficult to write humor for someone else unless both people are real professionals at their jobs. To be safe, use anecdotes—narratives that don't depend heavily on the style of delivery. Good anecdotes give you an opportunity to show a visual that illustrates the narrative. Pictures aid retention.

At each rehearsal do more trimming. Sometimes you'll find whole chunks of copy to delete. Do that, but add transitions so the speech won't become choppy. You need to physically time the speech with a stopwatch. If you are writing the speech for someone else, attend rehearsals and time the delivery. When visuals are used, you'll have less copy because visuals take more time than the actual showing. There's lost time in the movement from voice to video, even when the speaker is using a clicker or has someone handling the computer. You'll lose less time if you do have someone else handling the visuals so the speaker can concentrate on delivery and be more attentive to audience reactions. Time the whole presentation at each rehearsal. It should get shorter, up to a point. That's fine. Good presenters always leave the audience wanting more, rather than getting eager for the end. One thing to remember, though, is most performers plan for an "encore." Prepare some extra visuals with captions, if the audience asks questions about an aspect that was mentioned, but deleted when the speech was tightened for timing purposes. You also want the audience to feel satisfied and "compensated" for their time and attention.

Persuading

As you convey your three main ideas, keep in mind what you want to accomplish with this message. Do you want to move the audience to take some action? If so, you'd better let the listeners know what you want them to do, how they can do it and what their rewards will be. Perhaps you want to change their belief about something. Remember, a belief is acceptance of a truth—an acceptance based on experience, evidence and opinions. If you are going to try to persuade people to change a belief, you'll have to offer both logical proof and some emotional appeal.

Alternatively, you may only want to reinforce a belief. Many public relations speeches are of this nature. Give the audience reasons for retaining their belief, and inform them of reference groups who also hold the belief. This will reassure your listeners that they are right in believing what they do.

The Mechanics of Organization

A speech has three parts: an introduction, a body and a conclusion. Contrary to what you've probably done all your life, don't write the introduction first. Just as you wouldn't write an introduction for a speaker until you knew who the speaker was, you shouldn't write an introduction for a speech until you know what will be in it.

Start with a title. The title should keep the main point of the speech in the forefront of your thinking. After you have a title, write down your purpose: to entertain, explain, convince or motivate. Then list the three ideas you want the audience to retain. Next, state precisely what you want the audience to do as a result of hearing the speech. You should then be able to write a conclusion.

Go back now to the three main ideas you want to convey, and devise a theme to tie them together. You ought to be able to tie this theme in with the purpose of the speech. At this point, you should be ready to prepare an outline.

Begin the outline by listing the three main points on separate sheets of paper. Under each point, list the pertinent information you have gathered from your research, along with what you already knew. Keep this list on the left side of the page. On the right side, write a key word for an anecdote or illustration to go with each point. Narratives make points memorable. Now arrange all of the information under each point in a logical sequence, and you are ready to write.

Formal speeches have a format that you need to consider: response to introduction; greetings to audience and effort to build rapport with them; overview of topic; summary of three points to be covered; discussion of each point with verbal and/or visual illustrations; reiteration of three points in light of purpose of speech; desired response from the audience—what to remember and why; conclusion and thanks for the audience's time and attention.

Style

To be effective in stimulating images in the audience's mind, employ vivid words and expressive language. Be clear. Choose your words with precision. Be specific. Keep a thesaurus and a dictionary on hand to find precisely the words you need. For emphasis and retention, use repetition, but use it effectively. Think of a phrase that used for rhetorical emphasis will be recalled by audiences and captured as a sound bite. (See Example 13.1 for Ten Types of Sound Bites.) Use transitions not just to connect thoughts, but also to underscore a point by reiterating it. Confirm that all your words are appropriate to the purpose of the speech, to the audience and to the speaker. The audience always is global, either actually or potentially, so be sensitive to cultural issues. Remember that words have definitions. People give them meaning.

Involve the audience by using personal pronouns and asking questions that listeners must answer for themselves. Find some way to establish rapport—by citing common experiences or using familiar situations and imagery, for example. Use quotations if they are not

FIGURE 13.1

Ten Types of Sound Bites (Sometimes Spelled "Bytes")

1. **Similes, metaphors and analogies:** "It's as if Republicans and Democrats are planning a trip, but they disagree over whether you should start the trip from Buenos Aires or Greenland,"—*Howard Gleckman, Tax Policy Center.*

2. **Triples:** "We help ordinary people get rich without working on Wall Street, inheriting wealth or marrying a millionaire."

3. **Rhetorical questions:** "More than 600,000 Americans lost their jobs last month. How many more families need to lose their economic lifeline before Congress acts?"

4. **Constraints.** Conflicts or paradoxes: "Our food is fresh. Our customers are spoiled."—*FreshDirect, online grocer.*

5. **Definitiveness or power:** "We are in this to win."—*Gen. David Petraeus.*

6. **Superlatives:** "This is the biggest technological advance in 50 years in the oil business." *Philip Crouse, oil analyst.*

7. **Pop culture:** "There's a greater likelihood that I'll be asked by Madonna to go on tour as her bass player than I'll be picked to be on the ticket."—*Former Gov. Mike Huckabee (R-AR), assessing his chances of becoming Mitt Romney's vice presidential running mate in 2012.*

8. **Emotions:** "As a New Yorker, I am absolutely horrified by what happened in my city last night."—*Commentator on Daily Kos website about alleged police brutality at a local protest.*

9. **Surprise twist:** "I will not exploit, for political purposes, my opponent's youth and inexperience."—*President Ronald Reagan, diffusing accusations that he was too old for a second term.*

10. **Tweaked clichés:** "Money doesn't grow on trees, but it does grow faster in credit unions without those greedy big bank fees."

Used with Permission of *PRSA TACTICS*, January 11, 2013, p. 9 and Brad Phillips, president of Phillips Media Relations, a media and presentation company based in New York.

long and if they can be integrated with your ideas to give authority. Be direct. If you are ambiguous, an audience may leave wondering what you meant and may come up with the wrong answer.

In delivery, the speech should support its points with various timely, meaningful exhibits—audiovisual aids, statistics (not too many and give source, date), detailed illustrations and hypothetical or real situations. Comparison and contrast are effective too. Craft the speech to include these.

After you've completed the body of the speech, go back and write an introduction. The introduction is an integral part of the speech. It should lead smoothly, logically and directly into the body. It shouldn't appear to have been pasted on as an after thought. The introduction must create attention and build rapport. It should give the audience some sign of the direction the rest of the speech will take.

You can use various devices to create an effective introduction. For example, start with an anecdote or illustration to capture the audience's interest. Use a quotation or a bright one-liner that makes a startling assertion or asks a provocative question. You might even use a suspense gimmick, which you can then refer to throughout the speech and finally tie into the conclusion. Some speakers begin with a compliment to help establish rapport, but there is some risk in this. You could come off as patronizing. You never want to apologize for yourself or the speech. You shouldn't have to!

When writing for someone else, keep in mind that person's favorite words, expressions and normal speaking pattern—long sentences or short, snappy ones. One speechwriter records the speech-planning session and plays it during this part of the work. The basic speech is then personalized for the speaker.

After the speech, be prepared for responses from the audience, either formal or informal. Think of questions the audience might ask and have answers ready, in writing if necessary. Provide some examples of the three main points that can be developed extemporaneously and review these with the speaker to rehearse possible responses. If possible, take a real example from the speaker's own background, or use that background to create a story or metaphor that the speaker might have thought of to illustrate the point. Summarize the three points so the speaker can reiterate them.

Part of the job is finding out all you can about the physical location so you can think of appropriate gestures. You need to inform the speaker of the physical arrangements so appropriate delivery can be rehearsed and nonverbal expressions developed to reinforce the message. The physical situation is extremely important. For example, subtle gestures are lost in a large auditorium, whereas even the slightest movement is magnified by television cameras.

Be sure the speaker is comfortable with any visual aids or demonstrations. Go over these carefully with the speaker. If the speaker is not experienced in handling such equipment and time for training is limited, get an assistant and write that into the speaker's script. Be sure the technician is familiar with both the speech and the equipment. Mechanical failures can undermine a speaker's authority and poise. Eye contact is important. Audiences don't like to be talked *at*. The speaker needs to find individual people to look at to direct the message to them. Be sure these "point people" are scattered about the room so that attention doesn't seem to be focused in one spot. For a speaker facing a television camera instead of a live audience, the red light is the audience. Such situations occur when a speech delivered by an official is being sent technologically to remote audiences.

Setting the Stage and Writing the Finale

In addition to writing the speech, the public relations writer must provide a written introduction of the speaker. How the person with the message is presented is important to audience acceptance. Content has to be controlled. For example, it's common for the person inviting the speaker to ask for a résumé. The problem is that the résumé is often *read*. Such an introduction is lethal. In public relations practice, you should offer to write the introduction for the person who will be presenting the speaker. Since you probably don't know the introducer, keep your introduction short and simple and easy to read. Think about what this particular audience wants and needs to know about the speaker. What will best set the tone and context for the speech? The slant will change for each audience even if the speech is basically the same.

Another part of the presentation that you'll need to write for the speaker is what she or he says immediately following the introduction. The speaker needs to acknowledge the introduction and say something nice about the person who invited him or her to speak, or about the person in charge of the gathering or the members of the audience. It's not only good manners, but it's also good public relations. Do some research to write something meaningful, such as finding out who issued the invitation and why. The reason to prepare this is because some speakers have destroyed the positive atmosphere for their speech before they begin by some extemporaneous, inappropriate remark. Planning and rehearsing some sort of acknowledgement should have the effect of sincerity.

The other major writing job is to prepare a news release about the speech. Because the audience for the speech may be limited, a news release gives the message broader circulation. For a major address, an institution usually includes publication of the speech in the promotion budget. The format is similar to a brochure, with the introduction of the speaker included, along with a description of the occasion on which the speech was presented. Copies are then mailed to lists of important publics for the message who were unlikely to have been present, usually with a cover memo (rarely a letter) or simply a business card. Specifications for reprint are also usually included. Be sure you have a high-resolution headshot of the speaker to use for the brochure.

Reprinting the speech is usually permitted, although in some cases, the speech is copyrighted. When the latter is the case, it should be made clear so that those who want to use the speech or large portions of it will know that permission for use is required. When you post the speech on the organization's website, be sure to include the copyright symbol and the date if the speech is to be copyrighted material.

Presentation Scripts

Speeches, as discussed here, are presentations that a person delivers before a live or electronic audience. Scripts are formats for integrating visuals into a presentation by one or more persons. Some electronic presentations may be interactive such as PowerPoint and Webinars.

Differences and Similarities

Major differences between preparing a script and a simple speech are the technologies involved and consideration of the audience. A script is not tailored as specifically for a single audience or single event as a speech. Many audiences may be seeing it *individually* (as in the case of employee videos on benefits) or *collectively* (as when salespeople all over the world see it in their own company group). Ordinarily, scripts are expected to have a longer "shelf life" than a speech, even one given frequently. Furthermore, the audiovisual presentation may be an educational tool from which the listener/viewer expects to gain a skill or information to progress in the workplace.

Approach script planning by first determining what you want to accomplish. Then think about the various publics who might be exposed to the presentation. After you have identified these publics, make a list of what each needs to know about the subject.

Types of Presentations

Basically there are two types of presentations that involve public relations writers: the primarily informational and the primarily persuasive.

Informational presentations are generally to employees and/or organizational advisory groups, external advisory groups such as government regulatory or supervisory bodies or nongovernmental groups (NGOs) who are a special public because of their interest in issues related to the organization, educational organizations or associations or trade and professional groups. Some informational presentations are instructional, and these are usually more repetitive in content than strictly informational scripts. Safety instructions or how to use new equipment presentations are in this category.

Persuasive presentations may be directed to any of these groups too, but usually persuasive presentations are a call to action or a particular point of view. These presentations are often given by lobbyists to governmental staff or elected officials themselves or to special-interest groups that the organization is trying to enlist in a joint effort to affect policy. Persuasive presentations may be given to employees too, especially those given in connection with a campaign to get them involved in and supportive of the effort before going to other publics. One type of persuasive presentation that public relations people in agencies or firms are always involved in is new business solicitations in which it is the organization itself that is being promoted with the idea of persuading the prospective client to hire them.

Planning

List the principal ideas you want to convey in the presentation. Arrange these logically, so development is easy to follow. Use a narrative approach if you can. Make a master chart of the ideas, listing under each, as you would for a speech, the points you want to make. Beside each, describe in detail how you might present the point visually. Be sure each point has these elements: something to set the scene for the idea, something to carry the action of the line of thought forward and something to relate to a common experience that audiences can identify with.

Because scripts are more like a play than a speech, there must be an element of drama that builds. You can't put your punch lines first. You need to build to climaxes, give comic relief, offer suspense and/or surprise. You are more of a dramatist than a speechwriter—but it's not all that different from writing a television commercial or a public service announcement (PSA). (See Part 4 for Designing Messages for Controlled Content.)

Development

At the point of developing audiovisuals, there is no single path forward. Often because the speech is composed on the computer, the writer will prepare the major points as a visual or series of visuals. If graphs or charts are important, these are added. Of course, you can incorporate other art from the computer or use art that you scan into the computer. The presentation is projected to a large screen directly from the computer. The speaker can then go from one point to another easily and back up if there's a need to revisit a point. (For suggestions about when to incorporate computer graphics, see Table 13.1.)

If the scriptwriter is not handling the graphics personally, the writer has to work closely with the person preparing the graphics and other visuals, because these tell the story. The words are just there to help. There are two ways to go about this double-track operation: select your visuals and write a script that fits them, or prepare the script and then "illustrate." When the visuals come from outside the organization, it is logical for the script to come first.

If you are getting help with visuals, plan for a series of conferences. The first adds details not in the proposal. The writer can explain the outline of points and suggest how these might be told with visuals. If specific pictures are needed, a photographer then develops a shooting schedule, interpreting the intent of the script in terms of shots that need to be taken to tell the story. Additional visuals may have to be sought or created elsewhere.

After the first visuals are ready, another conference should be held to ensure that the visuals match your conception of the message. And when all are completed, another conference is needed to see what is missing or needs replacement. At this point, the stronger art should be selected. The most compelling illustrations must be arranged in the best way to tell the story. In addition, the script may have to be revised at this stage. The importance of flexibility can't be overstated—although it is sometimes difficult to be objective about finding the best way to tell the story.

After the art is chosen and the sequences are planned, the script is ready for polishing, if it has been written. If it has not been written, you are ready to start.

Matching Words and Sights

Visuals have the power to set a mood, inject drama and explain in powerful ways. The words of the script should help the visuals do this. Too many words interfere with the listener's ability to absorb the visuals. Allow time for the pictures to have an impact.

The question always arises as to whether the script should carry the same information that is being seen, perhaps on charts or graphs. Usually the audience is given the charts and graphs as a handout. These need to be in a suitable format for keeping as a reference. It's best to handle charts as they are handled in the print media. First the textual material prepares readers for the illustration by discussing it. Below the illustration there usually is a caption explaining the graph or chart and source or credit lines where necessary. Readers then expect to see the relationship between the illustration and the point being made explained further in the textual matter.

Writers with television-writing skills adjust easily to presentation scripts. Their experience with the medium transfers easily to writing scripts. Sometimes, though, they have

T A B L E 1 3 . 1	*Computer Graphics*

When should you use computer graphics?

- When you want to have a screen show at the touch of a key
- When the equipment is available and the technology would enhance your communication with the audience
- When your competitors are using it or a similar presentation mode

Creating graphics

Graphics can be either static (still) or dynamic (animated).

Examples

Still: Charts—Bar/line, organization, text, pie, area, high/low, etc.

Should be used for communicating information such as budget disbursement.

Animated: Product rotated on the screen, internal view of how something works, simulated growth history of sales in animated form, flow of information in a communication network, etc.

Should be used for communicating information such as product capability.

Hints for effective use

- Use graphic techniques and maintain audience focus and attention.
  Transitions include zooms, fades, overlaps, dissolves, and others.
- Use a different color in graphics to emphasize major points.
- Present only pertinent information. Avoid excessive details.
  Use as a guideline: No less than 28-point type
  Maximum of 33 characters per line
  No more than 6 lines of text per screen
  No more than 3 or 4 screens per minute

- Use upper and lower case (rather than all caps) for text. Headers can be upper case, if desired.
- For readability from across a room, use a very dark background and large, very light-colored type.

Contingency plan

- Before your presentation, check whether equipment is functioning properly.
- Have copies printed ready to use as handouts in case equipment failure prevents your computer screen show.

Know your material well enough that you can still give an organized presentation during a power outage (even if it means giving your presentation in the dark).

Source: Permission Gay Wakefield.

difficulty with the time period. Television writers are accustomed to working with fragments of time. In a presentation incorporating visuals, the time is usually about 30 minutes, but it can be twice that. In a long presentation, both unity and pace make the job quite different from that of writing an ordinary television script. For elaborate presentations consider the use of sound. It can add emphasis and recall. Think of music and sound effects to accompany the words.

Pace can be varied in both the script and visuals. And to keep audience interest, it is essential to employ some of the techniques of the dramatist—suspense, dramatic foreshadowing and comic relief among others. In a way, the script constitutes half of a dialogue and the visuals form the other half; together, both tell the story.

Just as in the case of speeches, promotion is involved in calling attention to the ideas presented in the script. Like speeches some presentations may be prepared as publications. A news release may be written if the presentation is for important or large groups or is a "traveling" presentation. If the production is a long presentation going to a number of audiences, a promotional brochure should be developed.

Computer Advantages/Disadvantages

Advantages seem fairly clear—retention and flexibility. Facts and visuals for the speech or script and various versions can all be stored as PDFs on a laptop or on disks for future consideration. Editing is simplified, and printed copies of various versions can easily be produced. Computer graphics programs can produce excellent transferable illustrations to integrate into the presentation. Illustrations can be changed easily on the computer. Some points can be highlighted, colors added, backgrounds changed and designs reconfigured. Digital images and audio can be imported and stored. When an observation calls for use of older visuals, these can be scanned in and used for something such as an historical observation.[1] Sound can be digitalized and imported too.

Computerized presentations can be developed using a program like Adobe software or Microsoft PowerPoint presentation software. Some computerized presentations are simply stored on a memory stick. A high-intensity overhead projector is needed for the presentation unless the computer is connected directly to a large-screen monitor.

When the presentation version is completed, it's best to copy that and a runtime version to a disk. The runtime version permits the presentation to be run on another computer without the software application, but it doesn't allow for revisions.[2]

Because one major advantage of computer presentations is flexibility, you always want to maintain that and keep open the opportunity for revisions, up to the last minute if necessary. Another advantage of computer-generated presentations is the opportunity to use the projected visuals as prompts for an experienced, knowledgeable speaker for whom the projection is the script. Preparing scripts for experts often means preparing just the points the speaker wants to make along with associated charts, graphs or other visuals. The speaker will use these to keep the presentation on track but will speak extemporaneously. This makes for a very persuasive presentation as long as the speaker's delivery is effective. You'll probably go through a number of designs for this sort of presentation until the speaker is comfortable with all of the computer screens that will be used. This must flow easily and nothing can be overlooked. Here the ability of the speaker to return to previous screens in a question-and-answer session following the presentation makes it necessary to have a script there for reference so the screen can be found promptly.

Disadvantages of computer presentations are not as obvious as the advantages. One disadvantage is having equipment problems. First make sure the equipment needed for the presentation is on-site and working. If the presentation is to a large group, you may be projecting to large screens or even to a remote site. In these cases, you need top-notch technical support. The equipment may check out fine in rehearsals and then break down while the presentation is going on. You want to be sure you have backup equipment, and someone there who knows the mechanics of the setup. That is a delivery problem, though. A not-so-obvious problem for the PR writer is inexperience in using PowerPoint or another presentation software effectively.

Presentation software offers endless possibilities, and some scriptwriters find it tempting to use all or most of them. The effects can be dazzling and dizzying. Shapes and forms that seem to melt into each other or surprisingly emerge wonderful color for background and type often are more of a detriment than an asset to the presentation. Before attempting a computer presentation script, reread guidance on message content and design in previous chapters. Much of the information there pertains to presentation scripts.

Other Speech/Presentation Occasions

Introductions and **acknowledgements** are two of the brief speeches that already have been discussed. Others are **award** and **recognition** speeches as well as **acceptance** speeches. Generally, the recipient is aware of the award or recognition and thus can provide biographical information so that it can be added to the speech that introduces the award and names the recipient. Introducing the award involves providing a brief history of the award or its inception. If this is the award's first recipient, explain the award's significance and then give the reason for the choice of recipient. The same pattern follows for types of recognition that don't necessarily have a physical award. Recognition is important, so be sure you know how to pronounce names correctly.

As mentioned earlier in the chapter, write pronunciation into the script, using the broadcaster's simplified phonics found in the *AP Broadcast News Handbook*. Representative sounds are given for vowels and consonants. Of course the person writing the script has to know the correct pronunciation or know where to find it in a reference book.

The broadcast handbook guidance will help with unfamiliar technical terms and the names of places, such as the Texas city Waco (WAY-KOH) or written (WAY-koh), using caps for the syllable to be stressed. For technical terms, titles and places, a dictionary will give you the standard phonetic alphabet, then you can craft an accurate, but quick read for an announcer. Foreign personal names are another matter. You may have to turn to a linguist for help. Even more common personal names you'll usually have to find out about pronunciation too. For example: Smythe can be SM-EH-TH or SM-EYE-TH or SM-EH-THE. Ask!

Background on recipients of any recognition always is needed because information that can be found about the person through electronic searches may need updating or confirming. A parallel to recognitions is **acceptances**. When someone is receiving an award, an off-the-cuff response is not always as thoughtful as a planned, gracious acceptance that recognizes the organizations giving it.

The organization will have some publicity about the presentation that usually includes the recipient's acknowledgement or acceptance. For that reason, some planning needs to occur so that the acceptance is genuine and brief. If you think of the ceremonies for the Oscars and Grammy awards, you will not have much trouble remembering some inappropriate acceptances. Although the recipients will not know that they will be chosen, being nominated suggests that a response be considered.

Some speaking opportunities are under less-controlled circumstances than what has been discussed so far. Two common situations are media interviews and news conferences.

Media Interviews

All media are included here. Some media interviews from traditional news organizations may come by telephone, landline or mobile, without any warning. That can be true too of interviews solicited by members of the trade press, although less likely. Although there is no specific warning, the calls should not be unanticipated. As issues are being monitored by the organization's public relations people, people likely to be called for comments should be notified and some talking points and positions should be discussed. That gives the persons likely to be called a chance to have at hand or at least in mind the background of the issue. Some news media go through the organization's public relations office to the contact, but often that is not the case. Contact information is easy to come by through websites and search engines. Responses to such unexpected media calls should be brief, but not abrupt, and should be consistent with the organization's mission statement and consider the effect of the comments on all stakeholders. Media training for likely respondents is useful, but speechwriters may get a call too to supply some background or statistics that can be sent quickly in an email. This is where backgrounders and position papers can be especially useful. Staff members fielding questions need to have these on hand, and even in a script format as issues evolve. Television interviews also can be unexpected when TV news crews are covering spot news. For more on this, see Chapter 14 on crisis communication.

However, television interviews are more likely to be structured because they occur in a TV studio. Normally in setting up the interview, you will have covered with the interviewer what you or the organization's representative will be discussing. If it is a friendly interviewing situation, the interviewer will meet with you prior to the show, although sometimes just before airtime or the taping. The interviewer wants a good show, and you want to make certain points, never more than three, and maybe less depending on the length of the interview. Get the most important point you want to make out in the first 15 to 20 seconds.

You need to organize your thoughts mentally because you will be speaking extemporaneously. Think of good sound bites, but use them appropriately. Listen carefully to the questions as they are asked, and respond specifically to the question.

Think carefully about how your response will be interpreted, and later could be taken out of context.

Keep a friendly, open demeanor, even if the questioning gets tough. You need to keep calm and relaxed, but be strong in your voice. You want to engage the audience so they'll remember your points. Be sure you know all of the information you are likely to be asked. Your preparation should seem effortless, though, and come out in a natural conversation.

If you are participating from another location, you will be wearing an earpiece. Be sure that it fits properly before the show or the recording starts. You don't want the distraction of fumbling to adjust the piece to your ear to get the right volume. Usually you'll be wearing a lapel microphone, but the sound staff probably will get this adjusted properly for you and test the pick-up of your voice before the interview begins.

News Conferences

Because you will have called the news conference, you have more control than you do in a television interview. It is your choice of site, your setting, your equipment and your staff. Be sure you have considered the site carefully. The background and setting carry their own message, and you want that to be positive for all who see the conference or news excerpts from it.

You want to be sure you have anticipated all of the questions. If you are responsible for having an executive interviewed, go through the types of questions likely to be asked and her/his general response. You should be working with a media-trained executive so she or he has some on-camera experience.

Occasionally news conferences call for demonstrations or injections of visuals. Be sure these work as expected and add significantly to the point of the news conference. Have microphones set up for news media to use them so their questions can be picked up by everyone, and also on your organization's video recording of the news conference that your staff is making. If the news conference is being carried in real time on your website, be sure the set is designed for easy viewing on a computer. The setting will have to be tighter than just for television.

In most news conferences, the executive or you will be speaking from a prepared script, although it should be brief. Afterward, you'll be responding to questions. Don't try to dodge them or be evasive in your response. Also, don't get defensive; it shows.

Since you are controlling the presentation, remember the broadcast rule: tell them what you are going to tell them, tell them, and then tell them what you told them. It's okay to be repetitive, just not redundant.

Some good advice comes from media trainer T.J. Walker who says that to evaluate your performance to improve, watch it within 24 hours of the airing or taping.[3]

Evaluations

Public relations writers, as well as presenters and certainly management, want to know if the speech or presentation was effective. What often is used on-site is a simple evaluation form. It may be handed to attendees at the presentation and either collected at the door or left behind on tables. Sometimes if the presentation is at a conference, the evaluation is sent later to those who attended and includes all of the speeches and presentations for respondents to evaluate.

Remember, these forms are generally distributed and collected by the organization where the speech or presentation was given, and when that organization is different from your own, you may or may not know the results. To assess the evaluation, you need a copy of the questionnaire used, the method for soliciting responses and how many completed responses were used in the assessment. Why? Because your job may be on the line. A presentation can get "bad reviews" that you get blamed for when your part of the job was fine. Or it may be that the opinion "survey" is not a good indicator.

When a presentation is an informative one, the best assessment is an evaluation some time after the presentation to test recall of information as well as what was best appreciated or liked about the presentation. This helps you design better presentations.

If the presentation is a persuasive one, the measures are more complex. You can't always judge long-term effects by short-term reports. However, you certainly can tell something about the presentation by the verbal and written responses the organization gets. You can document these and draw some conclusions from them, so long as you remember that those you don't hear from may be significantly different from those who make the effort to express themselves. Be alert to any pointed criticism about bias or insensitivity that a presentation may have aroused. Even one critic's message can be important here.

Exercises

1. You are the vice president of communication at O. Joyitz Funn Manufacturing Systems. OJF is a major producer of children's toys made of plastics. The management team recently got a confidential staff medical report confirming that OJF employees have a much higher incidence of respiratory illnesses than is normal in the surrounding community and region. The report cites as the probable cause a key ingredient used in the manufacture of several OJF products, although more study is necessary to confirm this chemical as the offending agent. Management immediately ordered more study for definitive answers. But it also decided to keep the information confidential until the results of these studies are known. Your task now is to come up with a persuasive rationale that will give support to running a story about the staff medical report in the company magazine now. What arguments will you use? Consult Chapter 7 on persuasion for some clues.
2. How would you treat this subject in writing a speech for the CEO to post on the website and how would you recraft it to present in person to:
    a. employees?
    b. a local civic group?
    c. an activist group for clean air in your city?
3. Develop a presentation script to recruit students to your school.

PART 5

Writing in Turbulent Times

Disasters of all kinds—both natural and human-caused—create crises in which public relations people and their writing play important roles. Chapter 14 is intended to make your crises less trying. In our crisis communication activities, we would do well to heed what Will Rogers said: "In time of crisis people want to know that you care, more than they care what you know."

CHAPTER FOURTEEN

Crisis Communication

EBOLA! That word evokes horror and fear of certain death. Until the fall of 2014, people in the USA believed Ebola was a problem for people in some far-away countries in Africa. But on September 30, 2014, the Centers for Disease Control (CDC) confirmed the first case of Ebola diagnosed in the United States: Thomas Eric Duncan, who had traveled to Dallas, Texas, from Liberia. USA's Ebola crisis had begun.

A few days after arriving in Dallas, experiencing fever and vomiting, Duncan went to the emergency room at Texas Health Presbyterian Hospital Dallas. The fact that he had traveled from Africa was put on his chart but "not communicated effectively among the care team," according to Barclay Berdan, CEO of Texas Health Resources. He was treated for his symptoms and released. He returned to the hospital on September 30 and was diagnosed with Ebola. He died on October 8. Two nurses who cared for him became infected but survived.

Because Duncan's travel from Africa was missed and his nurses became infected, the Ebola diagnosis and the related incidents made headlines across the nation. "The reputation and bottom line of Texas Health Presbyterian Hospital Dallas were damaged," wrote Kathleen Larey Lewton, past president of Public Relations Society of America (PRSA) in that organization's magazine, *The Public Relations Strategist*. Her article continued, "Physicians reported patients canceling appointments or wanting to have procedures done at other facilities, and there was a 25-percent drop in revenues in October. ... Nurses went public and accused the hospital of not providing proper training and protection. The public waited for the hospital to explain what had gone wrong, and *The Dallas Morning News* cited a 'deep loss of public trust' in a facility that was once known as one of the city's most prestigious."[1]

In his testimony before Congress, Dr. Daniel Varga, chief clinical officer of the hospital's parent organization, said that in its effort to be transparent and release information quickly, the hospital "inadvertently provided some information that was inaccurate and had to be corrected." The hospital's attempt to regain public trust and reputation continues.

General Motors Recalls

When Mary Barra took over as CEO of General Motors (GM) on January 15, 2014, she had no idea that a brew of GM problems had been fermenting for more than 10 years. Barra said she learned on January 31 about the faulty ignition switch that was responsible for numerous deaths and injuries. What a welcome to the leadership of the huge vehicle company!

The recalls began in February 2014—800,000 Chevrolets and Pontiacs. Before the end of the month, another 600,000 were recalled. To her credit Barra took the heat, saying, "We will hold ourselves accountable and improve our processes so our customers do not experience this again."[2] By the end of June, more than 29 *million* vehicles had been recalled. In the meantime the Justice Department had begun an investigation. GM was fined $28 million, lawsuits were filed, sales had dropped and shareholder's value had declined more than $3 billion.

Hopefully you'll never face a crisis of that size. Crises don't always come in big packages.

Whether it's called an emergency, a disaster or a crisis, the word means that something bad and/or unexpected has happened or is happening, and the organizations affected are expected to let their stakeholders know what's going on. That's the challenge of crisis communication.

Crisis communication isn't what it used to be. In the past, PR people were the first to provide public responses to catastrophes and, therefore, were in charge of what was said about the crisis. No more. As reported by MediaShift, "Nowadays, the type of media that will report on a crisis is often as unforeseen as the crisis itself." Handheld devices including the iPhone® equip many people to record and transmit photos and text messages worldwide instantly via the Internet.

"When Chesley Sullenberger, the captain of US Airways Flight 1549, executed a near-miraculous water landing in the Hudson River in January 2009, initial news reports came from the unlikeliest of sources—and beat the official corporate response by a long shot. One of the most iconic images of US Airways Flight 1549's bobbing hull came not from a fast-acting photojournalist but from Janis Krums, a regular guy on a nearby ferry who snapped a picture with his iPhone® and uploaded it to his Twitter stream. Before US Airways was able to issue even a preliminary statement confirming the incident, MSNBC had already broadcast the photo and interviewed Krums."[3]

What's it like to experience such a crisis? Only those who have been through such disasters could possibly know. But we do know that in every disaster people in all types of organizations are immediately and deeply involved. Police, fire and other emergency organizations are instantly impacted, along with government agencies at all levels. Charitable organizations must respond immediately, and news media from around the globe cover the crisis.

The Susan G. Komen for the Cure®, a highly respected foundation with a global presence dedicated to detecting and curing breast cancer, failed to respond quickly to an early 2012 crisis. Komen withdrew its funding from Planned Parenthood's nationwide organization. "Komen's decision was based on its new policy of withholding money from any organization being investigated by local, state or federal authorities," the organization said.[4]

"Planned Parenthood is under investigation by a congressional committee, which is trying to determine whether the agency has used public money to pay for abortions, a violation of federal law,"[5] the response explained.

The backlash was immediate, by phone, email and social media, but the reaction "seemed to catch the charity by surprise," said Marc Ramirez, a staff writer for *The Dallas Morning News.*

" 'We are witnessing the accidental rebranding of what is surely one of America's biggest and most well-known and even well-loved, non-profit brands,' North Carolina non-profit marketing consultant Kivi Leroux Miller wrote on her blog. 'Komen for the Cure, it seems, is no longer a breast cancer charity, but a pro-life breast cancer charity.' "

"According to Miller, the episode showed 'what happens when a leading nonprofit jumps into a highly controversial area of public debate without a communication strategy, stays silent and therefore lets others take over the public dialogue.' "[6]

Obviously Komen didn't anticipate the backlash, but they could have had a plan to deal with any unexpected situation. Finally, responding to an avalanche of negative responses, Komen CEO Nancy Brinker issued a statement that began, "We want to apologize to the American public for recent decisions that cast doubt upon our commitment to our mission of saving women's lives" and pledged to continue funding Planned Parenthood.[7] According to *The New York Times,* this response to the deluge of criticism "demonstrated again how social media can change the national conversation with head-snapping speed."[8] On PRSA's blog PRSAY, former PRSA Chair and CEO Michael Cherenson wrote, "Political opinions aside, the Komen/Planned Parenthood issue represents one of the biggest (if not *the* biggest) self-inflicted public relations misstep in modern business, and provides a lesson for all professional communicators."[9]

The matter became even more complicated when Komen's Senior Vice President for Public Policy, Karen Handel resigned, saying, "The only group that has made this political is Planned Parenthood." Handel is an anti-abortion Republican who ran for Governor of Georgia in 2010. The article says that Handel "made no secret of her anti-abortion politics and her longstanding opposition to Planned Parenthood."

Handel's position was well known to women's groups as well as is Brinker's. Women's eNews editor in chief, Rita Henley Jensen said, "Nancy G. Brinker may have reversed her decision to cut Susan G. Komen for the Cure's funding to Planned Parenthood, but she can't reverse what the event exposed: close ties to the GOP agenda of eliminating women's access to contraceptives and abortion." Jensen goes on to chronicle donors to Komen such as Tim Tebow, evangelical anti-choice Denver Broncos' star, and Donald Trump, a GOP presidential hopeful for a while in 2011. Brinker, "a Republican of long standing," was a George W. Bush ambassador to Hungary, a good friend of Bush advisor Karen Hughes and the one who hired Handel.

Politics aside, Jensen points out that Planned Parenthood spends only 28 percent of its donations on the organization in contrast to Komen's 45 percent spent on itself. The currency of the issue might have been temporary but, like many public relations crises, may resurface.

FIGURE 14.1

Public Relations Society of America Devotes Entire Magazine Issue to Crises

Immediately following the tragic shooting down of Malaysia Airlines Flight 17, Public Relations Society of America (PRSA) devoted the entire content of *The Public Relations Strategist*, its magazine for members, to crises. (See Figure 14.1.) In the publication's major articles:

- A veteran aviator "examines the confusing communications approach that officials took in the days, weeks and months following the disappearance of Malaysian Air Flight MH370"
- An experienced crisis management consultant "shares an anecdote about counseling a company whose CEO passed away suddenly"
- A media training expert "says that it's time to 'scrutinize your crisis communications strategy for the warning signs that you might be in trouble when a crisis calls and how to avoid them' "
- A nationally recognized expert in corporate communications and reputation management and senior manager of a major PR agency "outlines how organizations can strategically protect their reputations in the face of a cybersecurity crisis"
- A senior public relations faculty member and textbook author "looks at how a seemingly innocuous Twitter campaign from the New York Police Department turned into an epic 'hashtag' "
- And a counselor to leading business executives including heads of numerous Fortune 500 corporations "visits the ongoing public relations scrutiny that GM is facing during its historic recall crisis and how new CFO Mary Barra is fairing in the spotlight"

John Elsasser, the publication's editor, said, "A glance at the headlines every day shows that there's never a shortage of crises to manage or to learn from."

Source: John Elsasser, "From the Editor," *The Public Relations Strategist*, summer 2014, p. 1. Image and text copyright © 2014 PRSA, used with permission.

Planning for Crisis Situations

No one likes to think about calamities, but public relations people are expected to consider and plan for worst-case possibilities. If you work for a refinery, you need to assume that there will be a fire or explosion sometime, somewhere. If you work for a chemical company, there will be a "hazardous substance" case sometime, in some form, somewhere. If you work for an airline, you must know that, sooner or later, an accident will occur.

But you don't have to be involved in a "dangerous business" to encounter a crisis. For instance, a Dallas CEO was kidnapped and held for ransom; a truck crashed into a busy cafeteria; an angered employee went home, returned with a rifle and killed supervisors and fellow employees. And we're all familiar with tragic events involving shootings of school children. Anything that *can* happen, *will*. You need to be prepared for it.

The term *crisis communication* includes within its meanings *issues management,* because it is good public relations to intervene in a developing situation before it becomes a crisis. And issues management, in turn, is primarily a research function, the purpose of which is to identify and track trends and events likely to affect the institution and any of its publics.

A good example of *preventing* a crisis was the planning and execution related to the closing of highway I-405 in California in July 2011 while construction crews dismantled an overpass. The predictions of traffic tie-ups and inconveniences were typified by the *Los Angeles Daily News* that said, "Shutting down the busiest north-south freeway connection in L.A. over a summer weekend is expected to create traffic headaches in the Valley and the basin. It is estimated that on a typical weekend, some 500,000 vehicles travel the 405 between the Valley and the Westside."[10] But transportation officials from the city, county, state and regional agencies launched a public relations campaign, "Countdown to Closure," intended to "scare the heck out of everyone" and steer drivers away from anticipated trouble spots. They offered free subway rides, added extra buses, used flashing "countdown" signs and got "saturation" media coverage—even nationally.

It worked. As the *Los Angeles Times* reported, "The demolition went smoothly, enabling contractors to finish about 17 hours ahead of schedule, pocket an extra $300,000 in incentive payments and win acclaim from Los Angeles Mayor Antonio Villaraigosa and other officials who jockeyed for position in front of television cameras. 'Mission accomplished,' the mayor said, beaming as if he had just won a war."[11]

But beyond issues management, which involves all of the communication tools and planning previously discussed, there is the critical event—the serious unforeseen development. In this chapter, we will use the term *crisis* exclusively to refer to the critical event. Refer to Table 14.1 for a brief outline of what's usually included in planning for and dealing with a crisis.

Research suggests that there are only six types of crises—three in each of two categories. Review these in Table 14.2. The two categories are violent and nonviolent. Within each are crises that are caused by nature, by accidents or by deliberate acts.[12]

Corporate Information

Part of being prepared is a matter of routine. It involves maintaining current corporate fact sheets containing all necessary basic information in the files at all times. See Chapter 9 for more information on fact sheets.

The most important precrisis action, though, is getting your positive messages out daily and educating your publics so they are knowledgeable and you can draw on their trust and goodwill when the crisis occurs.

T A B L E 1 4 . 1	*Outline of Crisis Communication Plan*

Planning

1. Develop a series of scenarios that reflect the kinds of crises your organization may face. Pay particular attention to the worst cases. Evaluate realistically the probability of their happening. Review current policies and strategies that may be impacted.

2. Identify a crisis management team. Assign specific roles to team members. Designate one person to speak to external publics and another to keep internal publics fully informed. Rehearse the crisis management team regularly. Train and retrain the spokespersons, emphasizing the need for them to coordinate and share information so the organization is seen as speaking with one corporate voice.

3. Insofar as is possible, implement policies and strategies designed to minimize the impact of crises. If needed, lobby government and seek public support for changes in laws and/or regulations that may prevent crises or reduce their impact.

4. Review the entire plan at least annually. A quarterly review is better. Make sure that members of the crisis management team have copies of the current plan and can access them immediately.

Triggering Event

1. When a crisis occurs, activate the crisis management team immediately. Designated spokespersons should take charge of all communication functions.

2. Strive for a timely, consistent and candid flow of accurate information to both external and internal publics to allay fears and stifle rumors.

3. The organization should continue to function as normally as possible, leaving it to the crisis management team to contend with the crisis.

4. Make adjustments to policies and strategies as needed to arrest the crisis. Seek public support as needed.

Recovery

1. As needed, make changes in policies and strategies to speed recovery from the effects of the crisis.

2. If necessary, make changes to the structure of the organization. If these changes are needed and the organization has a history of an open management style, such changes are often slight.

3. Seek as soon as possible to re-establish the operation of the organization to the level it had before the crisis or even better.

Evaluation

1. Learn from the crisis experience. Evaluate its causes, the organization's responses to it and the outcomes.

2. Modify policies and strategies in light of this experience.

3. Update the crisis management/communication plan in light of this most recent experience.

T A B L E 1 4 . 2	*Crisis Typology*	
Source of Crisis	**Violent: Cataclysmic—Immediate Loss of Life or Property**	**Nonviolent: Sudden Upheaval But Damages, If Any, Are Delayed**
Act of nature	Forest fires, earthquakes, mud slides and floods, such as the one in Pakistan's Swat Valley in 2010 and Japan's 2011 earthquake	Droughts, epidemics, diseases, such as the H1N1 flu virus in 2009–2010.
Intentional	Acts of terrorism, including product tampering, when these result in loss of life or destruction of property. The most obvious in 2010–2011 were suicide bombings in crowded areas such as mosques, restaurants and attacks on military personnel in Afghanistan and Iraq, with one of the most horrific being the August 2011 downing of a U.S. Chinook helicopter in Afghanistan that killed 30 Americans, including 17 members of the U.S. Navy's elite Seals	Bomb and product tampering threats, hostile takeovers, insider trading, malicious rumors and other malfeasance, such as the Bernard Madoff Ponzi scheme that collapsed in 2008, leaving many individual and institutional investors facing large, if not total, losses.
Unintentional	Explosions, fires, leaks, other accidents, such as the BP Texas Gulf oil spill from the explosion of a deep water drilling rig April 20, 2010, which created the worst oil spill in U.S. history.	Process or product problems with delayed consequences, as in the egg recall in the USA in 2010 and various drug, toy and automobile recalls also in 2010.

Source: Reprinted with permission from Doug Newsom, Judy VanSlyke Turk and Dean Kruckeberg, *This Is PR: The Realities of Public Relations,* 11th ed. (Wadsworth Publishing Company: Belmont, Calif., 2013) p. 314.

© Cengage Learning

Crisis Planning

There is never a good time to plan for a crisis, but sooner is better than later. And it is critical not only to have a plan, but also to make sure that everyone understands it.

In a crisis, the media's first response often is to contact the creators of the institution's public relations image. But before the situation arises, it's important to develop a good plan and be sure everyone likely to be involved knows what to do. Seminars involving role playing can help those who might be responsible in a time of crisis to understand the plan. It's important for you, as the writer of the plan, to know who will play specific roles as well.

Crisis planning by organizations goes beyond communication to specific employee actions.

Most institutions where crises are especially likely—such as chemical plants, hospitals, prisons and banks—have employees who are crisis-trained. The way a situation is handled as it is occurring can make the public relations job easier or more difficult. For example, writing about hostage-taking, which is a fairly common experience in hospitals, clinical psychologist James Turner says that staffs need to be trained in handling the hostage-takers in the first few minutes, before police officers and negotiators arrive.[13]

According to the USA Centers Disease Control and Prevention, "The ability to deal effectively with disasters is becoming more relevant as the factors that tend to increase risk are also increasing." Some of these factors include the following:

- **Increasing population density.**
- **Increased settlement in high-risk areas.** There is greater settlement in such high-risk areas as floodplains; earthquake faults; coastal hurricane areas; unstable hillsides; areas subject to wild land fires and areas adjacent to hazardous waste landfills, airports and nuclear power plants.
- **Increased technological risks.** New technology is adding to the list of disaster agents at an ever-increasing rate. One of these is the 4 billion tons of hazardous chemicals that are shipped annually in this country.
- **Aging USA population.** The growing number and proportion of older adults is placing increasing demands on the public health system and on medical and social services.
- **Emerging infectious diseases and antimicrobial resistance.**
- **Increased international travel and trade** play a role in the development of microbial resistance.
- **Increased terrorism.**[14]

It is helpful to understand that, although each crisis is different, they all follow and have similar lifecycles:

1. Precrisis planning phase
2. Triggering event/initial phase
3. Communication during the crisis (See Table 14.3.)
4. Resolution of the crisis and recovery
5. Evaluation

Precrisis Planning

It's essential to examine and document the types of disaster that your organization may need to deal with. Your planning team should "brainstorm" each of the types of crisis that you may have to face. (See Table 14.2.)

At a time when your organization isn't involved in a crisis, you must take the opportunity to do precrisis planning. (See Table 14.1.) This is where much of work should be done. Whatever the crisis, there needs to be a **dark site** on the organizational intranet that can be updated periodically and activated immediately. For internal use the site needs to contain easy-to-follow procedures and one section needs to be activated for the public. The public access site area should have bios of the organization's leadership, information about the organization, mission statement and emergency contact information. Keep visuals as well as text in PDF or JPEG for instant loading. Keep thumb drives updated for key personnel. Separately, the organization's 24-hour online newsroom will be used for information about the crisis itself and the organizations efforts regarding it.

Types of disasters that your organization may need to address can be anticipated. Reasonable questions can be expected, and preliminary answers can be sought. Initial communication can be drafted with blanks to be filled in later. Spokespersons and resources can be

TABLE 14.3	*Assess the Communication Crisis Level*

Based on the level of communication required as listed in the criteria below, determine the crisis level of the situation.

Level	Communication characteristics
4 *Highly intense*	• Media have immediate and urgent need for information about the crisis. CEO may need to provide opening statement of empathy/caring. • One or more groups or individuals express anger or outrage. • Broadcast and print media appear on-site for live coverage.
3 *Intense*	• Crisis causes growing attention from local and regional media. • Media contacts non-CCT staff for information about the crisis. • In addition to the media, stakeholders and community partners are present at site. • Affected and potentially affected parties threaten to talk to the media.
2 *Moderately intense*	• Crisis situation may/may not have occurred; the situation is attracting slow, but steady media coverage. • External stakeholders (e.g., MSHA, NMA, State or Fed) receive media inquiries. • The public at large is aware of the situation/event but is attracting very little attention.
1 *Minimally intense*	• Crisis attracts little or no attention. • Pre-event information requests are received. • Public and/or media are virtually unaware of crisis.

Source: Copyright © (date unknown) National Mining Association, "Assess the Communication Crisis Level" Media and "Community Crisis Communication Planning Template," based on the research and teachings of Dr. Vincent Covello and Dr. Tim Tinker, both internationally recognized experts in the field of risk and crisis communication, this planning template was developed by Widmeyer Communications, Inc., p. 10. Used with permission.

identified. Training and refinements to plans and messages can be made. Alliances and partnerships can be fostered to ensure that experts are speaking with one voice.[15]

Identifying stakeholders is an important step in precrisis planning. For each type of crisis, you may have a different set of stakeholders. Given careful consideration, it is possible to anticipate questions that may be asked, develop supporting facts for each question and prepare responses to the questions.

The next step is to prepare a list of potential questions and concerns for each stakeholder group. "Questions and concerns typically fall into three categories:

- *Overarching Questions:* for example, 'What do people need to know?'
- *Informational Questions:* for example, 'When will the water be safe to use?'
- *Challenging Questions:* for example, 'Why should we trust what you are telling us?' "[16]

Research conducted by the Center for Risk Communication and other groups indicates that questions and concerns raised by stakeholders in emergency situations can be identified in advance. For example, Table 14.4 provides a list of the 77 most frequently asked questions by journalists during a crisis.[17]

TABLE 14.4

The 77 Most Frequently Asked Questions by Journalists Following Crisis Incidents

The list was generated by researching a large database of questions posed by journalists at news conferences immediately following disasters and distilling the larger list into 77 questions. This is an excellent resource for identifying potential questions for which messages should be developed. **Journalists are likely to ask six questions in a crisis (who, what, where, when, why, how) that relate to three broad topics: (1) what happened; (2) what caused it to happen; (3) what does it mean.**

Specific questions:

1. What is your name and title?

2. What are your job responsibilities?

3. What are your qualifications?

4. Can you tell us what happened?

5. When did it happen?

6. Where did it happen?

7. Who was harmed?

8. How many people were harmed?

9. Are those that were harmed getting help?

10. How certain are you about this information?

11. How are those who were harmed getting help?

12. Is the situation under control?

13. How certain are you that the situation is under control?

14. Is there any immediate danger?

15. What is being done in response to what happened?

16. Who is in charge?

17. What can we expect next?

18. What are you advising people to do?

19. How long will it be before the situation returns to normal?

20. What help has been requested or offered from others?

21. What responses have you received?

22. Can you be specific about the types of harm that occurred?

23. What are the names of those that were harmed?

24. Can we talk to them?

25. How much damage occurred?

26. What other damage may have occurred?

27. How certain are you about damages?

28. How much damage do you expect?

29. What are you doing now?

30. Who else is involved in the response?

31. Why did this happen?

32. What was the cause?

33. Did you have any forewarning that this might happen?

(Continued)

TABLE 14.4	(Continued)

34. Why wasn't this prevented from happening?

35. What else can go wrong?

36. If you are not sure of the cause, what is your best guess?

37. Who caused this to happen?

38. Who is to blame?

39. Could this have been avoided?

40. Do you think those involved handled the situation well enough?

41. When did your response to this begin?

42. When were you notified that something had happened?

43. Who is conducting the investigation?

44. What are you going to do after the investigation?

45. What have you found out so far?

46. Why was more not done to prevent this from happening?

47. What is your personal opinion?

48. What are you telling your own family?

49. Are all those involved in agreement?

50. Are people over reacting?

51. Which laws are applicable?

52. Has anyone broken the law?

53. How certain are you about whether laws have been broken?

54. Has anyone made mistakes?

55. How certain are you that mistakes have not been made?

56. Have you told us everything you know?

57. What are you not telling us?

58. What effects will this have on the people involved?

59. What precautionary measures were taken?

60. Do you accept responsibility for what happened?

61. Has this ever happened before?

62. Can this happen elsewhere?

63. What is the worst case scenario?

64. What lessons were learned?

65. Were those lessons implemented?

66. What can be done to prevent this from happening again?

67. What would you like to say to those that have been harmed and to their families?

68. Is there any continuing danger?

69. Are people out of danger? Are people safe?

70. Will there be inconvenience to employees or to the public?

71) How much will all this cost?

72) Are you able and willing to pay the costs?

73) Who else will pay the costs?

74) When will we find out more?

75) What steps are being taken to avoid a similar event?

76) What lessons have you learned?

77) What does this all mean?

Source: United States Environmental Protection Agency, "Effective Risk and Crisis Communication during Water Security Emergencies," pp. 2–7 and 2–8.

Now you need to prepare a Crisis Communication Plan. An important part of planning is consideration of crisis response strategies. (See Table 14.1.)

A Crisis Communication Plan   First, identify people likely to be the principal participants in the communication plan. Then decide what media to use in a crisis: the organization's intranet, Internet websites and online newsroom, email and text memos, social media postings, closed-circuit television, remote computer terminals, mobile telephones—whatever is likely to work in a given situation that could be global in scope. Remember that in many disasters, power is lost, so consider access to generators.

Message strategy is critical to consider in developing message statements. To a certain extent, the crisis itself shapes the response. However, some other considerations are the organization's reputation with its wide variety of publics, its history of responding to problems and issues, its mission statement and its tradition of social responsibility. Nonprofit organizations are especially sensitive to crises because there is a general understanding that they are functioning with the use of other people's money entrusted to them. For-profit organizations are expected to be responsible for their products and services, but are using funds the organization has generated itself, albeit from public support of its products and services.

You should create a system for checking message statements. Usually, an internal message for employees is developed first, and the external one is composed from that. You don't want employees and others close to the organization to hear about a crisis from outside sources unless this is absolutely unavoidable.

When time is critical and people are not where they are usually found, a telephone operation becomes particularly important. You or the person in charge of communications needs to be highly skilled in getting facts, taking questions and dispensing information accurately. You must act like a reporter first, finding out as much as you can about the situation. Anticipate questions from traditional news media. Have your own photographers and interviewers out gathering the story. If you don't take these steps, you won't have enough documentation later, and you will not know what the reporters are getting or how accurate their information is. Monitor the social media carefully and be set up to respond instantly to questions there and/or provide a link to the public area of the dark site. If disaster assistance is needed use text messages and social media postings, being very specific about what is needed and how to get it there. People who want to help don't like to be frustrated in their efforts to do so (See Table 14.5.)

Triggering Event/Initial Phase

The initial phase of a crisis is characterized by confusion and intense media interest. Information is usually incomplete. Don't hesitate to admit that.

Your first job will be to gather any accurate information that is available and prepare a statement on the severity of the disaster or crisis, working with someone in authority. You'll need to have the statement both in printed, audio and video forms. Then you'll need to develop a fact sheet telling what is known. Review this information with the organization's attorney—by phone if necessary—to assess the legal ramifications of the information you will be releasing.

"The initial statement should:

- Acknowledge the event with empathy.
- Explain and inform the public, in simple terms.
- Establish organizational/spokesperson credibility.

- Provide emergency courses of action (including how/where to get more information).
- Commit to stakeholders and public to continued communication."[18]

T A B L E 1 4 . 5	*Making Crisis-Related Messages More Effective*

Making Crisis-Related Messages More Effective

Professional risk communicators have developed several templates for developing effective messages, including the following:

Rule of 3	In high-stress situations, people can process only three messages at a time instead of the seven they could normally process.
Primacy/Recency	Spokespersons should state the most important messages first and last. In high-stress situations, listeners tend to remember that which they hear first and last. Messages in the middle of a list are often not heard or remembered.
Average Grade Level Minus 4	During crises, messages should be at the average grade level of the intended audience, minus four.
Triple T Model	(1) Tell people what you are going to tell them in summary form, i.e., three key messages; (2) Tell them more, i.e., the supporting information; (3) Tell people again what you told them in summary form, i.e., repeat the three key messages.
Negative Dominance	According to risk communication theory, people tend to focus more on the negative than on the positive in emotionally charged situations. For this reason, it is important to balance negative key messages with positive, constructive, or solution-oriented key messages; offering three positive messages for every one negative.
Anticipate, Prepare, Practice	Spokespersons should anticipate questions, prepare answers, and practice delivery ahead of time (never wing it).
Cite Third Parties	Spokespersons should cite third parties or sources that would be perceived as credible by the receiving audience. The greater the extent to which messages are supported and corroborated by credible third party sources, the greater the trust and the less likely it is that mental noise will interfere with the ability to comprehend messages.
Address Risk Perceptions	Key messages and supporting information should address emotionally charged factors that influence the way people perceive risks, such as lack of control, dread, unfamiliarity, uncertainty, and effects on children. Research indicates that the greater the extent to which risk perception factors are addressed in messaging, the less likely that mental noise will interfere with the ability to comprehend messages.
Use Graphics and Other Visual Aids	The use of graphics, visual aids, analogies, and narratives (e.g., personal stories) can increase an individual's ability to hear, understand, and recall a message by more than 50 percent.

Source: United States Environmental Protection Agency, "Effective Risk and Crisis Communication during Water Security Emergencies," pp. 3–12.

All information released on the dark site or through any other medium, from mobile phones to social media postings, should be drawn only from prepared and checked information.

Designated Spokesperson   The most important strategy in crisis communication is to have only one person communicating with the news media and other external audiences. You may sometimes use both an expert and a management representative, with the crisis determining who is the principal spokesperson. The other person is a support voice and should coordinate messages so these *never* conflict or contradict themselves. When the messages fail to match, a severe credibility problem develops. The best precaution against this is to develop a crisis communication plan.

Crisis Teams   The organization (corporate or nonprofit) involved will create crisis communication teams from staff members—as well as public relations and crisis communications consultants—to create the necessary level of expertise. These teams should be able to deal with the crisis so the organization can go on about its regular activities as normally as possible. Nothing contributes more to the atmosphere of uncertainty than involving all the institution's decision makers in the crisis and thus causing day-to-day business to come to a halt. When this happens, observers can conclude that there is not much depth to management and that the company needs everyone it can get to handle a problem.

Communication During the Crisis

"As the crisis evolves, you should expect continuing media interest and scrutiny. Unexpected developments, rumors and misinformation may place more media demands on communicators. Experts, professionals and others not associated with your organization may comment publicly on the issue and sometimes contradict or misinterpret your messages. Expect to be criticized for your handling of the situation."

"Staying on top of the information flow and maintaining tight coordination are essential. Processes for tracking communication activities become increasingly important as the workload increases.

Your communications during the crisis should:

- Help people more accurately understand their own risks.
- Provide background and encompassing information to those who need it. (How could this happen? Has this happened before? How can I prevent this from happening again? Will I be all right in the long term—will I recover?)
- Gain understanding and support for response and recovery plans.
- Listen to stakeholder and audience feedback and correct misinformation.
- Explain emergency recommendations."[19]

When a crisis first occurs, its announcement involves some sort of consultation within the organization. Ordinarily this is a face-to-face meeting, but it could be an electronic one—for instance, a telephone conference call. Of primary importance at this meeting is that a record be kept—a fairly detailed one—of the points discussed and the responsibilities assigned. In fact, it may be your specific responsibility to write and circulate a memo detailing this.

Almost immediately, and sometimes before such a meeting takes place, you will need to make a response release addressing the situation. The public affairs staff of a Houston-based pipeline company pledges to have a statement in the hands of the local spokesperson within 30 minutes after they are notified of a pipeline rupture or other triggering event, regardless of where it occurs. That involves fast, brief and absolutely accurate interviewing, but they deliver on their promise. You the writer must characterize the crisis in language that will become a symbol of the event. In doing so, you will need to check attributed quotes with the organization's attorney if the release contains any mention of responsibility or damages.

For the broadcast media, you should have an actuality of the statement from the spokesperson. And you will need your own photographer's pictures from the crisis scene—digital black-and-white and color stills and videos. Some companies maintain ENG (electronic news gathering) equipment so that they can receive pictures of the disaster immediately at corporate headquarters. Here, too, the art chosen should represent the way you want the event symbolized.

You may need to call a news conference so that news media representatives can pose questions. If you do, you should be prepared with a list of the points you want to make, and you should anticipate the reporters' needs and questions. Be very careful about the setting for the news conference. The more contained and orderly the setting, the better. On-site news conferences are often confusing and somewhat chaotic.

As news develops, you will be issuing bulletins to keep internal and external publics informed. All of these bulletins should be put in your online news site, on your website or the dark website. Additionally, you will be preparing print and electronic messages to various related publics to keep them aware of your control of the situation. For example, a university experiencing a number of fires sent letters to parents, and a company that found a problem with a certain lot of its product sent letters to all affected consumers it could identify through warranty cards. In some cases, you may need to plan special advertising. One utility that had gotten a bad safety review of its nuclear plant and several days of bad publicity thereafter felt it necessary to buy time and space for its own message.

Often crises involve materials or conditions that the average person (including reporters) may not know much about. With nuclear plant accidents and chemical-related stories, scientists often are called on to help reporters explain these situations. But because of scientists' concerns about being misquoted, the Scientists' Institute for Public Information provides a free service to journalists—a database clearinghouse with a computer file of thousands of scientists, engineers, physicians and policy makers who have agreed to answer queries from reporters.

Top management's role is critical in crisis communication. Their leadership and "voice" can result in either positive or negative impressions of the organization.

The Federal Communicators Network's *Communicator's Guide* provides the following tips on "What to Do When Crisis Occurs":

- Communicate. Don't hide behind "no comment." If you do that, you immediately lose control. Even if all you can say is that you don't know, say so, say why and when you think you will know. Reporters look favorably on people who are trying to be helpful.
- Never lie or speculate. Provide only factual, confirmed information.

- Put people first. Help the people most affected by the crisis. In the case of accidents, remember to deal with victims' families before any other group. If they want you to, intercede on their behalf with the news media. Be sensitive to legal restrictions regarding information, such as the Privacy Act and Freedom of Information Act. Know what kind of information is public and what must be withheld.
- Communicate your concern about the victims.
- Be available at all times to respond to your various publics. Know media deadlines and don't rely on news conferences alone.
- Don't be defensive. Be prepared for aggressive questioning. You might have to answer the same question several times.
- Provide brief, precise answers to questions. Don't ramble. Use plain language. Short answers also help alleviate nervousness.
- Take your time in explaining difficult issues to reporters.
- Monitor media accounts and quickly correct errors by contacting the reporter or correspondents.
- Don't attempt legal battles in the media. Express assurances that matters of litigation or potential litigation will be investigated thoroughly.
- Prepare key points you want to make ahead of time. Make them short and to the point. Try to repeat them several times during the news conference or interview.
- Stay with the crisis throughout its duration.
- Follow up with the news media to keep them updated about what preventive actions were taken after the crisis ended.[20]

Social media have become increasingly important in crisis communication and must be carefully integrated into your crisis communication plan. (See Table 14.1.)

In summary, from the Institute for Public Relations, "Three Things Research Teaches About Crisis Response:

1. If you act fast, you have a better chance of controlling the story and the outcome.
2. Treat employees, community leaders and officials as key contributors to helping you solve the problem.
3. Never miss out on the opportunity to learn from the mistake. The public is far less forgiving when you've had this problem before and you let it happen again."[21]

Resolution/Recovery

This stage is important and involves risk-avoidance and mitigation education directly after a disaster has occurred. Although you may believe that the crisis at hand will never end, it will. As the crisis resolves, there is a return to stasis, with increased understanding about the crisis as complete recovery systems are put in place. This phase is characterized by a reduction in public/media interest. Once the crisis is resolved, you may need to respond to intense media scrutiny of how the event was handled. You may have an opportunity to reinforce messages while the issue is still current. A public education campaign or changes to a website may be necessary. Research has shown that a community is usually most responsive to communication as the crisis "winds down" and should include the following:

- Improve appropriate public response in future similar emergencies through education.
- Honestly examine problems and mishaps, and then reinforce what worked in the recovery and response efforts.
- Persuade the public to support public policy and resource allocation.
- Promote the activities and capabilities of the organization (corporate identity reinforced—internally, too).[22]

Overall Public Relations Plan

Writing a crisis communication plan is much easier if your organization has an overall public relations plan. Let's examine the steps involved in developing and implementing such a plan. (See Figure 14.2.)

Review, Revise and Affirm the Mission Statement

The organization's mission statement establishes the scope, domain and fundamental purpose of the organization and provides a guiding philosophy. The mission statement should be a clear, simple statement of the overall purpose of the organization; provide a focal point for objectives, goals and activities; and define success for the organization.

To review the mission statement, answer the following questions:

- Is it current? Does it reflect the organization as it exists today?
- Is it explicit? Is there any room for misinterpreting what the organization is all about?
- Is it understandable?
- Is it brief?
- Is it memorable?
- Does it contain the key words that reflect the organization's focus?

If these questions can all be answered "yes," then the mission statement can be affirmed, and the public relations planning process can proceed. If there is a "no," the statement should be modified. Once this is done, most organizations require that the revised mission statement be approved by the organization's senior management or board of directors. Such approval will represent affirmation of the revised mission statement.

Examine the Present Situation

Now that the mission of the organization has been reviewed, changed if necessary and affirmed, you can begin the task of gathering relevant information, analyzing it and preparing forecasts.

FIGURE 14.2

A Dozen Steps to Make Public Relations Work

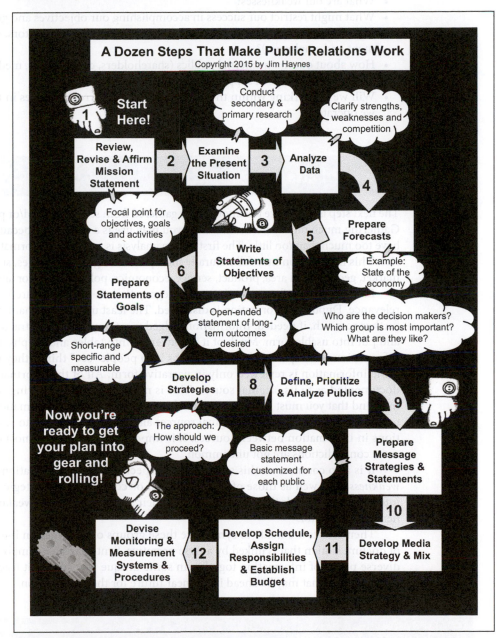

Source: Copyright © 2015 by Jim Haynes; used with permission.

Questions you will want to answer in this work include:

- What are our strengths?
- What are our weaknesses?
- What might restrict our success in accomplishing our objectives and goals?
- Will we have the support of our internal publics (board of directors, senior management and employees)?
- How about our main external publics (shareholders, contributors, media and others)?
- What level of financial support can we expect?
- Will we be working within the boundaries of the current cultures in the areas where we operate?

Analyze the Data

The next step is to analyze the information gathered from secondary and/or primary sources. Gathering much more information than you may use is a good idea, because it is better to have too much than too little. The first step in analysis is to sort the information into categories. This information may fall naturally into quite a range of categories, such as audience, market, geographical area, product, service, economics, politics, behavior and so on.

Each piece of information in each category then is reviewed carefully for its direct relevance. Duplicate information is discarded. The least useful information is set aside for further research, if needed. Information judged most important is extracted from the rest and put into usable form. Much of it is converted into tables and graphs, especially if the information is complex. Tables and graphs help people "see" things they might overlook if the information is reviewed only in narrative form. All of the information is carefully documented as to its original source. This is necessary because during the analysis you may find that you must refer to an original source for additional information or to clarify a technical point. Returning to original sources also may be necessary to resolve contradictions in information between sources. It is important to select the most credible source since contradictions are not uncommon.

It is also common at this stage to look especially at an organization's *strengths* and *weaknesses,* as well as those of the opposition or competition. Strategic planners covet information that leads them to match one of their strengths against a weakness of an opponent or competitor.

Then efforts are made to synthesize these groups of information into a cohesive set of documentation that is linked by a terse narrative. Synthesizing is simply the art of tying diverse pieces of information together in some unique way so that it leads to clear, new insights as to what may be ahead in the near future for the organization.

Prepare Forecasts

If the information is well defined, it will lead management to draw better conclusions about the future. For example, if the data indicate that the economy is static or in a downturn, this might be interpreted to mean that an organization may have a hard time reaching its profit or fundraising goal. This might lead to a cutback in goals' targets. On the other hand, if the economy is heating up, the organization might adjust its target upward.

The point is this: objectives, goals and strategies adopted for a program should be based on solid information, not whimsy, that supports the clearest possible view of the future. After the information is gathered and analyzed, conclusions can help you set achievable objectives, goals and strategies.

Write Statements of Objectives and Goals

Objectives and goals usually don't explain *how* the goal is to be met. That's the role of *strategies*. Keep reading! (See Chapter 6 for information on objectives and goals.)

Develop Strategies

Once objectives and goals are spelled out, you're ready to take the next step toward a plan—the development of a basic strategy. A strategy is an approach to solving a problem or capturing an opportunity and should answer the following questions:

- How shall we proceed?
- What approach will guide us?

For example, a nonprofit organization could adopt a strategy of public recognition of donors, calling attention to the benefits of their generosity to individuals and to the community. Good news and feature stories could be developed around success stories. If these could be tied to current programs in the community, the general awareness of both the organization's focus and the organization itself could be increased, thus making it easier to raise money.

Define, Prioritize and Analyze Publics

The next step in the planning process is to define your publics, often called audiences, constituencies or stakeholders. Each public is a group of people with similar characteristics (demographic and/or psychographic) that can help your organization achieve the objectives you have set, hinder your organization in achieving its objectives or hurt your organization in some way.

The basic questions to be answered are, "Who can make the decision (or take the action) that I want made? And what are those people *like?*"

Identifying the characteristics of publics—whether the public is made up of employees, shareholders or others—allows the public relations person to make communications more personal and relevant and therefore more memorable to the individuals composing the public. For example, if you work in public relations for an organization that sells pet-related products, knowing who owns pets can help you target your efforts and make your public relations program more effective. Or if you work in a corporation, you know that the company's shareholders have in common the ownership of shares of stock in the corporation.

Prioritizing Publics

Once you have identified your main publics and conducted as thorough an analysis as time and budget allow, you'll find it's helpful to list the groups in order of priority, with the most important first on your list. This small step will equip you to always consider your most important constituency first—when you allocate budgets and staff time.

Prepare Message Strategies and Statements

Notice that deciding what to say, how to say it and in what media messages should be conveyed are *not* decisions made at the outset of the planning process. Making those decisions before steps 1–8 have been completed would be like a physician prescribing medications before examining the patient.

Yet another step—developing message strategies—is important before messages are conceived.

Organizational, business and functional strategies collectively influence and shape message strategy. A basic message strategy focuses on what is the basic message to be conveyed to target audiences in every message. A good message strategy is simple, adaptable to any medium, applicable to all messages in the campaign and durable.

Develop Media Strategy/Mix

Media strategy/mix represents one of the most important areas of a public relations plan. However, it sometimes does not get the careful attention it deserves. It deals with what kinds of media will be used to deliver campaign messages, which specific media will be used and how they are mixed. It also deals with the timing of the delivery of messages and the frequency of delivery.

According to Forrester Research, "Media planning is ever more complex and dynamic. Americans use many different media—from TV to blogs—and their usage changes every year. Some media help drive brand awareness, and some drive loyalty. Some media have a young, urban audience; some have an older, rural one. Some media generate high consumer trust, some low. Some media form great cross-channel combinations; some don't. To get a first assessment on which media mix gives the best returns, marketers can use Forrester's media allocation tool (MAT). This model helps to optimize the media mix by combining Forrester's Consumer Technographics® data on media behaviors and attitudes with advertisers' campaign objectives and media costs."[23]

To select an appropriate media mix, you first would make a list of all the kinds of media—mass media, specialized media and digital media—that you can possibly use to effectively reach the publics that have been defined. In public relations, almost everything is a communications medium—from doorknob hangers to videos. The list might include such things as all of the local mass media and such specialized media as face-to-face contact, social media, brochures, annual reports, backgrounders, position papers, newsletters, direct mail, ads, public service announcements (PSAs), faxes, email, news releases and so on.

You then would apply several criteria to each of these media before you begin to make strategic decisions about them. These criteria are attending, persuasiveness, credibility, timing and effective reach.

Strategic Use of Media

Having evaluated the different kinds of media that could be used, you now can begin to create a basic media strategy for your organization. Three communication guidelines should be kept in mind here. First, you stand a better chance of getting the message across to your target publics if you use a multimedia approach. Research shows that people learn easier and retain information better if they get the same message from different kinds of media. Second, the media chosen should involve as many of the human senses as possible. Research indicates that this improves both learning and retention. It is easy to see how sight and sound can be involved in many of the media we've discussed. But what about touch, smell and taste? Are there things that can be done to engage those senses also? Third, some media should be used with messages designed to get the target publics intellectually involved.

Develop Schedule, Assign Responsibilities and Establish Budget

Having made those decisions, you would now develop a schedule or time line. You could divide the year into weeks and list them in columns across the top of a planning board or a spreadsheet software program. Down the left side you'd list the various media and activities that will be used, thus forming a grid. You'd then insert dates into appropriate blocks in the grid. When timing is critical, you may want to create specialized sub-schedules. For instance, you may want to create a special schedule that deals only with the days, times and locations of group presentations. Similar schedules might be made for individuals who will make the one-on-one presentations. Other sub-schedules can be developed as the need arises. A schedule grid makes it easy to track activities very closely. Of course, much narrative material about each of these activities will accompany the plan.

For each activity, one person with overall responsibility should be identified. Other people probably will be involved in various parts of the activity, but they do not need to be named in this overview of the plan.

A budget for each activity also should be included. Arriving at a budget may involve obtaining estimates from outside suppliers for printing, still and video photography and so on. Preparation for mailing and postage can be major costs in large projects such as annual reports and printed brochures. It's a good idea to add a contingency of 10–15 percent for unexpected costs. And be sure to add amounts for taxes as appropriate.

Tactical Implementation

When functional strategic plans are finished and approved, it is time to set them in motion. This is when the public relations writer begins to play a major role. Assignments are made for a range of tasks, often called *tactics*. Copy supervisors do careful reviews with the writers to make sure they know what they are supposed to do, what the basic message strategy is and how it can be interpreted in particular writing tasks.

Suppose you are assigned the task of writing a brochure that explains to current donors and potential donors the background and philosophy of APEX. There are countless ways this task could be approached. Because this brochure will be used as a "selling tool," you'll probably want to avoid a chronology, preferring to concentrate on the philosophy behind the organization that created its unique history. That provides a context in which you can tie APEX's history and philosophy to the new campaign. Of course, your work must be coordinated with that of designers and production people.

A key element, regardless of the writing task, is to be sure that what you write is consistent with the strategic thrust of the campaign. That's what makes a campaign a campaign. As more and more messages are created and distributed, awareness of what APEX is doing begins to rise.

Another requirement is that each message must be written so it will fit the format of the medium used to deliver it. Of course, every message should be directed especially to the target audiences. Yes, other people will see many of these messages. But it is a good idea to regard them as incidental receivers. Don't let them divert you from the basic strategy.

While you are writing, others are designing, recording videos and doing myriad other tasks, such as negotiating with vendors about printing a brochure or producing a PowerPoint-type slide show. At the same time, people in other functional areas of the organization are doing their own things, such as arranging for financing, clearing legal requirements for the use of copyrighted materials, securing releases from models and doing various other tasks.

Devise Monitoring and Measurement Systems and Procedures

Monitoring a program is essential. Functional strategies collectively define what is expected to happen to achieve stated goals. One of the primary functions of supervisors at all levels in every area is to monitor progress. This is a routine part of their jobs, but their efforts are mostly focused inside the organization. What about monitoring things that go on outside? That's a different situation. Certainly, the leadership of the communication program should routinely and regularly scan the environment for problems, issues, developments, trends, opportunities and other things that may affect the organization or the campaign in progress.

How can we tell whether the program is working? Do we go by intuition, or do we set some routine procedures to take the pulse of our target publics at regular intervals? One measure we might consider is to review progressive reports on the number of inquiries. If there is an increase in inquiries, how can we be sure the increase is a result of the campaign? Another measure might be to count the house at special events to gauge how well people are responding to the campaign. It may be that an overflow crowd attended a concert simply because of the quality of the singer but they will soon forget the sponsor, even if they ever realized who the sponsor was. If we are selling a product or service, weekly sales reports can give us some insights. But are contributions, sales or the number of orders a clear indication of how effectively we are communicating with our audience? Lots of variables—in addition to messages—affect those actions. If we are promoting a candidate or a political issue, telephone canvassing can tell us a lot, but can we predict with great accuracy a victory at the polling booth?

Although those indicators, as well as many others, may be prominent parts of many campaign plans, the information they yield is ambiguous about what the target public knows about us or whether there have been any shifts in attitudes toward us because of the campaign. These two issues deal exclusively with the communication function. The only way they can be evaluated objectively is to do systematic research on relevant publics at regular intervals. This means that we need incremental research on our relevant publics to get a clear picture of how the campaign is doing. Such information may help us spot problems that can be corrected during the remainder of a campaign. (See Chapter 6 for additional information on monitoring and measuring the effects and value of public relations, including the Declaration of Measurement Principles. Intended to "address the need for clear standards and common approaches to measuring and evaluating public relations results," adopted in June 2010 by delegates attending the second European Summit on Measurement in Barcelona, Spain.)

The monitoring process results in an assortment of writing tasks. Prominent among them are emails, memos, letters and social media interaction. Analytical reports may also be written, along with cover letters. If something is awry in the campaign and ways of righting it are found, then recommendations or proposals for specific actions will need to be written. Monitoring should be, of course, a part of every functional plan.

When a program is completed, it is necessary to evaluate its productivity. The most effective evaluations are those with known benchmarks in place at the time the campaign begins. For example, pertinent data gathered in support of the strategic plan would ordinarily contain a good bit of benchmark information. The idea is to determine "where we are" when the program begins with a benchmark study, then measure "where we are now" periodically or at the end of the program. Comparing the two findings will provide information on results. Depending on the nature of the organization, this information might be found in measures of attitudes and behavior, brand shares, market shares, sales volumes, unit sales, contributions and pledges received, aided and unaided recall scores and others.

Particular measures should be selected that are uniquely appropriate to the campaign and its parent organization. In the case of APEX, a critical measure is the dollar volume of contributions and pledges. The sources can be identified fairly accurately and compared to the levels from the preceding year. It is easy to see whether the organization met its goal. If it did not, efforts must be made to determine why, so that those mistakes will not be made in future campaigns. If the goal was exceeded, we need to know why.

Is the greater-than-expected increase due to the campaign, or is it attributable to some influence beyond the scope of the campaign? Is the awareness of APEX higher now than when the campaign began? Do people have more appreciation for APEX now than before the campaign? Clearly, many of these questions, and many like them, can be answered only if we expand the systematic research program that we used during the monitoring phase. Both monitoring and campaign evaluation cost money. This needs to be provided in the campaign budget. If there is not enough money for good monitoring and effective evaluation, then we can't really do these tasks correctly. An absence of evaluation cripples strategic planning for future campaigns.

Although many messages will be written as part of a campaign's final evaluation, the most daunting writing task is likely to be a thorough, lengthy report that summarizes the results of the campaign. Such reports must be highly persuasive, yet be careful not to mislead management as you try to marshal your arguments in support of conclusions. Much of the information in these reports is complex. That may make it useful to break out some pieces of information and recast them into backgrounders, position papers, letters and memos in support of forthcoming planning efforts. The reason for doing that, of course, is to make sure that the responsible managers get information that is in its most usable form without having to wade through a lengthy report.

Exercises

1. This is based on a real situation in which one of the authors was involved:

   You are Director of Public Relations for a petrochemical company headquartered in Dallas, Texas. It's just after midnight, and you get a phone call at home notifying you that your company's largest plant, at the edge of a small West Texas town nearly 500 miles away, has had a major explosion and now is burning. It is believed that three employees have been killed and several injured, but facts are limited. The plant's manager is on vacation and cannot be reached. Your experience and instincts tell you that this is going to be a national news story within hours. *You have a total of 30 minutes* to do the following:

   - Write a brief statement that the assistant plant manager can give to news media who call during the next few hours.
   - List, in sequence, the actions you will take during the next 24 hours.
   - You learn from a second phone call that the plant offices were destroyed, along with all of the public relations files and media lists. List the materials that you will need to reconstruct.

     Now assume that you are able to get a company airplane to take you and your company's president to the town near the plant where the explosion occurred. You are on the plane with the president.

   - Write a statement for the president to read to news media when the plane lands. Remember that the president's first concerns need to be (1) for those directly involved, including employees, firefighters and police, as well as their families and (2) for the safety of employees and neighbors.

- List the information that you will try to gather. (A good way to do this is to draft the news release that you would like to distribute, leaving blank spaces for the information that you will need.)

2. Select a public relations campaign that is now under way in your area. Get as many pieces of campaign materials as you can. Work out a clear set of statements that reflect that organization's mission, objectives, goals and strategy.

3. Using your work from Exercise 2, identify the message and media strategies in use by this organization. Write a short evaluation that judges the degree to which these strategies support what appears to be the organization's mission, objectives, goals and strategies. Is that the best plan for this organization? Why? If not, why not?

Notes

Chapter 1

1. Paula LaRocque, "Learning Leads from Nursery Rhymes," *Quill*, 98(4), (July/August 2010): 53.
2. Doug Newsom, Judy VanSlyke Turk and Dean Kruckeberg, *This Is PR: The Realities of Public Relations*, 11th ed. (Boston, MA: Wadsworth Cengage Learning, 2012), p.3.
3. John Bussey, "CIOs Eye the Corner Office: At *The Wall Street Journal*'s CIO Network Conference, Chief Information Officers Made It Clear that They Had Left Their Narrow, Geeky World Behind," *The Wall Street Journal*, February 11, 2014, p. R1.
4. Frank Wylie, "The New Professionals," Speech to the First National Student Conference, Public Relations Student Society of America, Dayton, Ohio, October 24, 1976, published by Chrysler Corporation, p. 5. (Wylie is now deceased but I have his handwritten note giving me permission to use any of his writings.)
5. David Tisch, Global Alliance for Public Relations and Communication Management, "8 Ways You Can Use the Global Alliance's Melbourne Mandate," News sent May 29, 2013. The Melbourne Mandate was produced from the Global Alliance meeting in 2013 on measurement of communication results.

Chapter 2

1. See www.stockholmaccords.org also www.globalalliancepr.org
2. Bart Ziegler, "Old-Fashioned Ethic of Separating Ads Is Lost in Cyberspace," *The Wall Street Journal*, July 25, 1996, p. B1.
3. John Pavlik and David Dozier, research quoted in "Study Details Bumps to Watch Out for on Info Superhighway," *pr reporter*, August 5, 1996, p. 2.
4. Terry Maxon, "Weighing the Financial Fallout of Speaking Out," *The Dallas Morning News*, January 14, 1996, p. H1.
5. Go to the USA government websites for information about laws and to the sites of the regulatory institutions for their decisions and new regulations. Also note the following section in this chapter on government regulators.

6. For more information look on the Internet for the Nike case, and see the law chapter of *This Is PR: The Realities of Public Relations*, 11th ed., Doug Newsom, Judy VanSlyke Turk and Dean Kruckeberg (Boston, MA: Wadsworth Cengage Learning, 2012).

7. David Ardia, "Case That Upended Truth Defense in Libel Actions Ends with Jury Verdict for Defendant," *Digital Media Law Project*. Posted by David Ardia October 15, 2009, Massachusetts Defamation, a Blog. Search DMLP (Digital Media Law Briefs).

8. Patrick Healy, "'Rebecca' Publicist Sued over E-Mails to Investor," *The New York Times*, Theater, January 29, 2013. http://theater.nytimes .com/2013/01/30/theater/rebecca-producers-sue-publicist-marc-thibodeau.html?hpw&_ r=1& (accessed Jan 31, 2013).

9. Cayce Myers, "Is Your Social Media Account Really Yours? Guidelines for PR Practitioner and Organizations to Determine Social Media Ownership," Research Conversations: The Institute for Public Relations (IPR) is an independent nonprofit foundation dedicated to the science beneath the art of public relations™ focusing on research that matters to the practice (accessed June 9, 2014).

Chapter 3

1. William Zinsser, *On Writing Well*, 2nd ed. (New York: Harper & Row, 1980), pp. 56–57.

2. Robert Gunning, *The Technique of Clear Writing*, rev. ed. (New York: McGraw-Hill, 1968), p. 1.

3. National Assessment of Adult Literacy (NAAL), Nation's 12th Graders' Math and Reading Scores Stagnant Since 2009 News Release, accessed June 21, 2014.

4. Greg Toppo, *USA TODAY*, posted January 18, 2009, http://www.usatoday.com/news/ education/2009-01-08-adult-literacy_N.htm (accessed December 28, 2011).

5. Gunning, p. 51. Also see Cynthia Crossen's article, "If You Can Read This, You Most Likely Are a High-School Grad," *The Wall Street Journal*, December 1, 2000, pp. A1, A11, for a quick history of readability formulas and their uses.

6. Gunning, p. 44.

7. Paula LaRocque, "Look Out for Persistent Mistakes," *Quill*, 97(7), (September/October, 2009): 33.

8. LaRocque, "Actively Demystifying Passive Voice," *Quill*, 98(2), (March/April 2010): 33.

9. LaRocque, "Words for Wordsmiths," *Quill*, 98(5) (September/October 2010): 33.

10. H. W. Fowler, *Modern English Usage* (New York: Oxford University Press, 1965), p. 148.

11. Kenneth E. Andersen, *Persuasion Theory and Practice* (Boston: Allyn & Bacon, 1971), p. 126.

12. LaRocque, "End-of-Year Potpourri of Poor Writing," *Quill*, 99(6) (November/December 2011): 33.

13. Albert Einstein, "On the Electrodynamics of Moving Bodies," *Annalen der Physik,* 17 (1905): pp. 891–929, reprinted in *The Principle of Relativity*, trans. W. Perrett and G. B. Jeffrey (New York: Dover, 1952), p. 39.

14. Rudolf Flesch, *The Art of Plain Talk* (New York: Collier Books, 1962), pp. 158–162.

15. William Zinsser, *On Writing Well*, p. 114.

16. *pr reporter*, "Panel Issues Guidelines for Reporting Scientific Research," *pr reporter*, March 16, 1998, p. 2.

17. William D. Lutz, "Language Appearance and Reality: Doublespeak in 1984," an excerpt from *The Legacy of Language—A Tribute to Charlton Laird*, ed. Philip C. Boardman (Reno, NV: University of Nevada Press, 1987), appeared with permission in *ETC*, 44(4) (Winter 1987): 382–391.

18. Lauran Neergaard, "Researchers Explore Benefits of Simplifying Jargon," *Fort Worth Star-Telegram*, November 25, 2002, p. 5D.

19. "Hacking Through the Paper Jungle," *Public Relations Journal* (August 1981): 26.

20. Teresa McUsic, TMcUsic@SavvyConsumer.net, *Fort Worth Star-Telegram*, June 21, 2014, pp. 1B, 6B.

21. Isaac Asimov, *Opus 100* (Boston, MA: Houghton Mifflin, 1969), pp. 89–90.

22. Bruce Brown, "Shedding Light on the Aurora," *National Wildlife*, 23(2) (February–March 1985): 51. Copyright 1985 by the National Wildlife Federation. Reprinted with permission.

23. Paula LaRocque, "This Analogy Clinic Fits Writers' Needs Like Cabretta Gloves," Clinic Column, *Quill* (September 1996): 32.

24. Kathleen Tinkel, "Taking It In," *Adobe Magazine*, 7(4) (April 1996): 40–44.

Chapter 4

1. Gilbert Highet, http://www.brainyquote.com/quotes/authors/g/gilbet_highet.html (accessed June 23, 2014).

2. *The Oxford English Dictionary* has quarterly updates and is available online with new words, phrases and uses. *Merriam-Webster*'s 2014 collegiate dictionary added 150 new words, many from social media.

3. Tom Herman, "Tax Report," *The Wall Street Journal*, June 26, 1996, p. 1.

4. Luther Brock, "In Direct Mail, Ignore Friends—Pay Attention to What Pays," *Southwest Advertising and Marketing* (December 1975): 20.

5. Luther Brock, "Two Professionals Disagree on the Need for Purity in Language," *Southwest Advertising and Marketing* (March 1977): 11.

6. Robert Gunning, *The Technique of Clear Writing*, rev. ed. (New York: McGraw-Hill, 1968), p. 265.

7. Stephen Wilbers, "Tarrant Business," *Fort Worth Star-Telegram*, July 13, 1998, p. 13.

8. Ibid.

9. Ibid.

10. Ibid.

11. Gunning, *The Technique of Clear Writing*, p. 121.

12. Rudolf Flesch, *The Art of Readable Writing*, 25th anniversary ed. (New York: Harper & Row, 1974), p. 163.

13. See "datum," http://dictionary.reference.com (accessed June 23, 2014).

14. Theodore Bernstein, *The Careful Writer* (New York: Atheneum, 1965), p. 288.

15. Flesch, *The Art of Readable Writing*, pp. 9–10.

16. William Strunk and E. B. White, *The Elements of Style*, 3rd ed. (New York: Macmillan, 1979), p. 78.

17. "Updates to *AP Stylebook* include 'over,' hyphenation of Wal-Mart," www.copydesk.org/blog/2014/03/25/updates-to-ap-stylebook (accessed June 23, 2014).

18. Howard Kahane and Nancy Cavender, *Logic and Contemporary Rhetoric: The Use of Reason in Everyday Life*, 8th ed. (Belmont, CA: Wadsworth, 1998). See Chapter 2, "Background Beliefs and World Views."

19. "10 Common Errors 'Spell Check' Won't Catch," www.copydesk.org/blog/2014/03/25/updates-to-ap-stylebook (accessed June 23, 2014).

20. Paula LaRocque, Words & Language column, "Don't Start the New Year Wrong," *Quill*, 97(2) (March 2009): 27.

21. Christopher J. Moore, *In Other Words: A Language Lover's Guide to the Most Intriguing Words Around the World* (New York: Levenger Press, Division of Walker & Company, 2004).

22. Paula LaRocque, "Readabililty: Dump Dense and Arcane Writing," *Quill*, 18(4) (July/August 2013): 13.

Chapter 6

1. "PR Needs Its Own Research Modes, Not Borrowed Ones," *pr reporter*, January 4, 1993, 1–2.

2. "Wikipedia: About," http://en.wikipedia.org/wiki/Wikipedia:About (accessed December 24, 2014).

3. See, for example, Irving L. Janis, "Personality as a Factor in Susceptibility to Persuade," in *The Science of Human Communication,* ed. Wilbur Schramm (New York: Basic Books, 1963), pp. 54–64.

4. Southwest Airlines, "The Mission of Southwest Airlines," http://www.southwest.com/html/about-southwest/index.html (accessed December 24, 2014).

5. Jens Manuel Krogstad and D'Vera Cohn, "U.S. Census Looking at Big Changes in How It Asks about Race and Ethnicity," FactTank, News in

the Numbers, Pew Research Center, http://www
.pewresearch.org/fact-tank/2014/03/14/u-s-
census-looking-at-big-changes-in-how-it-asks-
about-race-and-ethnicity/ (accessed December
24, 2014).

6. Katherine Russell Rich, "Language Lessons," *The
Rotarian*, May 2010, pp. 23–24.

7. Charlene Li and Josh Bernoff, *Groundswell:
Winning in a World Transformed by Social Technologies* (Boston, MA: Harvard Business Press,
2008), p. 89.

8. Ibid.

9. WordPerfect Corporation Company History, https://www.princeton.edu/~achaney
/tmve/wiki100k/docs/Corel_Corporation.html
(accessed December 24, 2014).

10. Microsoft, "Test Your Document's Readability," http://office.microsoft.com/en-gb/
word-help/test-your-document-s-readability-
HP010148506.aspx (accessed December 24,
2014).

11. David Geddes, "Framework, Standards, and
Metrics: PR Research Priorities Part 2," http://
www.instituteforpr.org/2011/11/framework-
standards-and-metrics-pr-research-priorities-
part-2/ (accessed December 24, 2014).

12. Jerry Swerling and Burghardt Tenderich,
"USC Annenberg Releases Results of Eighth
GAP Study Assessing PR Industry Trends
and Practices," http://www.instituteforpr.org/
topics/usc-annenberg-releases-results-eighth
-gap-study-assessing-pr-industry-trends
-practices/ (accessed December 24, 2014).

13. Association for Measurement and Evaluation
of Communication (AMEC), "Barcelona Declaration of Measurement Principles: Validated
Metrics, Social Media Measurement," http://
www.instituteforpr.org/wp-content/uploads/
BarcelonaPrinciplesOct2010.pdf (accessed
December 24, 2014).

14. Ibid.

15. Angela Sinickas, "Calculating a Return on
Investment (ROI)," *ComPRehension*, http://
comprehension.prsa.org/?p=239 (accessed
December 24, 2014).

Chapter 7

1. Edward L. Bernays, *Public Relations* (Norman,
OK: University of Oklahoma Press, 1952), p. 130.

2. Kang-Hoon Sung and Sora Kim, "I Want to
Be Your Friend: The Effects of Organizations'
Interpersonal Approaches on Social Networking
Sites," *Journal of Public Relations Research*, 26
(2014): 235–255.

3. Gregory D. Saxton and Richard D. Warren,
"What Do Stakeholders *Like* on Facebook?
Examining Public Reactions to Nonprofit
Organizations' Informational, Promotional,
and Community-Building Messages," *Journal of
Public Relations Research*, 26 (2014): 280–299.

4. Jeff Elder, "Social Media Fail to Live Up to Early
Marketing Hype," *The Wall Street Journal*, June
23, 2014, pp. B1, B2 (New York: Dow Jones &
Company).

5. Reed Albergotti and Elizabeth Dowoskin,
"Facebook Study Spurs Ethical Questions," *The
Wall Street Journal*, July 1, 2014, pp. B1, B2, B4
(New York: Dow Jones & Company).

6. Reed Albergotti, "Facebook Lab Had Few Limits, Data Science Group Conducted Experiments on Users with Little Oversight," *The Wall
Street Journal*, July 3, 2014, pp. A1, A2 (New
York: Dow Jones & Company)

7. Otto Lerbinger, *Designs for Persuasive Communication* (Englewood Cliffs, NJ: Prentice Hall,
1972).

8. Stephanie Clifford, "When a Founder Is the
Face of a Brand," *The New York Times*, http://
www.nytimes.com/2013/06/021/business/
media/when-a-founder-is-the-face-of-a-brand
.html?ref-bueiness&r=1&

9. See, for example, Irving L. Janis, "Personality as
a Factor in Susceptibility to Persuasion," in *The
Science of Human Communication*, ed. Wilbur
Schramm (New York: Basic Books, 1963),
pp. 54–64.

10. Milton Rokeach, *The Nature of Human Values*
(New York: Free Press, 1973).

11. William J. McGuire, "Persuasion, Resistance, and Attitude Change," in *Handbook of*

Communication, eds. Ithiel de Sola Pool et al. (Chicago: Rand McNally, 1973), p. 221.

12. Stanley Lehmann, "Personality and Compliance: A Study of Anxiety and Self-Esteem in Opinion and Behavior Change," *Journal of Personality and Social Psychology*, 15 (1970): 76–86. Cited in McGuire, "Persuasion," p. 233.

13. David J. Therkelsen and Christina L. Fiebich, "Message to Desired Action: A Communication Effectiveness Model," *Journal of Communication Management*, 5(4), (2001): 374–390.

14. Everett M. Rogers, *Diffusion of Innovations* (New York: Free Press of Glencoe, 1962). Also see Everett M. Rogers, "Mass Media and Interpersonal Communication," in *Handbook of Communication*, eds. Ithiel de Sola Pool and Wilbur Schramm, et al. (Chicago: Rand McNally, 1973), pp. 290–310.

15. Wilbur Schramm, "The Challenge of Communication Research," in *Introduction to Mass Communication Research*, eds. Ralph O. Nafziger and David M. White (Baton Rouge, LA.: Louisiana State University Press, 1963), p. 29.

16. The statement provided is not always true, however. See B. Sternthal, L. Phillips and R. Dholakia, "The Persuasive Effect of Source Credibility: A Situational Analysis," *Public Opinion Quarterly*, 42 (Fall 1978): 285–314.

17. Lerbinger, *Designs*, p. 25.

18. McGuire, "Persuasion," p. 231.

19. Duangkamol Chartprasert, "How Bureaucratic Writing Style Affects Source Credibility," *Journalism Quarterly*, 70 (Spring 1993): 150–159.

20. Aristotle, *Rhetoric*, trans. W. Rhys Roberts (New York: Modern Library, 1954).

21. McGuire, "Persuasion," p. 234.

22. William J. McGuire, "Nature of Attitudes and Attitude Change," in *Handbook of Social Psychology*, eds. Gardener Lindzey and Elliot Aronson (Reading, Mass.: Addison-Wesley, 1969), p. 225.

23. Ibid., pp. 228–229.

24. Everett M. Rogers, "Mass Media and Interpersonal Communication," in *Handbook of Communication*, eds. Ithiel de Sola Pool and Wilbur Schramm, et al. (Chicago: Rand McNally, 1973), pp. 292–298.

25. McGuire, "Nature," pp. 230–231.

26. Andrew Beaujon, "AP Will Use Robots to Write Some Business Stories," Poynter, Latest News, Media Wire, published June 30, 2014, updated June 30, 2014 (accessed July 15, 2014).

27. McGuire, "Persuasion," p. 231.

28. Elliot Aronson, Judith Turner and J. M. Carlsmith, "Communicator Credibility and Communication Discrepancy as Determinants of Opinion Change," *Journal of Abnormal and Social Psychology*, 67 (1963): 31–36.

29. James E. Grunig, "Communication Behaviors and Attitudes of Environmental Publics: Two Studies," *Journalism Monographs*, 81 (March 1983): 9–14.

Chapter 8

1. Jason Cochran, "Cool USB Flash Drive Press Kit Designs," http://jasoncochran.com/blog/cool-usb-flash-drive-press-kit-designs/ (accessed May 6, 2015).

2. "2015 Online Newsroom Survey Results," TEKgroup International, www.tekgroup.com/marketing/online-newsroom-survey-report/ (accessed May 6, 2015).

3. Ibid.

4. Tony Harrison, "The ABCs of CD-ROMs," *Public Relations Tactics*, Public Relations Society of America (New York, September 1996), p. 14.

5. Katharine Q. Seely, "White House Approves Pass for Blogger," *The New York Times*, http://www.nytimes.com/2005/03/07/technology/07press.html?ex=1267938000&en=53aba0fd77cf623d&ei=5090&partner=rssuserland (accessed January 26, 2015).

6. American Society of Plastic Surgeons, "Press Room Guidelines for Plastic Surgery 2011," http://www.plasticsurgery.org/news/annual-meeting-press-room-guidelines.html (accessed January 26, 2015).

7. Todd Brabender, "Turning Your Media Pitch into a Media Hit," http://www.evancarmichael.com/Public-Relations/286/Business-Publicity-

Turning-Your-Media-Pitch-Into-A-Media-Hit .html (accessed January 26, 2015).

8. California Association for Health Services at Home, "Media Relations," undated, http:// cahsah.org/documents/313_hcmonth_media .pdf (accessed January 26, 2015).

9. Katrina M. Mendolera, "State of the Media Report 2014," http://lp.prweb.com/Global /FileLib/Guides/Vocus_-_State_of_the_ Media_2014.pdf (accessed January 26, 2015).

10. "How the Press Uses and Values Public Relations and Other Media Resources," a national study by Cision, Inc. and The George Washington University Graduate School of Political Management, http://www.gwu.edu/~media/ research_report.pdf (accessed January 26, 2015).

11. The Earth Institute, Columbia University, "Writing and Submitting an Opinion Piece: A Guide," http://www.google.com/ur l?sa=t&rct=j&q=&esrc=s&frm=1&source =web&cd=1&ved=0CB8QFjAA&url=http %3A%2F%2Fwww.earth.columbia.edu%2F sitefiles%2Ffile%2Fpressroom%2Fmedia_ outreach%2FOpEdGuide.doc&ei=CnPaTsvgE-vfsQLchpHPDQ&usg=AFQjCNEgPQ9Zd6F-zXj0iPJcHo6zyJzulQ&sig2=FEawXRXV82jjE5a PnXVt6Q (accessed January 26, 2015).

12. Based on United Nations Association of the United States of America, "How to Write Opinion Articles," http://www.unausa.org/global-classrooms-model-un/how-to-participate/ model-un-preparation/position-papers (accessed January 26, 2015).

Chapter 9

1. Katrina M. Mendolera, Editor in Chief, *inVocus* "State of the Media Report 2014," Vocua®Marketing Cloud.

2. Greg Beaubien, "Confidence in News Media at Record Lows," Editor's Column in *Public Relations Journal*, 8(2), (June 20, 2014). Public Relations *Tactics*, Public Relations Society of America online.

3. Elena Verlee, "Do You Still Need Traditional Media for PR?" http://prinyourpajamas.com/ traditional-media-for-pr/ (accessed November 4, 2011).

4. Janet Kolodzy, August E. Grant, Tony R. DeMars, Jeffery S. Wilkinson, "The Convergence Years," *Journalism and Mass Communication Educator*, 69(2), (2014): 200–201, pp. 197–205.

5. Georgia Wells, "Real-Time Marketing, How Advertisers Are Using Social Media to Promote Their Brands at a Moment's Notice," *The Wall Street Journal*, March 24, 2014, p. R3.

6. David Jarmul, "How to Write an Op-Ed Article," http://newsoffice.duke.edu/duke_resources/ oped (accessed November 9, 2011).

7. Suzanne Huffman, "Writing Radio News," Chapter 6, in *Broadcast News Handbook*, eds. C. A. Tuggle, Forrest Carr and Suzanne Huffman (New York: McGraw-Hill, 2001), p. 74.

8. Kelli B. Newman, "A Strategic Subspecialty: Defining the Comprehensive Value of Broadcast Public Relations," *Public Relations Tactics*, June 2006, p. 18.

9. Eric Alkire, "ABC's of Long-Form Video Edits," *News Photographer*, January 1997, p. 15.

10. David Eisenstadt, "How to Make Video News Releases Work," *Public Relations Quarterly*, 47(4), (Winter 2002): 24–25.

11. Tom Moore, "TV News Directors Report High VNR, SMT Usage; Cite Favorite Topics," *PR News*, 48(45), (November 16, 1992): 8.

12. "Use of Video News Releases as a Public Relations Tool," Public Relations Society of America Ethical Standards Advisory ES12, October 2009.

13. "The 8 Types of Images That Increase the Psychological Impact of Your Content," FeedBlitz@ mail.feedblitz.com on behalf of Copyblogger, feedmanager@copyblogger.com, from Copyblogger, Tuesday, June 24, 2014.

14. Matthew McClone, "Persuasive Communication: Health," *Ideas & Work*, University of Texas Moody College of Communication (Austin, TX: The University of Texas, 2014), p. 18.

15. "Final Rule: Selective Disclosure and Insider Trading, Securities and Exchange Commission, 17 CFR Parts 240, 243, and 249, Release Nos. 33-7881, 34-43154, IC-24599, File No. S7-31-99, RIN 3235-AH82, Selective Disclosure and Insider Trading," Washington, D.C., October 23, 2002, http://www.sec.gov/rules/final/33-7881.htm (accessed November 9, 2011).

16. Silicon.com Staff, "Lowdown on SOX," San Francisco, CA, undated, http://news.com.com/Sarbanes-Oxley+cheat+sheet/2030-7349_3-5465172.html (accessed November 9, 2011).

17. Cayce Myers, "Disclosure: New FTC Social Media Guidelines for PR," from Research Conversations—The Institute for Public Relations (IPR), info@instituteforpr.org (accessed February 24, 2014).

Chapter 10

1. Cision, "2013 Social Journalism Survey," http://us.cision.com/ty/Social-Journalism-Survey-USA-120513.pdf (accessed January 26, 2015).

2. Michael Muchmore, "The Best Web-Based Email Services," August 29, 2012, http://www.pcmag.com/article2/0,2817,2408983,00.asp (accessed January 26, 2015).

3. Gale Holland and Seema Mehta, "UC San Diego Admissions Gaffe Dashes Students' Hopes—Again," *Los Angeles Times*, April 1, 2009, http://articles.latimes.com/2009/apr/01/local/me-ucsd-reject1 (accessed January 26, 2015).

4. "McAfee Labs Report Sees Mobile Malware Abuse Trust in Early 2014," http://www.mcafee.com/us/resources/reports/rp-quarterly-threat-q1-2014.pdf (accessed January 26, 2015).

5. "Sophos Security Threat Report 2009," http://www.securitytrust.co.kr/data/tb_notice/sophos-security-threat-report-jan-2009-na.pdf (accessed January 26, 2015).

6. Virus News, "2012 by the Numbers: Kaspersky Lab Now Detects 200,000 New Malicious Programs Every Day," http://www.kaspersky.com/about/news/virus/2012/2012_by_the_numbers_Kaspersky_Lab_now_detects_200000_new_malicious_programs_every_day (accessed January 26, 2015).

7. Natasa Lucic, "How Motorola Uses Social Media to Manage Information Overload," http://www.simply-communicate.com/case-studies/company-profile/how-motorola-uses-social-media-manage-information-overload (accessed January 26, 2015).

8. Marguerite Reardon, "Americans Text More Than They Talk," http://www.cnet.com/search/?query=in+the+second+quarter+of+2014%2C+found+that+Americans+each+sent+or+received+357+text+messages+a+month%2C+compared+with+just+204+phone+calls (accessed January 26, 2015).

9. "Negative Aspects of Text Messaging," http://www.notepage.net/may-2014.htm (accessed January 26, 2015).

10. Statistics from the National Highway Traffic Safety Administration published by Edgar Snyder & Associates®, http://www.edgarsnyder.com/car-accident/cell-phone/statistics.html (accessed January 26, 2015).

11. AOL, "Think You Might Be Addicted to Email? You're Not Alone," http://ir.aol.com/phoenix.zhtml?c=147895&p=irol-newsArticle&ID=1354021&highlight= (accessed January 26, 2015).

12. Elliott Bell, "Are Your Emails Too Long (Hint: Probably)," *theMuse*, https://www.themuse.com/advice/are-your-emails-too-long-hint-probably?ref=search (accessed January 26, 2015).

13. "Who Is the Sorriest Airline?" *The Wall Street Journal*, http://online.wsj.com/news/articles/SB20001424052702303973004580019262484065450 (accessed January 26, 2015).

14. Brad Allen, IR Magazine, "The Annual Report Endures, NIRI Survey Finds," http://www.irmagazine.com/articles/earnings-calls-financial-reporting/19232/annual-report-endures-niri-survey-finds/ (accessed January 26, 2015).

15. *NIRI (National Investor Relations Institute), "Annual Report Survey 2008,"* http://www.google.com/url?sa=t&rct=j&q=&esrc=s&source=web&cd=1&ved=0CB8QFjAA&url=http%3A%2F%2Fwww.niri.org%2FOther-Content%2F0810annualreportslides

.aspx&ei=HeWyU83TC8OVqAb0tYK
YDg&usg=AFQjCNHj-pKbppiha0cX_
o1FfQ1JrY9ppA&bvm=bv.70138588,d.b2k
(accessed January 26, 2015).

16. Ibid.

17. Broadridge Financial Solutions, Inc, "Notice and Access FAQs for Shareholders," https://www.shareholdereducation.com/faq.asp (accessed January 26, 2015).

Chapter 11

1. *The Huffington Post*, "The U.S. Illiteracy Rate Hasn't Changed in 10 Years," *The Huffington Post*, http://www.huffingtonpost.com/2013/09/06/illiteracy-rate_n_3880355.html (accessed May 13, 2015).

2. Mark Brownlow, "Email newsletter frequency," http://www.email-marketing-reports.com/emailnewsletters/frequency.htm (accessed January 26, 2015).

3. Gary F. Grates, speaking on "Maintaining Reputation in a Time of Global Change" at the *Corporate Communication Institute*, http://www.google.com/url?sa=t&rct=j&q=&esrc=s&source=web&cd=3&ved=0CCkQFjAC&url=http%3A%2F%2Fwww.corporatecomm.org%2Fpdf%2FCCI_Grates_Reputation-Deck_2112706.ppt&ei=hbq1U4mhHpGhqAaNlID4BQ&usg=AFQjCNEUR6GXWiscmNne_Hsa3KpYZQ72Wg&bvm=bv.70138588,d.b2k (accessed January 26, 2015).

4. Robyn Reilly, "Five Ways to Improve Employee Engagement Now," *Gallup* Business Journal, January 7, 2014, http://businessjournal.gallup.com/content/166667/five-ways-improve-employee-engagement.aspx#1 (accessed January 26, 2015).

5. Ibid.

6. Ibid.

7. Tamara Snyder, "Seven Key Studies on the Business Impact of Employee Engagement," http://www.edelman.com/post/seven-key-studies-on-the-business-impact-of-employee-engagement/ (accessed January 26, 2015).

8. Jacci Howard Bear, "Top Desktop Publishing Software for Windows," http://desktoppub.about.com/od/softwarehardware/tp/Desktop_Publishing_Software.htm (accessed January 26, 2015).

Chapter 12

1. Miles Maguire, "Mapping the Size and Scope of a Nonprofit Media Sector: The Case of Magazine Publishing," *Journalism & Mass Communication Quarterly* (Columbia, SC: Association for Education in Journalism and Mass Communication, Autumn 2008), p. 647.

2. Alliance for Audited Media, http://abcas3.auditedmedia.com/ecirc/magform.asp (accessed July 7, 2014).

3. "How Word Choice Impacts Employee Communication," *Mid-America Communication Foundation*, 2(1), (1996): 47–55.

4. Don Fabun, "Company Publications," in *Lesly's Public Relations Handbook*, ed. Philip Lesly (Englewood Cliffs, NJ: Prentice Hall, 1971), p. 135.

5. "Top 10 Trade Magazines," http://www.allyoucanread.com/top-10-trade-magazines/ (accessed July 7, 2014).

6. Ibid.

7. Noel Ward, "Translating the Languages of Color," *Desktop Publishing Journal*, March 1995, pp. 26–27.

8. Ibid.

Chapter 13

1. Barbara A. Ross, Sarah V. Beckman and Linda V. Meyer, "Learning to Produce and Integrate Presentations, Videos and Stills." *T.H.E. Journal*, (September 1995): 78–81.

2. Ibid.

3. *tips and tactics*, 41(10), May 5, 2003, pp. 1–2.

Chapter 14

1. Kathleen Larey Lewton, " 'Reputation Recovery,' The Ebola Patient Crisis in Dallas," *The Public Relations Strategist*, Public Relations Society of America (New York, Winter 2014): 22–24.

2. Bill Vlasic, "G.M.'s Barra Promises to Investigate How Recall Was Handled," *The New York Times*, March 4, 2014. http://www.nytimes.com/2014/03/05/business/gms-barra-promises-to-investigate-how-recall-was-handled.html?_r=0 (accessed February 4, 2015).

3. Mark Hannah, "In Hudson River Landing, PR Pros Were Not First Responders," http://www.pbs.org/mediashift/2009/02/in-hudson-river-landing-pr-pros-were-not-first-responders036.html (accessed February 5, 2015).

4. Sheri Jacobson, "Komen Reaction Strong from 2 Sides," *The Dallas Morning News*, Dallas, TX, February 2, 2012, pp. 1A and 6A.

5. Ibid.

6. Marc Ramirez, "Outrage, Praise Fill Social Media," *The Dallas Morning News*, Dallas, TX, February 2, 2012, p. 3B.

7. Tom Benning, "Komen Apologizes for 'Recent Decisions,' Pledges to Continue Funding Planned Parenthood," http://thescoopblog.dallasnews.com/archives/2012/02/komen-apologizes-for-recent-de.html (accessed February 3, 2012).

8. Jennifer Preston and Gardiner Harris, "Outcry Grows Fiercer after Funding Cut by Cancer Group," *The New York Times*, http://www.nytimes.com/2012/02/03/us/komen-foundation-urged-to-restore-planned-parenthood-funds.html (accessed February 4, 2015).

9. Michael Cherenson, "Who Really Owns the Komen Brand?" http://prsay.prsa.org/index.php/2012/02/07/examinining-brand-ownership-in-wake-of-the-komen-pr-crisis/ (accessed February 4, 2015).

10. Dakota Smith, "Residents Brace for Closure of 405 Freeway," *Daily News*, http://www.dailynews.com/news/ci_18212978 (accessed February 4, 2015).

11. Kenneth R. Weiss, Molly Hennessy-Fiske and Andrew Khouri, "Carmageddon: 'Mission accomplished,' says Villaraigosa as 405 Freeway Reopens Early," http://articles.latimes.com/2011/jul/18/local/la-me-0718-405-open-20110718 (accessed February 4, 2015).

12. Jack C. Horn, "The Hostage Ward," *Psychology Today*, 21(7) (July 1985): 9.

13. Doug Newsom, Judy VanSlyke Turk and Dean Kruckeberg, *This Is PR: The Realities of Public Relations*, 11th ed. (Belmont, CA: Wadsworth, 2013), p. 314

14. Based on "A Changing World," in Crisis and Emergency Risk Communication, 2012 Edition, Centers for Disease Control and Prevention, http://emergency.cdc.gov/cerc/resources/pdf/cerc_2012edition.pdf (accessed February 4, 2015).

15. Ibid.

16. Ibid.

17. Ibid.

18. "Crisis Communications: Planning to Attack the Crisis Before It Attacks You," http://homeless.samhsa.gov/ResourceFiles/wcg0ta5g.pdf (accessed February 4, 2015).

19. "Writing Communication Plans," http://govinfo.library.unt.edu/npr/library/papers/bkgrd/chapter3.html (accessed February 4, 2015).

20. Institute for Public Relations, "Three Things Research Teaches About Crisis Response," http://www.instituteforpr.org/three-things-research-teaches-about-crisis-response/ (accessed February 4, 2015).

21. "Post Event," Emergency Risk Communication CDCynergy, http://www.orau.gov/cdcynergy/erc/content/phase4/phase4.htm (accessed February 4, 2015).

22. Lisa Bradner and Kim Le Quoc with Jaap Favier and Jean-Yves Lugo, "Choosing The Right Media Mix: North America from Creating Awareness to the Act of Purchase," https://www.forrester.com/Choosing+The+Right+Media+Mix+North+America/fulltext/-/E-RES47054 (accessed February 4, 2015).

23. Ibid.

Index